Dreamer Who's Been Extremely Blessed

Dreamer Who's Been Extremely Blessed

Edgar Francis Poree Jr.

iUniverse, Inc.
Bloomington

DREAMER WHO'S BEEN EXTREMELY BLESSED

Copyright © 2013 by Edgar Francis Poree Jr.

All rights reserved. No part of this book may be used or reproduced by any means, graphic, electronic, or mechanical, including photocopying, recording, taping or by any information storage retrieval system without the written permission of the publisher except in the case of brief quotations embodied in critical articles and reviews.

iUniverse books may be ordered through booksellers or by contacting:

iUniverse
1663 Liberty Drive
Bloomington, IN 47403
www.iuniverse.com
1-800-Authors (1-800-288-4677)

Because of the dynamic nature of the Internet, any web addresses or links contained in this book may have changed since publication and may no longer be valid. The views expressed in this work are solely those of the author and do not necessarily reflect the views of the publisher, and the publisher hereby disclaims any responsibility for them.

Any people depicted in stock imagery provided by Thinkstock are models, and such images are being used for illustrative purposes only.
Certain stock imagery © Thinkstock.

ISBN: 978-1-4759-7530-7 (sc)
ISBN: 978-1-4759-7529-1 (hc)
ISBN: 978-1-4759-7531-4 (ebk)

Library of Congress Control Number: 2013903314

Printed in the United States of America

iUniverse rev. date: 03/14/2013

PREFACE

A story about an African-American male, who against tremendous odds and challenges, remained focused, ignored naysayers, and overcame the numerous obstacles confronting Black males during the transition from segregation to integration of the South.

My story depicts the struggles, failures, disappointments, grief, successes, and the constant inner turmoil in dealing with deeply rooted racial, ethnic, inter-ethnic, class, skin color, hair texture, religious discrimination, and prejudices of family, peers, and significantly older members of the African-American community.

Although some names, identities of places and institutions in my story have been changed, they represent real people, real places, real experiences, and real divisions that really occurred during my life experiences. This story is being told, not to cast aspersions or single out individuals or institutions that consistently created road-blocks and enormous challenges, but instead, it is my hope the information will embolden, encourage, and inspire the readers to stay focused on their visions and aspirations, never giving up on their dreams, so they too will be blessed.

Dedication

To my parents, Edgar Francis and Gertrude Boyd Poree, who departed this life June 25, 1964, and October 17, 1990, respectively, and who were passionately dedicated to the educational growth, development, well-being, and independence of their five children.

Acknowledgement

During every phase of my life, I've been extremely fortunate to have people around me whose encouragement, support and love made a tremendous difference in my life. They filled my voyage with incredible learning experiences. They often made me appear better than I was. Some of them, like my Mother, were obvious, and they are featured in the text of the book so they hardly need mentioning here. There are others, however, who were not as obvious in the storyline that were barely mentioned. Yet if not for all of them, I would not have experienced such an incredible blessed life.

I've often felt that while I might not be the fastest or the most athletic runner in the race, over the years, however, I've always felt if I would work hard enough, and I would be quick and crafty enough to be the winner in the race. I still worry it is impossible to give credit to all persons who contributed so much to my successes, over the years. If I have omitted anyone who played a role in my life, please accept my apologies. If my words of thanks seem insufficient, my love, appreciation and gratitude are everlasting and true.

I first need to extend my thanks, gratitude and appreciation to my wife, my life-long sweetheart, Gloria, for her patience, endurance and unconditional love. She's my best friend, my uncompromising confidant. Gloria has been more than just understanding and patient during my seven and a half years of working on my memoirs. I want to thank my two terrific kids, Deidra and Edgar, III, because I know it's not always easy to have Edgar Poree Jr. as their dad, but they always made it very easy for me. My Daughter, Deidra gave Gloria and me two of the most fantastic grandchildren, Troy Dion, II, and Alexis Kirsten, who have greatly enriched our lives and who will be even more important part of our lives going forward.

I had many good teachers and role models that had a profound influence on my life, especially during my formative years. I thank my Father, the self-taught, highly intelligent scholar with a relentless thirst of knowledge, for inspiring me to read and to think critically. He had a major influence in helping me to "think outside the box" when developing resolutions and in overcoming extreme challenges. To my oldest sister, Edna Floe, to compensate her adequately for her compassion, caring, advice, unwavering support, respect of our parents, siblings, family, elders, institutions and fervent compassion and uncompromising integrity, would require tens of millions. Everyone who was fortunate to experience Edna Floe left with a new appreciation of spirituality and decency. Thanks for Edna giving us the capacity to exercise ethical behavior during challenging situations. To Juli Rose, my second oldest sister, I give my thanks for her willingness and patience, teaching me how to sew, crochet, embroider and fixing delicious stewed bananas. To Natalie and Anna Lea, my third and fourth sisters, respectively, I thank them for tolerating all of my many antics over the years. I'm thankful to my surrogate sibling, Dolores Thompson Aaron, for her love, life-long support and unlimited generosity to my Mother, my siblings and me.

To Octavia Glapion Douglas, my first cousin, surrogate mom, generous benefactor, who treated me royally like a son, I am forever grateful for her unconditional love and generosity. To Beverly Saulny, owner of Dot's Home Beverage Company, I am grateful and thankful for the job opportunity, the affordable rental home, and his courageous leadership fostering a robust community awareness activism. To A. P. Tureaud, Jr. my friend, classmate, and coworker, I cannot thank him enough for his tremendous assistance enabling my enlistment in the U.S. Army Reserve, one day before recruitment expired. Much thanks to Sister Elise, Chairman of Xavier University's Music Department, for being instrumental in my being awarded a full scholarship to Xavier University. She was also a major influence in resurrecting my singing career after a dismal failure as freshmen featured vocalist in the university's annual opera. Sister Elise's encouragement, support and intensive voice training restored my confidence and my performance such that I had several leading roles in opera performances during my junior and senior years.

To Dr. Walter Austin, distinguished Economist and Professor of Economics at Southern University at New Orleans, my gratitude and thanks for the tremendous assistance he provided during the development of my Sales Tax Strategic Plan Proposal for Orleans Parish Public Schools. I am indebted to Dr. Edwin Stump, Associate Superintendent, Orleans Parish Public Schools, for support and recommendations of a leadership position in Orleans Parish Public Schools' Revenue Initiative Campaign and a supervisory position in the U.S. Department of Labor, both of which I was appointed. Much thanks and gratitude to Daniel Vincent, Executive Director, Total Community Action, Inc., for support and appointments to senior leadership positions in the agency. To Dr. James Bobo, Dean of Louisiana State University—New Orleans and Executive Director of Goals Foundation, much thanks and gratitude for selecting me as an Associate Director of the Foundation from a list of more than sixty candidates.

To Mr. Murray Fincher, State Vice-President-South Central Bell Telephone Company, I am forever indebted for his support and appointment of me to a management position in Corporate America. My gratitude and appreciation will always be etched in my heart. To Bill Cangelosi, District Manager, BellSouth, I'm grateful for the trust and confidence he gave, affording me an opportunity to demonstrate my competence and effectiveness in administering the duties and responsibilities of his office. That opportunity made it possible for his superiors to assess my performance as a potential senior management candidate. When Bill was selected as an Alfred P. Sloan Fellow Program at Stanford University, I was appointed District Manager and Chief Spokesman for the Company, succeeding him. To Fred Nodier, Assistant Vice President, Corporate and External Affairs BellSouth, I extend my heartfelt gratitude and appreciation for the extra-ordinary commitment of fairness and genuine concern for his senior associates as well as his subordinates. Fred was one of the true gentlemen of Corporate America, and I will always cherish his friendship. To Herschel Abbott, Jr., President BellSouth Louisiana Operations, I thank you for including me in your corporate leadership endeavors, challenges and successes. Murray Fincher, opened the door to Corporate America for me, Herschel Abbott, Jr. gave me a corporate master key to open corporate doors and opportunities that previously had not been available to me. Thanks Herschel for treating me as a colleague, confident, advisor, counsel and for being a true friend.

To Leah Chase, culinary, humanitarian, much thanks and gratitude for the tremendous contributions she and she husband, Dooky made on behalf of justice and community betterment. Most of all I thank Leah for her many acts of kindness, generosity and accommodations she afforded my family as well as the hundreds of families and organizations with unselfish and unconditional love. Leah will always be an endeared, loved, revered member of our family.

Finally, to Dian Kent, my highly competent, trusted and devoted Administrative Assistant, Keith Hitchens, my incredibly talented negotiator and affable Staff Associate and Mary Ann Francois, Staff Manager, three individuals who were my protectors, my supporters, my eyes, my ears, my safety shields and safety nets, enabling me to effectively initiate enhancements of our company's image, prosperity and fostering greater community's well-being. Thank you, from the debts of my heart for your support, dedication, trust and your genuine caring love of my family and me. Whatever successes, accomplishments and awards I attained, much of the credit I owe to Dian, Keith and Mary Ann, individually and collectively, my endeared and beloved extended family.

Table of Contents

I.	Birth of the Beginning	1
II.	Bienville Street House	25
III.	High School	51
IV.	College Here I Come	73
V.	Starting New Career	104
VI.	Fulfilling A Commitment	153
VII.	Strategic Tax Plan	163
VIII.	New Opportunities	174
IX.	Business Interest	208
X.	Career Ladder to Corporate America	220
XI.	Breakup of Bell System	269
XII.	1990: Year of Highs and Lows	291
XIII.	Company Reorganization, Pluses and Minuses, and Retirement	328
XIV.	Hurricane Katrina and the Aftermath	335
XV.	A Year of Festive Family Celebrations	347

Appendices 371

CHAPTER I

BIRTH OF THE BEGINNING

The 19th Century

My story had its beginning fifty years before I was born, during the twilight of the nineteenth century. On August 25, 1886, my Father, Edgar Francis Poree, was born in the bedroom behind the family's barber shop in New Orleans. Father was the second child and first son of the marriage of Thomas and Sara Francis. Louise, his oldest sister was two years old at the time of his birth. My grandparents were extremely elated as the first son of their marriage union had arrived. Grandfather was a free man of color and a barber since his early teens. Following family tradition, my Father was a third-generation barber—a family trade since the time of the emancipation proclamation. Louis, the youngest son of the family was born several years after my Father. The Poree family and Aunt Ethel Lou, settled in a house at Conti and North Roman streets at the turn of the twentieth century in New Orleans.

Father, a handsome eligible bachelor gentleman, only completed eight grades; however, his passion and relentless pursuit of knowledge enabled him to become a highly intellectual self-taught scholar. He read hundreds of books, publications, newspapers, business journals, and listened to the news on the radio, while practicing his trade throughout his 59-year career. Father would play an important role in promoting and fostering a thirst of knowledge among his peers, customers, and family members. Father was an incredible resource for hundreds of college students who visited his barber shop to do their research with the hundreds of books and publications he acquired during his nearly six decades career. His barbershop library had many books that the two historical Black colleges in the City either had limited available volumes for multiple use or did not have at all during the late 1940's, 50's, and early 60's.

Poree's Barber Shop would also play a major role in articulating the importance of reading and being better informed. Students would also benefit tremendously from Father's extensive knowledge and awareness of what was happening nationally and internationally during their research visits. Father believed the way of "breaking" the enslavement of ignorance cycle was to read, do research, and become better informed about what's going on in the community, the nation, and the world. His love and search of knowledge would be an inspirational and motivational force in my quest and pursuit of knowledge of those prerequisites of competence, ethical behavior, and ability to excel and would contribute to the betterment of our community.

This visionary, philosopher, and self-taught scholar was affectionately called the Judge by all who knew of his exceptional and extraordinary mastery of the King's English (language) as well as his interpretation, his opinions, and his assessments of events and situations that influenced or adversely affected the lives of our community.

Turn of Century

My Mother, Gertrude Boyd, the older of two children of Thelma Boyd was born on May 31, 1900, in Mandeville, Louisiana. My Mother came to New Orleans to further her education in high school because there was no high school in Mandeville for *Colored people*. Grandmother and Alma, Mother's sister, later moved to New Orleans to live. Prior to the Boyd family moving to New Orleans, working the fields most of the year with little schooling opportunities was the norm during the turn of the twentieth century for colored children in Mandeville.

Mother lived with the Poree family in New Orleans, while attending McDonogh #35 High School. The Poree and Boyd families were extremely close friends. It was a very difficult decision for Grandmother to allow my Mother to move to New Orleans while she and her other daughter, Alma, remained in Mandeville. Although painful, Grandmother's decision to allow Mother to leave home and be separated for years was greatly influenced by her desire to afford Mother an opportunity to further her education and improve her economic conditions in the future.

Grandmother Thelma recognized at the beginning of the century just how critically one's future depended on getting an education. It was that compelling reason for which she relinquished seeing her daughter every day at home so that Mother would be afforded an opportunity to see a better day in the future. Grandmother and Alma remained in Mandeville where they continued working for the same plantation owner Grandmother had worked for, practically all of her life. The separation of Grandmother and Alma from Mother for educational and economic considerations would eventually have a very profound influence and impact upon their relationships during subsequent years and their young adult lives.

Distinct Differences

The relationship between Mother and Alma would be tremendously influenced and adversely impacted by not only the forty plus miles separating them from each other between New Orleans and Mandeville, but more profoundly, their distinct differences in appearances. Grandmother Thelma had keen features with extremely dark complexioned skin and rather coarse hair. Alma was extremely dark complexioned with broad features and hair that was rather coarse and kinky. Mother was extremely light complexioned with extremely keen features and hair that was naturally curly. These distinguishable differences in complexion, features, and hair texture would prove to be very defining factors in relationships, associations, acceptance, and affiliations—socially, economically, and most of all class, especially by the natives of New Orleans.

Mother and Alma were as different as night and day. Neither of them knew their Father. It was rumored that the plantation owner for whom Grandmother worked for was Mother's Father. Alma, on the other hand, may have been fathered by someone other than Mother's Father. Unfortunately, there was little evidence linking Fathers of either Mother or her sister, so the trail of discovery remained a mystery to this day.

When Mother moved to New Orleans to live with the Poree family, complexion, features, and hair texture did cause much dissension and animosity among some of the family's friends, especially the girls in the neighborhood. Although the Poree family welcomed Mother with "open arms" in their home, her presence and association with my Father created quite a bit of controversy and strained relations. Before this light complexioned girl from Mandeville moved in with the Poree family, many of the neighborhood girls got plenty of attention from my Father. However, that situation changed when Father began giving more attention to my Mother instead of the neighborhood girls. That once friendly chatter and laughter among young Edgar and the neighborhood girls, before Mother's arrival, turned into resentment and ugly remarks. "Why is he spending so much time with that yellow so and so? She thinks she's better than us; she needs to go back where she belongs in the country!"

Many girls living on the St. Louis Street side of the railroad tracks weren't as light complexioned or as plentiful as the girls who lived in Treme were many more multi-colored, multi-racial families living next to one another; colored folks, white folks, and light skinned (complexioned) people of color, commonly called *Creoles*. Many light-skinned people of Treme, especially those living in the Seventh Ward of the City, discriminated among themselves, using the brown paper bag test. If you were fortunate to be lighter than a brown paper bag, you could become a friend, a husband or a wife of a light-skinned person of color, and you may also be accepted into social circles of events and social clubs. So before one considered bringing someone home to meet his family to dating or marriage, she better be no darker than a light brown paper bag; otherwise, she could be out of luck because his family won't be too happy with his selection.

Many Creoles of Color during Father's youth spoke French fluently, and many were extremely good tradesmen. Another factor distinguishing people who lived on one side of the railroad tracks from the other was religion. Many of the residents living on the Treme side of the railroad tracks were mostly Roman Catholics. On the other hand, many individuals living on the St. Louis Street side of the tracks were mostly Protestant. Skin complexion, facial features, and hair texture created much animosity among individuals lighter than brown bags and those that were not. Because of these differences, even some members of the Poree family thought my Mother was getting too much attention, they, like many neighborhood girls, became disenchanted, rude, and distant from Mother.

We don't know the real reason, maybe it was the difference in complexion, features, and hair texture, among family or how it appeared, but Mother was treated with kid gloves and courtesies by light skinned neighbors, who mistakenly assumed she was one of them. Unfortunately, Mother's sister, didn't get kid glove treatment, friendly courtesies, or to socialize with many of the neighborhood natives. Mother, then fifteen years younger than my Father, began developing a very close friendship which eventually led them to fall in love.

After graduating from McDonogh #35 High School in 1916, Mother began working at a haberdashery store on South Rampart near Canal Street. After a short period of time, she became manager of the Haberdashery. Many store customers thought Mother was white or Creole. When my Father came to the store, near closing, many customers thought he was Mother's family house boy, helping her clean up, closing, and carrying packages that needed to be delivered to her family's home.

In 1917, on a snowy Christmas Day, my thirty-two year old Father and seventeen-year old Mother were married. That marriage was not very acceptable by many of Father's friends and family members. Many felt Father took advantage of that poor young country girl. Even some family members believed that the reason that my Mother didn't turn him down was because she was so appreciative of what Father's family had done for her. Others suggested the only reason Father married her was because she was high yellow and looked more like being white than any of the girls in the neighborhood. The newly married couple simply ignored naysayers and began their new life happily together.

My parents honeymoon did not last very long because shortly after their marriage Father was drafted in the U.S. Army's 805th Pioneer Infantry, where he served with great distinction. He was recognized, commended, and acknowledged by the Commanding Colonel of the 805th Battalion for his dedication, loyalty, and especially for his decision-making and leadership, cited in a Letter of Commendation written in June of 1918 on the battle field of Normandy. After Father's Honorable Discharge from the army, he returned home to resume his short-lived honeymoon with his lovely wife, and he got back into growing his barber business in the family's barber shop.

Father was very civic minded and a registered voter in the 4th Ward, 3rd Precinct. He was appointed a Commissioner of Election in the Republican Primary Election held on September 14, 1926. After several years of honeymooning, his barber shop customers were growing, and Father began setting his sights on starting a family. In November of 1926, the first child, Edna Floe, a daughter, was born. Like clockwork, another daughter, Juli Rose was born in July of 1929; another daughter, Natalie, was born in June of 1931; and, still another daughter, Anna Lea, was born in July of 1933.

Time was running out, still no son. When Father was forty-seven years old, the clock must have been ticking a bit slower, and prospects for that long awaited son's arrival to carry the Poree family's name was fading. Father was getting a little panicky about the prospects of having a son since he was nearing fifty. In spite of his anxieties, he continued hoping his dream would come true and a son would arrive.

Great Divide

Just as complexion and hair texture factors had a profound influence in the selection of friends, associates, and attainment of social status, during the turn of the twentieth century, generation after generation endured heavy burdens associated with this behavior. Unable to overcome bias, diminishing dreams, aspirations, animosity, and even hatred among families appeared even more demeaning and discriminatory than racial bias. One was being driven by ignorance, the other being self-inflicted. Unfortunately, like so many families in our community, the Poree family did not break the shackles associated with the wounds and the great divide that skin complexion, facial features, and hair texture preferences created.

Nomads

Poree's' Barber Shop was like Nomads, moving from one location to another throughout the Fourth and Fifth Wards during the first half of the twentieth century. The barber shop was a neighborhood landmark in the Fourth and Fifth Wards. During early 1900, the barber shop was located on the corner of Conti and North Roman Streets across from the Coliseum, the largest arena in the city at that time. The Coliseum was the place where all major championship fights and wrestling matches were held. Those were the days when champion wrestlers had to win two out of three falls to be declared winners, unlike today's theatrical wrestling matches.

Some of the world's most famous fights and famous celebrities could be seen at the Coliseum. The location of Poree's Barber Shop made it possible for Father's customers to have a front row seat for some of those great events. Back then, there were no air conditioners in the Coliseum, and the building's windows were extremely large. When events were held in the Coliseum, all of the large windows were opened to allow fresh air in and to let the smoke-filled arena release its toxic smoke outside. Because of its location, Father's barber shop was the most sought after place to be when special events were at the Coliseum. The window on the Roman Street side of the barber shop was perfect for seeing inside the Coliseum's very large "opened" windows. When world championship events were scheduled at the Coliseum, coincidently those were Father's busiest days of the years. The Roman Street side of the barber shop was the place to be to see the events.

After many years on Conti Street, Poree's Barber Shop had to move because the landlord wanted his house for relatives who were moving to New Orleans. Father found a house, across the tracks, three blocks away on Lafitte and North Prieur Streets in the fall of 1934. The front room was converted into the barber shop and once again the family's barber shop was open for business. This house would later become the birthplace of Father's long awaited special gift.

Finding a house a landlord who would be willing to allow a portion of the property to be converted into a business was not an easy task. Since there were no laws, protecting renters from being evicted without just cause, the Poree family was constantly looking for potential locations in the event their landlord gave them a hastily notice to vacate the property without just cause. Being a good tenant was not always a guarantee to be safe from eviction, especially if an owner's relatives move into the city. The Poree family realized in order to avoid that major reoccurring obstacle, it would have to eventually buy a house; the big problem, finding the money to pay for it. The combination of a lack of owners' willingness to convert their properties to store front businesses, such as barber shops coupled with the lack of laws protecting renters, subjected the Poree family to living at the mercy of the landlords. Consequently, Poree's Barber Shop moved on numerous occasions during the early 1930's and 1940's to various locations in the fourth and fifth wards of New Orleans.

Another Generation

Almost a half century after Father's birth in a room behind the family's barber shop, in 1886, one evening on the fifth day of October in 1936, a mid-wife delivered a nine pound ten ounce baby boy in a room behind the family's barber shop on the corner of Lafitte and North Prieur Streets. At last, Father's long awaited dream came true, the fifth sibling his son. My Father, the Judge, with his extraordinary mastery of the English language, his enormous knowledge of literature, and awareness of current events confronting our nation; jubilantly, audaciously proclaimed, "My son, my son has finally arrived." The Judge was fifty years old when I was born. He was one jubilant Macho Man. Back in those days, a man was seemingly unfulfilled unless he fathered a son to carry on the family's name and legacy.

Several years after the family's barber shop opened on the corner of Lafitte and North Prieur Street, once again the family barber shop had to move. This time it wasn't the landlord wanting the house for relatives; instead the Federal Government was building the first public housing project for colored people in New Orleans. The Lafitte Housing Project for Negroes, "Colored People," would be built on acres of land stretching eight blocks from North Claiborne to North Rocheblave Streets. Once again, Poree's Barber Shop moved two blocks away from the Lafitte Street location to 2013 Orleans Street between N. Prieur and N. Johnson Streets.

From the front window of Father's barber shop, our family and his customers could see the construction of the Lafitte Housing Project, literally rising up from the ground. After several years of construction, the Lafitte Project, the city's first public housing project for colored people, became a reality. The barber shop on Orleans Street was right across from the newly constructed Lafitte Project. Families who had been displaced by the project were given priority or "first" option to live in a housing unit. The Lafitte Housing Project Units were far superior to most houses in the neighborhood. Each unit had a kitchen with a gas stove, refrigerator, hardwood floors, separate bedrooms, closets, front porch with screen doors, and hot and cold running water.

The project was the finest housing in the neighborhood. Unfortunately, the public housing project did not allow for any type of businesses to operate in its facility; consequently, living in the newly constructed housing was not an option for the Poree family. Furthermore, my parents wanted a house where the barber shop and the living quarters would be together so there would always be an adult home, especially when the children came from school. Mother worked at Haspel Brothers clothing factory as a seamstress, and she didn't get off from work until 5:30 p.m. each evening. Fortunately, having the barber shop located in the family home allowed Father to be home when we arrived home from school, greeting, supervising, communicating, and assisting us with our homework, the prerequisites for our growth and development. In spite of the numerous relocations, the Poree family, all seven of us, managed to live together under one roof with the exception of a brief period of seven months.

We lived on Orleans Street for quite a few years. My oldest sister Edna Floe attended Dillard University. She walked to and from school most of the time. My second oldest sister Juli Rose and her friend Beverly Bart would take me to Hume Child Development Center before going to school at McDonogh #35 on Rampart Street in the morning. During most evenings after school, they would pick me up from Hume Center and take me home. Edna Floe's best friend Dolores Thompson Aaron also pick me up from Hume Center on days that she got out of class earlier than Juli and Beverly.

Natalie and Anna Lea, my other two younger sisters, also attended McDonogh # 35 High School while we lived on Orleans Street. After attending pre-school at Hume's Center, I began attending Joseph A. Craig Elementary School on St. Phillip Street in Treme. Several years after the Lafitte Project was built, my family was once again forced to move because our landlord wanted his property for his relatives. Father challenged the landlord's short notice demand by appealing to the Rent Control Agency, the Office of The Housing Expedition in Dallas, Texas. Unfortunately, bureaucratic processing delays eventually led to the landlord's filing suit against our family and getting a favorable judgment from the First City Court of New Orleans, evicting our family from the $20 a month rental home at 2013 Orleans Avenue.

Chicken, Chicken, a Food for All Occasions

Mother and Aunt Louise were excellent cooks. They knew how to stretch even the smallest amount of culinary meals into meals for a small army. During World War II, meat was rationed, all over the nation. Families could only get a very limited amount of meat, especially seasoning meat. Just the thought of not having any meat to season red beans, mustard greens, turnip greens or meat to bake or stew was unimaginable. Well, Mother and Aunt Louise knew just what to do to solve that problem. They changed and transformed chicken feet to pickle flavored seasoning meat substitute by using a special family formula handed down from our ancestors, that seasoned many chicken feet with salt and other family secret ingredients, then saturated the chicken feet with vinegar and a fermenting agent. They placed the chicken feet in a very large jar, sealing the lid tightly. After the fermenting process concluded, the chicken feet were transformed into pickled flavored seasoning meat. Mother and Aunt Louise knew exactly when it was ripe for opening the glass jar. The transformed chicken feet were the best pickled meat available for seasoning red beans, mustard greens, and turnip greens.

Mrs. Goins, who lived across the street from Aunt Louise's, owned Goins' Chicken Shack, located on the corner of Dumaine and North Galvez Streets. Every Saturday mornings, I went to Goins' Chicken Shack early to get in line for today's freshly killed chickens for Mother and Aunt Louise. Unlike most customers in line, I was there to get chicken feet, not chickens. When the line moved and I got closer to the front, if I didn't see enough chicken feet available, I would step aside, tell the customer standing behind me in line that I was waiting for the Dominick (black and white) hen's shipment to come in. The real reason I kept delaying my order, I was waiting for the chicken feet customers didn't want. After waiting in line, on some occasions for more than an hour, Mrs. Goins gave me two big bags full of chicken feet, one for Mother and one for Aunt Louise.

Those two bags of chicken feet would become the best pickled meat, fried chicken meat, baked chicken meat, and stewed chicken meat. That's right, one day we had red beans with pickled chicken feet, another day we had stewed chicken feet with green peas and potatoes salad, another day we had fried chicken feet with mashed potatoes and cold slaw, and on Sundays we had baked macaroni, string beans, candied yams, and good old baked chicken feet. Even Mother's file' gumbo would have some of those delicious chicken feet that you could suck the meat off the bones.

Third Grade Failure

Families faced really difficult times during the 1940's, and I was about to face a really bad time, being kept back in the third grade. I still remember that day and how devastated I was when Miss Gwendolyn Walker, my third grade teacher, called the names of all my buddies who were going to fourth grade and my name was not called at all. I couldn't stop crying as those great big crocodile tears kept rolling down my face. Miss Walker told me she loved me and that it was difficult for her to make the decision not to allow me to go to fourth at that time. I certainly did not understand how she could love me dearly on one hand and in the same breathe tell me that I had to repeat the third grade for another year. Much worst, I would be in her class again for that year.

I wasn't a dumb kid; I was the class's clown. I helped my buddies with their class work many times; unfortunately, I spent so much time clowning I didn't always complete my assignments on time. When it was time to turn in class assignments, my buddies I had helped finish their assignments turned their completed work in on time. Unfortunately, my clowning prevented me from finishing my assignments on time; consequently, my buddies' got good grades and I got unsatisfactory grades. When I became a young man, Mother told me that she knew I would be repeating third grade a month before the closing of school. She also told me that she and Ms. Walker had agreed earlier that it was in my best interest to repeat third grade. That was a shocking revelation to find out my Mother agreed with my teacher to make me repeat the third grade for another year with the same teacher. That's got to be the strangest kind of love ever administered to a third grader!

Once again our landlord gave our parents a short notice to move this time. Unfortunately, they did not have enough time to find a house that could be converted into a barber shop; consequently and hastily, Father had to find another alternative quickly in order to salvage his business and retain some income for our family. The only available property Father could find was a vacant garage next to the Duplantier family's home located on the corner of St. Ann and North Galvez Streets. For the first time, Poree's Barber Shop would not be in the same house where we lived. Our family lived in three separate locations for nearly seven months while Father's barber shop was housed in a garage. Father continued looking for a house during those seven months that could be converted into a barber shop so our family could be reunited together again.

Living with Relatives

When Poree's Barber Shop opened in the garage, Mother, Father, Edna, Natalie, and Anna Lea lived with Willis Joseph's family on St. Ann Street between North Roman and North Prieur Streets, two and a half blocks from the barber shop. Julie Rose lived with Mrs. Katie Wickam, National President Beautician Association and owner of Katie Wickam's Beauty School on Dryades Street near Jackson Avenue. I lived with Aunt Louise and Uncle Glapion (aka Glap) at 2229 St. Ann Street, only a half block from Father's shop. On weekends I stayed with my parents and three sisters, returning to my aunt and uncle's house on Mondays after school.

When I came from school each day, I stopped at Father's barber shop to see what he wanted me to do. Then, I went to my aunt's house to see what errands she had before returning to the barber shop for my daily chores, which included bringing a bucket of hot water to the shop, for Father to use for shaving customers and cleaning his razors. There wasn't any hot or cold running water in the garage. Sweeping the shop, cleaning outside, and taking dirty towels back to the house and washing them were part of my daily routine. Later during the evenings I brought Father something to eat that Aunt Louise fixed for him. After completing my daily chores, Father would review and help me with my homework, asking questions and making suggestions, and when I completed the assignment, he would give me a pat on the back and say, "That's my boy."

Living at my aunt and uncle's house was quite different than our house. I was one among five children at home; consequently, I wasn't the center of attention. My first cousin, Octavia, affectionately called Tavee and her husband, Wall, lived with my aunt and uncle. Tavee treated me like I was her son just like a little prince. Uncle Glap's elderly Aunt Katherine, affectionately called Tante, also lived at the house in a tiny room at the back of the house on a porch behind the kitchen. Tante was extremely light complexion with snow white silky hair. Tavee didn't have any children so she treated me like I was her child, giving me practically anything and everything I wanted, even things that I was forbidden from having at my house.

One afternoon, we were playing football on the Miro Court across the street from Dooky Chase in the Lafitte Project, and the football accidentally went into the street and a city bus rolled over and crushed it. That ended our football game. We later played with a stuffed raggedy old football for weeks. Tavee bought me a genuine leather football, and I became the most popular boy in the neighborhood. One evening, while playing football on Miro Street, two boys on a bicycle stopped to watch us play. After our team scored a touchdown, the kid sitting on the bike's handlebars asked, "Can I see your football?" Without any hesitation my friend threw him the football. When he caught it, they took off like lightening on the bicycle with my brand new football toward their neighborhood around Craig School.

When my friends and I realized that the only real football in our neighborhood was being stolen, we ran after those boys on the bike. After chasing them for more than seven blocks, we caught up with the two thieves a block from the municipal auditorium. The boys gladly gave us the football and ran off leaving the bike behind. One of them dropped a wallet, which apparently had been stolen. When we returned to our neighborhood with the bike, we discovered that the bike had been stolen from Mr. Lester, owner of the Orange Room Bar on the corner of North Galvez across from Father's barber shop. Mr. Lester thanked us for getting his son's bike, and he bought us another leather football. The wallet belonged to one of Mr. Lester's customers.

My parents didn't allow me to have a toy pistol at all because they felt that guns were bad to have, even toy ones. Most of my friends had toy guns when we played cowboys and Indians. Only a few of us didn't have a toy gun. I was one of the few. I made a homemade rifle by cutting off the straw portion of a broom's wooden handle and nailed another piece of wood on the end for the big shoot-out. My friends always laughed at my homemade rifle, but they allowed me to be an Indian. Most of my friends living near my aunt and uncle's house were light skinned with an olive complexion and Roman Catholic. They were always the cowboys in the shoot-outs. Those of us who were dark complexioned were always the Indians. I don't have to tell you who won the fight. Tavee bought me a Hopper Long Cassidy gun and holster, and I became one of the top guns in the neighborhood shoot-outs.

I had my toy gun the entire time I stayed with my aunt and uncle during the time Father's shop was located in the garage, on St. Ann Street. As long as my parents didn't know I had a toy gun and holster, it was safe. Unfortunately, a day after my family moved from Willis Joseph's house, where they had been living for seven months, to Bienville Street, I forgot to take the toy gun and holster out of my little suitcase. I used to save my clothes in the suitcase when I went back and forth from my parents' temporary home and my aunt and uncle's house. That was a big mistake because I never saw my toy gun and holster since then. I suspect Father discovered the gun and holster and that was the end of my shoot-out days and the end of my gun story.

Living at my aunt and uncle's house was quite a different experience for a third grader than the one I had living on the St. Louis Street side of the railroad tracks. There were many experiences that I couldn't understand, and there were memories that I cherished and others I'd rather forget. Unlike in Treme where so many of my aunt and uncle's neighbors were light skinned or olive complexioned and Roman Catholic, many of our neighbors living on the St. Louis Street side of the railroad tracks were not. Many of our neighbors were dark complexioned and protestant. Aunt Louise like Father was dark complexioned with rather course hair, and Uncle Glap was an olive complexioned Creole; both were Roman Catholic.

Many of Father's family were also Roman Catholics. Father followed that faith until my sisters were born. Mother looked like other Creoles, because of her light complexion, keen features, and good hair, was Methodist. Mother felt that the family should attend church together. For a long time, Father attended early mass at St. Katherine Catholic Church on Tulane Avenue, then he began attending the 11:00 a.m. service at Grace Methodist Church with Mother and my sisters. Our church was located on Iberville and North Prieur Street. After many years of attending both services, my Father became more involved with Mother's church activities, and he officially joined the Methodist Church when I was born.

Mother and Aunt Louise were so very different. Mother, a former store manager, normal school teacher, seamstress, and poet laureate, who could recite Paul Lawrence Dunbar's poetry so vividly that the characters she imitated seem real. Mother had an endearing personality and a keen sense of humor. Aunt Louise, on the other hand, like so many women during those days seem satisfied with serving and satisfying Uncle Glap's desires without giving much consideration of satisfying any of her own interest or aspirations. Mother was outgoing and caring, always willing to undertake challenges that others chided away from. Aunt Louise seemed content on cooking, washing, ironing clothes, cleaning up, preparing dinner, and satisfying Uncle Glap and her son-in-law's desires. Mother was active in many organizations; she baked more cakes and made more Calais (tastier than Beignets) than any small bakery during the year. Aunt Louise's social activities seem to be limited to attending church, occasional weddings, or funerals. Aunt Louise did however have a very special ability or expertise of identifying whether newly born babies would retain their light complexioned skin as they grew older or whether the hair of the babies would be curly or coarse when they grew older.

    I remember seeing Aunt Louise examining the skin around new born baby's fingernails which apparently was a way of determining the complexion and color of the baby when they got older. She would also place her thumb in front of the baby's ear, pressing down and sweeping backward along the side of the head, which apparently was a way of determining whether the texture of hair would be naturally curly, coarse or kinky. Complexion and hair fortune telling were Aunt Louise's specialty and expertise. If she didn't smile during her complexion and hair examinations, you could bet the baby's complexion and hair would not pass the "brown paper bag tests."

    Uncle Glap's eighty-five year old Aunt Katherine, Tante, spoke French fluently. She hardly came out of her bedroom other than peeping through her door to play her numbers (lottery) with the neighborhood bookie or getting her food from Aunt Louise. Tante would get a bottle of white port wine from the Orange Room bar every other day during the week. I went to the Orange Room every other day to get a pint of white port wine for Tante and a fifth of claret, red wine for uncle Glap and Aunt Louise for dinner. Tante never let me in her room when I brought her wine. Instead, she opened her door slightly enough to slip the pint of wine through. She never gave the money to buy the wine in my hand; instead she gave me a white handkerchief tied very tightly with the exact amount of money for the wine along with a small paper bag to carry the wine in. Aunt Louise gave me the exact amount of money for the red wine in a small canvas cloth sack with a pull string.

    When I went to the Orange Room service window to get wine, Mr. Lester, the owner, knew exactly what I came to get without me telling him, what I came for. He placed the bottle of port and the white handkerchief in the paper bag, and then he put a bottle of claret in the pull string sack and told me to tell Tante and Aunt Louise hello. Every time I made that trip to stand in line to get those bottles of wine for Tante and Aunt Louise, I felt embarrassed because many of the older people standing in line appeared to be drunk. The more I stood, waiting in line to get liquor for Tante and Aunt Louise, the more I began to dislike liquor more and more.

Neither Aunt Louise nor Uncle Glap got to go into Tante's room either. When Aunt Louise brought Tante's meals, she would open her door slightly enough to allow the plate through. No one other than the priest got to go in her room when he visited her to give Holy Communion or pray to comfort her during illness. On evening after school on a regular scheduled wine day, I knocked on Tante's door to get her paper bag and white handkerchief to go get her bottle of port wine, she didn't answer or open her door. I began knocking harder and harder on her door, still no answer and she didn't come to the door either. I told Aunt Louise that something must be wrong because Tante didn't answer nor open the door. Aunt Louise never did anything unless she first talked to Uncle Glap; consequently, nothing was done until Uncle Glap came home from work after six o'clock that evening. When he knocked on the door and called Tante several times and she didn't answer, he realized something was wrong. He forced opened the door and found Tante lying motionless in her bed, dead. That was a sad day because Tante was my good buddy and friend. That was the very first time that I had ever seen Tante's little room. It was very neat and tidy, just like Tante.

Captain Video

When television first came out during the late 1940's, I became one of the most popular boys in the Treme neighborhood. My popularity was directly related to Aunt Louise and Uncle Glap's having a "giant" twelve inch black-and-white Admiral television, radio phonograph combination set in the front room. Very few people had televisions in the neighborhood at that time, especially combination television set. Many youngsters in the neighborhood became my good friends, especially around five o'clock in the evenings when the television station came on the air. The big television show then was Captain Video. Every evening after school around 4:30 p.m. many of my friends sat on my aunt's steps talking about summer picnic across the lake. All of a sudden the topic changed from the picnic to, "How Captain Video got out of trouble yesterday." That was the usual sign for me to ask Aunt Louise if we could come in to see Captain Video. Aunt Louise allowed us to come and watch the show often. I suspect that's what made me such a popular boy in Treme.

Picnics and Church

During the summer time, Aunt Louise's neighbor, Ms. Meyers sponsored a picnic across the lake. Children from the neighborhood got an opportunity to ride in a big red truck, travel across the seven mile bridge over Lake Pontchartrain and go to the big picnic grounds for Colored people. The picnics were always on Sunday and that created a problem for me. My parents, especially Mother would not allow any of us to go anywhere on Sunday until we attended church first. Our family was Methodist, and the earliest service was Sunday school that began at 9:30 a.m. in the morning for young people. The regular Sunday Morning Service began at 11:00 a.m.; therefore, my chances of going on picnics were very limited.

I asked Mother if I could go to church with my friends in the neighborhood that had early morning service. She asked, "What church Junior?" I said, "St. Peter Claver Church." She said, "That's a Catholic church." "Yes, Mother, you said that we couldn't go anywhere until we first went to church; does it matter what church as long as it's a church?" Mother paused for a moment then said, "If Aunt Louise and Uncle Glap say it's OK." I asked them if it was alright if I went with my friends to St. Peter Claver's Mass, they said, "Yes." I told Mother Aunt Louise said yes, and she agreed to let me go.

I was so excited when I arrived at Mrs. Meyer's house to tell her I could go to the picnic; unfortunately, I forgot to bring my money for the ride. Mother brought the money plus some fruit, candy, and cold cuts for Aunt Louise to make sandwiches. I could hardly sleep Saturday night. I woke up at 5:00 a.m. Sunday morning to get ready to go to the 6:00 a.m. mass with my friends. When mass was over, we all raced back to get ready to get on that big red truck. The truck had hard wooden benches, bunched so closely together that you could hardly move because your knees were knocking your friend's knees sitting across from you. It didn't matter because we were getting ready to ride across that long bridge over the lake and along that winding dirt road surrounded by tall pine trees finally arriving at those big picnic grounds for us to have fun all day. We got on the big red truck at 7:30 a.m. Sunday morning and at 8:00 a.m., we were off and running to the picnic grounds.

Aunt Louise did not let this opportunity slip by because she always felt that her brother's children should be Catholic, since most of the Poree family was Roman Catholic. "Once a Catholic, always a Catholic," she said. Aunt Louise prayed for Father to return back to the Catholic faith after Father joined Mother's Methodist Church. Once Mother gave me permission to attend St. Peter Claver Catholic Church, it gave Aunt Louise an opportunity to get me to attend mass more often with my friends. She seized that moment to begin her plan to get one of her brother's children converted to the Catholic faith.

Most of the time, I went to Sunday school at Grace Methodist Church on Iberville and North Prieur Streets, our family's church. It was ten blocks from Aunt Louise and Uncle Glap's house. St. Peter Claver's was only four and a half blocks from their house. Aunt Louise asked Mother if I could go to St. Peter Claver Church with my friends on Sundays, since they kept asking her if I could go with them. I always attend my family's church on the first Sunday of the month for Communion Service. Mother allowed me to attend St. Peter Claver Catholic Church with my friends every other Sunday.

After a couple of weeks rotating back and forth from my church to St. Peter Claver Church, Aunt Louise always found a reason for me to attend St. Peter Claver with her. During mass she always encouraged me to follow closely what was going on. When we returned from mass, she questioned me about the mass. I learned to say the rosaries and the fourteen Stations of the Cross. Each week I attended Peter Claver, I learned something else about the ritual. Aunt Louise always questioned me about mass and my participation. She told Father that he ought to come and see how well I had learned to follow the Mass. This was part of Aunt Louise's plan to convince Father to come back to the Catholic Church and just maybe, he would allow me to convert to Catholicism. However, Father didn't take the bait, my parents continued to allow me to attend St. Peter Claver quite often with my friends.

One Sunday, when my buddies were about to take their Holy Communion, one of them said, "Come on Edgar and take Communion with us." I told them I didn't think I ought to do that, but they insisted so I followed them. When we reached the alter I opened my mouth just like my friends and took Holy Communion. When I got back to Aunt Louise's house, before she asked me what I had learned, I said, "Guess what I did today Aunt Louise?" "What did you do Junior? She asked with a big smile on her face. "Aunt Louise I did everything this morning." She stood there with a look of excitement in her eyes. I said with a great deal of pride, "I took Holy Communion this morning." Aunt Louise said, "What!" I repeated, "I took Holy Communion." Aunt Louise looked like she had just seen a ghost. She fell to her knees and immediately began praying for my forgiveness. She appeared to be in shock; I didn't know why she looks so pale and upset.

When she got up off her knees, she told me to get in the bedroom and stay there until she told me to come out. Aunt Louise went from appearing very pleased with what I was about to tell her into someone who had been double-crossed; vengeance was hers. She said, "Wait until I tell your Mother and Father what you did." I thought Aunt Louise would be happy with what I had done that Sunday. Little did I realize what a terrible thing I had done, unknowingly? When she told Mother what I had done, Mother said, "Louise he was just doing what his friends asked him to do, and he didn't know he was doing something that would upset her." Mother told me to apologize to Aunt Louise and promise not to do that again.

Aunt Louise was not satisfied with my apology. She felt she had to ask for forgiveness and do penance for what I had done. I still remember that look on her face and her seven day penance crusade at the Shrine of St. Ann. For seven straight days, Aunt Louise went to the Shrine of St. Ann on Ursuline and North Johnson Street to pray for my forgiveness. She crawled up the steps of St. Ann each day doing penance for my apparent grievous sin. During those seven days of penance, she hardly spoke to me even though she was praying for my forgiveness each day at the Shrine of St. Ann. I guess Roman Catholics could not talk to the ones who had committed such a grievous sin during the penance period of praying. I never could understand that about my aunt.

The Prince and His Servants

Aunt Louise was a devoted wife and Mother-in-law to both men who lived in the house, uncle Glap and Wall Douglas. Uncle Glap was an insurance salesman for the Venus Life Insurance Company located on North Claiborne and St. Phillip Street. Wall owned a ballroom on the corner of Bienville and North Johnson Streets. He was the most handsome, best looking man that I had ever seen. He was olive complexioned with jet black, naturally curly hair with extremely keen features. Neighborhood folks, especially the women, called him the beautiful "Turk." Tavee practically worshipped and adored him like he was some king. Whatever he wanted, he got from her, and she would be there for his every beckon call.

Every morning Aunt Louise got up early and pressed several of Wall's slack suits. Then she or Tavee placed the suits on the bed for him to select which one he wanted to wear that day. Slack-suits were very popular during those days, and Wall had more slack suits, sport shirts, and pants then anyone that I knew at that time. Several pairs of shoes were placed at the foot of the bed with several pairs of matching socks, and belts were also displayed for Wall's selection. After he made his daily selections, Aunt Louise or Tavee hung the other suits up for another day's selection. The clothing selection process was a daily routine. Once dressed and after splattering his favorite cologne on, Aunt Louise fixed his favorite breakfast, ready for his liking. In the meantime, Tavee cleaned the bathroom after his use. Aunt Louise fixed a plate for him with some snacks to take to work. Without any thanks, Wall was off to his Bienville Street barroom. On Saturdays, before I went to stay over the weekends with my parents at Willis Joseph's house, Aunt Louise got me to bring Wall's lunch to him.

Aunt Louise and uncle Glap's house was half of a double similar to a typical shotgun house where rooms were right behind each other. The front room was the living-room, the second room was Aunt Louise and Uncle Glap's bedroom, and the room next was a hallway with the bathroom. The next room was cousin Tavee and Wall's bedroom, followed by another bedroom where I slept next to the kitchen. There was a porch and laundry room between the kitchen and Tante's room. Aunt Louise used the bedroom where I slept to do her ironing and folding of clothes. She could be seen through the window humming and ironing all day long listening to her favorite soap operas.

One day as I was playing checkers in Ms. Meyer's backyard, the insurance man came in the yard to collect for her insurance policy. The insurance man said, "Ms. Meyers, I know some of your neighbors raised chickens, but I didn't know anyone had a cow." "Mister, that ain't a cow, that's my aunt humming," I said. All my friends were laughing because they knew it was my aunt.

Wall's barroom didn't close until early in the mornings, and many times he didn't get home until after two a.m. in the mornings. Consequently, he slept most of the mornings until noon the next day. When he slept, no one could walk or even tip-toe through that bedroom. If the front door bell rang while Aunt Louise was either cooking in the kitchen or ironing in the next bedroom, she had to walk through the alley way to see who rang the doorbell to avoid disturbing Wall's sleep. Even during the rain when Wall slept, everyone in the rear of the house used the alley way, except Uncle Glap, who usually was not home during his-son-in-law's sleeping tours.

One rainy morning, someone rang the front doorbell while Wall was sleeping; Aunt Louise was cooking in the kitchen. She got an umbrella and walked through the slippery alley way to see who was ringing the doorbell. Before she reached the front gate, I heard a loud noise and Aunt Louise holler. I looked down the alley way and saw Aunt Louise lying on the ground. She had apparently slipped down and couldn't get up from her fall. I went out to help her get up and practically held her up while we walked back through the alley to get to the bedroom. Both of her legs were badly bruised, and she had a cut below her left knee. I helped her sit on the side of the bed and went to the kitchen to get a bottle of apple cider vinegar. She told me to get an old pillow slip from the washroom on the porch. Aunt Louise tore the pillow slip into small strips like bandages, then she poured the apple cider vinegar on the bruises and the cut, and she wrapped the pillow strips around her legs. After resting for a little while, she got up and started cooking again. Wall never got up during that ordeal. Aunt Louise changed the dress that she wore when she fell and put on a very long smock so that Uncle Glap would not see her injuries when he came home from work. That's the extreme extent that she and cousin Tavee would go to please the beautiful Turk.

Uncle Glap was the treasurer of the Vidalia's Benevolent Association, an organization that my grandfather, Thomas Poree, was one of the founding directors. The association held their monthly meetings in St. James Church's Education Building on North Roman Street. The benevolent associate provided doctor home visits, paid for medicine, and provided burial plots for its members for two dollar monthly fee. Uncle Glap was responsible for collecting monthly dues, recording the amounts collected, depositing funds, and making financial reports for the

Association. Tavee, in addition to her regular job, did bookkeeping for several small organizations, and she volunteered to assist uncle Glap with the bookkeeping for the benevolent association. The association met on the second Sunday of each month.

Many members did not always pay their dues on time during the monthly meeting for various reasons; they gave I.O.U's. Consequently, some monthly financial reports were not always completed in time for the next monthly meeting due to unpaid I.O.U.'s and late payment fees. Because Cousin Tavee did the bookkeeping after she got off from her regular job, money would, on some occasions, remain in the house for several days before being deposited. This proved to be a very unfortunate situation. Cousin Tavee's husband was a big time gambler, and he apparently borrowed and lost a lot of money that he owed to some people who were hassling him. He was always asking Aunt Louise to loan him some money until the weekends when the bar had most of its business. He never told Tavee about borrowing money from Aunt Louise and other people to cover his gambling. His brother, a popular businessman, apparently stopped loaning him money and bailing him out to cover his gambling debts, so Wall was desperate for money.

Unable to get anyone else to loan him money to cover his gambling debts, he began taking money that belong to the benevolent association and other organizations that had not been deposited yet without being detected. This theft continued to go on and when he couldn't afford replacing money that he had been taking from the funds, my cousin detected missing funds during reconciling the association and organizations' accounts. At first, she thought maybe Aunt Louise had accidentally moved some of the boxes containing the money while cleaning up. She asked Aunt Louise had she moved any of the boxes containing the money when she was cleaning up and Aunt Louise told her no.

My cousin must have known in her heart that Wall had probably been taking some of the money. She confronted and questioned him about the missing money, and he denied taking any of the money. Tavee continued searching the house for the missing money unsuccessfully. When she once again confronted Wall, he finally admitted that he only borrowed the money, and he intended to replace it when his horse would win. He suggested that she "fix" the books for a while until he got some money to replace what he had borrowed. My cousin refused to do what he suggested. Unfortunately, by that time questions about the association and organization's funds became a hot topic of discussion at the meetings and an investigation began. Since my cousin handled the bookkeeping and accounting for the association and organizations, she became the prime suspect of the theft, even though she did not commit the crime. Because of her graveyard love and devotion for her husband, she took the wrap for him instead of proving her innocence. She served nine months in Parish Prison for a crime that her despicable husband committed. A crime she paid the ultimate sacrifice, her reputation and her freedom.

Each time I went with Aunt Louise to visit Tavee in prison, we all cried as we embraced her. Tavee was a devout Christian, kind, caring, loving, and extremely generous always helping others during very difficult times. Personally, Tavee was like my guardian angel, she was my mom away from home. With big crocodile tears rolling down my cheeks I asked her, "Tavee, when are you coming home?" She always said, "Junior Tavee's coming home soon!" What a terrible injustice to such a decent, generous and loving person whose only real crime was her "graveyard love" for Wall, that no good husband.

Wall, no longer had my cousin to lean on, while she served, what should have been his time in prison. He no longer had her brain to depend on for making sound decisions, her financial support to bail him out of his gambling debts, or her managing skills which enabled him to operate the barroom business. You see, Wall without her was like an empty shell, just a "pretty face" without any substance. His barroom business turned for the worst, his gambling debts exceeded his sales, and the business closed. Ironically, one of Father's customer's famous saying, "If you want to see a fifty dollar hat on a nickel head, go to the corner barroom, you'll see one standing behind the bar." He was describing my cousin's husband.

Without Tavee's support any longer, Wall continued drinking excessively and gambling. With the barroom business gone and his friends deserted, he fell on very hard times, eventually becoming homeless. He became a pitiful site picking up rags and bottles, going through garbage for food, picking up cigarettes butts to smoke, and sleeping on the neighborhood streets. This once handsome, beautiful Turk was now a pitiful homeless drifter whose bedroom was the streets instead of the privileged bedroom at Aunt Louise and uncle Glap's house. After many months living on the streets, one of Aunt Louise's neighbors found him dead in an alley way only three blocks from Aunt Louise and uncle Glap's house.

A Shocking and Devastating Experience

After operating his barber shop in a garage for seven months and our family living apart in different houses, Father finally found a house on Bienville Street to rent for us to live; his barber shop would be located in the front room. At last, our entire family would be reunited once again in one house with Father's barber shop. The weekend before our family was scheduled to move to the Bienville Street home, I got up early Saturday morning full of energy and excitement. This Saturday was my last day carrying buckets of hot water from Aunt Louise and uncle Glap's house to Father's barber shop. This Saturday would be the last day that Father would be cutting hair and shaving customers in a garage. It was a new beginning for the Poree family, reunited living together and having Father always present to receive us when we came home from school or some other activity outside our home.

Saturday night after shaving and cutting his last customer's hair in the garage, Father closed the shop for the last time at that location. Apparently, the thought and excitement of being reunited with his family once again in the same house as the barber shop, Father stopped at a neighborhood bar. Mother became concerned when Father didn't get home several hours after closing the shop. Late Saturday night, one of Father's customers stopped to tell Mother two of his friends helped Father get to the steps on the corner of St. Ann and North Roman Street, after drinking excessively at the bar.

When Mother and I reached the corner, Father was lying on the steps in a stupor, mumbling unintelligently. I was devastated for I had never seen Father like this. As I helped Mother lift Father up and helped her physically hold him upright, while walking to the house, my world changed drastically. When we reached the house and got Father into bed I told Mother, "You will never ever see me like this during our lifetime." I promised to never ever take one drink in life! Seeing Father, the Judge, the learned scholar lying on those steps drunk, coupled with the embarrassment of having to stand in line at a barroom's window to buy liquor for relatives, was too much for a third grader to cope with. These experiences would have a lifelong impact upon me.

CHAPTER II

BIENVILLE STREET HOUSE

I was ten years old when my parents rented a house at 2115 Bienville Street in 1946. Our family would never be separated again. It was a shotgun house in which the front room was converted into Father's barbershop. The second room was Mother and Father's bedroom. The third room was for three of my sisters, and the fourth very small room was shared by my oldest sister, Edna Floe and me. Next was the kitchen, and the bathroom was the last room in the house. We had a wide-side yard and a big back yard where we raised chickens.

My Grandmother's sister, Ophelia Dumas, and her son, Roy, moved in with us in a tiny room in the back yard. They lived with my parents for about three years and the only place they would go would be to church or to the doctor's office. No one was allowed to go in the room while they live there. They both died in that room about three years later. Roy died first and Ophelia died eight months later. That was the only time that my folks got to see the room, when the undertaker removed their bodies.

When we first moved into the house, there were so many things my parents had to overcome before we could utilize all of the rooms in the house. The house was built during the turn of the twentieth century, and it had sustained some serious structural as well as roof problems. The first three rooms of the house were structurally sound and were under the same roof; however, the next room, kitchen and bathroom were attached portions of the house with a tin roof that had many problems. Unlike the structurally sound first three rooms of the house, the rear portion had upright boards which had drifted apart due to the settling of the house over the many years. This separation caused plenty drafts of air flowing through the cracks in the walls of the house.

Although the roof in the rear section of the house had been patched many times, during hard rains, like Morton Salt, it poured rainwater through the roof. During a hard rain, it sounded like a symphony orchestra in the kitchen, as the rain drops from the leaks in the roof splashed down into the different size pots and pans placed in the rooms to catch the rain water. Bong, bing, and beep were the sounds of the rainwater splashing in the pots and pans. Some of the boards of the floors in the rear of the house had some separations, allowing drafts flowing through the floor. In spite of these problems with the house, being together as a family far out-weighted those inconveniences. With grit, determination, and a little creativity we corrected many of the structural problems, and our house was transformed into our home.

The first three rooms of the house had plastered walls; the rear section that had foot-wide upright boards on the exterior walls and one-by-four inch upright boards for the interior walls. Bienville Street was a busy two lanes of traffic on both sides of the medium, and big trucks used this route daily. On several occasions when big trucks passed, it caused some of the plaster to crack. After several months of heavy traffic, some of the plaster fell from the walls creating huge holes in the wall. My parents did not have enough money to hire a plasterer to repair the plaster so we had to find another alternative to repair the wall. One such alternative was the use of corrugated cardboard boxes used for crating bicycles.

There was a bicycle store on North Claiborne and St. Peter Streets across from the Lafitte Project. Father and I would go to the store and get some of the discarded cardboard boxes thrown away for trash. The bicycle boxes were approximately four feet tall, six feet long and about a one foot wide. When boxes were fully opened, they covered an area approximately eight feet by fourteen feet. Father's wealth of knowledge and thirst of creative use of discarded materials enabled him to think out of the box. He asked Mr. Martin, his longshoreman customer, who worked at a chinaware packaging company, "What did they do with the surplus cellulose used in packing chinaware for shipping. Mr. Martin told Father they discarded it as trash. Father asked him to bring some of the trashed cellulose to the barber shop because he wanted to use it as insulation. Mr. Martin asked, "Judge where in the hell did you get that wild idea?" Father said, "From reading." He brought many bags of trashed surplus cellulose to the barber shop.

The surplus cellulose became Father's creative insulation. Before covering the damaged plaster walls, Father removed two of the top wooden slats along the entire wall, then he poured the trashed surplus cellulose into the wall cavities. After filling all of the wall cavities, he nailed the wooden slats, previously removed back onto the wall. We began covering the entire walls with the cardboard boxes we got from the bike store. This creative wall processing treatment, hid holes in the plaster and allowed for insulation as well as provided smooth surfaces for wallpapering. After repeating this routine over and over, I became proficient in hanging wall paper, enabling me to earn much needed money when I became a teenager.

Cardboard boxes also proved to be a much needed source of floor insulation. Because of the poor condition of some floors in the house caused by decades of house settling, there were numerous slight separations of floor boards. During winter, drafts pouring through those separations make it rather uncomfortable in some of the rooms. Father covered the floors with cardboard boxes and newspaper before placing the linoleum on top. The rooms no longer had cold spots in them. The toilet's water storage tank in the bathroom was attached high on the wall of the bathroom. A chain hanging from the water tank was used for flushing the toilet. There was a cast iron tub and a small face bowl in the bathroom. The space between the face bowl and the tub was so small that you practically had to turn side-ways to use the toilet. The bathroom's floor had so many bad boards that we had to put cardboard boxes under the linoleum there also. In the winter time we took our baths in a large galvanized tub in one of the bedrooms because there were too many drafts in the bathroom, and it was too small to place an upright heater in there.

Unlike the kitchens in the Lafitte Housing Projects, we did not have a refrigerator; instead we had an ice box. We would get fifty pounds of ice twice a week. The ice man delivered our ice on Tuesdays and Saturdays. Mr. Bird, the ice man, was one of Father's best friends. He was so white looking that everybody who saw him thought he was white. Mr. Bird was a hard worker and a very quiet man. He and Father, however, always got into heated conversations every time he came to the barber shop.

Chicken Little

It was a very difficult time for my family, and money was very hard to get. Most families, in the neighborhood were on rations, and Father and Mother were not making much money at the time. My family raised chickens in our back yard to supplement our food supply. Juli Rose fed the chickens often, and she became very attached to one of the black and white Domino chickens. Juli could get that chicken to do anything she wanted. She called that chicken her pet and named it Chicken Little. When Juli told Chicken Little to stand up on one leg, Chicken Little would do so. If Juli told Chicken Little to lie down and play dead, Chicken Little would roll over, close her eyes, and pretend to be dead. Every command Julie gave Chicken Little, she would do it.

I can remember one week Father had only a few customers all week, and Mother's clothing factory did not have very much piece work for her to do, so they had very little money available to make groceries. Things were really tough that week, and my parents had to make one of the most difficult decisions. The cupboard was bare, and all but one of the chickens had already been eaten, all but one, Chicken Little. That day my parents made the tough decision. Juli's pet; Chicken Little was the only available option. When Father went to the chicken coop to get Chicken Little, Juli screamed, "Mama you can't let daddy kill Chicken Little; she's my best friend in the whole-wide world."

Mother tried to explain to Juli Rose that we had no other choice. Rent had to be paid, Edna Floe's tuition had to be paid, the light bill had to be paid, and there was not any money left until next Friday, four days from now. Juli said, "Mama I don't need to eat. I'll eat a piece of stale bread and drink water." Unfortunately, by that time Father had done the most terrible thing that my sisters and I, especially Juli Rose, thought at that time, that he had broken Chicken Little's neck, plucked off her feathers, and prepared her for cooking. Mother even shed some tears as she was stewing Chicken Little for dinner.

During dinner everyone except Juli Rose was eating. I was very sorry Father killed Chicken Little, but I must confess it was the best finger licking tasting chicken I had ever eaten. From the looks on my other sisters' faces, they must have had the same experience, but they did not say one word. When I asked Mother for another piece of chicken, she told me the only piece left was for Juli Rose, who had not eaten anything. When Juli saw our facial expressions of apparent enjoyment, she reached, picked up the last piece of Chicken Little's drumstick and reluctantly began eating. While Juli was eating, slowly her teary eyes began transforming from sadness into a sparkling gleaming light expression. To our amazement, Juli Rose said, "Mama, we got to raise more little Chicken Little's because she was the best tasting stewed chicken I've eaten!" We all said in unison, "Yes, mama and daddy, let's get plenty little chicks and raise many more Chicken Littles."

Lottery, Books and Culinary Delicacies

Father was such an avid, serious reader; he bought volumes of great literary works and books of some of the most renowned great philosophers. Confucius, Socrates, Plato, and such legendary epics like the Iliad and the Odyssey written by that great European writer, Homer, were just samples of books found on shelves of the barbershop and in the bedrooms of our home. Father was also an avid culinary practitioner of gourmet foods and wild game. Solar's, on Royal Street in the French Quarters was Father's favorite gourmet store. Raccoons, *coons,* alligators, deer, rabbits, pheasants, squirrels, quails, venison, wild ducks, and muskrats were just a few of the many wild game found on the plates of Father's customers and friends.

Due to foul odors, Mother would not allow father to cook wild game in the house. Father had to cook the wild game outside the house, in the yard. He had special pots to cook wild game in and he bought a special pot for cooking muskrats outside on the barbeque pit. Mother refused to let him cook in the pots she prepared the daily family meals, especially muskrats. Father claimed muskrats were the cleanest of all wild game; washing everything that they ate; however, Mother declared, "Ain't no rats being cooked in her pots! No matter how clean they were!"

Father was a regular player of lottery. Although, lottery was not legalized, it was a popular bookie's wager. The bookies were like nomads, operating from one place to another, always moving one step quicker than the police. Bookies visited neighborhoods daily taking bets from customers, writing their numbers bets on pieces of paper. Customers wrote their numbers down on little pieces of paper to give to the bookies. Those pieces of paper were the customer's number for the day. This was done in case the police stopped the bookie; there would be little evidence to arrest the bookie for illegal activity. When the winning numbers list came out, the bookies returned in the evenings to make the pay-offs for their winning customers.

When Father won, he split his winnings three ways, one third for Mother's household needs, one for books, and one for culinary delicacies and wild game. Over his fifty plus years as a barber, avid reader, intellectual scholar, and knowledgeable current event student, Father acquired over five hundred books, publications, newsletters, and journals for his extensive barber shop library. His array of books played an important role in the growth and development of many African-American students, who attended the two historically African-American Universities, Dillard and Xavier Universities, in New Orleans, during the 1940's, 50's, and 60's. Father's barber shop had such a wide diverse collection of books and journals that many students from Dillard and Xavier came to Father's barber shop to do their assignments and research papers. Since Father read most of the books in the barber shop, the college students' research experience was greatly enhanced by Father's insight and knowledge of the books that they were reviewing. Hundreds of class assignments and research papers were completed using Father's barber shop library books and journals.

The Poree's kitchen table was the college students' desk, Father was their subject matter research advisor, and Mother was their culinary chef during their research tour. When Mother got home from work at Haspel Brothers in the evenings, four or five students would be doing their assignments on the kitchen table. Mother provided the very best meals and desserts for her extended students family members. She was a source of inspiration and wisdom, encouraging them to keep God in their plans, to honor their parents, and to be grateful to them for the tremendous sacrifices they made in making it possible for them to get a college education.

Mother was a seamstress at Haspel Brothers, makers of men's Palm Beach clothing. Haspel employees were allowed to select and purchase for a very monomial price clothing items that did not meet Palm Beach Brand's clothing standards. Mother gave numerous pairs of slacks and coats with slight flaws to the many male students who did their class assignments at our home that she purchased at work. For many of the female students, Mother gave them hand-me-down clothing from rich white folks, given to relatives who worked as domestics. She also did alterations on students' clothing brought to her during their research sessions at the Poree's. Father's barber shop was the off-campus library for hundreds of college students from Dillard and Xavier. Mother's kitchen was the best restaurant, student wisdom building resource center and clothing alterations shop. This bond and union among Father, Mother, and college students lasted more than thirty years between the 1940's and the 1960's. My parents and their extended student families, who studied, ate, advised, counseled, inspired, and dressed, created an incredible wholesome environment which resulted in life-long friendships and family ties.

Sunday Dinners at the Poree's

After decades of interacting with college students from all over the country attending Dillard and Xavier Universities, my parents, especially Mother, experienced unbelievably long-lasting relationships with many families whose daughters and sons studied and ate during their college days. Although college dormitory students, especially freshmen and sophomores, were prohibited from visiting off-campus homes without parental approval and university authorization, my parent's home was the exception for Dillard's students. Edna Flo, my oldest sister, a graduate and active alumna of Dillard encouraged university officials to allow dorm students to attend Grace Methodist Church's services, accompanied by chaperons. Edna felt that it would be beneficial for the students' spiritual and social growth and development. The university agreed to a limited trial of her proposal. Edna encouraged several members of our church, who had automobiles to provide transportation for the dorm students to and from the campus on Sundays. Guess where most students ate after church, the Poree's. Mother's kitchen was the favorite restaurant for dorm students as well as their parents who attended Grace Methodist Church's service. That off campus trial lasted over three decades.

Father's Barber Shop, Its Characters and Stories

My Father, the scholar, and his friend, Mr. Bird the iceman, who looked white and sophisticated until he opened his mouth, were known as the combative friends. Mr. Bird was as limited (unintelligent) as he could be. Father told Mr. Bird if you would just nod your head when people talk to you instead of opening your mouth, no one would know how ignorant you were. I never understood how these two men claimed to be the best of friends since they were constantly arguing all the time. After having their usual arguments every time, Mr. Bird delivered ice, and Father vowed never again to cut that ignorant man's hair any more. Mr. Bird vowed never to deliver any ice and never to let Mr. Intelligent, as he called Father, cut his hair. Like clock-work, the following Monday, after Saturday's big argument, Mr. Bird showed up just as he did every other Monday for his hair cut. Mr. Intelligent and Mr. Ignorant had the strangest relationship that I had ever known at that young age.

Another one of Father's good friends was Mr. Jones, a Jahncke Concrete truck driver. The side yard and back yard on Bienville Street were covered with shells. When Mr. Jones finished delivering concrete to constructions work sites, he had to clean out any excess concrete in his truck. Instead of going to a dump to clean out his truck, he came to Father's barber shop to clean out his truck. He had a wheelbarrow on his truck, and he let Father use it to carry the excess concrete to the back yard for paving areas as large as the concrete would cover. I also carried some of the excess concrete in my little red wagon while helping Father paving the yard.

After many, many years and many blisters and back pains, Father and I had completed paving most of the side yard and most of the back yard with excess concrete. Thanks to Mr. Jones' generosity and Father's hard work, we could now play in the yard without getting all scratched up when we fell. What was once a dusty old shell yard was now a beautifully covered concrete surface yard. The only section of the yard that was not paved was a small section of the year near the back fence. That was the area used for raising chickens.

The Poree family and the Cooper families were very close friends. Arthur and Edna Cooper had eight siblings, three boys and five girls. His brother, Walter, and his wife, Valerie, had one daughter. Arthur, Walter, and Father had been friends since early childhood, and Mother and their wives were very close friends. Whenever Mother cooked something that she knew Arthur or Walter liked, I made a trip to Conti Street and then to North Tonti Street to deliver that good tasting cuisine. Mother loved to bake, and she always sent some delicious pastries for Edna and Valerie to mince on when I brought the men's cuisine.

Arthur and Edna were extremely fair complexioned. If you didn't know who they were, it would be impossible to think they were colored. Their features and hair texture appeared more like Caucasian then even some Creoles. Walter, unlike his brother Arthur, resembled more closely with the majority of the folks who lived on the St. Louis Street side of the tracks. He was olive complexion with hair that was typically rather coarse yet manageable. Walter was a very tall stately well groomed gentleman who was the best dressed man that I had ever known.

Mr. Arthur Cooper was a Pullman porter on the Sunset Limited Railroad, the train that traveled from New Orleans to Chicago. Because of his appearance, he was always the most questioned Pullman porter on the train. Pullman porters were colored, and they mostly look colored. Mr. Arthur, however, looked like every other passenger traveling on the train's *white* section; consequently, it created a lot of curiosity among some of the white male passengers that they just had to question Mr. Arthur about himself. Mr. Arthur said the white passengers were always very cordial and nice, and the men always gave him good tips before they found out something about him.

Mr. Arthur would always tell the story about his trip to Chicago to customers in Father's barber shop when he returned home from his round-trip tour. He said the train ride through the state of Mississippi was longest on the route to Chicago. By the time the train got almost to the northern border of Mississippi, white male passengers, always asked him the same question, over and over with smiles on their faces, "Young man I bet your Father was one of our kind, one of us?" Mr. Arthur made sure that he had gotten all of his tips first before answering that ultimate Father question. He knew that once he answered, the tips, the niceness, the smiles, the cordial and polite acknowledgements would come to a sudden halt for the rest of the trip to Chicago. Once he got all of the possible tips, Mr. Arthur always paused a few moments before replying, "No, it was my Mother who was one of you."

Natalie, my third sister's godfather, Oscar Bell, was a soft spoken gentleman who worked for one of the rich white families on St. Charles Avenue. He was a divorcee who always came to the barber shop on the weekends for he knew Mother would always prepare take-home meals for him since he lived alone. Parraine Bell always brought clothes home that the rich white family's children had out grown for my sisters and me. Those were really expensive clothes, and Mother altered them to fit my sisters and me. He also brought wild game for Father that the rich family caught during some of their hunting trips.

Parraine Bell lived in a one-room apartment upstairs above a famous liquor store on the corner of Cleveland and South Robertson Street. When he came to the barber shop, especially on Saturday, he always brought a fifth of Jack Daniels Whiskey for the boys; Father's regular customers who had their usual Saturday night bull-session after the barber shop closed. Parraine Bell also came to our house after church services on Sundays to eat Mother's tasty cuisine and get his take-home *doggie bags* for his dinner during the week.

One of Father's favorite customers and colleagues was Professor O. C. W. Taylor, a public school principal, radio and television announcer, public relations consultant, and the first Editor of the Louisiana Weekly Newspaper. Father always appreciated time he and Professor Taylor spent in the shop because they both had so much in common. Their conversations always focused on educational, economic, and social issues of the community, nation, and the world. As Father's regular customers would say, "The Judge and the Professor were in some heavy discussions about the world." They sat and listened attentively during Professor Taylor's and Father's assessments of international issues as well as national and local issues.

Because of Father's avid interest and appetite for reading, especially about great philosophers, Professor Taylor brought references of some philosophic messages he discovered during his research for their barber shop conference. Those messages would be the topic for discussions, analyses, and assessments by Professor Taylor and the Judge, during their barber shop great debates. Professor Taylor also brought some books from his research for Father to read. Additional, he also brought journals and books of which he had multiple copies for Father to keep in his barbershop library. I would be so excited when Professor Taylor came to the barber shop because I knew I would learn something new and exciting about what was going on in the community and in the whole wide world. Professor O. C. W. Taylor and Father were on the same wave length in discussing heavy issues.

Mr. Walter Cooper, a dealer in a white private club on Canal and St. Charles Avenue, was a tall handsome gentleman who was the best dressed person in the entire neighborhood, perhaps in the city. He wore four piece suits—coat, vest with snap on collar, pants, and well-polished high top shoes. He always wore a matching necktie and handkerchief in his coat pocket. His derby hats, his long expensive cigars, and his long chain gold pocket watch complimented his attire. Although he was recognized as one of the best dressed gentlemen around, his real trademark was silver dollars. Mr. Walter always paid his bills with silver dollars. When he came to the barber shops, customers would exchange a couple of their paper dollars bills for his silver dollars. He was known as the Silver Dollar King.

When we were living on Orleans Street, something very exciting happened to me, on my third birthday. Mr. Walter Cooper affectionately called Parraine Cooper came to the barber shop, and he gave me three brand new silver dollars for my birthday. I was rich, and excited Parraine Cooper gave me the biggest and best birthday gift, three silver dollars. I showed Father my three brand new silver dollars and when Mother came home from work, I showed her my three new silver dollars that Parraine Cooper gave me for my birthday gift. My Mother saved my gift for me, and something very special happened years later when I became a young man with that gift.

Another one of Father's customers he truly enjoyed was Professor Leonard, an English Professor at Dillard University. Like O. C. W. Taylor, Professor Leonard's conversations with Father were always about education and its importance for Negro people in their quest for greater independence. Professor Leonard also brought Father some of the university's discarded library books, especially books containing works of great philosophers and ancient history. Father's barber shop library was getting so large he began placing many of the books throughout the house. These books coupled with others Father purchased plus those Professor Taylor gave him became tremendous resources for students from Dillard and Xavier Universities over the years.

Another one of Father's favorite conversationalist was Anna Lea's godfather, Mr. Willis Joseph. We called godfathers Parraine back in those days. Parraine Joseph was a supervisor in the U.S. Post Office. He was a very handsome and a very imposing looking man, standing well over six-feet-four tall with very broad shoulders and a powerful melodic speaking voice. He was known as the kind gentle giant with the big generous heart. He was the most supportive member of Grace Methodist Church where our family belonged. Parraine Joseph was always leading and or providing tremendous leadership in raising funds for the church and its outreach ministries. Whatever goals he established to raise money for the church, he always reached and in many cases exceeded.

Parraine Joseph was a very smart businessman with great organizing and planning skills. When he took on any project, he knew how to effectively utilize people skills in giving them assignments and challenges. When he came to the barber shop, you could always expect the conversation to be focused on strategies, new techniques, and timetables for successfully completing projects. Father and Parraine Joseph would debate the local and national state of affairs, including recommendations for resolving that state of affairs. Father, the Judge, and Willis Joseph, the kind gentle giant, discussed more problems and resolution strategies than the state legislature or the U.S. Congress during hair cutting sessions.

Alton Smith better known as Boot Mouth and Edwin Johnson better known as Smokey were two of Father's childhood friends who came to the barber shop every day. Boot Mouth, always known for putting his foot in mouth, as the old folks used to say for people who always seemed to say wrong things at the wrong time. He was a very pleasant man with a great sense of humor. Smokey was a very tall thin man with an extremely dark complexion and thick kinky hair. He and Boot Mouth used to hang out together, and they always seemed to get the blunt of all of the barber shop's jokes and skidding. Boot Mouth used to sweep the shop and clean up in front of the barber shop. I never knew where he worked or what he did other than hang around the barber shop and go on errands for Father.

Many of my Father's customers, loved wild game, and they would order alligator, muskrat, deer, and rabbits with him. One of Father's customers, Mr. Fred, was a house porter for one of the city's wealthiest families that went wild game hunting every hunting season. Father would give him a list of orders with money for purchasing wild game his customers requested. Mr. Fred gave the list and money to his house master when left for the hunting trip. The house master bought wild game from some other trappers, and he gave Mr. Fred some additional wild game that his hunting party caught. When Father received crates full of wild game, he and Boot Mouth separated the wild game into customer orders. Moot Mouth and Smoky delivered Father's customers wild game requests. In return for their assistance, Father gave each of them equal portions of alligator, deer, muskrat, and rabbits, free of charge for their service.

Dan's Grocery—My First Official Job

When I turned eleven years old I went to Mr. Dan, owner of Dan's Grocery Store, located on the corner of Bienville and North Prieur Streets, to ask him if I could clean his store. It was a typical corner grocery where all products were behind the counter. The grocery was located on the corner side of a double house. The customer's waiting area was in the first room of the house, typically the living room in a residential home. In that same area was a meat display box and a counter on each side of the meat box. The next room, which was separated by very large ten-foot pocket high doors, had additional shelves and large metal barrels used to store boxes of groceries that had not been stored on the shelves yet.

Mr. Dan had red beans mixed with soup, pet milk, flour, dog food, candy, sugar, rice, and even household items like tooth brushes and shoe polish on the same shelves. On many occasions when customers requested a certain item, Mr. Dan took so long finding the item the customers told him which shelf the item was on. Mr. Dan usually had one other person working with him in the grocery. He always had very young girls working for him in the grocery. Every time a new girl began working at Dan's Grocery, the older women in the neighborhood would say, "That old fool's got another one of those young girlfriends whose going to rob him blind again." In spite of that, Mr. Dan continued to get fooled, robbed, and fell in love with each new young worker every other month.

When I told Mr. Dan I could clean and straighten his grocery so he could find things quicker when customers asked for a certain item. He said, "OK my boy, let's see what you can do." I began work, removing all groceries from shelves and placing them in boxes of similar eatable items. I placed non-eatable items in separate boxes. After separating all of the different grocery items, I painted shelves a bright white. I then straighten out the second room and built some shelves on the one of the pocket doors to place household items, such as soap powder, scrubbing brushes, rat traps, toilet paper, and matches. Then I nailed large nails on the rear of the pocket door to hang brooms and mops.

While cleaning the second room, Mr. Dan told me to throw away everything in the very large metal barrels that looked soiled or damaged. Many cans were rusty or swollen, and others had nothing in them. After throwing most of the damaged items in the barrels away for trash, I saw a greasy looking paper bag at the bottom of the barrel. I attempted to lift the bag, but it was extremely heavy, so I opened the bag and found a sack inside that was tied tightly with a small rope. I called Mr. Dan to see what I had found. He didn't know what was in the sack so he got a knife, cut open the sack, and to his surprise it was money. He apparently hid that money many months or years ago and forgot about it or didn't remember where he put it. Mr. Dan counted the money in the sack, and it was more than nine hundred dollars. He patted me on the back and said, "Thank you my boy for finding that sack, I forgot I had it."

I worked a total of fifty-five hours cleaning and straightening Dan's Grocery that week. Many of Mr. Dan's customers were very complimentary about the new look and how much more convenient it was to shop there. Food items were separated by brands, types, and paper packages. Household items were separated from food items, and the freshly painted shelves and pocket doors made the grocery look brighter and more attractive. Customers no longer had to wait very long to get requested items. Mr. Dan no longer had to search all over the grocery to find what the customers requested. Mr. Dan paid me $5.50 for the fifty-five hours I worked, ten cents per hour. When I brought the $5.50 to my Mother, she said, "Son, we are poor, but we aren't that poor to work for pennies." "You never ever have to work at Dan's Grocery any more, baby," Mother said.

Special Punishment Treatment

After moving to Bienville Street, repeating third grade, and having to cross railroad tracks daily to go to Craig School, I had to make friends with the boys across the tracks, especially those living in Treme. When our family lived on Orleans Street, Craig School was the school children living on the Orleans Street side of the track attended. Now that we lived on the Bienville Street side of the tracks, I should have attended McDonogh #37 Elementary School. My parents wanted me to remain at Craig School where I had attended since first grade, especially since my oldest sister, Edna Floe, was doing her student teaching there and Mother's former high school classmate and good friend, Mrs. Maude Dedeaux Crocker, was principal. My parents could get a daily report of what I was doing in class.

I don't know what was worst, having to fight boys who lived in Treme when crossing the tracks going to school, or facing Father after getting a bad report from my teachers, Edna Floe brought home. Father had a very special way of responding to a bad behavior report. It wasn't a spanking with his belt; it was something much worse. He would tell me to sit in the barber chair, and with a triple zero hand clipper, he began cutting my hair all off in the middle of my head first. Then he would continue cutting until my head was bald as an old worn out basketball. Unlike a spanking that hurts while it's going on, a bald head meant I would get in trouble at school, especially during lunch time. A bald head was neither fashionable nor very cool back then, especially during lunchtime. When I stood in the lunch line, boys from the Treme would spit in their hands then slap me on the back of my bald head. Pushing, subbing, and fighting began after the slapping incident. After getting many bald heads and many run-ins with boys from Treme, finally they accepted me and my bald head as one of their friends. I no longer had any problems getting special punishment haircuts from my Father.

Chasing Girl of My Dreams

It was during my second year in third grade that I spotted something very interesting at Craig School. Many students who previously attended St. Peter Claver Catholic School were now attending Craig Elementary School. There was a pretty little girl in third grade class, next to my class room that caught my attention. During lunch time I would follow her everywhere in the school yard and attempt to talk to her. She would always tell me, "Leave me alone disgusting boy!" She would tell the teacher I was bothering her all the time. As a punishment for bothering this little girl, my third grade teacher made me stand up in the corner of my classroom with my hands folded until lunch time was over.

One evening I followed her after school to see where she lived. I followed about a block behind her so she wouldn't see me. At last I found where she lived in the Lafitte Housing Project at 711 North Claiborne Avenue. Once I found out where she lived and the route she took home, I waited on the corner of St. Phillip Street and North Claiborne Avenue after school, so I could say, "Hello Gloria." Apparently, she told her cousins who attended Craig School I was a pest because the next time I waited for her to pass, her cousins chased me all the way home across the railroad tracks. Every time I tried to talk to her she told me, "She was going to tell her cousins I was messing with her again!"

I was hard-headed and didn't take her advice so I ran a lot after being chased by her cousins over the tracks so many times over the years. In spite of being rejected and chased over and over, I didn't stop chasing my dream girl, Gloria. Year after year, I continued chasing Gloria, unfortunately with the same results. She continued ignoring me, her cousins continued chasing me home after school as usual, and I continued being ignored and rejected my dream girl.

Pastor without a Caring Heart

I sang in the junior choir at church. Choir rehearsal was every Tuesdays at church. Our church was located five blocks from our house. Anna Lea and I were walking to church to attend choir rehearsal when a girl sicked her big dog on us. We started running, and the big dog began gaining on us, I managed to push Ann Lea through a screen door on a side porch of a home on North Prieur Street to prevent the dog from biting her. Unfortunately, the big dog bit me on the back of my thigh. When I hollered loudly, "The dog bit me!" The girl and her dog that attacked us ran away.

When Anna Lea saw my wounds, she said, "Edgar, you're bleeding badly; we better get home so Mother can stop the bleeding." An elderly lady, who saw the dog attack, told us to go to the church and ask the pastor to bring us home. Anna Lea took her scarf and wrapped it around my leg to help stop the bleeding. We walked to our church in the next block and saw the Pastor's car in the driveway so we thought we were in luck. When Anna Lea rang the church parsonage's door bell, our pastor came to the door and asked what she wanted. She told him what happened showing him my wounds, still bleeding. Our pastor said, "Darling, you better get your brother home quickly so your parents can take care of his wounds." Anna Lea and I stood there confused; we thought our pastor would take us home in his car, but he didn't.

I couldn't understand how a man of God didn't offer us a ride home, especially after seeing me bleeding from a dog bite sustained on our way to choir rehearsal. Perhaps the pastor did not want to get any blood stains on the seats of his car as his reason for not assisting us. Anna Lea and I walked home. When we got home, Mother soaked my wounds with peroxide and apple cider vinegar, wrapped some strips torn from a sheet around the wounds, and put me to bed. Anna Lea told Mother she thought the pastor was a man of God, someone who cared for his fellowmen. She couldn't understand why he didn't offer to bring us home. Mother said, "Perhaps the pastor was going to see someone in the hospital or he was bringing Holy Communion to someone who was sick at home." Mother always had some reason or reasons for justifying someone else's misdeeds. I guess it was just another one of those character building experiences that I needed to experience becoming a better person. After several days of anger, when I returned to school and spotted Gloria, my daily chase resumed and I forgot about the pastor. Just as I had done in third and fourth grades, the results were the same, Gloria continued ignoring me, and her cousins continued chasing me home every evening.

Big Sister's Determination and Academic Achievement

The same year my family moved to Bienville Street, Edna Floe reached a tremendous milestone in our family's history. She graduated "Cum Laude" from Dillard University, a Historic Black Methodist University, in the Class of 1946. She was the first in our family to graduate from college, and she did it at a ripe old age of nineteen. Most of her classmates were twenty-one and twenty-two years old at graduation. Everyone in our family was extremely proud of Edna Floe, and graduation day was a jubilant celebration for the Poree family. Edna's graduation celebration party was the first big event held in the backyard on Bienville. It was a wonderful family gathering. Edna received a Scholarship from Northwestern University in Evanston, Illinois, in which she subsequently successfully completed graduate work earning a Master's Degree in Education from Northwestern.

What made her accomplishments even more amazing; Edna Floe achieved academic excellence during extremely difficult time for our family. During most of the time she attended college we lived on Orleans Street except for a brief period of seven months when our family lived in three separate places. Dillard University was located approximately three miles from our Orleans Street home. Edna, as she was affectionately known, got up extremely early in the mornings to get to school on time for her eight

O'clock class. The seven cents public service bus route ended a mile from the university so she walked three miles to and from the university most of the time. Edna rode the public transportation bus mostly during rain or extremely cold weather. Otherwise, you could see this attractive young lady with a beautiful smile strolling along the three mile hike daily.

Edna was hired as an elementary school teacher at Nelson Elementary School near the colored St. Bernard Housing Project, a rather undeveloped rural like neighborhood. Nelson was located approximately a mile and a half from Dillard University and a mile from the nearest public transportation bus stop. There was no regular public transportation bus service in the Nelson School/St. Bernard Project community. The only transportation to Nelson School area was provided by an old run-down school bus operated by St. Bernard neighborhood residents. The five cents bus service was not very reliable, breaking down so frequently that most residents living in the area walked to and from the end of the regular public transportation bus route a mile away. Edna found herself walking a mile daily to and from Nelson School, like her old college days. On a few occasions she was given a ride by a coworker; however, that was rare because most coworkers didn't have cars at that time so they walked together to and from Nelson School daily.

Pastor's Rejection of Sister's Leadership Appointment

The same pastor who refused to provide transportation assistance when I was bitten by a dog going to choir rehearsal years ago once again demonstrated his lack of caring and obvious self-serving agenda. Edna, with impeccable credentials and years of devoted church service, was unanimously nominated by the Finance Committee to become Chairperson for the Conference Year. She was one of the most honest, competent, devoted, and loyal supporters of the mission and ministries of our church. She had successfully served in leadership capacities of our church and was highly respected by our congregation as well as other member churches of the Methodist District.

During the Church's Confirmation Meeting, the pastor rejected Edna's nomination as chairperson in spite of being unanimously nominated by the Finance Committee. The pastor told the congregation he had final say in whomever he desired to serve as committee chairpersons. The pastor was a tall, handsome, and charismatic speaker that could mesmerize members of the congregations with his fire and brimstone sermons. Our congregation allowed him to have his way for everything. Unfortunately, back then church pastors were treated like kings of the flock. Congregations did whatever the pastor desired without any degree of accountability to the congregation. It was obvious this pastor wanted sole control of the church's finances. He did not want anyone with impeccable integrity, competency, and honesty who was devoted to the mission of the church as Edna.

Family Cosmetologist

My second oldest sister, Juli Rose, attended Xavier University, the Black Catholic University in the Carrollton-Gert Town section of the city. She majored in English and Home Economics. Unlike Dillard University, the Black Methodist University Edna Floe attended, public bus transportation was very good. Juli Rose got to school practically all the way by public transportation for seven cents. During the summer, Juli attended Katie Wickem's Beauty School (Beauty Culture College) on Dryades Street in central city. Mrs. Wickam, owner of the beauty culture college, took a special interest in Juli, teaching her every aspect about the business. Juli was trained in every phase of the business, including managing, marketing the business, and how to supervise student trainees.

Mrs. Wickam was the National President of the Beautician Association. When she was out of town conducting the association's business, she allowed Juli Rose to assist in the management of the college. The owner and her husband practically adopted Juli as if she was their daughter allowing Juli to stay at their house, which was located above the business for weeks at a time. Juli Rose became an outstanding cosmetician and an excellent instructor at the beauty college which allowed her to earn additional money for college. She was also very skillful in sewing, embroidery, and crocheting. I loved watching Juli crocheting, using a hooked-like needle going in and out interlocking and looping stitches formed with tread creating beautiful capes or scarps. Sometimes, she allowed me to loop and interlock stitches of thread during her needle work crocheting. She even allowed me to help during embroidery work. I eventually learned how to crochet and embroider very skillfully over the years after being taught by Juli Rose.

Natalie, commonly called Nat, my third sister, and Anna Lea, my youngest sister, were in high school during the time Edna Floe and Juli Rose were in college. Nat had previously attended St. Mary's Academy, a Catholic School in the French Quarter. Unfortunately, due to an increase in tuition, my family was unable to afford sending her to St. Mary's. Nat later enrolled at McDonogh #35 High School where Anna Lea also attended.

Hardwood Floors—The Start of a Business

When I was in seventh grade, my teacher, Mrs. Laws, told in our class that she no longer had anyone to polish her hardwood floors after her husband became ill. She indicated she did not know anyone to call to get her hardwood floors polished. I raised my hands and told her I knew how to polish hardwood floors. She said, "You do." I paused for a moment before I responded because I had to think of something I had done that would qualify me to do her hardwood floors. Although, we did not have hardwood floors at home nor did Aunt Louis's house, I was an expert scrubbing wooden steps at both houses with crushed red bricks so I did have experience with cleaning hardwood, even though they were steps not floors so I said, "Yes."

The next thing I told Mrs. Laws was a little lie because I didn't have a floor polisher. I said, "Mrs. Laws, our floor polisher was broken and the repair shop told us it would be several weeks before it would be fixed because they had to order some parts." Mrs. Laws said, "I have a brand new deluxe floor polisher you can use." That was my first hardwood floor polishing job and what an experience it was. Mrs. Laws lived in a two story red brick house on the corner of London Avenue and Hope Street. The house had seven rooms with hardwood floors plus the stairs. I bought a two pound can of Johnson Paste Wax for $0.25 at Dan's Grocery, a gallon of kerosene for $0.15 at the corner Gulf Coast gas station, and Mother gave me some old rags to use. I rode the Galvez Bus for $0.07 to London Avenue and walked six blocks to Mrs. Laws' house.

I started stripping the old wax off the hardwood floors with kerosene at 8:30 a.m. Saturday morning. I finished polishing all of the floors at 7:30 p.m. that night. It was extremely hard work and after telling Mrs. Laws I could do it, I had to prove I could indeed do it. Mrs. Laws was extremely pleased and paid me $5 for my service. Because it was night time, she drove me home in her husband's car. My total expenses for supplies were $0.47 cents so my profit for working eleven hours was $4.53, approximately $0.41 an hour. Domestic workers made $3.50 per day, approximately $0.43 per hour.

On Monday, Mrs. Laws told seven coworkers at school how beautifully I had polished her hardwood floors. As results, I got seven new customers. She allowed me to use her floor polished until I was able to buy a used polisher for $7 after completing the third house. Another good fortune happened during the week after I bought my used floor polisher. Several crates of grocery supplies fell from a delivery truck on its way to the big market in the neighborhood. The market sold the damaged two pound cans of Johnson Paste Wax for $0.10. I bought twenty cans for $2.00; therefore, my expense for each house was reduced to $0.40 instead of $0.54 (paste wax $0.25, kerosene $0.15, bus fare $0.07 one way, and two-way bus fare $0.14).

After completing four houses, I knew how to stretch supplies, reduce time, and complete the jobs much sooner. I had to maintain the $5 house service charge in order to remain competitive with the going wages for domestic workers that had increased to $3.75 per day. Since the five dollar per house charge, covered all sizes of houses, I had to look at more creative ways to make my services have *greater value* for customers. As my customer base grew, fortunately, many had cars and they picked me up and drove me home after completing their floors, further reducing my expenses fourteen cents. Additionally, some of my customers began paying for my supplies so my profit was a clear five dollars per house.

Value Added Home Service

One Saturday, before leaving to go to one of my hardwood jobs, Mr. Brown, an elderly customer of Father, stopped over to talk to Father on his way to work. Mr. Brown always carried an old wooden carrying case with him when he came to the shop. I was curious what was in the wooden case, so I asked Mr. Brown, "What's in your case, Mr. Brown?" When he opened the case, it had large cans of VIM Shoe Polish in black, oxblood, tan, neutral, and brown. He also had all sizes of old rags and a piece of mahogany in the case. I thought Mr. Brown was a bootblack *(shoe polisher)*, so I asked him if he was a bootblack, he said, "No." Mr. Brown took the piece of mahogany out of the case, began rubbing oxblood shoe polish on it, then took a rag, and began wiping the polish in a circular motion until the mahogany began shining like glass. He gave me one of the rags and told me to wet it for him. When I brought the wet rag to him, he dragged it lightly over the shinning mahogany; bubbles began appearing all over the piece of mahogany. I wondered why Mr. Brown put the wet rag on the shining mahogany after polishing it. When he began blowing the water bubbles off the piece of mahogany, the shine appeared even brighter.

Mr. Brown told me placing water on wax crystallizes the wax making it harder; therefore, you won't have to polish the item again for a very long time. He asked me if I had ever seen or heard of a spit shine. I told him Father told me when he was in the army they always gave their boots a good spit shine before going on a mission. That protected the leather on the boot and prevented his foot from getting wet when walking in water. I had also seen bootblacks (shoe polishers) spit on shoes after brushing, and then finished the shine with a soft cloth.

Mr. Brown also told me wood was porous; therefore, when rubbing shoe polish into wood the polish goes into the grains, giving it greater definition than the top layer of the wood. It brings out the beauty and design in the wood when polished. He told me he was a furniture curator for antique shops in the French Quarters. He said once he completed polishing furniture with shoe polish and wiped it down with wet rags, the highly polished appearance lasted for months. The only thing you had to do to maintain a beautiful bright shine was touch-up around the handles of furniture where finger prints occurred from frequent use.

Mr. Brown's demonstration and explanation afforded me an additional *added value* service for my customers, furniture polishing and maintenance service. I purchased large cans of VIM Shoe Polish in every color available. Once I added the furniture polishing maintenance service with my hardwood floor polishing services, my home care service increased from $5.00 to $7.50 per house. The additional $2.50 was for polishing and maintaining furniture brilliance. Business continued growing, and more and more customers had venetian blinds in their homes. One Saturday, I decided to clean the venetian blinds at one of my customer's house. When I arrived, I removed the venetian blinds from the windows and hung them across the cloth lines in the yard. If a hose pipe were available, I sprayed water on the blinds; if not, I threw buckets of water on the blinds, leaving them to dry in the sun. After completing the floors and furniture, I placed the clean sun dried venetian blinds back in the appropriate windows. My home service fee increased an additional $2.50 for cleaning and servicing venetian blinds. My once $5.00 floor polishing service was now a $10 Home Maintenance Service; including hardwood floor, furniture, and window blinds maintenance.

After many years of basic home cleaning service, my services expanded to grass cutting, automobile washing, polishing, and detailing, babysitting, and even grocery shopping. The $5 per house service in 1949 had blossomed to an excess of $50 per house for many customers, seventeen years later. What started out as a seventh grade floor polishing opportunity grew and expanded into a full fledge business that played a major role, in later years, in helping me realize and fulfill dreams and commitments.

Seventh Grade Cupid

Seventh grade proved to be a growing-up experience for me. My cleaning and polishing hardwood floors began expanding into a wide variety of services enabling me to become more efficient in providing greater services for customers. While in seventh grade, I was afforded additional opportunities to further develop my skills in basic carpentry. Mr. King, our Manual Training Teacher, taught us wood working and basic carpentry skills. As a result of this basic carpentry training and wood working class, I had an opportunity to do some minor repairs for some of my existing customers which generated additional dollars for my home care service.

The manual training shop was located in the basement next to the eight grade brick masonry classroom. Whenever we had a break, if I had finished my wood working assignment, I would always go next door to the brick masonry classroom and peep at what the eighth grade students were building. Mr. Lee, the brick masonry teacher, always asked, "Boy, what are you peeping at?" I told him I was watching the students laying bricks because I wanted to learn how to lay bricks also. "You better learn how to use a hammer and a level in your carpentry class before you think about laying brick," he responded.

During lunch time, I'd always go and ask Mr. Lee if he wanted me to get his lunch from the cafeteria? That was my excuse for getting to see what the eighth grade boys were doing. It also gave me an opportunity to ask Mr. Lee to allow me to lay a few bricks. On some occasions, he allowed me to lay a few bricks after I brought his lunch from the cafeteria. Mr. Lee called me a pain in the neck every time I came to his classroom; however, in spite of that, he allowed me to lay a few more bricks each time I went to get his lunch. He ate lunch with my homeroom teacher many times, and I got to lay bricks after getting their lunches from the cafeteria. I became Mr. Lee's personal delivery boy which proved to be a plus for me, especially when I delivered notes to my homeroom teacher. Sometimes, I delivered several notes on the same day to my homeroom teacher, and I got an opportunity to lay more bricks. He always sealed his envelops with tape when he sent me on an errand to deliver the note to her. He always told me, "Don't give this note to anyone but my homeroom teacher, do you understand." My homeroom teacher was very attractive, like a model with bright red hair. She appeared much younger than Mr. Lee.

As a seventh grader, I got to lay more bricks then many of the eight grade brick masonry students because of the many errands I ran for their teacher. Those errands afforded me more and more opportunities expanding my skills in brick masonry such that when I got to eight grades I was more advanced in brick masonry skills than most of my classmates. This was a result of my becoming the delivery boy for the masonry teacher and getting opportunities to practice laying brick during lunch time and after school.

One day during lunch time while playing in the school yard, Mr. Lee asked me to bring an envelope to my homeroom teacher. While playing, I accidentally dropped the envelope and one of my classmates ran over the envelope ripping it opened. I was frightened to death because I didn't want Mr. Lee to know I had not delivered his note. When I picked up the torn envelope, a note fell out and to my surprise it was a love note. Mr. Lee was proposing to my homeroom teacher. I went to the custodian's house and asked him for an envelope just like the one I had and he gave me one. I placed the note in the envelope, sealed it tight, and brought it to my homeroom teacher.

Not long after the note carrying incident, the masonry teacher and my homeroom teacher were married. I guess you could say his pain in the neck had become his official delivery cupid. I delivered the official proposal for marriage note to my homeroom teacher from the masonry teacher. When my family received an invitation to the wedding, they were quite surprised; however, I knew the invitation was really for me, the groom's personal delivery cupid. My parents and I attended the wedding ceremony and reception.

King's Simonize Shop

King Simonize Shop was located across the street from Grace Methodist Church, the church our family attended. This shop did auto detailing, washing, waxing, and polishing new and used cars for some of the city' largest automobile dealerships. Mr. King had four full-time workers, including himself. He also had several part-time helpers he used when needed. Every now and then, Mr. King gave some of the fellas in the neighborhood a shot at compounding and detailing really dirty cruddy old cars. Some used cars were in such bad conditions, you couldn't tell what color they were, especially the dark colored cars. What may have appeared to be a blue car turns out to be purple or black after compounding with a wet potato sack.

Detailing a car was quite extensive. It included cleaning the interior, trunk, motor, and compounding and polishing bumpers. Additionally, it required cleaning and polishing rims, dressing tires with black wall paint, and cleaning windows. Your pay for detailing a car ranged from one dollar to two dollars per car. Every summer I hung around the simonize shop to see how the pros compounded and polished cars hoping I would get a job during the summers when I graduated from high school.

Multiple Wedding Receptions

In August of 1950, Juli Rose, my second oldest sister, was the first of the Poree sisters to get married. Something apparently happened between Juli and Father regarding her wedding plans. Juli was a very private person so no one knew what really happened between her and Father. Apparently, there must have been some disagreement about the wedding reception, because little was being done at our house in preparation of the wedding. It was rumored that Father did not want the wedding reception at our house. Apparently, Mack, my soon to be brother-in-law, must have told his parents that Juli's family hadn't planned a reception. Perhaps, his parents have begun preparing a wedding reception for the newlyweds. Meanwhile, Juli told Mrs. Katie Wickam, owner of Katie Wickam's Beauty School, about the wedding reception dilemma. Mrs. Wickam immediately began purchasing food, liquor, decorations, and all the other frills for Juli's wedding reception.

Several weeks before the wedding, Mother decided the wedding reception was going to take place at our family's home on Bienville Street in spite of Father's reluctance in having the reception at the house. When Mother puts her foot down, decisions were final. With less than a month to transform our yard from accommodating chickens to reception, we had to work around the clock getting the place ready for Juli's reception. I had to clean out, clean up, whitewash the chicken coops, weed the garden, scrub the steps with powered red bricks, and clean all the windows in the house. The yard was pretty large, and we had an old shade in the rear of the house next to where we housed the chickens. We brought all our chickens to my aunt's house on St. Ann Street a week before the wedding, so I could start cleaning up the place for the family's first wedding reception.

Two weeks before the wedding, many family members still didn't know where the reception would be held. In spite of this uncertainty, Mother, the groom's Mother, and the beauty school owner were all apparently preparing to host Juli Rose and Mac's reception independently of each other. The official wedding reception was at our home on Bienville Street. According to Mac's talkative cousin Edward, better known as *Radio*, Juli's wedding had three receptions. He was correct; there were actually three receptions for Juli on her wedding day. Cousin Edward said after the wedding that he came to the Poree's reception first because he wanted to make sure he got to eat Mrs. Poree's best tasting food in town. After eating Mother's finger licking food, *Radio* left our house and went to Katie's Beauty School's reception to drink his boozes. After drinking a variety of booze he left the beauty school to go to Mac's house to get a few more boozes and some desserts. Finally, *Radio* returned to our back-yard reception to get some highly involved conversation with Father and drink more booze. At the end of the day, there were more people over stuffed from food and drunk from too much booze than you could count at those receptions. Juli's wedding receptions were all festive and full of merriment at all three locations.

CHAPTER III

HIGH SCHOOL

Just like my elementary school days when my oldest sister, Edna Floe did her student observation and teaching assignment, while I was in seventh and eighth grades at Craig School, when I entered ninth grade at Joseph S. Clark High School in 1950, Juli Rose, my second oldest sister, was a Home-Economics and English Teacher there. Once again my parents got first-hand information about my behavior and academic performance daily. It was like being in boot camp all over again. Joseph S. Clark High School was once the former all-white Benjamin Franklin School on Bayou Road, converted to a school for Negroes. The school board changed the name to Joseph Samuel Clark because it wanted to retain the Benjamin Franklin name for an all-white school.

The board also closed the main entrance of the former Benjamin Franklin School when the school became Joseph S. Clark for Negroes. The new main entrance of the school was relocated to the former side entrance of the school on North Derbigny Street. I suspect the school board felt changing an all-white school to a Negro school didn't mean Negroes should be allowed to come through the same main entrance "Front Doors" white students once traveled through. Clark School didn't have a cafeteria, or gymnasium, or locker room, or auditorium, or adequate restroom facilities. Instead the school's basement was the multi-purpose room serving as the school's cafeteria, gym, assembly hall, physical education classrooms, and rainy-day activity facility.

Many of the school's textbooks were ten years old tattered and torn discarded by white schools; the library books were grossly inadequate; biology labs did not have any test tubes; and most of the microscopes were so old and dysfunctional that two or three students had to use the same microscope completing projects. Desks and other basic equipment were not only old but dysfunctional at best. In spite of these many shortcomings, the administrators, teachers, and counselors at Clark were so incredibly committed and dedicated in developing the intellectual and critical thinking capacity of every student enrolled that those impediments were overcome with excellence.

Enrollment at Clark High School grew so rapidly that during its first two years the school board allowed the former all-white Edward Douglas White School building on Dumaine Street to become a school for Negroes making it Joseph S. Clark High School's Annex in 1949. The annex had two buildings located across the street from each other, and most students had classes in both buildings. If it rained, most students got wet going from one building to the next class across the street. That wasn't so bad, especially during spring time because it cooled you off for the next class; however, during the winter it wasn't very pleasant being wet and cold in class. Hardly anyone wanted to take an umbrella to school. The truth of the matter was that very few of us had umbrellas. The Annex was located five blocks from the main campus. Ninth grade students who sang in the choir or played in the band traveled to the main campus for practice. In spite of this, we took it all in stride, and the new experience and new friendships began a new chapter in our lives as high school students.

Ninth grade was rather uneventful for me other than having to get adjusted to new teachers, learning short-cuts to classes across the street at the annex buildings when it rained and learning to duck sooner when sky-larking. In case you are not familiar with sky-larking it means boxing. Ninth grade also proved to be a year that I discovered that being the biggest does not mean being the best. One day during the Thanksgiving holidays break from school, Will, one of my Father's good customers, always challenged me to a sky lark, boxing match. Will was a rather skinny built man, and although I was only fourteen at the time, I was much bigger than he was. After getting his hair cut he said, "Come on junior, let's sky-lark." Will was a World War II veteran and a junior at Dillard University, when I decided to take him on.

Will lost four fingers on his right hand during the war, so he only had his thumb and a nub on the hand. We began sky-larking boxing. I hit him with a left jab to his chest, and he almost fell down. I said, "Will I hit too hard, you better give up." Will struck me rather hard on the nose with his right nubby hand, and it stung me for a moment. He said, "Junior, we better stop because I accidentally broke one of my classmates nose with that nub." "You didn't break my nose so let's keep boxing," I said. Little did I realize that skinny little man's punch would require emergency surgery six weeks later from our sky-larking boxing match? I thought being bigger than Will that I could win the boxing match. What I didn't realize was that Will's lost fingers meant his nub was solid bone when it struck my nose; the weaker of the two gave way. The boxing match proved to be another learning experience that taught me bigger doesn't mean better.

Near the end of the ninth grade semester, everyone was excited about going to the main campus on Bayou Road for tenth grade. We really never felt like we were in high school at the Annex so we were looking forward to next school year, being on the main campus. Because of the geographic location of the main campus of our high school, many students who previously attended St. Mary Academy, an all girls' Catholic school in the French Quarter, and many of the young men and young ladies who attended Xavier Prep Co-ed Catholic high school uptown on Magazine Street enrolled at Clark. For many of those students who had attended Catholic schools for most of their lives, enrolling at Clark was their first time attending public high schools. This was a totally new experience for most of us attending Clark High School. Clark was located in the Sixth Ward on the fringe of what was known as the Creole part of town, the Seventh Ward. Many of my classmates were rather shy about mixing with those of us who were not from their part of town. Creoles tend to socialize and associate with each other.

Brown Paper Bag Influence

Clark school was located only six blocks from one the Seventh Ward's most popular and largest social and pleasure clubs which used the brown paper bag test to determine eligibility for membership in the social club. If you were not as light as a brown paper bag, you couldn't join the club. Many of my new classmates' Fathers and other male relatives were qualified members of that social club; consequently, establishing comrade friendship with many of those classmates, initially was rather rare, an exception rather than the norm. Additionally, many of the students living in that part of the city were Roman Catholic. In sharp contrast, many of my friends who lived on the other side of what was once the old Basin Canal were Protestant.

Long before the federally mandated school integration in 1960, Joseph S. Clark High School, because of its location and the large number of younger generation of Creoles enrolled, became a melting and mixing pot of cultures and religious affiliations in our city. Students of Clark High School made tremendous contributions in establishing genuine friendships and associations based on common interest, mutual respect, and wholesome experiences provided by those visionary and compassionate teachers, administrators, and Mr. Jesse Richards, Principal, in diminishing the brown paper bag influence among the younger generation of Creoles as a litmus test of selecting friends.

Ms. Dolores Thompson Aaron, Helena Winchester Burrell, and Mr. Enos Hicks, physical education teachers, had incredible rapport with students, and they were instrumental in helping break those barriers previously preventing Creole students from socializing and becoming too friendly with non-seventh ward students. Square dancing was a major catalyst in fostering and developing friendships and rapport among students with diverse backgrounds. During square dancing classes, you didn't only dance with your partner of choice, but before the dance was over you, you danced with many other partners as you circled back and forth doing the *dose-se-doses* dance sequence. By the time square dance classes were over, everyone was exchanging pleasantries, enjoying laughter, and getting to know one another as classmates and friends.

Although we didn't have a gymnasium, the basement was a classroom, cafeteria, dance studio, basketball figure-eight drill court, auditorium for PTA meetings, and a giant stage for operetta practice. Because of the close proximity and multiple use of the basement, students constantly came in contact with each other practically the full school day; consequently, it wasn't the easiest thing to avoid mingling with one another. The brown paper bag influence dwindled more and more as students went to class together, square danced together, ate in the basement cafeteria together, met between classes together, and socialized more and more as friends.

Platoon—Early Morning School

Another adjustment we made on our main campus was getting accustomed to attending school on a platoon schedule. Because of overcrowding, Clark had two separate schedules, a morning session and an evening session. The morning session began at 7:00 a.m. and ended at 12:00 noon. The evening session started at noon and ended at 5:00 p.m. in the evening. I was fortunate to attend the morning session which allowed me to work in the evenings. Of course, there were some disadvantages going to school in the morning sessions; it appeared that most of the pretty girls attended the evening session. That prevented opportunities walking them home after school, particularly if you worked after school. Another disadvantage was the number of special requests for your assistance running errands because your school shift was over and teachers always had some task for those of us who were morning students.

Working for One of City's Most Influential Family

Attending the morning shift at Clark High School afforded me an opportunity to continue developing my home cleaning business in the afternoons and evenings during the school week. I had been working mostly in the Sugar Hill neighborhood near Dillard University where some of the city's most affluent citizens lived. One of my customers recommended my hardwood polishing services to Mrs. Celestine Cook. That recommendation proved to be one of the most defining developmental periods in my young life. Mrs. Cook and her husband, Jesse, were wealthy benefactors known for their goodwill and philanthropies throughout the city, state, and nation. She maintained one of the most extensive data bases of national, professional, business, political, educational, civic, and social-service organization. As President of the National Links, she met with many of the power brokers of America, and her business development and networking skills were tremendous. Whenever worthwhile organizations sought advice and assistance in enhancing their programs and resources, Mrs. Cook was the first source of consultation.

Mrs. Cook told me she had heard I did outstanding work polishing hardwood floors so, she was going to give me an opportunity to clean and polish the hardwood floors in her living room and dining room. She told me if I did a good job in those rooms, I would have a weekly job of maintaining all hardwood floors in her home. I accepted the challenge, and two days later, I successfully cleaned and polished the living and dining room hardwood floors with a brilliance that almost looked like glass. That was the beginning of a business development schooling opportunity enabling me to grow and expand my floor polishing business into a full service home maintenance provider.

What started out as a performance challenge satisfying a customer, afforded me an incredible opportunity to experience first-hand business development, networking, and financial planning under the mentorship of Mrs. Celestine Cook. When the Cook family moved into their new home in the Sugar Hill neighborhood, I was given a set of keys to their residence so I could perform my weekly services whether they were in town or not. In addition to providing complete home service and automobile maintenance for the Cook family, I became their prime babysitter for their son and daughter. The one-time work performance test with the Cook family during ninth grade was a major influence in helping me understand the importance of education in strengthening my growth, development, and independence. Being present while Mrs. Cook was transacting business either over the telephone or with associates at her home was like being present in a major corporation board room where major investors were planning expansion plans. Mr. and Mrs. Cook were indeed members of the business elite. I learned more about business in their home than any business course I had in college.

Developing Lifelong Friendships

As we began to close our ninth grade school year, our classmates from the different parts of the city began to know one another better and friendships and *mixing* with the folks on the other side of the tracks began to increase. One good thing about being in the same place, school together, you get to pick and choose with whom you like to associate, and many lifelong friendships began at the close of our ninth grade school year.

Tenth grade was a very exciting and challenging time for me because it was a time when competition for being one of the best in algebra I and algebra II classes. Elbert Durden and I were the top two students in

Mr. Grubbs's algebra I and II classes. After every exam, our classmates remained after class to see which one of us did not have a perfect score. Elbert and I continued to maintain a perfect score throughout the semester. When I had one incorrect answer on the semester's final exam, my string of perfect scores was over. I felt that Elbert had won the competition. When Mr. Grubbs finished correcting our final exams, he said to the class, "After a full semester the string of perfect scores had finally been broken, and I'm about to announce the winner of the competition." At that moment, I somehow felt somewhat alone and disappointed for I knew that I had missed an answer that ended my chance of finishing "first" in the competition with Elbert. Mr. Grubbs paused for a moment then said, "The winner of the algebra I and algebra II competition is, I mean the winners of the competition are Elbert and Edgar; they both missed the same problem on the final exam so their semester grades are the same." Both Elbert and I shook hands and embraced each other, and our classmates applauded and congratulated each of us. That was an exciting moment in my high school career.

Ford Foundation Scholarship Challenge

As tenth grade students, our class advisors told us we had an opportunity to compete for a Ford Foundation Scholarship for college, a very ambitious program initiative which afforded tenth grade students who successfully passed a special college admission examination admission to college after completing tenth grade. Successfully passing the examination, students would be awarded a full scholarship to Morehouse College in Atlanta Georgia. I couldn't image going to college after completing tenth grade. Students maintaining an excellent grade performance during the first semester and the first-half of the second semester were eligible for taking the Fords Foundation's Special College Scholarship Examination.

As mid-term approached, to my amazement I qualified and became eligible to participate in the Ford Foundation's Special College Scholarship Examination Competition. Three of my classmates, Joseph Jack, Peter Chartard, and Juanita Crawford also qualified to participate in the competition. All four of us were very excited and somewhat overwhelmed by this honor. When the examination was over, the initial report indicated that three of us had successfully passed the examination, Joseph, Peter, and I. Our class advisor cautioned the three of us that the initial report was not official until Clark Senior High School receives the Foundation's Official Finalist of College Scholarships Awarded. Two days later, my English teacher advised me the initial report indicating I had successfully completed the scholarship examination was in error, Unfortunately, the final official tabulation report indicated my examination score was one point shy of successfully attaining the scholarship's qualifying score.

At first I was devastated when she told me I missed a college scholarship by one point. My English teacher embraced me said, "You may be disappointed now; however, when you think you were one of only four students in the entire tenth grade class eligible to take the Ford Foundation College Examination that in itself was a great accomplishment. When I got home and gave my parents a copy of the official report, they too embraced me, telling me how proud they were of me and what an honor of having been chosen to compete for such a prestigious scholarship.

After a few days feeling sorry for myself, I suddenly realized how was I going to adjust to college campus life at fifteen, when I was still adjusting to high school life at this time. I received a phone call from three of my buddies, and they told me they were sorry I didn't get the college scholarship; however, they were very happy I would be with them for our junior and senior years at Clark High School. One of my friend's Father treated four of my friends, his son, and me to sandwiches at Mule's and a movie at the Claiborne Theatre, which was a most enjoyable evening. Shortly thereafter, I regained my enthusiasm and energy once again. The Ford Foundation experience was another character building experience.

Another factor helping me getting over my frustrations was the upcoming marriage of my oldest sister, Edna Floe. Once again I had the distinct honor and privilege of having to sanitize and clean up the chicken coop in the back yard for the wedding reception. Unlike Juli Rose's three-in-one wedding reception, Edna Floe's wedding reception was rather subdued compared to Juli's celebration. Perhaps, one of the reasons for the more conservative celebration was the lack of "boos." Since the groom's Father was a preacher, most of the real drinkers brought their private boos, and they went outside in the front of the house to take a "nip" from their bottle.

Little Lord Fauntleroy

While attending high school, unlike most of my classmates, I had the distinction of wearing many expensive clothing outfits. Those expensive clothing outfits were given to my Father's cousin, who was a domestic worker for a rich white family who lived in the Garden District. Although most of the outfits were expensive I wore to school, they were also rather out of the ordinary for what the majority of the boys were wearing to school at that time. Roebucks Jeans, Keds, and Chuck Taylor's Converse All Star sneakers were very popular with colorful shirts. I was the only boy at Clark School wearing knickerbockers (baggy pants with elastic at the knees) with plaid socks and oxford shoes, while my classmates were wearing the popular Roebucks, Keds, or Converse All Star sneakers.

When I wore my knickerbockers, some of my classmates use to say, "Here come little Lord Fauntleroy, the best dressed Englishman in New Orleans." I had the dubious distinction of being expensively dressed but didn't pass the school's daily acceptable style. At first I was rather embarrassed being called Little Lord Fauntleroy; however, like many other experiences; I took it in stride as another character building experience. It isn't what you wear it's how you wear it, that counts.

Eleventh and twelfth grades were very exciting for me. I went out for the junior varsity basketball team and made the team as a starting guard. Whenever the senior varsity team outscored the competition, I even got to play in the game as a junior varsity player. During my senior year, I went out for the varsity football team. That's rather late to attempt to get on the football team. In spite of the late start, with hard work and a burning determination to make the team; bingo, I made the team. Back then, players would play both offense and defense, so my chances of really playing in a game were rather remote at best, especially as a senior. Because most of the football players on the team had been playing for several seasons, I knew that the only way that I could have a chance was to be a strong tackler.

During scrimmage, the coach would put me in front of the best offensive players, and each time they knocked me down I would get up and get knocked down again and again. This of course was to discourage me; however, it didn't work. I was determined to prove I could withstand the knock downs and still make the tackle of the ball carrier. The coach allowed me to practice with the first team unit at center. He placed me at that position because I could long-snap the football on punts. When I started out at spring practice, I wasn't even listed on the roster. After five day of grueling practices, the coach called my name to be on the final roster.

As a player on my high school team, I learned another character building lesson. That lesson began with the idea that a small football player is as good as a big football player. That's what the coaches would tell us all the time, especially at practice. Well one day while we were having a controlled scrimmage with Dillard University, I was playing center linebacker on defense. Dillard's halfback was only five feet six inches tall but weighed two-hundred five pounds. His legs and thighs were huge like tree stumps, and he ran extremely low to the ground making it very difficult for any one tackler to stop alone. This steam rolling halfback was the leading rusher in the college conference.

During a controlled scrimmage, the university team called a delayed trap. The quarterback fakes giving the ball to the running back then hands the ball to the halfback deep in the backfield. All of a sudden, the halfback took off up the middle like a bullet fired from cannon. The only thing separating this fireball was a one-hundred seventy-five pound first year player, who had only played varsity football for eight weeks. I stooped over preparing to make the tackle and all of a sudden when our two bodies collided; my helmet went one way my head and my body another; and, that's the only thing I remembered. I was knocked out momentarily tackling the fireball halfback. In spite of the collision, I still made the tackle.

Unfortunately, that experience adversely impacted my willingness to aggressively tackle in the future. That controlled scrimmage collision significantly impacted my fearlessness and aggressiveness to a level of uncertainty while tackling. Each time I lowered my head to tackle someone, I thought about that violent collision I had and I began missing tackles. My guts and my heart were no longer the driving force; therefore, my playing time in the two remaining games of the season was minimal.

Backyard Wedding Reception Place

In December of 1953, my senior year in high school, Natalie, my third oldest sister, was married. Like my two older sisters, who previously celebrated their wedding reception in our backyard, once again I had the dubious task of cleaning and sanitizing the chicken coops. Unfortunately, it rained on the day of the wedding so the reception was held inside our home instead of the backyard. Everyone had a good time in spite of being a little cramped together in our shot-gun house.

Blowing State Championship

I made the varsity basketball team during my senior year, and we had a very successful season. I played guard and even got to started a few games. We had a great season, and for the first time we were successful in beating the powerful perennial champions, Booker T. Washington, for the City Championship. We were quite confident about possibly winning the State Championship because we had already beaten each of the teams that we were scheduled to play in our bracket. During the fall of 1954, the National Basketball Association (NBA) began televising its basketball games. All of our players on the team watched the NBA games on TV. Perhaps, looking at the NBA games on television diverted our normal game plan execution. During the state playoff championship tournament, we were playing a team from a very small town from North Louisiana that we had beaten during the regular season by ten points.

At half-time we were leading by twenty-two points. We could just taste that state championship. Many of our classmates, thinking the game was all but won left the gymnasium to go to the store to get refreshments, so they missed most of the second half of the game. When the second half started, we began taking shots like we saw the NBA players were taking on television. Unfortunately, unlike the first half of the game, the ball stop going in the basket. To further complicate the matter, our key players began making silly fouls, and our two best players fouled out of the game with only three minutes remaining. We were still leading by five points at that time. The small town team had an identical set of twins playing for them, and everything they shot or threw up scored points.

With only a few seconds left in the game, and we were leading by two points. One of the twins threw up a miracle shot from all most half court which went straight through the goal, and the game was tied with three seconds left. Our starting quarterback on the varsity football team caught an inbound pass, and he was fouled with one second on the clock. He only had to make one free throw, and we would win the game. The score was tied 70 to 70. He walked up to the free throw line and took his first shot; it hit the backboard and fell to the right of the goal. At that moment every one of our classmates in the gym was speechless so that you could hear a pin drop striking the floor. This time he took a deep breath then took his second free throw. For a moment it appeared to be going in for the win. Unfortunately, the ball rimmed out of the basket, and the game had to go in overtime.

Our basketball team head coach was also our school's football team's head coach. He was so furious. He called us gutless, quitters, losers. He said. "If we lose this game, we would pay the price dearly." When the overtime started, the identical twins set the basket on fire; that small town North Louisiana team scored the first eleven points in the overtime, and we lost that playoff game that we were leading by twenty-two points at haft time. Our head coach, who was also our English teacher, never said a word to any of us personally after that loss. Even in his class, he never called any of us either to participate in class discussions or to perform any request that he made during class for the rest of the year.

As for the coach's statement, if we lost that game, we would pay dearly—we certainly paid dearly. Even though we won the City Championship, we never received the traditional City Championship Silver necklace, nor did we receive the City Championship Emblem for our Varsity Jackets. I guess that was another one of those character building experiences in growing up. The lesson I learned from this experience is never take anything for granted; never become over confident about an outcome until the entire process or event is over.

State Choral Finalist

Another good experience that occurred during my senior year in high school was being selected as Clark School's bass/baritone contestant in the state soloist competition. Under the direction and tutelage of Mrs. Lillian Jenkins, one of the finest music instructors in the city, I received the top rating Superior for my individual performance in the bass/baritone soloist category. Clark's choir, one of the top choirs in the city and in the state, also received a Superior performance rating in choral competition. Booker T. Washington High School was our greatest competitor in the state's annual choral and individual soloist competition. The four ratings used included Superior for top performance, Excellent for second best performance, Outstanding for third best performance and Honorable Mention for fourth best performance. The four individual musical soloist categories were: soprano, contralto, tenor, and bass/baritone. Coach Enos Hicks used to say after a ball game, "If Poree had done as much exercising his body strength and practicing tackling as he did exercising his vocal cords, he would have been a fierce superior tackler on the football field."

First Date with Girl of My Dreams

One of the most fantastic things that occurred during my senior year in high school was in April of 1954. For the first time in nine years of chasing that elusive very special young lady who always responded to any of my requests negatively, this time it was positive. When I asked her if she would consider going to the school's sports banquet with me, she said, "Yes." I couldn't believe it. I just stood there speechless, and then said, "You actually said yes!" Her response was, "If you ask me again, the answer might be something else." My heart skipped a beat, beating faster and faster.

After being chased by her cousins for years and after being told leave her alone over and over, my very special girl of my dreams, finally said, yes. Oh what a fantastic day in my life. When I realized what had happened, I said to myself, don't utter another word other than just say graciously, thank you so very much. I turned around abruptly and began walking with a quicken pace over the tracks, where I had previously run for years from Gloria's cousins. This time, however, I ran the last two blocks at a torrid speed. Years of persistence and perseverance appeared to have paid off. I had a date with the girl of my dreams. I still remember that moment vividly, after many decades. That was my first and most fantastic date of my young life. I was beginning to feel my oats; feeling confident the brick wall that previously prevented me from even getting any conversation with the girl of my dreams now appeared to have crumbled. At least, that's what I thought back then.

At the banquet, Gloria was simply beautiful; the dress she made was awesome, and I was as proud as peacock to be her escort. She was extremely polite yet extremely cautious with her response to my request during our conversation at the banquet. I was not very talkative during the banquet, which was totally out of character because I didn't want to ruin my dream girl's evening. Most of my classmates were quite surprised to see Gloria with me, since she always rejected my advances over the years. Additionally, Gloria's boyfriend was a freshman at Grambling State College in North Louisiana and was still the boyfriend of record. In spite of the odds and the circumstances, no one was going to spoil my date with Gloria that night.

After, the banquet while we were walking home, I asked Gloria for her telephone number and surpassingly she gave it to me. Man, my confidence was really flying high, and I began feeling my oats, reflecting on those long years of persevering. Maybe this was the beginning of a turning point, possibly in my favor. When we arrived at 711 North Claiborne Avenue, her home in the Lafitte Project, I thanked her for allowing me to take her to the banquet and for giving me her telephone number. Then in an instance of boldness, I attempted to kiss her on the cheek, she gracefully withdrew with lady-like precision saying, "Good night Edgar," promptly opening the front door then closing it. Even with that setback, I had had the most fantastic time that night in April 1954. A date, that remains very vividly in my memory even after some fifty-seven years.

Three days after my banquet date, I made my first attempt calling Gloria one evening, and she politely advised me that she didn't have time for talking on the telephone because she was studying for an English exam. Each time I attempted to talk to her on the telephone, she always had a good reason that prevented her for doing so. The brick wall of separation appeared to have risen again, and opportunities to get to see Gloria at best appeared remote. Her family, especially her Mother, did not give me the time of the day. When I would stop over to Gloria's house some evenings after school, her Mother would give me the coldest treatment and response. I would always greet her saying, "Good evening Mrs. Thelma, how you are doing today?" Her usual response, "Hello," period! Guess I was not welcomed because Gloria's Mother and most of her family were so crazy about the college boyfriend that I was perceived as an outsider with no apparent ties or morays associated with their family. In spite of the cold treatment by Gloria's Mother and the lukewarm reception from some other family members, I continued to pursue her.

One afternoon after school, I decided to make a very bold move so I asked Gloria would she consider allowing me to take her out after our high school graduation. Gloria told me that graduation was almost two months away, and she had many other important things to think about before considering whom she's going to go out with after graduation. I thought that was at least encouraging, since she did not say that she was going out with the college boyfriend of record. In spite of the circumstances, there was a possible chance I might be lucky enough to be the graduation date. The odds against that happening were extremely great, but I remained optimistic.

Considering I had been chasing Gloria for nearly nine years unsuccessfully, I decided to change tactics from asking for a graduation date to a movie date. To my surprise, she agreed to allow me to take her to the Claiborne Theatre on the corner of North Claiborne Avenue and Ursuline Street, only four blocks from her home. While in the movie, I once again attempted boldness, putting my arm around the back of her seat, not around Gloria. The results were the same as when I attempted to kiss her on her cheek after my very first date. Gloria politely removed my arm from the back of her seat placing it back onto my armrest. I didn't attempt that again and I remained silent during most of the movie.

When the movie was over, on our way home I asked Gloria if she would allow me to take her out on graduation night. I repeated my request, and this time to my surprise, she said, "Yes!" I was so thrilled and excited I got an extra bounce in my steps as we walked back to the famous 711 address residence. I practically floated across the railroad tracks going to my house on Bienville Street that night, overjoyed with my graduation date!

Gloria was an extremely talented seamstress who worked during the summers at Rex Clothing factory to help her parents supplement income for the family. She also was the Guichard's family chief "in house" seamstress making casual and dress clothing for her Mother and her two sisters, Gwendolyn and Catherine. Gloria also was the main seamstress for her aunts, Grandmother, and cousins living in the Lafitte Projects. Her sewing skills were recognized in a featured story on the front page of Black Weekly Newspaper. On the front page of The Louisiana Weekly Newspaper's Easter Edition was a very large photograph of Gloria and her two sisters, Gwendolyn and Catherine Guichard, attired in their beautiful Easter dresses that she had made. The headlines read "Ladies in the Easter Parade." The front page feature story highlighting Gloria's extremely talented skills, both in designing and making beautiful clothing, and also showcased her radiantly stunning beauty. What an incredible young lady, and what an incredible date. One thing that I will always remember Gloria saying after making so many clothing outfits for her family members, she said, "The day I can spell able will be my last day on the sewing machine!"

Half-A-Chicken Dinner with Two Plates

As high school days neared their end, I was selected as one of the Co-Masters of Ceremony for our 1954 Graduation Class Night. Class Night was held at Carver Theater on Orleans and North Johnson Streets, only a half block where we once lived across from the Lafitte Project. After Class Night, I took Gloria to the famous Dooky Chase Restaurant for dinner. When the waitress gave us a menu, I told her I wanted a *"half-a-chicken dinner with two plates."* The waitress asked "What about the young lady, is she eating?" I said, "Of course, why do you think I asked for two plates; we are going to split the fried chicken dinner between us." The waitress looked rather perplexed then she asked, "Is there anything else you want besides the fried chicken?" I said, "I want a bottle of Barq's and a Coke-Cola for my Gloria, my date." The fried chicken plate was a $1.39, and soft drinks were $0.15 each. The bill including tax was $1.74. I gave the waitress $2.00 and told her to keep the change for her tip for her service. Some big tipper!

High School Graduation

At last, it was graduation day. Everyone was very excited about finishing high school. Edna Floe, our family's guardian angel, once again demonstrated her generosity. She bought me a pair of extremely expensive black Edmond Clapp shoes, socks, dress shirt, neck tie, cuff links, and pocket handkerchief. Not many of my graduating classmates were wearing Edmond Clapp shoes. We had a very large graduating class, more than four hundred fifty graduates, and the ceremony would be held in the Municipal Auditorium. The class of 1953 was the first Black graduating class at Clark High School to hold its graduation ceremony in the City's Municipal Auditorium so we were excited about being the second graduating class to march up the aisles of the auditorium onto the stage to get our diploma.

The speaker for our graduation exercise was Attorney Israel Augustine, an outstanding Civil Rights Activist Lawyer. Attorney Augustine said, "Tonight is the very last time all of you gathered here would be together." As young immature graduates, we didn't really understand just how profound that statement was at that time. As we grew older, however, we understood just how profound and prophetic that statement was on graduation night. The speaker recognized once our graduation ceremony was over, as graduates and members of their families departed from the auditorium, life circumstances would prevent the entire group from ever again being assembled all together in one place and any other time during our lifetime. What a profound prophecy, Attorney Augustine made to the four hundred fifty plus classmates before leaving and separating from one another on that 1954 graduation night.

After the graduating ceremony ended and the family members and graduates exchanged congratulations, we were off and running to celebrate finishing high school. The Municipal Auditorium was only three and a half blocks from Gloria's home and all of her family members who attended the graduating ceremony were standing together outside of St. Ann Street side of the auditorium waiting to greet and congratulate Gloria. After being congratulated by my family, I left them to go over to meet Gloria, since we were scheduled to go out and celebrate our graduation together. Oh! What a big surprise I would get before the evening was over.

Darling, Was that Meant for Me?

When I met Gloria, we began walking over toward her family. I was eagerly waiting the moment when she and I would be off for an evening of celebration. Remembering past experiences, I could not be too confident about promises. As we met Gloria's family, relatives, and friends, they began hugging, kissing, and congratulating her with great joy and enthusiasm. Gloria's Grandmother was the only one in her family to congratulate me. All of a sudden to my surprise, Gloria's Mother began walking toward me and with a great big smile on her face saying, "Darling, Darling." I was dumbfounded because Gloria's Mother hardly gave me the time of the day. I had my robe in one hand and my diploma in the other hand, so when Mrs. Thelma got closer to me I threw my robe over my shoulder and tucked my diploma under my arm, anticipating Gloria's Mother unexpected and shocking congratulations.

As Mrs. Thelma opened her arms wide and walked toward me enthusiastically saying, "Darling, Darling," I opened my arms awaiting her embrace and congratulations only to discover that her Mother's affectionate welcoming was not for me but for Gloria's boyfriend, Wendell "Choo," as he was affectionately called, who was standing behind me. Mrs. Thelma embraced and kissed Choo saying very passionately, Choo's here! Choo's here! All of a sudden, I was the odd man out. Family member were embracing him, telling him how much they missed him, and how glad he was back home with the family. As we walked back toward Gloria's house, Choo got all of the atta-boys and high fives while I got silent treatment from the family. I was walking all alone at the back of the family members because Mrs. Thelma insisted that Gloria walk with Choo during our stroll to their home.

Graduation's Strangest Date

When we arrived at the house, the whole conversation was centered on Choo's return to the city and his being back at home where he belongs. Family members and friends continued their warm welcoming as they ate, drank beer, and celebrated Gloria's graduation. During the merriment, Gloria said, "Mother we were getting ready to go out." Her Mother asked, "What we"? Gloria said, "Edgar and I are going out." Gloria's Mother responded very abruptly, "If you ain't going out with Choo, you ain't going out at all!" Gloria was quite embarrassed and speechless, and I was stunned as I looked at Gloria, as she looked at me apologetically, and we both seemed resolved our graduation date was over.

Gloria's Grandmother went over to Gloria, whispered something in her ear then she went over to Mrs. Thelma, her daughter, and told her something also. I didn't know what was said, however, to my surprise, Gloria went over to Choo and told him something then she came to me saying, "We are still going out, Edgar." I was confused but not yet beaten, for what was to follow would be one of the most astonishing and memorable experience that I have ever had. Gloria kept her promise by going out with me on graduation night in 1954. With one major and incredible exception, Choo, at the insistence of Gloria's Mother, accompanied Gloria and me on the date. That's right! My date with the girl of my dreams turned out to be a threesome date, Gloria, Edgar, and Choo, the college boyfriend of record.

In spite of the adverse circumstances surrounding this evening, Gloria, Edgar, and Choo probably created a first for the Guinness Book for the most crowded graduation date in 1954. This trio graduation date was the talk of graduation night. In spite of this unusual situation and the embarrassing moments that transpired on this evening of long awaited anticipation, this date proved to be another one of those many character building experiences that helped to develop my capacity and ability to cope with uncertainties in the future.

The summer of 1954 proved to be full of new discoveries and learning experiences for me. Living a few blocks from one side of the track to the other side meant far more differences than simply distance. I did not realize just how many differences existed among neighbors living in the same neighborhood, but the summer of 1954 gave me a much greater understanding of the marked differences existing among neighbors and families living within the same neighborhood. I began visiting Gloria on several occasions during the summer of 1954, and I discovered even though our families lived only eight blocks from one another, yet our families were miles apart from one another.

First of all, my family was Protestant, members of the Methodist Church. Gloria and most of her family were Roman Catholics. Ironically, I was fortunate to get a four year scholarship to Xavier, the Black Catholic University in our city and the nation. Gloria who was Catholic enrolled at Dillard University, the Black Methodist University. Gloria was the first of any generation of her family to ever attend college. I was the third member of my family to attend college during my generation. Although we lived only eight blocks from each other, our two families differed so much in ways we perceived what was important. That was so evident when I began visiting Gloria and meeting members of her family who practically lived next door to one another in the housing project. Gloria's great aunt and uncle lived only two doors away and her Grandmother, aunt, and uncle, and her four cousins lived only a half block in the St. Peter Court around the corner from her 711 North Claiborne residence.

Making a Cow

Another distinguishing difference I discovered visiting Gloria's family was the way they socialized. Practically every weekend family members and some friends made a cow—contributed money buying beer, chickens, turkey necks, and potato chips. After icing the beer in a tub, family members fried chicken and boiled turkey necks, corn-on-the-cob, and red potatoes for the party. When friends and family members knocked off work the party began. They gathered on the porch, drank beer, and ate fried chicken, turkey necks, corn-on-the-cob, and red potatoes, then they second lined upstairs in to the living room. The longer the drinking lasted, the louder the party got. My family on the other hand rarely exhibited this sort of party atmosphere. The only thing comparable to the lively *cow* gathering that was routine for Gloria's family parties was when Mother made homemade ice cream and cake and Father's customers, my sisters, and some neighbors sat in our back yard and enjoyed the ice cream and cake. No music, no fried chicken, no beer, or any second lines—what a boring difference.

Because of the close proximity of Gloria's relatives' homes to her 711 North Claiborne Avenue residence, I got to meet her family members most of the time I visited her during the summer. I discovered there was a basic routine to be followed when Gloria and I went out on a date. Gloria's Mother had to be the strictest person living at that time, and she ruled her family with an iron fist. Whatever she said was gospel, the rule of law, with no exceptions, and I learned that the first time I met her. Ten o'clock was my curfew when I visited Gloria. If I happen to be there one minute beyond that time, I would be severely penalized by not being able to visit her for a while. Gloria was the oldest of three daughters and the prettiest too. Gloria's Mother was extremely strict on her and her youngest sister, Catherine, "Cat." Gwen, the second oldest sister, was her Mother's favorite. Mrs. Guichard always appeared to be more lenient with her, allowing her to do things that neither Gloria nor Cat could do. When Gloria and I went to the movie, she would have to pass her Mother's rigid inspection before we could go. If we were going out to a party, Gloria would have to get additional inspections from her great aunt, aunt, and Grandmother before we would be off to the party.

Acquiring the American Dream

After eight years of renting and living at the 2115 Bienville Street home, my parents acquired their American Dream by purchasing our home from Commonwealth Savings Association on April 27, 1954, for Four Thousand Dollars. That was a truly major accomplishment; buying a home then for Father and Mother's combined income was extremely meager. Edna Floe, who was a public school teacher at the time, provided 70%, $1,400 of the $2,000 down payment required for the purchase. Father provided 20%, $400, and one of his good customers and neighbor, Mr. Blanks, a Pullman porter loaned my parents the other 10%, $200 of the down payment.

Edna made it possible for our parents to purchase the Poree's American Dream Home. She made an extremely big sacrifice which almost depleted her savings. My parents insisted the $1,400 she provided was a loan; they pledged to repay her in full over time. Had it not been for Edna, our family would not have been able to buy the 2115 Bienville Street home. Like so many other acts of generosity by Edna Floe, our family had been the beneficiaries of her unselfish deeds.

Gulfside, A Working Vacation?

The summer of 1954 was also another opportunity for me to experience working; this time it was in another state. The Methodist Church owned a resort on the beach in Waveland, Mississippi. The resort was called Gulfside, and during the summer months many Methodist throughout the Gulf South Region traveled to Gulfside for Christian educational training as well as recreation activities. It was the only section of the beach where colored folks could enjoy the beautiful comforts of the beach and water. You could literally walk out in the Gulf of Mexico for blocks, and the water was only at your waistline.

Gulfside had cabins for visiting guests and a full service cafeteria that served three meals a day. I worked in the cafeteria as a dish washer and janitor. My pay was fifty cents per hour plus free room and board. I got up at 5:00 a.m. every morning, seven days a week, reporting to work in the cafeteria at 5:30 a.m. My duties included helping set up tables for morning breakfast, washing pots and pans used in preparing breakfast. At 6:30 a.m. breakfast began being served. After all of the guests, faculty, and staff were fed, we would eat breakfast. After breakfast, we began cleaning the cafeteria, preparing it for lunch. Lunch was served at noon each day, and dinner was served at 6:30 p.m. in the evening. The routine was the same, three times a day, washing pots, pans, and dishes too, mopping the floors, and cleaning the restrooms before, during, and after three meals served daily.

I was excited when I heard I would be working at Gulfside, particularly because of the opportunity to enjoy the outdoors and the beach. However, after two weeks of hard labor in the cafeteria, I had second thoughts of the wonderful time on the beach. By the time we were finished working in the cafeteria; we were too tired to even walk over the highway to relax on the beach. When my six weeks summer working vacation was over at Gulfside, I was ready to get back in school, so I could get some much needed rest between classes. Gulfside proved to be another character building experience that made school even more important. The first thing I did was called Gloria to see if I could come over and see her and share my summer experience at Gulfside. I was really excited when she said, "Yes, it was Ok." I guess those six weeks I was away allowed Gloria some peace of mind during my absence.

CHAPTER IV

COLLEGE HERE I COME

I was fortunate to be awarded a four year music scholarship to Xavier University in New Orleans. This was especially helpful to my parents because tuition was $225 per semester. For many families it was very difficult to afford college tuition especially if they had other children in Catholic schools at the same time. Because of the numerous odd jobs and the steady growth in my domestic house cleaning and floor polishing customers, the scholarship afforded me an opportunity to give my parents some money to help in the household necessities. I was really excited about becoming a college student. I was seventeen at the time, and I was going to be a "big" freshman at the Black Catholic College at seventeen. I used to think if I had not been kept back in third grade, I would have been a sixteen-year-old freshman. Edna, my oldest sister, finished college at nineteen; that girl was some smart.

When I entered college, it was a totally different environment from my previous high school experience. Unlike high school, Xavier University had some strict rules regarding what male and female students could and could not do. There were designated stairways for females' use and stairways exclusively for male usage only. Any male or female students violating using the restricted gender's stairways were subject to suspensions. Male students could not wear any tight fitting shirts or sweaters revealing their physical build. Female students could not wear any tightly revealing clothing clinging to their bodies or dresses that were above the knees or blouses (tops) revealing cleavage. Male and female dormitories were strictly confined to the same sex. Religious classes were mandatory and required at every classification, and attendance at convocation was mandatory with no exceptions except death. There were additional rules and regulations for freshmen. I thought they treated us too much like children rather than young adults.

Being seventeen and getting used to a completely different environment took a lot of adjustment in my behavior. Being a Methodist, I somehow resented the mandatory Catholic religious classes required for all students. I felt one's religious affiliation was a personal choice, and mandatory attendance at any type of religious classes should be voluntary. However, I was fortunate to get a four-year scholarship, so I felt obligated to not resist attending religious classes, even though I did not agree with the policy.

As a working freshmen student, I also didn't agree with some of the seemingly demeaning chores upper classmen dictated, such as carrying their books to class, picking up litter they created, and standing in the middle of the campus repeating crazy statements like, "I'm a silly stupid crab of the freshman class, honored to obey the masters of the upper class." I resisted many of the intimidating initiation tactics imposed on freshmen by upper classmen; consequently, I didn't become one of their favorites during my initial semester on the campus.

A Shocking Revelation

On my eighteenth birthday, Parraine Cooper, affectionately known as the "Silver Dollar King, gave me eighteen brand new silver dollars in recognition of my eighteenth birthday, just as he had done since my third birthday. For fifteen years, Parraine Cooper gave me the equivalent of my age in silver dollars each year. It was a routine I had become so accustomed to over the years on each birthday. He always said, "Happy birthday my boy; hope you can use a few silver dollars for something you like on your birthday." This time, however, Parraine Cooper said something extremely out of character as he placed the eighteen silver dollars in my hand. Instead of the usual birthday greeting, I was accustomed for fifteen years, Parraine Cooper said, "Junior, you think I'm quite a man, don't you." I said enthusiastically, "I think you're the greatest; you are the finest gentleman I know."

Parraine Cooper looked me straight in the eye, saying, "I'm a fraud, a liar, a cheat; I'm not that greatest and finest gentleman you think I am." I stood there in disbelief and shock for a moment, speechless. I said,

"Parraine Cooper, you've been the kindness and most generous person I've known for years." "You've given me silver dollars on birthdays, holidays, and from time to time what you called rewards for my doing something special over fifteen years." I went into my pants pocket, pulled out an envelope Mother gave me earlier that morning and said, "Parraine Cooper Mother gave me this envelope containing the original three silver dollars you gave me on my third birthday." Parraine Cooper looked me straight in the eye then said the most incredible and shocking revelations I had ever heard or experienced in my eighteen years. He said, "Junior, I never gave you one dime during all those years; it was your Father who gave you the money, not me." I said, "Father rarely gave me money." Parraine Cooper said, "Son, I merely exchanged silver dollars for the paper dollar bills your Father gave to me for you." I simply gave you silver dollars on birthdays, holidays, and on other occasions your Father felt you earned rewards for something that you did in recognition of your accomplishments."

I was shocked and dumbfounded as I stood there in disbelief and speechless. I had been thinking Parraine Cooper was the greatest thing that walked the earth for the past fifteen years, and all of a sudden my little world had been crushed in shambles right before my very eyes. I just shook my head; told Parraine Cooper that was quite a story he told me because I knew he was joking. Parraine Cooper said emphatically, "Junior, I'm no longer going to live this big lie. I can't deceive you any longer. The greatest man in your life is right there in the barber shop, your Father, the Judge!" Parraine Cooper left the barber shop and did not return for several weeks.

I asked Father if he had given the money to Parraine Cooper to exchange for silver dollars to give to me. He looked me straight in my eyes and said, "Son, you know you can't believe what a gambler says." Parraine Cooper was a blackjack and poker card dealer in one of the city's rich white social clubs downtown. He was the best dressed man in town and a smooth talker. Father told me Parraine Cooper was famous for telling tall tales. Parraine Cooper always came to Father's shop on Tuesdays, Thursdays, and Saturdays every week, at 5:30 p.m. just like clockwork. For three weeks after telling me Father provided the money all of those years, not him, Parraine Cooper was strangely absent from the barber shop.

On the last Friday of October, after returning home from class during a stormy afternoon, Father was alone in the barber shop. I walked up to him looked straight in his eyes and asked, "Daddy, was it true what

Parraine Cooper told me about the silver dollars he gave me over the years." Father paused for a moment and then said, "Yes." We both stood there in a moment of dead silence. Finally, I asked, "Why Daddy did you do that for all those years?" Father that very proud extremely intelligent person, said, "Son, when I saw how your eyes lit-up with such brilliance and adulations when Parraine Cooper walked into the barber shop, I decided I would not be the one to dim your dreams and aspirations!" What an incredible, remarkable giant of a man my Father was. What an eye opener for me.

Father told me he saw how I admired Parraine Cooper and since my admiration was so very obvious, he decided to allow me to live out my dream through Parraine Cooper. He was willing to sacrifice himself for what had appeared to be the trend-setter for my dreams and aspirations. That was a shocking revelation which occurred on my eighteenth birthday that I still remember vividly today. Sometimes we are fascinated by what appears to be of worth without knowing the true substance and worthiness of those things that attracts us and or get our attention. This shocking revelation of October 5, 1954, was an incredible awakening for me, and it completely brought a 360 degree turn-around in my respect of and my relationship with my Father. For fifteen years, I had been living a fantasy influenced by gifts of silver dollars and a highly revered hero benefactor. Oh, how wrong I was about the real hero benefactor during those years, my Father. That was a tremendous character building experience for me.

Opera Star Flop

In the Spring of 1955, as a freshmen, I had the honor and distinction of being selected for the featured "leading" role in the university's inaugural performance of Clarence Cameron White's Opera *Ouanga*, depicting the rise and fall of Haiti's Emperor Toussaint L'Ouverture. I played the role of Toussaint L'Ouverture in the opera. Everyone in the opera had an understudy, back-up performer but me. I was being touted as the next "outstanding" baritone at the university. Like a typical rookie, unlike many of the seasoned upper classmates in the opera, during rehearsals I would sing with full throttled basso volume. The more seasoned upper classmates sang with much greater reservation, preserving their vocals cords and voices for the main opera performances. Things were really looking great, and I seem to get better at every rehearsal.

During the dress rehearsal performance, I was terrific and the faculty and staff were excited as to the quality of my performance at dress rehearsal. Everyone was eagerly waiting tomorrow for the opening performance of *Ouanga,* the opera. I was really pumped-up, ready to perform right then and there. The morning of the "big" day was here; I got up so early the sun was not out yet. After getting dressed and prepared to go on stage opening night, I was confident and ready to demonstrate my talent with the audience.

When the curtains opened and it was time for me to perform, I handled that moment with great ease and melodically performing my solo beautifully. Throughout the opera, I seemed to get more at ease, and my performance appeared getting better and most appealing to the audience, evident by the tremendous applauds. Backstage the staff and cast were all beaming with great pride as we prepared for the final act where I had the featured solo in the climax scene. With great confidence and a sterling performance throughout the previous acts, I took my place on the stage for the final spotlight and something very traumatic happened that would abruptly shatter negatively my confidence and ability to sing for several years thereafter.

I began the featured aria solo with great energy, vigor, and melodically with great perfection, while approaching the climatic highest note of the solo, all of a sudden my voice cracked while struggling to reach the highest note of the aria which left a "deafening hush" in the audience and tears flowing down my cheeks. My voice instructor, standing in the wings of the stage immediately behind the curtains, where I was standing, sang the final notes of the closing solo as I lip-synched the final words of the aria. My world, which appeared to be a most promising, collapsed within seconds. The audience stood and applauded graciously and compassionately as I stood motionless, petrified, embarrassed, and my spirits severely broken.

Many of my family members rushed to the stage to console me, and most of the cast also came over to give me words of encouragement during my most devastating moment of failure. In spite of those who tried so diligently to comfort and console me, my confidence was indeed at an all-time low. The head of the music department, who was my dearest supporter and mentor, placed her arms tightly around me saying, "It's all right to cry, remember you thrilled the audience with your incredible portrayal and performance of the Emperor of Haiti, Toussaint L'Ouverture, so don't you ever forget that; we are all very proud of you." I remember how Mother embraced me with her warmth and kissed me saying, "We are very proud of you and what you have done for the Poree family; we love you so very much." As I began to walk out of the auditorium, dozens of persons from the audience came and embraced me and consoled me during this very difficult time of my life. In spite of the overwhelming support and consolation, my heart and spirit were severely broken, and the heavy flow of tears was evidence of my disappointment.

The major newspaper story was highly complementary of the overall performance of *Ouanga* the opera; however, it pointed out the youthful featured leading soloist demonstrated very promising performance during the opera; however, he experienced much difficulty in struggling to crescendo to the highest scale during the opera's finale. Attempting to sleep that night was extremely difficult, especially the flashback of those moments of collapse. Since I did not have an understudy like my co-performers, I had to face the audience the next performance with a broken voice that could hardly reach the mid-level of higher note of the scale. My voice instructor reassured me he would be behind prepared to sing in case my voice gave way during my performance. He said, "In case your voice gives out, I will sing your part just continue to lip-sync as if you are singing, and everything will be all right. I sucked more than a dozen lemons throughout the day, hoping to restore my voice quality I had obviously loss the previous night.

Well, I made it through the performance singing most of my parts with a rather scratched voice but clear enough for the audience to understand. Unlike the previous teary eyed performance at opening night's final act, I maintained a tear free performance, in spite of the inner turmoil that literally played havoc inside of me. When it was over, basically my singing career was finished. I did not sing a note for almost two solid years. Much worst, I had to face those upperclassmen I had resisted freshmen initiation dictate. When I returned to the campus, several days after the opera, I could feel the extreme "cold" reception awaiting me, especially by the upperclassmen. As I walked toward my first class, I had to pass the men's dormitory. Hanging from the second floor windows was a very large banner which read, "The boy with the golden voice had no voice at all!" Once again my eyes became full of tears, and I experienced another one of that character building episode that I would never ever forget. The opera experience ended my music career, and I lost my four year music/math scholarship, eventually changing my major to elementary education.

Summer Job at Sears

During the summer of 1955, I got a job as a porter (janitor) at Sears's downtown department store. Juli's father-in-law, Mr. Mac, was the "head" building man, responsible for cleaning up the store. He had keys to every door, office, desk, and even the money drawers at the store. If anyone had a problem at the store just call Mac, as he was affectionately called. I used to get so upset when those teenage sales girls would send for Mr. Mac, and they never called him Mr. Knox, instead they always said. "Come here Mac and do this." or "Mac, this mess has to be cleaned up." Mr. Mac would always address those teenage sales girls, "Alright, Miss Susan or Miss Rogers." I would get so angry when Mr. Mac addresses those sales girls, young enough to be his grandchildren; however, that routine greeting had been going on long before I got there.

I was responsible for cleaning the entire third floor which included straightening out the displays and merchandise shelves, sweeping and mopping the floors and emptying trash cans. After completing my duties on the third floor, I had to go to the fifth floor where all of the offices were to help clean that floor. The employee responsible for that floor always made overtime while those of us responsible for other floors did not get any overtime. Every night after finishing cleaning our assigned floor, we had to rush to the fifth to help finish cleaning the fifth floor.

One evening while we were on break, I told the older full-time workers, I didn't think it was fair for them not to get any overtime pay, especially since they had to help clean the fifth floor business offices in addition to their floor assignments. I said, "Apparently you're not doing a good job cleaning your floor thoroughly enough because you have to rush to get upstairs to help clean the fifth floor business offices." "The janitor on the fifth floor is making all of the overtime pay and you're not getting overtime." I don't know what happen the next night, but none of the workers finished cleaning their assigned floors in time enough to go up to the fifth floor before normal closing time. I didn't finish my floor assignment that night on time either to get up to the fifth floor so all of us had to work overtime cleaning the business offices on the fifth floor. Oddly enough, none of us finished our floor assignments that week in enough time to get upstairs to the fifth floor before ten o'clock closing time, so we all got to work over-time the whole week.

Unfortunately, after the personnel director questioned each of us individually, apparently one of the older workers told the personnel director I had encouraged them not to finish their floors on time, so they could make overtime. The personnel director told Mr. Mac to take me off the third floor cleaning assignment and reassigned me to clean the "White" and "Colored" only restrooms, drinking fountains, elevators, and empty all waste trash cans on all floors. I guess I would have been fired had I not been Mr. Mac's daughter-in-law's little brother. When I started working on my new assignment, I found the strongest possible cleanser to clean the restroom fixtures, the floors, and the toilets. I also used that strong cleanser to scrub the doors of the "White Restrooms" and the doors of the "Colored Restrooms." I also used the strong cleanser to clean the walls where the drinking fountains for white were located and where the color drinking fountains were located.

Apparently, in my efforts of wanting to do the very best job cleaning of the restroom doors and walls where the drinking fountains were located, I apparently must have scrubbed too hard with the strong cleanser that I eradicated the *For Whites Only Restrooms* signs and the *For Colored Only Restroom* signs off the glass doors and the *For Whites Only* and *For Colored Only* signs off the walls where the drinking fountains were located. As a result, mass confusion—colored people were going in the white only restrooms and white people were going in the colored only restrooms. Colored folks were drinking out of the white only drinking fountains, and whites were drinking from the colored only drinking fountains. What a mess.

Mr. Mac had to hire a sign painter, who happened to be colored to paint the appropriate designations for the restrooms and drinking fountains. This time Mr. Mac reassigned me to resume cleaning the third floor and the elevators for the three remaining weeks of my summer employment. Mr. Mac was so glad when I finished my last day at work at his store. He told me everyone wished me much success in college.

My First Car

During my sophomore year in 1956, I bought my first car from Gloria's uncle, Elliott. I paid $35 for his 1940 black Plymouth four-door sedan that was $10 too much based on the condition of that car. The grill was missing; the "A" frame was so out of alignment, and I had to replace the two front tires every three to four months. The gas gauge didn't work, the car was burning about a gallon of motor oil a week, and the seats covers of the car were so worn they were as thin as toilet paper. In spite of these minor defects, my 1940 Plymouth sedan had great potential, and it would provide a means of transportation for my growing home care business. I didn't tell my parents I bought a car so I parked it around the corner on North Johnson Street before my parents actually found out about it. I think Father, the genius, figured I had the car because every day I would go around the corner with a bucket of water to clean the car.

Three months after I got the car, I had an opportunity to tell Mother diplomatically that I had a car. She was going to see Ms. Jenkins, one of her good friends at Flint Goodridge Hospital on Louisiana Avenue. Mother had to transfer three times on public service buses to get from our house to the hospital. I told Mother, "I'll take you to the hospital." She said, "Junior, how are you going to take me to the hospital?" I told her to wait at the Galvez Street bus stop. I walked around the corner where I had been parking my car for three months and drove my 1940 Plymouth sedan on Conti Street to the bus stop because I didn't want Father seeing me driving. Mother asked, "Junior, whose car is this?" "It's my car Mother." She said, "Junior, you better get some gas since we are right here at the gas station." I said, "We don't need any gas Mother."

Well as faith would have it, when I got to Washington Avenue and North Robertson Street, seven blocks from the hospital, the car began jerking and the engine sounded like it was missing. Mother asked, "What's the matter Junior?" I said reluctantly "I think I'm out of gas." She said, "Junior, didn't I ask you if you needed gas while we were at the bus stop?" I said, "Yes, I thought I had enough gas because I had put five gallons in the car three days ago." Normally I kept a few gallons of gas in my trunk because my gas gauge didn't work. Unfortunately, when I opened the trunk to get the gas can, it was empty. Mother walked the next seven blocks to the hospital because she had food and dessert for Ms. Jenkins, and she wanted to spend enough time with her before visiting hours were over. She gave me two dollar to get some gas.

I walked two blocks, got five gallons of gas, then drove to the hospital. When visiting hours were over, Mother asked, "Junior, do we need any more gas to get home?" I told her, "We didn't need any gas." Then we drove home without any more car problems. That's when Mother found out I had a car. When we got home, Mother asked Father if he knew I had a car. He said he figured that out after the third day I went around the corner with a bucket of water, a potato sack, a can of car wax, and some old rags. "I knew he wasn't polishing any hardwood floors especially around the corner," he said. That was the official acknowledgement of their son's car ownership. I couldn't fool Father, the Judge.

Riding Hot Seat

One Sunday afternoon, Gloria and I went riding; she complained the car appeared to be on fire. I explained to her the car did not have rings on many of the cylinders so the engine emitted an unusual amount of smoke. As I continued driving, Gloria said, "Edgar, stop the car because I feel like something is burning!" I slowed down, pulled on the side of the road, got out of the car, and raised the hood up. It was the usual amount of smoke coming from the engine so when I was about to close the hood of the car, Gloria jumped out the car screaming, "The front seat is burning!" She was right; the front seat was burning, apparently one of the spring's coils in the front seat must have sprung loose striking the battery terminal located under the driver's side of the front seat setting the fire. I rushed over and pulled the front seat out the car, and it became completely engulfed in flame.

I suspect the worn out bushings on the car was responsible for causing the front seat spring coil to strike the battery terminal after hitting a big bump in the road, igniting the fire. Gloria was right. The car was on fire while we were both sitting on top of the fire. The flames hadn't broken through yet. Once the fire was extinguished, I removed the back seat of the car and put it in the front, so we could drive home. There was a slight problem; however, the back seat was wider than the front seat. After putting the back seat in the front of the car, getting Gloria seated, and taking my place in the driver's seat, I attempted closing my door without any success. After failing repeatedly closing the driver's door from inside, I got out of the car and slammed the door shut. The only way I could get in the driver's seat now was to get in through the back door and climb over the seat. Gloria was not very happy about that Sunday outing.

I went to several junk yards looking for a front seat for my 1940 Plymouth without much success. I didn't find a front seat until four weeks later. During those four weeks, when Gloria and I went on a date, my routine was to get Gloria seated, slam the driver side door, go through the back door, climb over the seat, and start the ride. Once I replaced the front seat, I was full of creative and imaginative ideas of fixing up and transforming my 1940 Plymouth into an upscale version. I went to a used car lot to trace the shapes of the 1940 Plymouth's front grill on paper bags to use as templates, patterns for making my grill. I also made two cardboard fender skirt templates for the rear fenders of my car. I took the grill strips and fender skirt templates to New Orleans Roofing Company to use for cutting out galvanized grill strips and fender skirts.

While talking to the shop's owner I noticed the tinsmiths throwing away scrapped galvanized strips into a trash bin. I asked the owner if I could have some of the scrapped galvanized strips in the trash bin. He told me to take as much as I wanted. Most of the scrapped galvanized was wide enough to use for my grill strips. The owner did not charge me for the scrapped galvanized for my grill. He told me I had a clever way of making a grill and fender skirts. When I asked, "What's my bill? The owner said, "$30." I was shocked; I paid only $35 for the car. The shop owner said, "Young inventor, the only thing you'll have to pay for this job was to bring your 1940 Plymouth back here when you finish, so we can see it." Man. I was so relieved. I bought chicken coop wire, aluminum paint, and screws from the hardware store to use along with the galvanize strips to rebuild the front grill of the car. Finally, I bought some inexpensive red vinyl from Woolworth's on Canal Street to cover the seats and the door panels. When I finished the renovation of my up scaled 1940 Plymouth, I drove over to New Orleans Roofing Company to make my final payment to the owner. When I arrived, to my surprise the owner and his tinsmiths stopped working, came out, and inspected my renewed 1940 Plymouth. They gave me thumbs up and took pictures by the car. The owner placed the picture of my 1940 Plymouth sedan with his workers on the wall of his shop.

My 1940 Plymouth sedan had its newly constructed front grill, new red vinyl seat covers, door panels, and fancy rear fender skirts. I now turned my attention to jazzing up the exterior of the car. During the 1950's whitewall tires and red rims were very popular, especially for black cars. I bought two used oversized rims and two used Buick Roadmaster whitewall tires with boots inside and two used 16 inch whitewall tires from the used tire graveyard on the corner of South Galvez and Gravier

Street. You could buy used oversized tires with boots in them for $3 to $5, depending on the size of the boot inside the tire.

Because I had to replace the front tires every three months because of the crooked "A" frame alignment problem, the tire graveyard was the most economic priced tire available. I painted the newly purchased oversized front rims and the two existing 16-inch rear rims bright red. With my newly rebuilt, refurbished, jazzy 1940 Plymouth four-door sedan, I now had a personal transportation means to accommodate my growing home cleaning business plus expand my opportunities to stay beyond the "get-out-of-here" 10 o'clock curfew imposed by Mrs. Thelma when I visited Gloria.

Catholic's Midnight Sandwiches

Gloria's family was devout Catholics, and they did not eat meat on Friday at all. Since I now had a means of transportation, there were occasions when I was able to stay beyond my 10 o'clock curfew. That's when Gloria's Mother wanted to eat those delicious Creole hot sausage sandwiches from Mule on LaHarpe Street. Because they did not eat meat on Fridays, they would wait until 12 o'clock midnight before eating hot sausage sandwiches from Mule. When Mr. Gus, Gloria's Father, had the company's parcel delivery truck over the weekends, he took Mrs. Thelma, Gloria, and her two sisters to Mule to get hot sausage sandwiches. When he did not have the company truck, I crossed my fingers hoping that Gloria's Mother would allow me to stay beyond the 10 o'clock curfew to bring them to Mule for those midnight hot sausage sandwiches.

Unfortunately, I never knew when or if I would be afforded the opportunity to stay late. It depended on Gloria's Mother moods. If 10 o'clock arrived and I didn't get the usual get-out-of-here directive from her Mother and the parcel truck was unavailable, it appeared I might get to stay until the midnight ride to Mule. Often times, when I thought I might be allowed to stay for the midnight ride to Mule, Gloria's Mother's change of mind results in a, "What's you're still doing here boy? You better get across those tracks in a hurry." ending my date abruptly. When Gloria's Mother spoke, everyone listened and obeyed. The purchase of Gloria's uncle's car did, however, afford me extra opportunities to see her.

Pickup and Delivery Service

My 1940 Plymouth afforded me an additional job opportunity. There was a Laundromat located on North Broad near St. Bernard Avenue. The Laundromat specialized in washing, drying, and folding customer clothes. Customers dropped off their dirty clothes in the morning; laundry workers washed, dried, and folded the clothes for pick-ups in the afternoons and evenings. I asked the Laundromat owner if he would allow me to provide "Pick-Up and Delivery Service" for his customers?" The owner asked, "Who's going to pay you for that service"? I said, "The customer." The owner said, "As long as I don't have to pay for it, you can try at your expense." I made the following sign on a bright yellow poster hung it up on the wall near the service counter where customers dropped off and picked up their clothing.

> Home Pick-Up and Delivery Service
> $0.25 for Pick-Up
> $0.25 for Delivery

I also made a Sign-Up List for customers who wanted the service. To my surprise 10 customers signed up the first day. At the end of the week, a total of 22 customers had signed up for the delivery service. My new venture helped pay my automobile expenses as well as some of my college expenses. It also afforded me an opportunity to further develop my planning and organizational skills. As I became more efficient in organizing, scheduling, and routing my customer delivery services, I shortened customer's delivery time, significantly reduced my automobile expenses, and increased my earnings and profits. Uncle Elliot's old beat-out 1940 Plymouth turned out to be a bargain investment after all.

Television Debut

My sophomore year also afforded me an opportunity to audition for an acting role in a television series on CBS. I competed with three students from Dillard University, a junior and senior from Xavier, and four other persons from the community. After several auditions, I was selected for the role in the CBS's Television Tracer Series. The series was about an insurance investigator looking for missing heirs of deceased wealthy persons. I played the role of a butler of a wealthy plantation family during the turn of the century. The story took place over a fifty year period of time so they had to transform me from a young servant butler in his early twenties into an elderly servant in his seventies. The setting for the television shooting was at a plantation on the River Road. I got paid seventy-five dollars a day. My part was to be shot in two days; however, when we went to the shooting location; it rained for four days so instead of being paid for two days, I was paid for a total of six days, $425. I thought I was rich; tuition was $250 per semester at that time. The series was broadcast on CBS, and I appeared in two episodes which aired in two weeks.

During my junior year in college, Sister Elise, Chairman of the Music Department, who was responsible for me getting a scholarship to the university, encouraged me to resume my singing training. Sister Elise had been my mentor since my freshmen year. I joined the choir and began taking voice classes even though my major was now in elementary education. Sister Elise got me a partial scholarship, I was selected for the concert choir, and I had regained my confidence in singing. After intensive voice training with Sister Elisa, I was selected once again have leading roles in an operas. I played the role of *Zuniga* in the University's annual opera, *Carmen.* The fellows, who in my freshmen year ridiculed and made fun of my voice-loss during my leading role as Toussaint L'Ouverture, Emperor of Haiti, in *Ouanga,* in the University Opera production in 1955, gave me a standing ovation with very vocal "Bravo!, Bravo!, Bravo!" for my performance in *Carmen.* That was indeed another incredible character building experiences in my life.

My home care business and Laundromat pick-up and delivery service had grown so much that my gasoline, motor oil, and upkeep of my 1940 Plymouth were getting extremely expensive. One morning as I was getting ready to begin my daily pick-up and delivery service, my greatest fear became my worst nightmare. When I went outside to get in the car, the front end of my 1940 Plymouth was resting on the ground. The two front tires were lying side-ways resting under the car. The front "A" frame collapsed completely as results of corrosion. My major source of transportation was dead on arrival. I called the junk yard to see if they would buy my junk 1940 Plymouth, and they agreed to tow the car and pay me $25.

I went to a used car lot on Canal Street and to my surprise there was another black four door 1940 Plymouth sedan that appeared to be in much better condition than my initial car. I paid $75 for my new used car so it was only $50 out-of-pocket money plus the $25 I received for the junked Plymouth. Because of the quick purchase of the new 1940 Plymouth sedan, I only missed a few days of pick-up and delivery service. My new 1940 Plymouth really gave me much better service than the first one. My operational expenses were reduced, and I no longer had to replace two front tires every few months nor did I have to replace the motor oil weekly. Finally, I didn't have to worry about running out of gas because my gas gage was working, and I was getting much better gasoline mileage. In other words, I had a real good operating vehicle this time.

Guardian Angel

Buying a newer used 1940 Plymouth sedan, opened an additional sources of underwriting of my gas and motor oil expenses. I discovered a transportation guardian angel at the university during my junior year. That guardian angel priest was the Assistant Chaplain and Religious Instructor. I had a full day of classes on Fridays, and my guardian angel always asked to use my 1940 Plymouth to go downtown. He always talked about how much he loved walking through the French Quarter and riding the ferry across the river. Every Friday morning my guardian angel would be standing in front of my first scheduled classroom. When I reached my class, he always asked, "Edgar Poree, can I use the car today?" My response, "You sure can, Father."

My guardian angel was the most understanding, free spirited member of the university's chaplains. He was not a typical priest at all and he was fun to be around. He always returned my car just prior to getting out my last class. More importantly, he always filled up my gas tank and added any motor oil needed. I allowed him to use my car some weekends, and I gave him a key of his own so he could use the car anytime I was in class. I also gave him a copy of my schedule so he could use the car at his convenience. My gas and motor oil expenses were substantially reduced when Father used my car. I never knew where he went every Friday all day long with my 1940 Plymouth sedan, and I never asked him where he went. One thing I knew was that his use of my car significantly reduced my gas and upkeep expenses.

Many years after my guardian angel used my car; one of my former classmates told me our favorite priest, my guardian angel, was married with a family living in Arizona. My hunch, after all was right, my guardian angel was not a typical priest, and perhaps he was visiting his future bride while using my 1940 Plymouth sedan during those college days. As previously stated when I was a seventh grade cupid delivering love notes to my homeroom teacher from the brick masonry teacher at Craig School, resulting in their marriage. Perhaps my Guardian Angel's frequent use of my 1940 Plymouth cultivated an early relationship that mushroomed into marriage. My 1940 Plymouth sedan could be classified as an Automotive Cupid.

Air Conditioned 1940 Plymouth Sedan

More and more new cars had been air-conditioned. I decided to upgrade my 1940 Plymouth with air conditioning. I bought two flexible oven-range vent pipes, a box of metal screws, and a big roll of duck-tape at the neighborhood hardware. Then I bought two used air-condition exterior in-take vents, and two interior cone vents. I also bought an old used Coca Cola ice chest from a used appliance shop. Now it was time to convert my 1940 Plymouth Sedan into an air-conditioned car. First, I cut out a circular template pattern to be used as my guide for cutting the circular holes in the rear side panel of the car. Then using my home made drill, ice pick and hammer, I punched tiny holes close to each other following the circular template pattern on both rear side panels of the car.

I repeated the hole making process on both sides of the ice chest, plus on the top of the ice chest as well as the two additional holes on the rear back panel behind the car's back seat. Using a chisel, I punched out the circular sections from the car and the ice chest so I could install the oven-range flexible pipes through the holes of the car's side panels into the trunk. Then I placed the flex pipes into the sides of the ice chest. Next, I attached the flex pipes into the used exterior in-take vents and secured it with the duck-tape. I then attached the used exterior in-take vents to the rear side panel of the car with the metal screws. Finally, I installed the remaining two flex pipes into the top of the ice chest and connected the other end of the flex pipes to the two interior in-take vents in the back seat rear panel. The only things left to do were to get ice and to see if it works.

I went to the ice house, bought a fifty pound block of ice, placed it in the ice-chest, and then started the real test of the newly converted 1940 Air-Conditioned Plymouth Sedan. I picked up two of my college buddies for the big road test. When we got to Chef Highway, the big test began. We rolled the car windows up, I began speeding up, and to our amazement, the car began getting cooler. The faster I drove, the cooler the car got. There was, however, a slight problem, condensation. The faster I drove, the foggier the windshield got because of the increased condensation inside the car. So as far as the air-conditioning test, we passed it. We just had to make a few adjustments—make sure to have extra towels and a cooperating passenger in the front always available for wiping the condensation from the windshield while the windshield wipers were working. My 1940 Air-Conditioned Plymouth was the talk of the campus.

After many months of enjoying the cooling of the Coca Cola used-chest air-conditioning during the summer months, an unusual happening occurred. Three of my classmates and I were going over to Dillard University's campus during Homecoming Week before the Turkey Bowl Football Game between Dillard and Xavier in my car. When we crossed over the Elysian Fields' overpass, we heard a tremendous boom that sounded like an explosion. All of a sudden the rear end of the car started pulling from side to side, and we heard something dragging. I thought I had struck something in the roadway that was stuck under the car, so I pulled to the side of the road and to see what was causing the problem.

Guess what, I didn't hit anything in the roadway; however, there was something else hanging underneath the trunk of the car, the Coca Cola ice-chest. During the installation of the air-conditioning project, I forgot a critically important item, putting a drain at the bottom of the ice-chest, to allow the water to drain out of the car's trunk bed. Instead the water drained in the trunk under the matt, eventually rusting out the bottom of the trunk's bed causing the ice-chest to fall through the corroded trunk's floor. That was the end of my air-conditioning!

College Junior Year

During our first class with Sister Cyprian, affectionately referred to as Sister Cip, our general science teacher; every student gave a brief introduction of himself, parents, church affiliations, hobbies, etc. I told Sister Cip our family was Methodist, and my Father's name was Edgar Francis Poree. Before I could give Mother's name, Sister Cyprian, said, "Your Father's middle name Francis is a Catholic name." I told Sister Father used to be Catholic; however, when my sisters were born, Father began attending Mother's church with the family. When I was born, Father joined Mother's church so we all would attend church together as a family. From that moment on, after each general science class' opening prayer, Sister Cyprian asked the class to pray for Edgar Poree's Father to return back to the faith, the Catholic Church. Needless to say, my classmates' prayers went unanswered.

Another one of those memorable moments in Sister Cyprian's class, one morning before our general science class, some of my co-conspirator classmates wanted to filler-buster so we wouldn't have to endure Sister Cip's regular subject matter. When we finished our class opening prayer, after everyone was seated I remained standing in a prayerful stance. Sister Cip, asked, "Edgar, is there something wrong?" I paused for a few moments, and then withdrew from my prayerful stance throwing my arms wide open saying, "I can't help being overwhelmed by the magnificent and omnipotent power of God creating the solar system with a mere whisper, that's incredible Sister Cyprian!" After my declaration, the remainder of the class was about the wonders of the solar system, not our scheduled class assignment. The filler-buster was successful, according to the co-conspirators, and our classmates seemed to enjoy the general science class very much.

My junior year also brought some unpleasant experiences as the results of my antics and rather non-compliance of some of the university rules and regulations. The Dean of the University was my math instructor and was a "no non-sense" tough and firm administrator, especially when it dealt with university policy and practices. I don't know if it was my personality or my continued resistance in conforming with accepting many of the practices and morays of Catholicism that somehow presented a somewhat compelling challenge to the Dean. Whatever her reason for taking a special interest in me, she somehow tolerated me in spite of my resistance to conformity. I'm quite sure that on many occasions her tolerance and patience became very strained.

Suspension

Italian shirts were really popular then. I made a bet with the fellows who lived in the dormitory that I would wear an Italian shirt to class, and they dared me to do so. The University had a very strict dress code and the Italian shirt violated every word of the code. Male and female students were prohibited from wearing any type of revealing clothes. Female students couldn't wear blouses that were low cut or tight-fitting or shear garments. They couldn't wear pants at all or tight fitting skirts or dresses, and the hems of the skirts and dresses had to be well below the knees in length. Male students couldn't wear T-shirts or shirts too tight, revealing their body contour. Italian shirts were not only tight-fitting with a deep cut "V" neck, but they also had sleeves that stop at the shoulders. When I showed up in class the next morning with that green and white sleeveless, low cut "V" neck Italian shirt, Sister Sip, my general science instructor, covered her eyes saying, "Edgar Poree, get out of here and go to the Dean's office immediately."

When the Dean saw me, she said, "You are suspended!" I responded, "Sister, you don't know the full story why I'm wearing this shirt." The Dean, always seemed to want to right my wrong doing said, "Edgar Poree, go into my office while I say a special prayer, asking God to give me strength of controlling my anger." When Sister returned to her office about a half-hour later she asked, "Edgar, what possible story are you going to give me this time that will prevent me from suspending you?" I said, "Sister, while I was cutting grass for my next door elderly neighbor, the lawn mower struck the shrubbery disturbing a bee nest and I was stung by several bees on my upper arms. I couldn't have anything touching my skin. She said, "You could have worn a white long sleeve shirt." I told the Dean that the doctor told me I shouldn't have anything touching my skin for a few days to allow the medication to draw the stingers out and help reduce the swelling. However, the real truth, I only needed a day to win my bet. I also told the Dean I really needed to be in class because we were getting a review for mid-term exams. I said, "Sister, my education was too important to miss the mid-term exam review so my wearing the non-compliance shirt was for health reasons not defiance of the university's dress codes. The Dean looked at me with a pessimistic "here-we-go-again expression" then said, "Edgar Poree, this is the very last time I will listen to any more of your crafty creative testimonies. Once again I avoided a suspension.

Big Problem

Because I was always working before and after school with my pick-up and delivery service, I would always arrive just a few minutes before class. Student parking was designated in a lot a block away from the main building, where most morning classes were scheduled. Because I arrived only a few minutes before class time, I parked as close to class in order to get to class before roll-call was over. If you had excessive tardiness, you could be suspended and fined, so I did not want either.

The campus administrator placed parking tickets on students' cars that were parked illegally outside the designated student parking lot. There were, however, certain students who were apparently given special treatment and privileges because of possible close family-social ties with the campus administrator. When they parked their cars in the same non-student parking areas where I parked my 1940 Plymouth, my car got the parking ticket and they did not get any. Each time I got parking tickets, I took the license plate numbers, the colors, make and models of all of the other cars parked in the same location that did not have a parking ticket on their windshields during that time the ticket was issued to my car.

One morning when I arrived for my science class, there was a notice posted with the names of students who were not allowed to attend any class until further notice. Those students, listed, had to report to the Dean's office for disciplinary action. There were only two students' names on that list; of course, one of them was mine. The other student's car had a broken axle, and he did not have money to get it towed so he had multiple parking tickets like I did. When I entered the Dean's office, I was advised I would not be able to return to class until I paid all of the outstanding "parking tickets' and the "fines" on my 1940 Plymouth. I had accumulated ten parking tickets and the tickets and fines totaled $100. Tuition for a semester was $225. The other "option" to satisfy the tickets fees and fines was to work in the cafeteria, cleaning up the gym and being prohibited from participating in any social activities on the campus for thirty days. Students unable to pay the penalties and fines or were unwilling to "work-off" the penalties and fines would be suspended from the university.

The Dean was on a retreat that morning so the campus administrator was in her office handling disciplinary cases, including parking violation tickets. Students complying with payment of penalties and fines or agreeing to "work-off" those penalties and fines were allowed to return to class. Students refusing to comply with those options were suspended. I decided to challenge those "options" for I felt I had been discriminated against. When I told the campus administrator I did not think I had been treated fairly when others did not get any ticketed for the same violation, he said, "You are suspended until further notice!"

Now I had taken that brave stand, and I could not go home and tell my parents I had been suspended from school. I left school and began completing most of my scheduled deliveries that afternoon. When I got home, I remained silent about the suspension. The next morning, I went to the Dean's office to see if I could get an appointment with her to explain the situation. When the Dean saw me she said, "I understand you've been suspended until further notice and since there has not been any reconsideration notice issued, Edgar get off of the campus now!"

Pleading My Case

This situation was really serious, and my luck of avoiding suspension appeared in jeopardy. I left the campus and began picking up and delivering the Laundromat customers until 4 o'clock that evening. I then headed back to the campus to the Dean's office because it was Thursday, and the Dean always routinely corrected math class exams and assignment papers on Thursday evenings after 5 o'clock. When the Dean arrived, she said, "Edgar, what are you doing here?" I said, "I just had to tell you why I did not pay the penalties and fines and why I believe the parking tickets were issued unfairly and in a discriminatory way." The Dean said, "You parked in the no parking area for students, didn't you?" "Yes," I responded. Then she said, "You continued parking in the student no-park area even after you got tickets, didn't you?" "Yes, I did." "Then why do you feel you were discriminated against, Edgar?"

"First of all, Sister, there are at least three or four students who routinely park daily in the no-park student area, and they never get any parking tickets and I have proof of that." I can give you the license plate numbers, the makes, the models, and the colors of the three or four students' cars that did not receive any parking tickets when I got my parking tickets as proof of me being discriminated against. Then the question is, "Why did they not get any tickets, and I always got tickets for the same violation? The first reason I got parking tickets and they did not is that they were Catholic and I'm Protestant. The second reason is that they were all light skinned students with naturally curly hair and I'm dark skinned with kinky hair. The third reason is that their families are socially connected with some of the campus administrator's family, and the fourth reason is that my family does not belong to any of the socially elite clubs. Those are the reasons I feel I have unfairly treated and discriminated against in this situation."

When the Dean heard my reasons for feeling discriminated against, she removed her handkerchief and began to wipe her tearful eyes; then said, "Edgar, you can return to class on Monday." She told me she planned to investigate whether my story about other students not getting parking tickets in the no-park student area to see if it had merit. If not, the Dean said my suspension would be reinstated, and the penalties and fines must be paid in full before I could return to class. Apparently, the Dean did get some information about certain students being given "special treatment" when they violated parking restriction codes. I did not get any other notification from her office about being suspended. So once again, I dodged the bullet.

Student-Teaching Taxi Service

Since the Dean had given me so many chances of redemption for my somewhat challenging behavior and non-conformity, I volunteered to work in the cafeteria and to help clean the gym. I guess it was my way of an act of penance. On the more favorable side of my tenure as a junior at the university, I provided taxi service for five of my classmates to and from the Joseph S. Craig Elementary School in Treme, where we were doing our student observation. The bus fare on public service buses at that time was seven cents, and you could transfer three times on that one fare. Elvira Day, Ann Depass, Ursula Lagarde, and Joyce and Joyclyn Joseph, my classmates, gave me ten cents each for transportation accommodations. I would go to the gas station on the corner of North Claiborne and Lafitte Street, tell the station attendant, and "Give me half." The attendant always asked, "A half tank of gas?" My response was, "No, half-dollar of gas." Gasoline was only twenty-three cents a gallon during those days.

Job at King's Simonize Shop

Many years after I hanged around King's Simonize Shop during those summers when I was in junior and senior high school, hoping to get a job waxing cars. At last I would get an opportunity to demonstrate my skills. During the summer of 1957, Mr. King hired Mitch, who was dating his daughter to work at the shop. Mitch and I were college classmates and good friends. I would go over to the shop and ask Mr. King if he would let be clean a car and his response was always the same, "You can't do this hard work, college boy." After several unsuccessful attempts to get Mr. King to allow me to clean a car, Mitch asked him to give me a shot at working there with him.

Mr. King placed a wet potato sack with red compound on it in my hand, and then said, "Let me see you clean this hood." The car was extremely dirty and the hood was the most difficult part of the car to compound because of the heat from the motor. It took me practically a half day to compound the whole car. When I finished, I was physically exhausted. The next day when I showed up, Mr. King said, "Boy, you're back for more, today?" "Yes Sir," I responded. Mitch asked Mr. King if it would be OK to let me detail the cars he was responsible for polishing and he said, "That's up to you, son." Mitch gave me half of the four dollars he was paid for waxing, polishing and detailing the car. Mitch and I worked as a team, and we split the four dollars, two dollar per car for each car that we did.

Looking back on those days in the yard of King Simonize Shop, I still remember those heated and jovial conversations and experiences. They were priceless, character building, and memorable. Alvin, *Fats,* remained the very best polisher ever; the youngest Moore brother later sang with a big band and became a top salesman for a beverage company, Richard, a.k.a. *Belly,* Pinero became one of the first Black public service bus drivers in the city, Leroy, a.k.a *Pickle,* Horton after many years in and out of college got his degree in social work and became a case worker for the State's Social Services. Mitch became a teacher, counselor, administrator, Neighborhood Youth Corp Director, youth development program director, and educational consultant for Orleans Public Schools. He also inherited King Simonize Shop after the death of his Father-in-law and held it until Hurricane Katrina destroyed it. Unlike Belly's prediction, I would remain rubbing on cars and dreaming, I did get to fulfill my dreams, working downtown and becoming a part of Corporate America.

    Working at King Simonize Shop afforded me still another opportunity to further develop skill sets that enabled and broaden future opportunities in supplementing my income. Mitch who helped get me that $2 per car job at the simonize shop during the summers while we were in college would in later years be greatly rewarded and compensated for his assistance. Ten years later after our detailing and polishing job, as fair play would have it, when I was appointed Personnel Director of Total Community Action, I recommended Mitch as my replacement as Director of the Neighborhood Youth Corp In-School Program. Mitch was selected and appointed and his salary was tens of thousands of dollars per year. Mitch and I always joked with each other as to who got the better deal. Was it the $2 a car summer job he got me at his Father-in-law's simonize shop or the director's position he got making tens of thousands of dollars per year that I got him ten years later? After years of debate, we both concluded each of us got the best deal at the time of the occurrences. That's what true friends and friendships should be, helping one another. Our friendship remains strong, sixty years and still counting, today.

College Senior

    At last, my senior year in college had come and Mother asked me to please make a concerted effort to avoid getting into any type of confrontation at school. I promised Mother that I would be a model student, and since I would be doing my student teaching during the fall semester, the chances of my getting into any trouble on campus would be minimal. Additionally, my home cleaning business had grown so much, and I had just purchased a 1951 black Mercury two-door coupe so I wouldn't have much time to be on campus.

Coca Cola Commercial

My senior year also once again afforded me a great opportunity to do something very exciting. Debra Brown and I auditioned for a Coca-Cola commercial. Debra was one of my closest friends, classmate, and one of Xavier University's greatest mezzo-soprano opera performers and pianists. We were selected for the commercial which was going to be shown in all "Colored" Theaters in the City. We were each paid $75 for the commercial, and we went to every Colored theater to see it when it was scheduled to run. It was really fun seeing how the people in the theaters reacted after seeing us in the Coca-Cola commercial then seeing us at the concession stand buying pop-corn. "Hey, that's you in the commercial," they said. Our response, "That's us." It was a good feeling seeing how well received we were among the movie customers. The Coca-Cola commercial played throughout the first semester of school and again during the spring of our senior year.

Major accomplishments followed the Coco-Cola commercial run. After successfully completing all of my course requirements, successfully passing the senior comprehensive exam, and the National Teacher's Exam, I was ready for graduation. More important, I successfully passed my job interview for a teaching position in Orleans Parish Public Schools. No confrontations, no suspensions, and only a few weeks to go before my college days would be over. Two weeks before graduation during the ceremony practice, we began following traditional elements of the university's graduation exercise, including the kissing of the Archbishop's ring. I told the class adviser I didn't think it was fair to impose non-Catholic students to kiss the Archbishop's ring at the graduation ceremony.

I also told her I respected the rights of the Catholic Church to expect its members to adhere to its traditional practices; however I would not voluntarily kiss the Archbishop's ring. My reasons were, first, I was a Methodist, and the second and most important was based on health considerations. Since, I was number one-hundred and twenty-seventh in line to receive a diploma, kissing the ring that the previous one hundred and twenty-six classmates had kissed before me was obviously not healthy at all. The class adviser told me the altar boys wiped the Archbishop's ring off after each person kissed it. I responded, "They wipe the ring with the same cloth; that's certainly not very healthy, either." The class adviser, laughed and said, "Edgar, kissing the ring won't kill you." Well, I told them that I would not kiss the ring; I don't think they believed me.

Breaking Class Night Tradition

Debra Brown and I were Co-Masters of Ceremonies for Class Night. Traditionally, class nights at Xavier were rather boring and uneventful for graduating seniors. Debbie and I had gigs (jobs) singing in night clubs all across town during our college days. We established great relations with many entertainers and bands in the City. We decided to liven-up class night by scrapping the originally planned program and replacing it with a "very special treat," unknown to all, especially, our class adviser. We arranged for Danny White and the Cavaliers, one of the hottest bands in the city, that we used to gig with at night clubs to make a surprise appearance in the university's auditorium about mid-way of the planned class night program.

The auditorium was jam packed and all of the Nuns, Sisters, Father Farrigan, my Guardian Angel, students and parents were all comfortably seated listening to classmates talk about their experiences as students of the university. Meanwhile, I was back stage getting ready to sneak members of Danny White's band through the back door for that really "big surprise." When the speeches were over and applauds dwindled down, I looked at Debbie and asked, *"Are we ready to rock?"* Debbie said, "We're ready to roll!" I said, "Debbie, you mean rock and roll!" She said, "Yea! Let's Rock and Roll!"

All of a sudden, the curtains opened, the band started playing, and I took the mike and began singing, Buddy Johnson's Hit Tune "I Surrender." Elvira Day stood up, started screaming, and all of a sudden the students got up rocking and screaming. The Nuns and Sisters vacated the auditorium as if the Black Plague had attacked. We jammed for over a half-hour, and class night rocked and rolled until everyone in there joined the celebration. I knew that we were going to be in big, big trouble, but we started a new tradition full of excitement and fun; however, we knew that there would be some harsh consequences to follow.

Our class adviser, a very young nun, told Debbie and me that we were going to be in big trouble. My guardian angel never left the auditorium during the live performance; his only comments while leaving, "They'll never forget class night 1958," with a smirk smile on his face. Our class advisor's facial expressions during the rhythm and blues performance gave the impression that she too was having a really good time enjoying the show! My Mother and Debbie's Mother just looked at us with faces full of anguish and asked, "Why did you two have to do that?" We said, "Our class needed something exciting to enjoy and to remember about The 1958 Class Night."

As faith would have it, our parents had to accompany us at a conference with the Dean the following Monday of the class night incident. After being admonished by the Dean for behavior unacceptable and detrimental to the reputation of the university, she turned to my Mother and said, "Mrs. Poree you have been a wonderful, loving supporter of the university, and I have seen and talked with you more over the years than any other parent. I cherish your friendship and your love." Then the Dean walked over toward me saying "Edgar Poree, you can hardly wait for graduation, guess what, I can hardly wait for it too, because I'll get a long awaited vacation from seeing you!" She placed her arms around me saying, "Thank you Heavenly Father for giving me the courage, the strength, and the ability to endure the numerous challenges and tests of my faith over these years!" I realized that the Dean, like my third grade teacher, Gwendolyn Walker, truly loved me, in spite of me being me.

College Graduation and Breaking Tradition

At last the big day was here, and my family was excited about attending the graduation ceremony of their son and little brother from college. Edna Floe, my oldest sister, bought me the most expensive shoes I have ever had, a pair of $42 black Edmond Clapp shoes. I had a good looking dark blue patch-pocket suit with a white-on-white dress shirt, and a beautiful complimentary blue neck-tie. In other words, I was sharp as a TAC. My parents, sisters, their husbands, and other family members assembled at our home on Bienville Street for a family prayer. After the family prayer, I left early in my 1951 Mercury coupe with a big smile on my face and a feeling of great satisfaction in my heart to set foot on Xavier's campus for that big graduation march in the university quadrant.

Well, after the speaker completed his address, the final moments of our college days was nearing an end. The awarding of diplomas began with its formal and traditional "kissing" of the Archbishop's ring when the graduate's name was called before receiving his diploma from the Dean of the university. As my classmates, who preceded me, stood proudly facing the audience with their diplomas in hand, you could tell where the families were seated by the location of the thunderous applauds. At last, only a very few classmates were standing before me, waiting to get their diploma.

When my name was called, I walked proudly up the steps to get my diploma from the Dean and when I faced the Archbishop for the traditional "kissing "of the ring, he stuck out his hand, and to his surprise, instead of me kissing his ring, I shook his hand. For a moment, the Archbishop seemed mesmerized and shocked. There was a deafening silence in the audience for a moment; then, all of a sudden there was thunderous applause from many of my classmates and some of my family members. Of course, I knew that there would be some consequences as the result of my action, but I had completed all of my graduation requirements, passed the National Teacher's Exam, successfully completed my job interview, and had been offered a teaching position in Orleans Parish Public Schools.

After the graduation ceremony, the Dean came over to my parents and advised them that the President wanted to have a conference with them regarding the ring incident. The Dean stated that my action was an embarrassment to the university. My parents and I met with the President and the Dean two days following my graduation. My parents, of course, apologized for my behavior, and I attempted to explain my reasons for not kissing the Archbishop's ring. However, the president said those reasons did not justify my behavior at all. She told us that she was sending a letter of apology to the Archbishop on behalf of the university. The Dean suggested that I send a personal letter of apology to the Archbishop as an act of repentance for my actions. In an effort to ameliorate the situation to which I had subjected my parents and in an attempt to appease the university's administration, I agreed to send a letter to the Archbishop.

The letter that I wrote to the Archbishop, however, was not a letter of apology, but an explanation of my reasons for not kissing his ring. To my surprise, I was contacted by one of the Archbishop's senior staff members who told me that although the Archbishop did not condone my actions at graduation ceremony, after reading my letter explaining my reasons for not kissing the ring, he commended me for standing up for my convictions. This of course was another one of those character building experiences.

It's ironic, the next year, when an African-American was appointed Auxiliary Bishop in New Orleans; strangely enough the tradition and practice of administering Holy Communication in the Catholic Church changed. The traditional placing of the "Host" (Holy Communication) on the tongues of the parishioners by the priest became optional. Parishioners no longer had to allow the "Host" (Holy Sacrament) to be placed on their tongues; instead the parishioners could accept their Holy Communion in their hands. I wonder if that change, in practice, had anything to do with the newly appointed African-American Auxiliary Bishop administering Holy Communion in the Church.

Church Summer Camp

During the first six weeks of summer of 1958, I volunteered to operate a six week trial summer camp at my church for boys and girls between the ages of six and twelve. I used the word volunteered because my pastor told me that since there wasn't any money in the church budget for the camp, he would personally provide a $10 a day stipend to run the camp.

My pastor felt a camp would provide both wholesome recreational as well as personal development experiences for youth in the neighborhood. He said that we would charge $2 per day per child, depending upon the parents' ability to pay.

He promised if they had any funds left over from the camp, he would divide that money between me and any regular volunteer that assisted in running the camp. I agreed to that most generous offer, and we had a very successful six week summer camp on the church grounds. By the way, since we were able to get $2 per day from most of the youth, the pastor only had to subsidize my salary for two weeks. I was able to pay my sophomore college assistant six dollars a day. The six week summer camp was a great success. We had a culminating program on the last day of camp and 90% of the parents were present.

Chicago Here We Come

After summer camp was over and before I would begin teaching school in the fall, Anna Lea, the youngest of my sisters, was getting married. Ann was living in Chicago with our cousin Edna, and the wedding was scheduled to be held at Selfridge Air Force Base in Michigan. Father was unable to take the long trip to Michigan, so I was going to be his stand-in to give Anna Lea away for marriage to Robert Tillage, the groom. Edna Floe, little Mose, her son, and I planned to drive to Chicago to visit relatives there then drive to Michigan for the wedding. Gloria had already purchased Greyhound Bus tickets for Chicago to visit her stepbrother, Gilbert, who lived there. Since we were driving to Chicago and then to Michigan for the wedding, I thought it would be a good idea if Gloria rode back home with us. It would save her the cost of a bus ticket back home, and she would get back home earlier than the bus' scheduled arrival.

Great idea, however, how would Gloria's Mother, Mrs. Guichard, react to that proposition? I told Gloria about my suggestion to get her reaction. To my surprise; she thought it was neat idea. The next step was the more challenging one, convincing Mrs. Guichard that it was a good idea. I spoke to Mother about my idea, and asked her if she would talk to Mrs. Guichard about allowing Gloria to ride back with us from Chicago instead of taking the Greyhound Bus back home. Mother agreed to talk to Gloria's Mother. I knew if anyone could convince a strong-willed person to change her opinion, position, and mind, Gertrude Poree could. Mother called and talked to Mrs. Guichard, assuring her that Edna Floe Pleasure, my oldest sister, was the very best chaperon who would be with us during the entire trip back home. Gloria's Mother agreed to allow Gloria to return home with us.

The day before we were scheduled to drive to Michigan for the wedding, I asked Cousin Edna where the closest barber shop was. She told me that Susan her next door neighbor was a barber/ hair stylist, and she would ask her to trim my hair. Susan agreed to give me a hair trim and a hair wash. I told Susan that I was meeting Gloria for a ride on the subway that afternoon, and she told me she would be finished in time for my date. After Susan finished trimming my hair, she gave me a hair wash. She told me the hair wash would give my hair a nice luster look.

When she finished my hair, I looked in the mirror, and to my surprise; I had more than a slight luster to my hair, my hair look like silk. When I reached the subway stop where I was to meet Gloria, she was already there. When she saw me I knew that it was obvious that she was some upset with my hair. Gloria said, "You look ridiculous with that hairdo; you look like you got a conk, a process job. I'm not going anywhere with you with that head." I knew that I had goofed. Gloria took the next subway alone to go back to Gilbert's house. I knew the new hairdo had to go. The next morning I went to a barber shop down the street and told the barber to cut it all off. I had a shiny bald head for Anna Lea and Robert's wedding. On our drive back home Gloria hardly had any words with me during the entire trip. I knew I had to do something spectacular to overcome the Chicago blunder.

Fortunately, after explaining to Gloria that I didn't realize the barber/hair stylist used a hair relaxer rinse which gave me that awful looking process job, she said, "I forgive you, but don't even think about another date until you get rid of that funny looking shinning bald head." For the next few weeks my date with her was at 711 N. Claiborne Avenue, her home. After my hair reached an acceptable height with a well groomed and neat appearance, she allowed me to take her to the movie. This was another one of those embarrassing moments, with Edgar.

CHAPTER V

STARTING NEW CAREER

After the camp, I decided to take a long overdue vacation for several weeks, since my teaching career would begin in August of that year. I re-scheduled all of my home-cleaning customer appointments for one month later. I got one of my closest friends to handle my pick-up and delivery service customers so that I could get some much needed relaxation. While on vacation, I got an opportunity to spruce-up my 1951 Mercury Coupe Sedan. I bought some brand new wide whitewall tires, painted the rims bright red, lowered the back, and installed fender skirts. The summer of 1958 seemed to fly by overnight. After the Fourth of July Holiday, I began preparing for my teaching career. I bought new suits, sport coats, slacks, dress shirts, colorful neck-ties, shoes, and a pair of Chuck Taylor's all-star sneakers.

My first teaching assignment was as at Lockett Elementary School near the city's largest housing project, Desire. Since my two oldest sisters had been teaching for several years, I had a wealth of information and classroom resources that I could use for my sixth grade class. The principal of the school used to be my algebra and math teacher in high school. Many of the newly assigned teachers were former high school and college classmates so I was looking forward to the opening of school. New teachers had to attend in-service training workshops and when we completed the workshops, we began decorating our classroom and attending faculty meetings in preparation of the opening of school. One of the things that I enjoyed about working at an elementary school at that time was the fact that there were so very few male teachers in elementary schools. Consequently, we were treated royally by the older faculty members and we became prime matrimony candidates for many of the newly appointed young female teachers.

Our elementary school had been an incubator for three other elementary schools in the neighborhood. Because of the rapid growth in student population, a new elementary school under construction was expected to be completed in time for the opening of the 1958 school year. Unfortunately, many of the classrooms were still unfinished at the time of the opening of school. Students assigned to the new school had to attend classes at my school. In spite of housing twice the number of students for which our school was built, the school administrators managed to do an exceptional job of coordinating the scheduling of classes. Additionally, at the time of the opening of schools, both principals had to coordinate the scheduling of some forty-four school buses daily to facilitate and accommodate transportation needs of the student body. In order to avoid students getting on the wrong bus, students were assigned buses according to the neighborhoods in which they lived in and by the classroom teacher that they were assigned.

Coworker's Taxi Service

The opening of the 1958 school year also brought another "first" for me. Gone was my 1951 black Mercury Coupe and in came a sparkling green and white 1954 Mercury Monterey hardtop coupe with leather seats, power steering, an automatic transmission, and yes, air-conditioning. Just like my junior year in college, when my car was the "taxi" for classmates doing our student teaching observations assignment; once again my 1954 Mercury was the taxi for several of my coworkers during the first two months of the new school year. What an exciting way to start a teaching career, with a new car and new suits.

My first sixth grade class had forty-five students; many were almost my age, give or take a few years. I was twenty-one at the start of the school year and nine students in my class were sixteen years old. Most of the over-age students migrated with their families from the rural areas of Mississippi and Alabama, where they worked on the farms and fields more months in the year then they attended school. What helped my students, however, to overcome this obstacle were their devoted and supportive parents who knew the importance of getting an education. Blessed with a good core of students and dedicated parents, I reported to work an hour and a half before school officially started. I was eager to start teaching.

Berlin Crisis vs. Teaching Career

In 1958, there were growing tensions between America and Germany and the possibility of war was becoming increasingly possible. A.P. Treaud, the son of a famous civil rights lawyer and a second year teacher at my school, enlisted in the Army Reserve, in the summer of 1958. A. P.'s classroom and mine were next to each other, and every day he would encourage me to join the Reserve. Each time he would attempt to get me to consider enlisting in the Reserve, I would change the subject. A.P. said, "Poree, if you join the Reserve, you only go on active duty for six months, then you come back home and play soldier in the Reserve for five and a half years. Then you will have fulfilled your military obligation. That's better than being drafted and having to be on active duty for three years." Every time A. P. attempted to encourage me to enlist, I would always change the conversation. Little did I realize that I would get the shock of my life in a few months? A.P. was scheduled to begin active duty on the last day of October. He would complete his active duty training, the last day of April and resume teaching in May.

Two months after school opened, A. P. was preparing to begin his active-duty on Friday, October 31, 1958. On Thursday, A.P.'s last teaching day, a group of us had a "going-away" party for him at Café Roux, one of our favorite night spots. When I got home from the party, Mother told me that I had a letter from Selective Service. I stopped dead in my tracks and asked, "From whom?" Mother said, "I think it's from the Draft Board." I was horrified, speechless, and then I ran to the telephone to call A.P. "A.P., you got to call that Recruiting Officer and see if you can get me in your unit!" A.P. said, "I thought you weren't interested in the Reserve?" I shouted, "A.P. I just got a letter from the Draft Board to report to the Custom House for an examination in two weeks for the Draft.

A.P. called the Recruiting Officer to see if there was any possibility for me to enlist. Unfortunately, the Officer told him that his unit's quota had been filled for the last quarter. The Recruiting Officer told A. P. to tell me to call the new Recruiting Officer tomorrow about next year's First Quarter's recruiting slots. I told A.P. that next year's Reserve slots won't save me. I asked A.P. to call the recruiter again to see if he could get me in his unit. A.P. agreed to call again. At 1:30 a.m., Friday morning, October 31, 1958, I got a phone call from the Recruiting Officer. He told me there was a slight possibility of me getting into the unit, if one of the recruits fails to report by noon. The Officer said he would call me at 12:05 p.m. if the recruit failed to report by noon. I gave the Recruiting Officer the telephone number of the principal's office. When I hanged up the telephone, I fell on my knees and prayed all night that the missing recruit would not show up for induction by noon.

I didn't sleep at all that night, and when I got to school that morning, I told Mrs. Mable Honore, school's secretary, and Mrs. Marion Harris, school's clerk, that I was expecting a very important telephone call at lunch time. I also told them I asked Lloyd Richards, my coworker, to keep an eye on my class while I waited in the office for the call. At exactly 12:05 p.m. the telephone rang, Mrs. Harris answered and said, "Poree, it's for you." When I answered, the Recruiter said, "You better get down here immediately to the Port of Embarkation and get sworn in the U.S. Army Reserve Unit." I shouted, "Yes Sir!"

I told Mrs. Honore to advise the principal that I had been notified to report immediately to the U. S. Army Reserve Unit at the Port of Embarkation to be sworn in for the U.S. Army Reserve Unit that was shipping out at 4:00 p.m. today for Fort Chaffee, Arkansas, for six months active duty. I also told her my Mother would get whatever information or documents that I needed for the school board regarding my request for a "Leave of Absence" for military duty. Since I did not have time to tell my coworkers I was leaving, I did however tell my students that I was leaving for the Army for six months. I embraced and kissed all forty-five of my students and told them to continue to do their very best while I was gone. I'd be back in May. There were many tears in the classroom, including mine as we said, "Goodbyes."

I got in my car, drove over to the Recruitment Center, and enlisted in the Army Reserve unit that A.P. was in. Then I drove home and told my parents that I was leaving today for Fort Chaffee, Arkansas, for six months active duty. I threw a few clothing items in an old "beat-out" suitcase, called Gloria to tell her that I was leaving for the Army Reserve, and asked her if she would drive me to the train station. Gloria was shocked. She said, "When did you say you were leaving for the Army?" "At 4:00 p.m. this evening," I responded. She agreed to take me to the train station.

I asked her to keep my car over the weekend until my brother-in-law returned from vacation. He was going to keep the car during my training. With a kiss from Gloria and tears in my eyes, I boarded the train and sat next to A.P. for our destination, Fort Chaffee, Arkansas, our new home for the next six months. At 4:00 p.m. the train conductor said, "All aboard," and the train began rolling out on its route to Fort Smith, Arkansas.

Army Life—An Entirely New Experience

The train ride to Fort Chaffee was long and tiring, especially since I didn't get any sleep last night. A.P. kept laughing throughout the ride repeatedly saying, "Edgar, didn't you tell me that joining the Army Reserve was the last thing in the world you wanted to do, Ha, Ha!" When we finally arrived in Fort Smith, Arkansas, we boarded an Army bus to our new home for the next six months. It was night time when we arrived at Fort Chaffee, and the next few hours proved to be a wake-up call/experience for all of us. As we got off the bus, we were assembled in the middle of a large field for roll-call.

One thing very obvious to A.P. and me, there weren't many Colored recruits in the more than two hundred plus members of the Reserve. Another very obvious thing we noticed during roll call, most of the White recruits had on military uniforms. The Colored recruits had on civilian clothes. I asked A.P., "Why did the Whites have on military uniforms, and we did not have any?" A.P. said, "Whites belong to the National Guard, there weren't any Colored folks he knew of in the National Guard." That was the first of many firsts that we experienced during our six months army reserve training in Fort Chaffee, Arkansas.

After roll-call, we were allowed to go to a barracks of our choice that night. At 5 o'clock the next morning, lights were turned on, the piecing burgle sounded during Revelry, followed by a ranting, raving, shouting, huge-muscular field sergeant's commands, "Git up you worthless, no-count, useless, poor excuse of men, it roll-call!" After getting out of bed, standing at attention, the sergeant told us to get rid of those civilian clothes, and he didn't want to see them again, ever! He shouted, "Do you idiots understand?" "Yes Sir!" everyone shouted.

After roll-call, we went to the mess hall for breakfast. After breakfast, we were issued bedding, military uniforms, weapons, equipment, and our new wardrobe for the next six months. We were also assigned to platoons and to our specific barracks. A.P. and I were assigned to different platoons and different barracks. My new bunk mate was Paul Pellerin, a little French speaking White boy from Lafayette, Louisiana. Paul was a fiery passionate and combative individual, ready to take on anyone regardless of his size. I wondered how Paul and I would get along as bunkmates for we were from two different cultures and backgrounds. That question was answered the first night that we settled in as bunk-mates. Paul asked "Can I have the top bunk?" "You certainly can," was my response. I didn't relish jumping up and down getting into my sleeping bunk.

Penalized For Being Educated

The corporal assigned to our platoon visited our barracks the first night to establish his "power" and "authority" over us and our lives during the eight weeks basic training. He ordered each member in our platoon to report outside in front of the barracks to be given assignments essential in maintaining "spotless" quarters and dominant competitive squadrons. Once assembled, the corporal said with the heavy southern dialect, "I want you to raise your hand for every question that I ask if your answer is yes. Do you understand?" he shouted. The recruits shouted, "Yes, Sir!" "I want to see the hands of recruits who finished high school." All but a few recruits raised their hands. "How many completed one year college?" A much smaller number of hands were raised. The corporal then asked "How many completed two years of college." The number of hands was even less than before. Then the corporal asked "How many completed three years of college?" Still fewer hands rose. The next question the corporal asked, "How many finished college?" Only one hand rose, mine. The corporal then said, "Since you got more education than everybody, and you're smarter than everyone else in the platoon, let me see how smart you are in cleaning up the latrine (toilets)."

I said "Sir, I don't think it's fair for you to make me clean the latrine just because I'm the only one who finished college." The corporal said "I'm the one who determines what's fair here; I give the orders; fairness isn't even a consideration of mine; so you are ordered to clean the latrine." The corporal asked me "What do you do back home Private?" I said, "Sir, I'm an elementary school teacher." The corporal said, "You got a choice, clean the latrine or you will never set foot again in the classroom to teach for the rest of your life! You're in the Army now, boy, and you'll do what I say or you will face the consequences for not obeying a direct order by your superior! Do I make myself clear, private?" Realizing that my personal freedom was non-existent here, I reluctantly said, "Yes Sir." The corporal shouted, "What did you say, private?" I said in a much louder voice, "Yes Sir! With my pride and self-esteem shackled, I was determined that I would not allow myself to "loose control" by the overzealous treatment that I would be subjected to during these six months.

Since I had been accustomed to cleaning bathrooms and restrooms for years in my home care business, I decided to clean the latrine better than it had ever been cleaned before to prove that I could not be intimidated by any demeaning orders. I polished the brass to a sparkle that had never been seen, the mirrors and window glass had no streaks, and the concrete floor was clean enough to eat your dinner on. When the platoon captain inspected the barrack's latrine that I cleaned, he asked "Who cleaned the latrine?" I said "I did, Sir." The platoon Captain said, "Private, you did a great job." He told Corporal Bush, who ordered me to clean the barrack's latrine "I want Private Poree to select and train a crew to clean the barrack's latrine." Corporal Bush asked, "What do you mean Sir?" The Captain repeated: "I want Private Poree to select a crew, train them, and monitor the crew's progress in cleaning the barracks' latrines."

Rather than selecting individual crew members, I asked for volunteers from our barracks, to join the latrine clean-up crews. The very first person to volunteer for becoming a "Waste Buster" the code name for my latrine clean-up crews was my new bunk-mate, Paul Peligrim, a Cajun (coonass) native of Lafayette, Louisiana. The other volunteers proved to be very efficient team members. What began as a very challenging obstacle for me on activity duty transformed into a great opportunity for me? Our "Waste Buster Crew" was recognized as the top performing and top rated "White Glove" Competition Winner in the Monthly Platoon Company Barrack's Cleanup Contest. This proved to be another character building experience for me.

The next great challenge for us was basic training for it required a tremendous test of stamina, mental and physical toughness, and the building of confidence and trust among squadron members. My bunk mate, Paul, and I developed a tremendous trust in one another during basic training. That trust and friendship proved to be a great motivating factor and force as we excelled in so many of the intricate drills and exercises that we had to perform during those eight weeks of grueling basic training. Marching and jogging for miles daily, up and down the hills of Arkansas. Crawling in rain-soaked muddy fields during combat engagements exercises, applying first aid by putting raw meat on "black eyes" received from being "kicked" from the recoil of our M-1's weapon during target practice on the firing range, and pulling K-P, kitchen police in the company's mess hall were just some of the many character building experiences we had during basic training.

After the sixth week of basic training, we were allowed an R & R "break" for the weekend. Paul and I decided to go into town, Fort Smith, for some rest and recreation. After sight-seeing in the town we decided to take in a movie. Paul got in line to buy two tickets for the movie. I was standing next to Paul in the line. When Paul asked for two tickets, the cashier asked him for whom was the second ticket, and he said my bunk-mate, pointing at me. The cashier told Paul that he could go in the movie, but we don't allow Colored people in our movie. Paul became ferrous and with his heavy French dialect he said, "You can keep your stinking tickets, and we ain't gonna spend a damn dime in this hick town!" Paul turned to me and said, "Let's git out this so and so town, and we ain't never gonna come back other than passing through to go home!" Both of us attended the movies on the Army base for the remainder of our six month activity duty time.

Separate Army Service Clubs

When we returned to the Army base, Paul suggested we go to the main service club near our barracks. When we arrived at Service Club # 1, together, there weren't any other Colored soldiers in the club. Paul asked recruits in our platoon, "Where were the Colored soldiers?" The recruit told him they were probably at Service Club # 2, which was about a mile-and-a-half from our barracks. A hillbilly band was playing at the Main Service Club. Paul said back home, Cajun music was hot, and he didn't care for hillbilly music at all. I agreed with him whole heartily. We decided to take the walk to Service Club # 2 down the hill. When we got there, the joint was jumping. The club was only a third the size of the Main Service Club, but the dance floor was filled from wall to wall with dancers. The band was playing those good old rhythm and blues, which the juke box played at home. Paul said, "Edgar, I guess I'll be the only White boy in Service Club # 2." We laughed and enjoyed the music and the sights for more than two hours.

When we got back to our barracks, Paul asked one of the regular Army sergeants why weren't Colored soldiers at the Main Service Club # 1? The sergeant told him that most of the Colored soldiers preferred to go to Service Club # 2. On Friday nights, the Army base buses picked up women from Fort Smith and brought them to the service clubs. One bus picked up White women and brought them to Service Club # 1, and the other bus picked up Colored women and brought them to Service Club # 2. I must admit the musicians at Service Club # 2 were terrific and of course they were Colored. Because I sang with many bands and small groups back home, Service Club # 2 was going to be an outlet for me to release my frustrations of being in the Army.

There was a group of soldiers from Chicago stationed at Fort Chaffee that was terrific musicians. Every Friday and Saturday night they played at Service Club # 2. At that time, Jerry Butler had a hit tune, *For Your Precious Love*, riding high on the nation's hit chart. That was one of my best performing ballads. I asked the piano player to give me a cord in the key of "C." I was going to do my version of *For Your Precious Love*. When he began playing the cadence in "C," the guitar player joined in, and I began singing *For Your Precious Love*, while the band members sang back-ups. The folks in Service Club #2 started screaming, and the dance floor was filled with couples swaying and dancing to the beat of the song. When basic training was over, I sang with the Chicago group every Friday and Saturday night at Service Club # 2.

Word got out about the Chicago group and me, and the company commander requested that the band and I perform at the Main Service Club # 1 one Saturday night. For the first time, some Colored women were brought to the Main Service Club, and when I sang some of those groovy ballads with the Chicago "back-up singers," White soldiers and their White guests took the floor and began dancing to the music. The next weekend, there were so many White soldiers at Service Club # 2 with their White guests, and the dance floor could not accommodate the regulars. That's progress for you.

At last, only two weeks remaining in basic training, and everyone was looking forward to phase II of the activity duty tour. The final big test for all recruits in basic training was the obstacle course in which every recruit competes against each other and the clock. The recruit who accumulated the greatest number of points in the least time would be declared the "Best of the Best" award. The obstacle course was just that. It included most of the drills, exercises, and endurance tests taken during the eight weeks basic training plus a number of intricate track and field competitions. The major difference this time as compared to the drills and exercises performed during basic training was every competition was measured by proficiency and time.

At the close of our company's competition, the winner not only had to perform more drills, exercises, and endurance tests better than the competition, plus achieve those tests in the least amount of time. Paul Peligrin, my bunk-mate, and Edgar Poree finished the company's obstacle course competition, number one and number two in the entire company. We finished first and second in every one of the obstacle challenges, and our point totals were the highest points ever accumulated in the history of the obstacle course competition at Fort Chaffee, Arkansas. That was quite an accomplishment, especially for one who did not want to enlist in the Army.

Better Days after Basic Training

Having successfully completing basic training, testing, registering an I.Q. of 120, I was assigned to become an evaluator in the placement center for the remainder of my active duty time. At that time, Brook Benton just released a hit tune, "It's Just a Matter of Time." I bought that record and played it every night over and over until I fell asleep. I also had a "countdown calendar" that I would cross out each day that I completed on active duty, counting the days when I would be finished and back home. I did get to go home for a week's furlough after Christmas, and it was great seeing the family and especially seeing and spending most of my time with Gloria, affectionately called *Guich*. Returning back to Fort Chaffee after the Christmas furlough wasn't as bad this time for I knew that my stay was not for very long.

Although my assignment as an evaluator was not hard at all, I still had to fulfill those two most challenging and rather demeaning tasks, in my opinion, guard duty and K.P., kitchen police. In spite of my dislike of the Army and its routine, I mastered the art of "soldiering," the power of avoiding the task without having to perform the task. As a result of my tenure on active duty, I was assigned guard duty on nine occasions. Out of the nine guard-duty assignments, I only walked once. One could avoid walking the guard duty tour by being the "Best of The Rest."

Since my beginning on active duty when I was forced to clean the barracks' latrines because I was the only college graduate in my platoon, I made a commitment to myself to never allow the Army to get the best of me. My strategy was to be the best soldier that I could be when it was time to soldier. Guard duty was the best time to excel because it was extremely cold in Arkansas during the winter, and marching in snow was not the most pleasant recreation in the winter.

In order to avoid marching on guard-duty, one had to have the best tailored uniform, the shiniest boots, the cleanest weapon, the fastest disassembling and reassembling of your weapon during guard-duty inspection, and be able to answer every question about the Articles of War, including the Chain of Command in the Army up to the President of the United States of America. In eight of the nine guard-duty assignments, I was rated "Super Numeral Best of The Rest" so I only walked guard duty one time at Fort Chaffee, my first assignment. The two character building experiences that I am most proud of during my active duty tour in the Army Reserve were being rated Super Numeral eight out of nine times and finishing with the second highest point total ever accumulated in the Obstacle Course Competition at Fort Chaffee Army Base.

Biggest Day in Army Career

On February 14, 1959, Valentine Day, I went to the base telephone center to make a long distance call to Gloria. The lines were extremely long, some as many as twenty deep. At 3:30 p.m. that evening after waiting in line for more than an hour, I made the long distance call to New Orleans that would turn my life completely around. I called Guich, the girl of my dreams, asked her if she would marry me, and she said, "Yes!" I was so excited I stood up in the telephone booth at Fort Chaffee shouting, "Yes, yes, yes!" My Dream Girl, after some fourteen years of chasing her, finally said, "Yes." I did not want her to change her mind so I told her I would call her back later because we had a time limit using the public telephone because of Valentine Day demands. I really got the best Valentine Day gift of all times. My Gloria was finally mine—all mine! February 14, 1959, was a day of celebration, and I was in great spirits all day long, like Brook Benton's hit tune, *It's Just a Matter of Time*, before reuniting with my true love, Gloria.

Second Biggest Day of Active Duty Tour

Well with the countdown of days remaining before my active duty would be over, anticipation of being home grew more and more with each passing day. Finally, on April 30, 1959, the second biggest day of my active duty tour had arrived, and we were all getting prepared to begin the trip back home. My coworker, A.P., and my bunkmate, Paul, were exchanging so longs and goodbyes as we were getting ready for our trip back home. A.P. was going to see some of his relatives in New York before returning home. He took an earlier train headed north two hours before the New Orleans bound train would began rolling. Paul was getting a ride back home with his Father, who drove up from Lafayette to get him. Since the train to New Orleans that I would travel on was not scheduled to leave Fort Smith, Arkansas, until much later that evening, Paul's Father suggested that I ride with them back to Lafayette, Louisiana, and I could get a bus to New Orleans from there. I was so anxious to get back home that I accepted the offer to ride with them to Lafayette.

When we arrived in Lafayette at the Trailways Bus Depot, Paul and his Father exchanged parting goodbyes with me, and they drove off to continue their trip back home. I went in the bus depot to buy a ticket for the trip to New Orleans, and the cashier told me that the regular scheduled Trailways Bus which normally stopped in Lafayette that night would not be arriving because there were no advance sales passengers scheduled for the New Orleans destination. I asked the cashier when the next bus was scheduled for New Orleans, and she told me 6:30 a.m. the next morning. There were no other accommodating facilities near the bus depot and when the depot closed, I was stranded in a strange town with nowhere to go for some seven hours. Fortunately, my active duty training somehow prepared me to cope with this situation. I took my duffel bag and placed it next to the front wall of the depot, and there I sat for seven hours until the 6:30 a.m. The Trailways Bus arrived for the trip to New Orleans. Instead of arriving home much earlier than the scheduled train arrival, I got home eight hours later than the train's arrival in New Orleans. Sometimes it's better to stay on schedule even when great anticipation appears to be more attractive. At last I was home, and it was great sleeping in my own bed.

Back Home and School Again

With only one month of school left in the 1958-59 school year, I did not have any time for taking a vacation because my official leave of absence from my teaching assignment was only for six months. My vacation lasted only two days after returning from Fort Chaffee and my six month activity duty. On Monday following the week that we returned home, my Coworker and savior, A. P. Tureaud, who saved me from being drafted for three years in the Army, and I returned to Johnson C. Lockett, our originally assigned elementary school. Since there was only one month of school remaining before closure, A. P. and I were assigned as in-house substitute teachers. We were once again assigned to our regular appointments as sixth grade teachers for the 1959-1960 school years at the same elementary school. The principal of our elementary school was my former algebra and trig teacher in high school.

Army Reserve First Summer Camp

Two weeks after the closure of the 1958-1959 school years, I had to fulfill my Army Reserve two-week summer training at Ship Island in Mississippi. I was assigned to the 377th Transportation Company, a stevedoring unit responsible for handling, storing, and shipping Army equipment and supplies. Like my six months Army Reserve Training Unit at Fort Chaffee, Arkansas, the 377th Transportation Company had very few Blacks who were members of that unit. Most of the assigned Blacks were longshoremen/ stevedores whose skill-sets were essential in handling the duties and responsibilities rigging, loading, storing, and discharging cargo from large shipping vessels. This was the beginning of my five and a half year obligation of serving two weeks annual summer training camps as a member of the 377th Transportation Company. There were six additional Black Army reservists from New York's Transportation Unit assigned temporarily to the 377th to complete their final two weeks annual summer camp obligation before being honorably discharged from their five and a half year Army Reserve obligation.

The few regularly assigned Blacks of the 377th handled most of the rigging, loading, storing and discharging of the cargo during the two week training camp. Sergeant Armstrong, a twenty-seven-year reservist, was the stevedore responsible for directing and training the reservists in handling of bulk cargo activities. Sergeant Armstrong was extremely overweight based upon Army requirements associated with meeting health standards for continued service. I suspect his stevedoring skills were the determining factor for his being exempted from meeting mandatory weight requirements for continued service. Most of the officers of the 377th had little or no stevedoring skills at all; therefore, the success of the unit's two-week summer camp training was entirely dependent upon Sergeant Armstrong's and those reservists who were longshoremen responsible for handling of cargo exercises. His presence and his instructions were critical to the success of the 377th unit's training performance rating.

As the 377th Transportation Company's convoy left the port of embarkation on St. Claude and Poland Avenue at the Industrial Canal for its voyage to Ship Island in the Gulf of Mexico off the shores of Mississippi, our route was via Highway 11. When the convoy reached Slidell, Louisiana, the convoy stopped at the White Kitchen Restaurant. Members of the 377th began getting out of buses and trucks of the convoy and went into the White Kitchen Restaurant. The six Black Army Reservists from New York and I left the bus and entered the restaurant. Strangely enough, the few regular Blacks Reservist members of the 377th remained in the bus. When we sat down at the same table in the restaurant like all of the White Reservists, a waiter came to our table and told us that they didn't serve Coloreds here. The New York Reservists continued looking at their menu without looking up at the waiter. The waiter said, "You all got to leave; we don't allow Coloreds to eat here." I said, "We are members of the United States Army Reserve's 377th Transportation Unit, so we are waiting to place our orders."

The waiter again told us we had to leave. I told the waiter he had to talk to our unit officer, because we were a part of the 377th, and none of our fellow White Reservists were leaving, so we weren't leaving either. At that point the waiter, turned around, walked swiftly to the front of the restaurant, and spoke to the apparent restaurant manager. The manager came over to our table and told us that they don't serve Coloreds, and he said you have to leave. I told the gentleman that we weren't leaving because we were members of the 377th. I told him he had to talk to our unit officer.

The unit officer came over to our table and said, "The manager told him that they would fix anything on the menu that we wanted to eat and have it brought to our bus for us because they weren't serving Colored yet in the restaurant." He apologized for the situation, and then he asked us politely to leave. I said, "Sir, as members of the U.S. Army under the Code of Conduct all members of the unit's convoy would participate in all activities associated with the convoy." The officer stated that this was an unfortunate situation and since many Whites who were members of the 377th were already eating, and he was requesting us to leave in order to avoid any trouble. I said, "Sir, I'm not leaving voluntarily unless you order me to leave." The other Black Reservists from New York at the table said, "We're not leaving either!"

The unit officer went over to the commanding officer and apparently conveyed what we had told him. When the unit officer returned to our table, he again asked us to leave voluntarily. When we refused to do so, he said, "I command you to leave now!" We got up and I said, "Sir, we are leaving; however, we are going to file an official complaint with the Internal General's Office of this Code of Conduct Violation." We could see that the young unit officer's facial expressions reflected discomfort in exercising that eviction order. This was my very first summer training camp, and the New York Reservists' last training before discharge. My actions did not make many friends among the 377th leadership, especially for the remaining five years of fulfilling by Army Reserve obligations.

When we returned to the bus, the regular Black Reservists of the 377th were eating sandwiches brought to the bus. I suspect they had been doing this over the years. When I returned home from the two weeks training, *The Louisiana Weekly* newspaper's headline story: "Black Soldiers Denied Eating in White Kitchen Restaurant." The article described in great details the White Kitchen caper. You know who received the backlash from that article, not the person or persons who gave the story to the newspaper, instead it was Private Poree. Two weeks after the article appeared in the Weekly, I received a letter from Robert, one of the Reservists from New York who had just received his Honorable Discharge from the Army Reserve obligations, advising me that he was the one who gave the story to the newspaper about our White Kitchen experience. Robert told me he was extremely proud to have served with me, and he had great respect for my courage in challenging the injustice and discriminatory bias still prevailing in our Nation, especially the South. Most of the officers of the company felt I was the one who gave the story to the newspaper.

Another unfortunate injustice that occurred during my tenure in the Army Reserve was what happened to Sergeant Armstrong. After he thoroughly trained the White Reservists how to rig, load, store, and discharge huge balk cargo into and out from large shipping vessels and storage facilities, he was abruptly cut short of being able to complete his dream of reaching thirty years of service in the Army. For more than ten years, Sergeant Armstrong "overweigh" condition during annual physical examination had been given waivers, exemptions for meeting mandatory criteria for continued service in the U. S. Army Reserve. Now that the White Reservists had become proficient in stevedoring, his expertise was not needed.

I used to always tell Sergeant Armstrong to stop teaching those young 377th non-commissioned officers stevedoring skill sets if he wanted to reach thirty years in the service. He used to tell me it was going to be OK. I said, "Sergeant, if you continue teaching them how to rig, load, store, and discharge balk cargo, they are going to stop giving you a waiver for being overweight, jeopardizing your thirty years Army career." Unfortunately just as I had cautioned, once they became skillful, his weigh, which had been ignored during annual examinations, became a major factor in forcing him to retire at twenty-eighth year of military service. Discrimination and injustices continued to be a suppressing and adversarial force in our nation.

Church Bingo

Like my previous summer church volunteer job, this summer a group of young progressive church members decided to be more active in helping the pastor implement programs that would be meaningful for the young people in the community. This would require raising additional revenues to supplement the church's budget. After exploring many options, I recommended we begin a weekly bingo game, since many members of our congregation were weekly players at St. Gabriel Catholic Church's

Bingo, located only five blocks from our church. At first, some members were rather reluctant to consider my proposal. They felt traditionally, Methodist, especially Methodist Churches, did not condone such an activity. I asked several of our group members, "Did any of their family members play bingo at St. Gabriel." and most responded, "Every week!"

Several older members in the group stated they felt uncomfortable about sponsoring a church bingo. I said, "We as a group who just happen to be members of the congregation would sponsor weekly bingo nights in the educational building." That's not the church sponsoring the bingo; it's a group utilizing the church's facility in hosting a family oriented fun event. With some group members' reservations, we talked to Rev. Kennedy, pastor, about utilizing the educational building for weekly bingo nights, and he agreed to allow its use. To our pleasant surprise, many of the Catholic bingo players became weekly players at our group sponsored bingo night in the educational building. We were able to purchase furniture for the church foyer, recreational equipment for the youth, and help pay many of the church's utility expenses from revenues generated by the bingo operation.

Unfortunately, even though we were providing much needed funds to supplement the church's operating expenses; our young pastor was getting plenty of heat from some of the older more conservative members of the congregation about the bingo. What's ironic, many who complained that our church had become the gambling capital of the Methodist church were weekly bingo players at St. Gabriel. One of the more vocal anti-bingo critics sent a letter to the Methodist Conference's District Superintendent requesting those persons responsible for hosting weekly bingo at Bethany United Methodist Church be ex-communicated from the church.

When I found out about this, I asked Rev. Kennedy to allow us to purchase the communion glasses, trays, and associated items with the money we raised from bingo. I also asked him to speak just before the congregation began taking their communion. His response was, "Definitely not!" The pastor asked, "Edgar, what were you going to say to the congregation?" I smiled and said, "As information, I want to advise you that the communion glasses and the communion wine that you were about to partake were purchased with that money raised from bingo!" Rev. Kennedy's response, "I had already figured out your address, Edgar; perhaps it was divine intervention." He smiled, shook his head, and said, "Edgar Poree, you're going to get me shipped out to China!"

Well I guess that's just another one of those ex-communication attempts for the Porees.

Colored People's Bank

When school closed for the summer, there were many things that I had to attend to that were unattended during the time that I was on active duty, especially transportation needs. The 1954 Mercury Monterey I purchased during the summer of 1958 had a bad transmission. My brother-in-law, who kept my 1954 Mercury Monterey, while I was on activity duty, attempted to drive to Baton Rouge for Southern University's homecoming football game. Unfortunately, he never reached Baton Rouge due to transmission trouble. The mechanic told him the transmission had been doctored with saw dust. Many street mechanics and some unscrupulous use car dealer mechanics put saw dust in transmissions to help reduce noise and prevent detection of malfunctioning. Unfortunately, I bought a lemon car that looks good but didn't run good. I had to get the car repaired in spite of paying car notes for almost a year for a car inoperable. I needed transportation for my home service business.

My unexpected military duty plus the loss of significant income from my home care services, and my salary from teaching, during my six months activity duty caused a drain in my savings. I still had 14 months of car notes left to pay on my 1954 Mercury, and I owed several hundred dollars on Gloria's engagement ring. Consequently, I needed to get a loan to be able to salvage some of my remaining savings, especially for emergencies. During the 1950's Colored people did not have the benefit or the privilege of getting loans from the traditional banking community, no matter what profession or occupation you may have had. Additionally, it didn't matter whether you were of good ethical character or an outstanding community servant, neither, "qualified" you for loan consideration, by traditional banks. Unfortunately, the only available banking institutions for Colored people were the loosely regulated and notoriously unscrupulous loan companies that charged outrageous high interest rates.

With no traditional banking institutions available, for me to secure a loan, I went to the only source available to borrow $1,000. That source was the school teachers' loan company. That wasn't the formal name of the loan company; however, most of its customers were Black teachers and principals. The overwhelming appeal of this loan company was, "No payment in the summer time." Public School teachers, principals, and other faculty members were paid ten times a year during the nine months that they worked. School employees did not get paid during the three summer months; consequently, the no payments during summer months was most appealing to public school employees.

The owner of the loan company had very strong relations and allegiance with some public school principals. Several principals were very avid and vocal in promoting and soliciting customers for that company. It was rumored, among public school employees as to why some principals had such strong allegiance to the loan company's owner. Speculation was that some principals were apparently heavily in debt to the loan company, and perhaps they could get some relief from their debt by soliciting teachers and other school employees as customers. Instead of being paid commissions for recruiting new customers, apparently the soliciting principals were granted reductions in their debts.

Many of the older coworkers at school told me the owner of the loan company made a lot of money from Colored home owners, especially, the elderly. Before he started the loan company business, the owner was in the roofing business. Two elderly neighbors, who lived across the street from the school, told me that they had a little leak in the front room of their houses, and when Mr. Ben, the owner of the roofing company, inspected their roofs he told them that they needed to replace the whole roof. On several other occasions, some of my students' parents also told me that some of their elderly relatives had been victims of the same kind of scam. Mr. Ben would tell his customers that they could pay him as much as they could, and if they had a bad week, they did not have to pay him until they got some money.

What Mr. Ben did not tell them that he added "hidden" charges on each payment and missed payment he would get the elderly home owners to sign a promissory note for the full amount of the roof. In many instances, the owner was the only one who knew how much the elderly home owners had paid on the debt; therefore, many family members knew nothing of the debt. Unfortunately, when some of the elderly home owners died, their families were facing a tremendous roofing debt that in some instances exceeded the value of their houses. It was rumored that since Mr. Ben held numerous promissory notes of the deceased customers, many relatives of the deceased could not afford to pay the roof replacement debt, so Mr. Ben in many cases acquired the homes of the deceased customers.

It was also rumored that the owner of the roofing company made so much money from the roofing business that he became a "cash" cow with enough money to start a loan business. What was once his primary business, the roofing company, became his "phased out business" replaced by a more lucrative business, the Colored schools employees' loan company. That's the loan company that I was referred to by one of my coworker. Securing the $1,000 loan from the Colored school employees' loan company on Claiborne Avenue next to a truck repair shop was another one of those character-building experiences—one that I will never forget.

My loan was for two years with no payments during the summer months. I paid $72.50 for twenty payments during the two years. Those twenty payments equaled $1,500 total payments. That $500 payment for a $1,000 loan represented a 25% interest rate. I asked one of my White Army Reservist friends how much interest he paid on his $1.000 loan that he got from a local bank, he said "$60," that's an annual Interest rate of only 3%. Having to pay $440 more for the same amount of loan for which my White friend only paid $60 at a traditional bank was not only unscrupulous but unethical. What's so very disheartening about this unfair and unethical practice was the involvement of some of the public school's Colored leadership in the solicitation of customers for these unscrupulous predators. Separate but equal certainly did not apply to Colored people when it came to lending practices.

Developing Parental Support

The summer of 1959 was a very busy one because there was much to do in a very short time. Preparation for the 1959-1960 school years, catching up with my home care business customers, and most importantly, getting ready for marriage scheduled for November. At the end of the 1958-59 school years, we were given the names and addresses of students assigned to our sixth-grade class for the new school year. During the months of July and August, I contacted every one of my assigned students' parents for the purpose of introducing myself as well as encouraging them to actively participate in supporting programs designed in the students' growth and development. Meeting with my sixth-grade students' parents proved to be an invaluable resource for me during the first full year of teaching.

One of the things I recognized during by contacts with the parents, was their burning and sincere desire for their children to get the very best educational development possible. Many of the students in my sixth-grade class were as old as sixteen. In fact two of my students would turn seventeen before the end of the year. There was, however, a reason for most of the older teenagers in my class; most had come from rural areas of Mississippi and Alabama where they worked more months during the year picking cotton then they did attending school. Consequently, they were several grades behind when they migrated to the big city. In spite of their age, their thirst for learning was intense, and their willingness to obey rules and regulations was much greater than those students who were from the city who were of the normal age for that grade.

Recognizing the educational deficiencies attributed to the limited educational development opportunities of my students who had come from rural farm areas of the South, I knew I would have to work very diligently with my parents in order to enhance the educational development of my students. I also recognized the probability of my parents from rural farm areas like my students also lacked the educational development opportunities so I would have to be very tactful and very diplomatic in engaging them in class and school activities. Encouraging parents to become involved in the development of their children at school required some knowledge of the strengths and shortcoming of your parents. To that end, I made a concerted effort to get to know each one of my parents to help me to better understand how they could make contributions for the betterment of their children and the school's objective.

One-on-One Parental Meetings

In August of 1959, I scheduled one-on-one meetings at my elementary school with as many parents who were able to attend. The purpose of the "one-on-one" meetings was to get to know the parents and to assure them that I had their children's interest at heart. Additionally, I wanted to assure the parents that I would never place them in a situation that they would feel rather uncomfortable which could be embarrassing. One of the techniques that I used during the one-on-one meetings with parents was to diplomatically and tactfully determine how well they could read. In order not to embarrass parents, I would ask them to sit near the back of the classroom just as many of the students would be seated during class. I began writing on the blackboard, "Welcome to My Sixth Grade Class." Then I asked my parent, "Can you understand my handwriting." I specifically did not ask, "Can you read what I wrote on the blackboard." There was a reason for this approach. By asking, "Can you understand my handwriting," it afforded my parents an opportunity to avoid being embarrassed if they couldn't read.

In many instances, some parents would say, "I'm sorry I did not bring my glasses, or the writing was too small and I've been having trouble with my eyes lately." Those responses were typically associated with reading deficiencies and inability to read very well so my "one-on-one" meetings with parents enabled me to more effectively understand their limitations as well as help me to better determine their strengths, utilizing their talents without placing them in situations that could be embarrassing to them. Additionally, it enabled me to establish a strong bond with my parents, so much so that they defended my every action, whether it was good or even not so good.

Big Risk Worth Taking

One of the things that I recognized that had to be addressed during my meetings with parents was the need to get our parents to become registered voters. That was a very big "No, No" back then because I could get fired swiftly. As a young, aggressive and future-oriented individual, I had a deep conviction that parents would not be able to provide the critical support and encouragement for their children unless they were a part of the political solution process. Therefore, I decided that I would include in my parental meetings instructions of how to successfully complete the Voter Registration requirements in becoming a Registered Voter in the community. My coworker's Father, A.P. Tureaud, fought so hard for civil rights. They could not exercise such rights unless they were registered to vote, and critically even more important, exercise that vote at every election. I had to be extremely careful in my efforts of providing assistance to my students' parents in mastering the very complicated voter registration process.

One of the most difficult sections of the voter registration processing was being able to figure out the specific time that the person's age was at the time of the actual registration. As an example, the voter registration applicant at the time of their registration had to list his age, the number of months, and number of days since their last birthday. This provision made it extremely it difficult for many applicants to complete their applications accurately, resulting in their being disqualified in as registered voters.

In order to overcome this difficult computation, I decided we would get our parents to apply for their voter registration applications as near as possible to their actual birthdays. This made it easier to figure out the complex formula used by the registration office. In order to assist each parent, I asked him to give me the date he planned to apply for his voter registration. I would work out his age, months, and days, counting before his scheduled date of registration. Each parent was given his age figures, well in advance of his scheduled application date. I encouraged all parents to call or contact me if they changed their original planned dates to apply, so that we could adjust the age requirements to reflect the changed application dates.

One of my oldest parents was so excited when he finally received his official voter registration cards, after failing on two previous attempts that he brought me a carbon copy of his Voter Registration Card along with his personal "Age" information. He wrote on the carbon copy, "Thank you, Mr. Poree," for making me feel so good about myself. In very large bold letters and numbers he wrote, "My birth date was October 15, 1916. I'm 43 years and two months old." He completed his voter registration application on December 16, 1959, at 10:00 a.m. that morning. All but two of the parents of my six grade class successfully completed their voter registration applications. The two that did not personally told me that they could not read. Was the risk of teaching my parents the importance of and how to accurately complete their voter registration application worth it? Yes, it was and it was indeed most gratifying with the tremendous success. Although we had to conduct this project undercover, it was a risk worth taking. A vote-less people was a hopeless people in the end.

Pre-Cana Conference

It was mandatory for all Catholic *mixed marriage* couples, those with one mate being non-Catholic to attend Pre-Cana Conferences in order to be married in the Catholic Church. Because I was Methodist, I had to comply with attending the conference if I was going to marry the girl of my dreams. The Pre-Cana Conference was supposed to be a learning experience for couples preparing for Catholic marriage vows. Gloria asked me before we left to attend the conference to please be quiet and refrain from antagonizing the conference instructors during their presentation. "Just listen, Edgar, please," she asked. I agreed somewhat reluctantly and promised to be good.

When we attended the Pre-Cana Conference, the first thing I noticed was the absence of any African-American couples who were program participants. When I mentioned that to Gloria, she again said, "Edgar please just listens and be good." "Ok!" I said. The Catholic priest was the lead instructor of the discussions, and all White couples gave examples of things and circumstances that occurred and how they overcame those challenges during the initial months of their marriage. That was the format that was used during the conference. I was quiet during most of the initial discussions and illustrations of the Pre-Cana Conference until the priest began talking in detail about "foreplay."

At that point, I raised my hand and asked the priest if I could interrupt his presentation, he said, "Yes." I told the priest I was rather confused with his discussion of foreplay, since I was of the impression that we would be getting from the newly married couples information of their "experiences," "challenges," and things they did to overcome those challenges. I also acknowledged I could have understood and perhaps accepted his explanation of foreplay if it were from a spiritual context and perspective rather than his explanation of the act itself! The priest immediately called a recess. Many candidate couples seem rather amused, nodding their heads in agreement with my observations. Some, however, seemed extremely annoyed and upset with my comments. The priest asked me to restrict my comments to questions for the participating married couples' examples and not question his presentation. Gloria asked me not to comment any further, since candidates had to "pass" Pre-Cana conference in order to be married in the Catholic Church.

Finding Rental Home before Marriage

With our wedding scheduled for November, the immediate agenda was locating a rental home. I asked some of my coworkers if they knew of any houses for rent in the area. The kindergarten teacher told me that one of my coworkers just bought a new home in the east, and they had been renting a house in the next block from school. I spoke to my coworker who purchased the new home, and she told me they planned to move into their new home on September 30th so the house they rented might be available in October. She told me the landlord didn't want to rent the house to anyone with children, so my chances may be good for renting the house. My coworker said that she would be happy to recommend to their landlord, Gloria and I as good candidates for the house.

Gloria and I met Ms. Dimes, the owner of the house on September 20, 1959, and she agreed to rent the house for $52 a month. It was a lovely one bedroom home with a living room, bathroom, kitchen and a wash shade. Gloria's cousin gave us her old wringer washing machine. The house had off-street parking, and it was located a half-block from a public transportation bus stop. I paid Mrs. Dimes the $52 for the rent for October, and she gave us the keys of our newly rented home. The next day Gloria and I began shopping and purchasing furniture. We were well on our way getting ready for our November 21th wedding date.

Jackpot Winner

On Saturday, November 21, 1959, at Corpus Christi Catholic Church at approximately 4:00 p.m., I won the greatest prize of all times, when my childhood dream princess said, "I do." Finally, we were married. Walter Mitchell, Milton Coulon, and Leonard Troullier were groomsmen. Minnie Wiggins, one of Gloria's dearest friends, was matron of honor, Gwendolyn, her sister, and Elvira Day Henry, our high school classmate and my college classmate were bridesmaids. Our wedding reception was held at the Brick Layers Union Hall on North Galvez Street, a block and a-half from my parents' home on Bienville Street.

All my buddies at our reception anticipated me taking my very first alcoholic drink during the newlyweds' toast. When champagne was poured into Gloria's glass, I pulled a bottle opener from my pants, and gleefully said, "Mitch, get me a bottle of 7-Up soda from the soft-drink machine." Mitch, my best man, reluctantly brought me a bottle of 7-Up, and after I filled my glass with the soda, our champagne toast was officially completed.

Our wedding reception didn't begin until 7:30 that night, and I was getting a bit restless because my Mother-in-law was still trying to call the shots. At 9:45 p.m. I was ready to leave to start my honeymoon. After chasing Gloria for nine years during our elementary and high schools, and five years during college and teaching, I was ready finally to have my Princess to myself. One of Gloria's aunts hadn't arrived at the reception, so my Mother-in-Law insisted that we wait for Auntie Buntee's arrival, so she could see Gloria before we left. After almost 15 years of waiting and submitting to my Mother-in-law's demands, I finally stood up like a man and spoke up like a man declaring my independence. "Aunt Buntee will have to see Gloria another day," I said. "Gloria is now Mrs. Gloria Poree as of 4 o'clock today, and Mr. Poree says it's time to go!"

As fate or luck would have it, Auntie Buntee walked in at that precise moment. She got to see Gloria for about ten minutes, and we were able to leave our wedding reception to begin our honeymoon on North Dergenoir Street. When we arrived at home, I picked my bride up, carried her over the threshold, closed the door, and at last began the beginning of my lifelong dream with my lifetime sweetheart. We lived only a half block from the school where I taught six grades.

Operating on Perilous Grounds

As a new teacher I was fully aware of the consequences of advocating such terrible notions as encouraging and promoting Colored people to become registered voters. The school system made it abundantly clear that there will be no advocating, educating, or even discussions about becoming politically involved, especially becoming registered voters. Any one reported advocating or promoting voter education would be subject to disciplinary action which could include termination of assignment. I knew that the educational development of my students as well as many other students' parents was directly related to the strength of and the number of registered voters that our school had. Therefore, I continued diplomatically and tactfully to encourage, educate, and cultivate as many parents of the school to become registered voters.

Because of the success of our efforts, we were able to get numerous parents whose children were many different grades to become Registered Voters.

After School Youth Development Program

In an effort to develop closer relations and bond among the parents, students of my class, I started an "After School Development Program" for the fourth, fifth, and sixth grade students on school's grounds. The program included math and English games, soft-ball, shuffle-board, square-dancing, and indoor games like Chinese checkers, checkers, fiddle-sticks, and jacks. Since there was no funding for the after-school program, we got many parents to donate equipment and games and also volunteer to help supervise the program.

Once the program was up and running successfully, a representative of the Colored school's physical education program offered to step in and provide some type after-school recreational activities. Instead of an opportunity to get paid by the Colored school recreation division and the City's Recreation Program, we turned down the offer. The recreational activities they wanted to provide did not include any academic developmental programs, a key element of our after school program. The Colored schools' physical education coordinator attempted to prevent us for operating an after-school program, citing all types of reasons why their recreation staff was more qualified to run such a program.

Because of the strong and good relations and relationships that we had established with parents, we were able to continue operating the after-school developmental program on the school grounds. No one got paid for assisting in the after-school program; we were non-paid volunteers. The parent volunteers were extremely supportive with their time and their donations of equipment and other developmental supplies, making the after-school program a great success. Additionally, the parental involvement in the after-school program played an important role in strengthening the Parent Teacher Association at the school.

Bigger Doesn't Mean Better

After singing with some of the city's most sought-after and popular bands and big orchestras, Edgar Blanchard, leader of the Gondoliers Band that I had been singing with for years, heard that a newly established local recording company was looking for a new face and talent to become its featured headliner recording artist. Edgar contacted the owner of the recording company and arranged an audition for me. When I completed singing the ballad, *Take My Hand, Lead Me On* and the swing tune *Come On Baby,* the owner was so impressed with my performance that he told Blanchard that he had found his headline recording artist for his record company's label. I was elated about the prospect of becoming the new face and artist of the local recording company. The owner told us that he would get back with us as soon as the paper work was completed.

During the same week of my audition, Edgar and his Gondoliers were doing some studio sessions at the city's premier recording studio, where major recording artists produced their recordings. Dave, a big band leader, agent, and producer for one of nation's biggest recording companies, had just finished directing a recording session for Fats when he spotted his friend Edgar Blanchard. The two of them exchanged greetings and Blanchard told Dave that Rich, the owner of a new local recording company, had offered me an opportunity to become his company's featured recording artist. Dave said, "Why would you want to take a chance with a small, recording company with a limited distribution outlet?" "Before you sign with Rich, let's do a recording session of the ballad and swing tune with my company and see if it gets thumbs-ups," said Dave. Blanchard told me that Dave's company had the greatest potential, so we decided to go with the national recording company instead of the local new recording company.

After completing the recording session for my ballad and swing tune, Dave, the studio band, and Edgar Blanchard gave a thumbs-up gesture and applauded. The tape recordings were shipped to California for further assessment for publishing. My oldest sister, Edna Floe, and two choir members from my church were back-up singers on both recordings. After the recording session, my sister and the two back-up singers were paid for their performance, and I had to wait for the decision of the recording company as to whether or not I would be offered a recording artist contract or be paid for the recording session. Everyone in the studio appeared extremely confident that both recordings were good enough to make the California record label.

Unfortunately, I received a congratulatory letter from the California recording company plus a check for the recording session; however, they indicated they were concentrating all of their promotion on two of their featured recording artists at that time, Ricky Nelson and Fats Domino. The new local recording company that we turned down to become its featured artist had a sensational opening hit, Johnny Adams, *I Won't Cry!* Bigger is not necessarily better.

Chaos, Uncertainty in The 60's

The beginning of the 1960's brought about a dramatic change in the New Orleans Public Schools. The Federal Courts ordered the once segregated public schools in the City to desegregate two elementary schools. One of the elementary schools, William Frantz located on the corner of North Galvez Street and Alva Street, was ordered to desegregate. It was located only nine blocks from Johnson Lockett Elementary School where I taught. The other elementary school, McDonogh # 19, was located in the Lower Ninth Ward across the Industrial Canal on Saint Claude Avenue. Both schools encountered tremendous civil unrest and racial tension and violence. Under the protection of U. S. Marshals, several Colored children were escorted to and from the two schools ordered to desegregate. White parents stormed the schools, took their children, and set up ranting, raving, and taunting mob-like gangs in the streets around those schools. The City was a city in crisis, and those of us in the teaching profession would experience some troubling times and uncertainties.

When schools were ordered to desegregate, Louisiana's Legislature, under the dictates of one of the country's most blatant segregationist, enacted legislation prohibiting the legally elected local school boards to operate the city's public schools. Because of the State Legislature's take—over of Orleans Parish Public School Board's operation of its schools, no funds were appropriated to operate the schools in spite of the Federal Court rulings. As a result of this legislative action, teachers and other employees were not paid for the first three months of the 1960-1961 School year. Consequently, employees did not receive any paychecks for the months of September, October, and November, causing severe financial chaos for most members of the city's public schools. Many teachers and other employees had to secure odd jobs to make ends meet and help prevent losing their homes, automobiles, and other essential possessions. Those were extremely tough times, and the city's retail businesses almost went bankrupt because the opening of the school year previously meant brisk and robust retail sales. Our city also faced an economic crisis as a result of the legislative action.

After three long months of not having any income, employees of the public schools were finally paid. The problem, however, did not end because no one wanted to take a risk of cashing state issue checks for public school employees. The reason was that banks as well as other businesses did not know whether the state had appropriated funds to cover the checks issued. We were caught in the middle of a cross-fire that seemed that there was no possible successful outcome. During the darkest days facing the employees of the city's public schools, Maison Blanche Department Store had the courage and convictions to take a tremendous risk by offering to cash checks issued to the employees of the city's public schools in December. That calculated risk that the department store took, cashing public school employee checks proved to be a tremendous plus in robust sales and especially opening of new customer accounts. Public school employees made Maison Blanche the store of first choice for most of their shopping needs in gratitude for the courageous and generous commitment of Maison Blanche's owners for helping alleviate the financial crisis of public school employees. I suspect every person who had his checks cashed at Maison Blanche opened a Maison Blanche credit account.

Maison Blanche Department Store had the most incredible "sales," more than any competitors. I remember the day when MB had its big men's day sale on name brand dress shirts. Ten and fifteen dollar name brand dress shirts were on sale for a mere one dollar. All of the men's department counters were full with name brand long sleeves dress shirts in a variety of colors and sizes. When I reached a counter where dress shirts were, I grabbed an arm full of dress shirts. A salesman said, "Mister, you got an arm full of different sizes of dress shirts." I said, "Name brand dress shirt for one dollar; who cares what size they are!"

The salesman told me the collars might be too large or too tight for me or the sleeves maybe too long or too short. I told the salesman, "If the collar was too big, I'd tighten my necktie, if too tight; I'd loosen my necktie and open the top button of the shirt to breathe a little better."

"If the sleeves were too long for me, I would simply turn the cuffs then button them." Finally, I told the salesman, "If my sleeves are too short, I would keep my coat on." I left Maison Blanche with two dozen name brand dress shirts of all colors and all different sizes. I bought two dozen name brand dress shirts for only $24, the same price that two $12 shirts cost previous to the big sale. That's was a terrific bargain.

Integration—The Decline and Deterioration of a Culture

Perhaps the single most debilitating impact of the decision to integrate the public schools was the devastating affect it had on the African-American community. More specifically, the negative influence it had on the thirst for knowledge and the dedication of committed school personnel in enforcing the discipline and governance once the pivotal standards governing the African-American segregated schools. Before integration, Black principals were the most respected and revered members of the Black community. They set the agenda maintained a high level of expectations and standards both for the teaching personnel and student body. Rules and regulations and hiring of teachers, faculty and staff were the responsibilities of the school's principals. Appropriate attire, appropriate behavior, and adherence to rules and regulations were determined by the school's principal.

The real role models in the Black community were principals, teachers, counselors, and social workers of the segregated schools. There was a strong bond and relationship among the parents and school personnel, where mutual respect and parental involvement were the norm. When a student broke the rules or standards, the administration's disciplinary codes and regulations were enforced. All parties, faculty, parents, and administrator, were in accord with the mandated corrective measures. The prevailing philosophy in the Black community during the pre-integration era was, "It takes a whole village to raise a child." Unfortunately, due to the School District's attempt not to subject its White principals, faculty, and staff members to the more rigid standards imposed in the Black schools, discipline, appropriate attire, and respect of authority were significantly diluted.

Prior to the integration of the public schools, Black teachers and other school personnel wore appropriate attire. Male teachers wore suits, sport coats, dress shirts with neck-ties; hair neatly cut and faces well shaven, and shoes highly polished. Female teachers wore suits, dresses, appropriate hair styling, make-up and shoes that were fashionable, professional, and comfortable. Once integration took place, the dress code mandated during the segregated school days in the Black community were greatly relaxed. The School Board in its effort to give the impression and appearance of having integrated faculties and staffs throughout the school district began to assign the very best, brightest, most experienced, and top performing Black teachers to previously all White schools. The rationale was that White parents would allow their children to continue their education at that school because of the faculty's make-up having the superior performing, highly qualified, and most experienced top Black teachers. Unfortunately, after displacing and the dismantling of the Black brain thrust, teachers, the pillars of educating Black children, the School Board replaced them with newly hired young hippies from Midwestern universities, low performing White teachers, and older White teachers waiting for their retirement.

Prior to integration of schools, Black teachers were constantly observed by the school district's supervisory staff, which by the way was always White personnel, assessing the teacher's proficiency in following the district's curriculum dictates. Much of the assessment appeared to be mostly in following the district's mandated rules and regulations based upon being on a certain page at a particular time of the year in a subject matter, rather than the quality of instruction. This practice was an instrument in determining whether or not the teacher was going to be retained after the three year probation period.

Black teachers always placed more emphases and efforts in providing individual attention and assistance in helping their students to grasp the fundamentals needed to improve their comprehension skills. That meant utilizing some non-traditional teaching methods to get their students to become more proficient in their comprehension skills. The school district's supervisory assessment personnel were more interested in following their traditional practices rather than allowing alternative initiatives that had positive results in enhancing the student's comprehension skills. Seldom, did you see Black teachers frequently checking out projectors, tape recorders, and art supplies for instructional purposes; instead, they were extremely resourceful in creating a learning environment.

A tremendous number of new teaching recruits hired by the Public School Board were not certified education major graduates. Many of them had all sorts of degrees other than education. Many of the newly appointed teachers were young, inexperienced college graduates, who came to New Orleans for Mardi Gras, fell in love with the partying atmosphere and Bourbon Street, decided to stay here and get a job. That job turns out to be a "teaching" one in the Black Public Schools. It appeared the only qualification those candidates needed to teach in Black Public Schools was a college degree with any major and being White.

Replacement teachers assigned to Black schools came to school wearing T-shirts, khaki pants, jeans, sandals without socks, and stringy hair. Black principals never would have allowed that kind of inappropriate attire during the segregated school days. Unfortunately, the School Board, in its effort to retain those young inexperienced teachers, forced the Black principals to relax their dress code requirement so as to retain as many of the replacement teachers. Dressing for success was no longer the norm in the previously all Black schools, so Black students became rather confused, and they began to wear clothing that previously were forbidden before school integration.

Unlike their Black coworkers, many of the older White teachers didn't spend much time providing thought provoking exercises for their students. Instead they frequently and routinely went to the school's office, checked out the 16 millimeter projector and Webcor tape recorder to either show short stories or listen to music. I assumed the listening exercise was for music appreciation. If their students weren't being shown stories or listening to tape exercises, they were having extended art and crafts sessions, instead of any thought-provoking comprehension skills exercises. This practice was not an isolated one but a frequent one used, especially with those waiting-to-retire teachers.

Prior to integration, Black teachers were constantly undergoing evaluations and assessments by White supervisors for determining competence. After integration, when the School Board began hiring more and more young White college graduates for teaching positions in Black schools, the aggressive and constant supervisory competence assessment of teachers mysteriously disappeared from the classroom once faculties were integrated. This was of great concern to the Black community because our children were being placed in the care of inexperience teachers whose background was not only foreign but for many in our classroom weren't adequately prepared in challenging and provoking critical thinking of our students. Instead, they were there because they came to New Orleans for Carnival, fell in love with Bourbon Street, and got a teaching job to support their partying in the French Quarter.

Discipline was another strong standard that deteriorated during integration of schools. White parents did not want Black teachers administering any type of discipline to their children. Black principals had very effective, correct measures and practices dealing with discipline during segregation. Unfortunately, when the schools were integrated, the School Board directed the Black principals to discontinue those effective corrective measures. When you put all the restraints that the School Board mandated on Black principals as to what they could do at their schools, now that they had been integrated, the negative impact that it had on the Black students was quite devastating. All of a sudden, Black teachers, seeing how their White coworkers were dressing, began wearing similar attire to school that was not only inappropriate but never allowed nor tolerated during segregated days. This drastic change in teachers dress was still another eroding of standards which were pillars and indicators of good moral character in Black schools and the Black community. The restraints placed on Black principals and administrators when schools were integrated was the beginning of a down-spiraling and marginalization of those traits, those values, and that insatiable thirst for knowledge which strengthen and sustained our culture during extremely difficult times.

Changing Administrations

Just as the beginning of the 1960's brought about chaos and financial crisis for the employees of the public schools, the 1960 school year brought another rein of uncertainty and trauma for the faculty and staff of my elementary school, a new principal. We thought the days of not being paid were traumatic. The newly appointed principal made those extremely dark and trying months of desegregation seem very trivial and uneventful. The new principal was my former fifth grade teacher, and he was a person who only marched to the beat of his drums. The principal was a very light skinned, devout Catholic, who treated female teachers like they were merely hired hands or mere sub-servant not professional. He had a Napoleon-like dictator style of running the school. His way was the only right way that counted. Dark complexioned faculty and staff members and non-Catholics were not treated with the same respect as those who were light complexioned. Additionally, the principal was extremely insensitive to the needs of the children who came from the housing projects.

Tyrant Principal

Although the first principal that I worked under had many similarities to the newly appointed principal (very light skinned, Catholic, argumentative, and moody), he would at least listen to others when it came to in resolving those critical issues that affected the well-being of the children. The new principal did not allow any input from his faculty or staff. His philosophy was doing as I say do or face the prospect of being shipped out. In fact, our school seemed to operate under siege and distrust. There were constant instances of clashes between the principal and those of us who refused to be treated like children. Anyone who did not agree with the principal's ideas, especially those teachers who were in their probationary period, risked being placed on the at-risk list for certification—becoming a tenured teacher. Intimidation was the principal's autocratic style of leadership, and he used it as a "fear factor," suppressing any thought of exercising critical thinking or other opinions contrary to his.

Unfortunately, I had many clashes with the new principal because I refused to be treated like a hired hand. Consequently, I was placed on the at-risk candidates' list that could have had an adverse affect on my receiving full certification for tenure at the end of my probationary period. Because of his dictatorial style of leadership, the principal on numerous occasions would openly criticize many of my coworkers in the present of other members of the faculty and staff. This was not a rare exception, but a frequent occurrence. I recall when we were preparing for our annual school operetta, which was being held at the George Washington Carver Senior High School's Auditorium. I was responsible for all the art decoration for the play. After successfully completing all of the major scenery for the annual school play, the day that we were scheduled to deliver the scenery to Carver, I had an emergency at Mother's home.

When I told the principal that I had an emergency at my Mother's home, and I needed to leave school. To my surprise, the principal said, "You're doing this on purpose; you don't have any emergency, you're just trying to put a monkey wrench in my school's play for selfish reasons." I told him again that there was an emergency at my Mother's home, and

I really had to go now. The principal advised me if I left school before the official close of the school day, he would place in my personnel file a memo for failing to adhere to his order. I told him that I had to do what was best for my family. It was 2:30 in the afternoon, only 30 minutes left before the normal school day ended. I asked Lloyd Richards, my coworker whose class was next door to my classroom, to supervise my class for the remainder of the school day. He agreed and I left school immediately to go Mother's home.

Gloria and I lived only a half block from school. She was a day-by-day substitute teacher, and she frequently worked at my school. Teachers would request that she work in their absence so she practically worked most days of the week at my school. Because the principal could not intimidate me and because he wanted to exercise his authority, he decided to look for a reason to justify limiting the number of opportunities that Gloria would have to substitute at his school. One Friday during the lunch period, Gloria was assigned duty in the school's cafeteria during the first half of the lunch period. After completing her duty, the principal decided that since she was a substitute teacher, he would extend her duty throughout the entire lunch hour. Gloria told him that she had completed her full duty tour and that she had not had lunch yet.

The principal told her he was in charge and that he instructed her to remain on duty during the second half of the lunch period. The ranking teacher, who assigned Gloria to the cafeteria, told the principal that Gloria had completed her tour of duty, but the principal said that he was in charge of the school, not her so he told Gloria to stay on duty. Gloria told the principal she thought it was unfair for him to deny her of her lunch, since she had fulfilled her scheduled duty. The principal said, "You do as I say do or you won't be here anymore." Gloria told the principal that according to the governing rule of assigned duties, she was entitled to have a lunch period. In spite of that, she remained on duty while eating lunch.

The principal notified personnel office that he did not want my wife to do any substitute work at his school. This was just another incident where the principal exercised his authority to intimidate his faculty members. The personnel director personally spoke with my wife about my principal's request. He told her she would not have any problems getting substitute work in the district because his office had received numerous commendations about her outstanding work performance from other principals across the City, and she would be working every day of the week.

The personnel director said he knew it was convenient for her to work at my school, because it was in walking distance from our house, however, in the interest of alleviating the current situation, take the substituting opportunities elsewhere and good things would happen, soon. Well soon was very soon, because a month after my principal demanded my wife not be permitted to substitute at his school, Gloria was appointed to a full-time teaching position at a newly constructed school only five blocks away from our home in the Desire Projects.

Jet Magazine Headlines

Later that same school year, our school had the dubious distinction of making national headlines in a syndicated Jet Weekly Magazine, as a result of our principal's irrational behavior. Some of our female faculty members were smokers. Apparently they smoked while using the ladies' restroom. Because of the principal's authoritative and somewhat dictatorial leadership style, he began to check the ladies' restroom throughout the day. Apparently after detecting evidence of some smoke on several occurrences, the principal instructed the school's head custodian to install a brand new lock for the ladies restroom. Additionally and immediately after the installation of the new lock, the principal instituted a new policy for female faculty members wanting to use the ladies restroom during the school day.

That policy required female faculty members who wanted to use the restroom to sign the usage log at the time they received the key for the restroom and again list the time they returned the key to the office after use of the restroom. Our school became the hottest gossip in the District as well as the subject of every conceivable joke around town. School principals during those days were like czars and administered their schools like they owned them. There were no teacher unions back then so principals pretty much ruled what went on in their schools.

After several weeks of this embarrassing and insane policy, it appeared that no one would dare challenge this policy, especially none of the female faculty members who were directly affected. I decided that enough was enough. Something had to be done to help alleviate this unfair, unethical, and discriminatory practice against female coworkers. One Tuesday morning as we assembled our classes in the yard for the traditional morning exercise, I brought a spittoon (more commonly called slop jar) with me to that assembly. When the teachers and children saw the slop jar on the ground next to me, they began laughing. Just as the morning exercise was about to begin, the principal spotted the slop jar and immediately notified the teachers to take their class to their classrooms. "Mr. Poree, report to my office immediately," he said most authoritatively.

Needless to say, I was in deep trouble again, the principal told me that I had embarrassed him and the school; therefore, he was placing a very serious reprimand in my personnel record. He also advised me he intended to request an extension of my Probationary Period for Teacher Certification for Tenure for an additional year. This was indeed a very severe disciplinary action. Then the principal told me to get my personal belongings and leave the school grounds until further notice. Just as I was about to leave his office, the telephone rang, and the secretary told the principal that it was Mr. Bison, the personnel director.

As fate would have it, the same day I was being admonished by the principal, our school had the dubious distinction of appearing in the Jet Magazine under the title *Need to Use the Restroom, Get Principal's Permission, First.* Before leaving the office, I heard the principal saying, "Mr. Bison, I was just about to call you about a very serious situation that occurred at school this morning, and the person responsible for that embarrassing incident is standing in my office presently." Apparently, the personnel director must have said something to my principal because all of a sudden, the principal said "Yes sir, I'll be right there!"

Isn't it ironic, my principal was attempting to get me disciplined for the slop jar incident, and he was summoned to the school board office to answer to and apparently being disciplined for the embarrassing article appearing in Jet Magazine, depicting him as an overzealous administrator. I escaped that disciplinary action by the skin of my front teeth. When word got around that the principal had apparently been admonished or disciplined, many of the female faculty members came to my classroom, gave me a big hug, kiss, and thank you. From that moment, I was a marked man with the principal; therefore, I had to be a bit more careful in what I did at school.

Staying Focus on Five-Year Commitment

In keeping with my commitment of getting Gloria into our home before our fifth anniversary, I had so many hustles and hustles (*jobs*) that it's hard to describe how I managed to get any rest. In addition to my regular teaching job, I continued to operate my home service residential cleaning service after school hours as well as on the Saturdays. At night on most weekends I had singing gigs with William Houston Orchestra and Clyde Kerr Orchestra at dances at the ILA and Labor Union halls. Additionally, on weekends I had singing gigs for matinees and nightly shows with two of the area's hottest bands, Danny White's Cavaliers and Edgar Blanchard's Gondoliers, at some of the hottest White night clubs including, The Conti House and Natal's Lounge on Chef Highway, Tropicana Club in Treme, and Club Sands on Jefferson Highway.

A Glorious Moment

In July of 1961, Gloria and I had our first child, Deidra Maria. Of course, as the only boy in the Poree's family, I was hoping for a little Edgar; however, when Deidra arrived, she brought so much joy and excitement that little Edgar would just have to wait a few years because Deidra was the "apple" of our eyes and the center attraction for Gloria and me. My parents were excited, especially my Mother, for this was her baby boy's first child. Deidra became my shadow, whenever you saw me there was Deidra right along with me. Gloria and I really had rotated during the night with our newly schedule life style. I even learned how to pin the diapers right and fix the baby formula. We were very fortunate to get a baby-sitter for Deidra who lived only two houses from where we lived. Joyce, our baby-sitter, gave as much love and care for Deidra that Gloria's "Goodbyes" in the morning were not as painful when she left for work.

Home Beverage Salesman Driver

During the summertime I worked as a salesman-delivery driver for Dot's Home Beverage Company, a Black owned business that provided beer and cold drinks, on consignment basis for many weekend "Suppers" held throughout the Black community and adjoining parishes as well as those regular customers that got semi-monthly deliveries. I made $10 a day, as salesman-driver, regardless of the number of hours worked, loading and unloading delivery trucks with hundreds of cases of beer and soft-drinks scheduled for Friday and Saturday deliveries. Each weekend delivery stops could range from a low of 30 stops to a high of 70 plus stops per day, depending on the number of cases of beverage a customer ordered. I had many deliveries in the housing projects and that meant carrying tens of cases of beer and soft drinks up the steps to the second floor apartments. Many of my friends and coworkers always asked me how I got so muscular. I told them from carrying those 52-pound cases of Barq's Root Beer up and down two and three flights of stairs. Barq's Root Beer was the most popular soft drink for "Suppers" even more popular than Coca-Cola at that time.

Mondays were the hardest day at Dot's Home Beverage and every weekend you hoped it didn't rain. If it rained, Monday would be a very tough "pick-up" day because all those "Suppers" sold hardly any of those hundreds of cases of beer and soft-drinks delivered on Friday and Saturday. It meant picking up a majority of "full" cases of beverage that you delivered on Friday and Saturday. Monday was also "collection" day; you had to collect full price for all returned empty cases and "short" cases (cases with two or more missing full bottles). Your math skills better be excellent or your ten dollar a day salary wouldn't be ten dollars.

When you finished your pick-up and collection route and returned to the warehouse, the owner would count the number of full cases of beer and soft drinks and the number of empty cases of beverage returned. That's the moment of truth for your total collection better be equal to the total cost for all empty and short cases or the difference would be deducted from your ten dollar daily salary. It was very easy to be short because many "supper" customers paid their bills with as much as twenty dollars in coins including, quarters, dimes, nickels, and pennies. If you had sixty or seventy customers and you were short three pennies each, your ten dollar day would be reduced to eight dollars and twenty cents. My accounting skills were greatly challenged each Monday.

Bigger House, Cheaper Rent

Working for Dot's Home Beverage also afforded me an opportunity to get a larger home for less monthly rent. Beverly Saulny, owner of Dot's Home Beverage Company, had a two bedroom house for rent on Marigny Street for $40 a month. He offered the house to me, since I had been a very good worker for him during the summer. I was somewhat reluctant to rent the house because it was only two doors from my in-laws and several miles from my regular teaching job; however, I could save $12 a month, and the location was more centrally located than where we lived.

The Marigny Street house was larger than our existing house, and Beverly allowed us to use his family game room, located on the first floor of the building. The house needed some serious cleaning and some minor repairs because the previous tenants were extremely negligent in the upkeep of the property. We had to scrub, deodorize, disinfect, and paint before moving in. In addition to working for Dot's Home Beverage during the summer months, I also worked for three weeks as a driver and delivery man for O'Donnell Brothers' Printing Company relieving Mr. Milton, one of my Father-in-laws best friends. I made $1.15 per hour, and I had over 140 delivery stops a day in Orleans, Jefferson, St. Bernard, and Plaquemine Parishes.

Another Embarrassing, Yet Enlightening Moment

Mr. Lloyd, my next door neighbor on Marigny Street, was a banquet captain at the Royal Orleans Hotel in the French Quarter. Every evening when I knocked off from work at Dot's Home Beverage, Mr. Lloyd told me he could get me a waiter's job making more money in fewer hours than I was delivering those heavy beer and soft drink cases. Every evening when I got home, he'd be sitting down relaxed on the porch reminding me how he works two banquets a day and be home relaxing for hours while I was still working hard all day long. After several weeks of hearing his daily ritual, I decided to take him up on his offer.

Just as he promised, Mr. Lloyd got me an opportunity to work a luncheon at the Royal Orleans Hotel. He gave me some tips of how to handle the food trays and how to place the food on the tables. He also suggested that I watch the older more experience waiters to see how they handled their luncheon guests before lunch was served. What I saw watching those older waiters greeting and assisting the seating of the guests was quite demeaning in my opinion. I thought their behavior appeared to be more like that of servants rather than banquet waiters. They were grinning and bobbing their heads, and all you could hear them saying was "Yes Mame! No Mame! Thank You Mame!" I certainly didn't plan to follow what I considered to be Uncle Tom behavior.

When it was time for serving lunch, it was amazing to see how those older more experienced waiters handled the trays containing ten or twelve luncheon plates. Even the smallest and slightest built waiters appeared to be like supermen when they picked up their serving trays from the kitchen. They lifted those fully loaded ten or twelve stacked luncheon plate trays with one hand, hoisted them above their heads, and walked through the swinging doors to the dining room, placing each plate in front of the luncheon guest on their assigned table. At six feet tall and one hundred and ninety-two pounds, I struggled lifting that fully loaded stacked luncheon tray with two hands. Once I got it up to my shoulders, I managed to place that extremely heavy serving tray on my shoulder. It felt heavier than those 52 pound cases of Barq's Root Beer that I was accustomed to carrying up two and three flights of stairs in the projects.

Unfortunately, my waiter's job didn't last very long. After struggling with my shoulder supported luncheon serving tray and successfully placing the plates on my assigned tables, my second trip from the kitchen ended in a disaster. As I was leaving the kitchen with my luncheon tray, I mistakenly went through wrong swinging doors and collided with the waiter returning from the dining room. My fully loaded stacked lunch plates and carrying tray crashed to the floor scattering the food all over the kitchen floor. Needless to say, after I finished cleaning the kitchen floor, I was relieved of my waiter's job that paid $8.50, the going rate.

After being relieved, I waited in the lobby of the hotel until the luncheon was over so I could apologize and thank Mr. Lloyd for giving me the opportunity. He told me that everything that looks easy isn't always the way it appears. One lesson that I learned on that day after the luncheon was over which has remained with me for almost five decades—things that appear to be demeaning to some are treasures to others. When I first observed those older more experienced waiters acting like what I thought were Uncle Toms, grinning and bobbing their heads with those little old white ladies, I discovered afterward was their cleverness in their trade. I saw them counting multiple big dollars in tips that they had gotten from those little old White ladies far exceeding their $8.50 basic salary rate for serving the luncheon. I realized they were not Uncle Toms; they were after all professional actors, extremely skilled in their art of persuasion, exceptionally polite and courteously working their mastery in generating big tips. Dropping the tray with a dozen plates of food was another one of those embarrassing moments of mine; however, it was also an enlightening experience. My interpretation and impression of what was a demeaning turned out to be a very in creditable acting performance. This proved to be still another character building experience.

Joining Brown Paper Bag Social Club

When the owner of Dot's Home Beverage was elected president of the brown bag social club, he encouraged me to join the club. I told him that I didn't think my complexion would pass the "brown bag" test, and he smiled and said, "We have folks in the club with your complexion." and I responded, "But their hair is naturally curly and mine's not!" We laughed and Beverly said, "Since I'm the new president, I might say a good word for you, then you'll be Ok." Since I did not have any air-conditioning at my house, I thought it might be a good idea to join the club because it was only $2 a month membership fee. The club had a Ping-Pong table, and there were several good players who were members. I was the runner-up in the Ping-Pong table tennis championship at Fort Chaffee, Arkansas, when I was in the Army Reserve so I wanted to test my skills against those good playing members. I became an official member of the former brown bag social club. After working ten or twelve hours at Dot's, I went to the club to cool off and rest before going home.

NORD Supervisor

There were very few supervised facilities, close to Johnson Lockett School where students could participate in wholesome recreational activities. I decided that I would volunteer with William Stevens, a coworker, to provide some supervised activities for our students on the school's play grounds. After getting approval for the use of the school's playground and some of the school's recreational balls, bats, and volley ball nets, we began an after school recreational program for our students during the spring. Eligibility to participate in the after school activity was based on two requirements, completing homework and permission from parents.

A major problem that existed before we began the after school recreation program; it was the use of the school's playground, especially the basketball courts by the neighborhood's teenagers. If we were going to have a safe and wholesome environment for our students after school, we had to address some of the obvious problems associated with the school yard being used by high school and non-school teens. The first thing that we had to address was theft and the use of profanity. Much of the school's playground equipment had been vandalized and many of our soft balls, bats, basketballs, and volley balls had been stolen. I used to go to the second floor of building B in the evenings to observe the teenagers playing or horsing around to help determine which ones were the trouble makers. I saw who seemed to boss the other teens, who frequently used profanity, and who were stealing.

I now had my candidates to help correct some of the problems that prevented the school grounds from being a safe and wholesome environment for the elementary school age students to play on. I made the teenager whom I observed frequently cursing the language assistant. He was in charge of preventing cursing and the use of profanity while playing in the after school program. I made the teenager I saw hiding a softball in his gym bag the equipment assistant. He would be responsible for making sure all of the equipment taken from the locker for use at the beginning of the after-school program would all be collected and accounted for at the close of the after-school program and locked up. Finally, I gave the teenager who appeared to be bossing others around on the playground the title of playground assistant. He would be responsible for making sure that all after-school program participants would get equal opportunities to play in all activities provided.

When we made the announcements of who would assist us, my coworker and me, during the after-school recreation program, many of the teens and elementary-age students laughed because they knew the persons that we selected were the leading trouble makers. However, if you allow trouble makers to become a part of a team in helping prevent trouble, sometimes it works and fortunately for our after-school recreational programs it was a great success.

One immediate benefit that occurred after naming our equipment manager was the return of most of the missing equipment that had been missing for a long time. The use of profanity was eliminated, and all participants of the program got opportunities to play in all games and activities. Our volunteer after school program was a big success. After a year of serving as volunteer supervisors, providing wholesome after-school recreational activities for our students and teens from the neighborhood, the New Orleans Recreational Department hired my coworker and me to run its summer program at Johnson Lockett Elementary School.

Drug Store Clerk

Sterling Henry, a pharmacy graduate and classmate of mine at Xavier, worked at Watkins' Drug Store on Hamilton Street after graduation. On Sundays he worked at the Circle Food Store's Drug Store for four hours, relieving the regular pharmacist. Sterling was paid $12.00, three dollars per hour as the Sunday's pharmacist, which at that time was the going rate. After several months relieving the regular pharmacist on Sundays, the owners grew tired of the regular pharmacist's erratic and unreliable behavior and offered the job to Sterling. He went to his mentor, Mr. Watkins, to get some advice as to how much he should ask for his salary. Mr. Watkins suggested a hundred fifty dollars a week. Sterling met with the owners and told them he would accept the job for $150 a week. The owners said, "Mr. Henry, welcome, you are our new Pharmacist, and we are looking forward to your taking over and making it better and bigger." Sterling was excited and thrilled, knowing he had gone from a Sunday-only $12 pharmacist to a $150 a week pharmacist. He couldn't wait to get home and tell his wife Elvira the good news.

After taking the helm as the new pharmacist of the drug store, Sterling began to improve the service, and the drug store began to grow and gain more and more customers every month. He hired addition clerks for the drug store from the market side of the business. Because of the increase demand of the drug store, Sterling needed a part-time employee to handle the additional demand. He asked me if I would be interested in working part-time after school and on the weekends and I said, "Yes." I became the first male drug store clerk at the Circle Food Store's Drug Store at the whooping salary of $0.65 per hour. Because my schedule was flexible, I could work as little as three hours an evening or as many as ten hours on Saturday depending on the grocery side of the business. I worked approximately 30 to 35 hours per week with an average weekly wage of between $18.50 and a whopping $21.75.

Since I was the only male clerk in the drug store, when female customers came in for personal items, they were at first reluctant to ask me for those personal items. They would always ask to speak to the pharmacist over the telephone. Sterling would then tell me what item or items to get for the customer. After weeks of this routine, the female customers finally began to ask me for their personal items as they got to know me better. This hesitancy to ask for personal items from the other gender was not limited to female customers only. Male customers who wanted personal items were hesitant to ask the female clerks for their requested personal items.

I'll never forget the day when it was raining really hard, and the owner of one of the neighborhood's largest restaurant came to the drug store. I was in the store room at the time so the female clerk asked the customer, "May I help you?" He told the female clerk that I was going to help him. When I got to the counter, I asked the customer, "How can I help you?" He told me he wanted a rain coat, so I reached up and got a plastic rain coat. The customer said, "No, no, not that kind of rain coat." Then I knew what he was asking for. I said, "You want a pack of prophylaxis, condoms!" The customer leaned over toward me and whispered "No, No, I want a pack of rubbers." I told the customer the next time he wanted to get some protection, ask for condoms not a rain coat. He laughed and said, "Yes Sir!"

Boy's Night Out

For months, Sterling and I didn't have any time to enjoy ourselves because we were both working practically around the clock. However, because of the drug store's tremendous growth, he was able to make Mertis, his part-time pharmacist full time. That made it possible for us to have a few Friday nights out on the town. Sterling and Elvira, his wife, began looking for a house to buy. When they found a newly built double house in the Lower Ninth Ward on St. Maurice Street, he told Mr. Mike, the owner of the drug store, they really wanted to buy a house; however, they didn't have enough cash for the down payment. Mr. Mike graciously agreed to loan them the money for the down payment, plus he allowed Sterling to pay only ten dollars per week on the loan with no interest. Since the house was a double, they rented the other side, enabling them to pay their house note, the ten dollar a week loan payment, plus start building their savings.

Two Friday night's each month; Sterling and I went out on the town. We scheduled our working tour on those nights to get off earlier. Our routine was that Gloria and I would drive to Sterling and Elvira's home and then we left those beautiful young ladies to have some quality time with each other while the boys were out on the town. Our first stop was J.T's Joy Tavern in Gert Town where we heard some of the coolest jazz and best rhythm and blues in town. Then we went to Okey Dokey's Club down the street from the Dew Drop and heard some of the best jazz around. The next stop on our way home was on Rampart and Erato Street, Sam's, the place that made the best ham sandwiches in town. Our final stop before getting back to our wives was in Melba's Ice Cream Parlor in Arabi in St. Bernard Parish to get some hand packed ice cream and bananas splits. Finally, when we reached the Henry's, the four of us pigged out with ham sandwiches and Melba's best. That was the official boy's night-out routine.

Political Abusive Power, Destruction of Black Business

Beverly Saulny, owner of Dot's Beverage Company, was one of our more progressive citizens. He recognized the importance of becoming more involved in the political process in the City if we were to improve economic conditions in our community. During the Mayoral Election, he decided he would become an active participant in supporting a young progressive white candidate, who was running for mayor. Beverly began escorting and introducing the young lawyer candidate for mayor to members of our community at as many places as humanly possible throughout the black community. When the mayor's political organization got word that he was introducing and encouraging members of the Black community to consider the candidacy of the young progressive mayoral candidate, a vicious and relentless attack was waged on Beverly Saulny's home beverage business.

In New Orleans, suppers and weekends were inseparable. There's a supper going on in every neighborhood in our community. Whether it's at church, school social club, or at your mama's or grand-mama's house, you could find one very easily in your neighborhood. Routinely, the home beverage business would deliver requested cases of beer and soft drinks to individual's households throughout the city on consignment. Customers did not have to pay for the requested cases of beverages on the day they were delivered. They would pay for only full cases and short cases used on Mondays, then pick-up unused ones over the weekend.

Traditionally, the City's Code Enforcement did not bother anyone having a *supper* at their home, or church, or organizations. However, when the incumbent mayor found out the owner of Dot Home Beverage Company was supporting one of his challengers in the next mayoral election, police began raiding neighborhood suppers, confiscating all of the beer and soft drinks cases at the suppers on consignment by the beverage companies. The cases of beer and soft drinks were held as evidence of violating the City's beer permit requirements. Strangely, all of the consignment cases of beer and soft drinks confiscated by the police belonging to the White-owned beverage company were always released fully to that White-owned home beverage company after a City hearing. Unfortunately, all of the consignment cases of beer and soft drinks owned by Dot's Home Beverage Company confiscated by police were never returned to Dot's Home Beverage Company after the City's hearing. Instead all of those cases were donated to the hearing officer's favorite charities, which were more than likely the mayor's political contributors.

This unwarranted assault on this Black-owned businessman's basic rights to participate in the political process of his choice was an example of blatant abusive political power. The tragic results, another Black family-owned business providing a decent living for more than fifteen families was severely impacted financially by this abusive political power. Sadly and unfortunately, this tragedy did not get the attention of the press, and even more disheartening, there wasn't any outrage from the Black community. Shame, shame on the Black community for not rallying and supporting Beverly Saulny, who sacrificed so much in attempting to enhance our community's fortunes.

Cashmere Overcoat and Lifelong Friendship

Maison Blanche had its annual fall sale where $200 men's cashmere overcoats were on sale for $100. I tried on a beautiful midnight blue cashmere overcoat, and it was a perfect fit. Just as I was taking my checkbook out of my coat pocket to pay for the cashmere overcoat, Bill Buchsbaum, a salesman at M.B. walked over to me saying, "Why pay for the coat today with your money when you can pay for the coat with someone else's money. Enjoy wearing it for a year for less than ten dollars a month." I asked Bill, "How can I do that?" He told me "Elmore Blache, one of his best friends, had opened an installment plan on Gravier Street, two blocks away from Maison Blanche that had extremely low interest rates during its inaugural promotional period to attract new customers."

I put my checkbook back in my coat pocket, Bill and I walked over to installment plan, I met Elmo Blache, signed some papers, got a brand new one hundred dollar bill, returned to Maison Blanche, and bought that sharp looking midnight blue cashmere overcoat. I only had to pay the sales tax on the coat with a couple dollars, pocket change—what a fantastic bargain! I paid nine dollars a month for twelve months for a total payment of $108. What a bargain that Wednesday evening at Maison Blanche and installment plan turned out to be. Bill's friend, Elmore, and later the next year one of Elmore's most competent and reliable employees, Rita Shremp, and their families became lifelong friend of the Porees.

CHAPTER VI

Fulfilling A Commitment

When I proposed to my wife, Gloria, I made three major commitments to her. The first commitment was that I would never disrespect her; however, I told her that I could not promise her that I would never embarrass her because I was a rather weird dude. I used to wear some weird looking outfits, when others were wearing what was considered "normal" attire so I wanted to be truthful to her regarding my commitments. The second commitment that I made to her was to have her in our home within five years of our marriage. The third commitment that I promised Gloria was to be debt free before I made fifty. Those were some might big commitments, especially from someone who had a sum total of $246.43 in his savings when I married Gloria.

As stated earlier, when I was in seventh grade I had my first $5 hardwood floor polishing job in 1949. Well what started out as a five dollar hardwood floor polishing job grew into a full fledge business, over a seventeen year period of time with more than 50 customer clients who paid fees ranging from $25 to $50 per household for my Custom Home Services. Little did I realize back then in 1949 just how much that "first" hardwood floor job and subsequent home cleaning jobs would contribute to the realization and fulfillment of one of the three commitments that I made to my fiancé during my proposal for marriage, that of having her in a new home in five years. That's a major accomplishment for someone who had less than $250 in the bank when married. Well thanks to those fifty plus customers over those seventeen years the realization of a new home was made possible.

In March of 1964, just after leaving Sunday school at my church, I decided to stop over at a Greenup's Real Estate Office to see if the newly developed section in the Pontchartrain Park Subdivision had any unsold lots. To my surprise, there were two remaining sites left in the Park. When the agent showed me the model homes that were to be built, I called Gloria and told her I was buying her a brand new three bedroom house with air conditioning, a built-in kitchen, and a carport. Gloria said, "Edgar, wouldn't it be nice if I got a chance to see the model before you decide to buy me a house?" I agreed, but we've got to do it immediately because two other people want the same house, and I've got to make an offer now! Gloria asked whether we could withdraw our offer if she didn't like the house, and I told her yes. Man, I was so excited that I made an offer for the house right there. The house sold for $25,700, and we were living in a rental house for $40 a month. That was a major decision going from a house that cost $40.00 a month to a $25,700 home.

When I completed the application for the house, I thought that I could qualify for a FHA loan because the down payment would only be about $1,700. Gloria and I had been saving for years to buy a home, and I knew that we could afford the monthly FHA mortgage house note of $95 for thirty years. I called my parents to tell them I was about to live the American Dream by purchasing our home and to say with pride that we had come from a very long way, since Father was sixty-year old when he and Mother bought our Bienville Street home. I was twenty-seven when we bought our new home. That was quite an accomplishment for our family but, little did I realize, there was a slight problem associated with purchasing the house.

Back then in the1960's, the wife's salary did not count when you applied for a FHA loan. Since there was always the possibility of a wife getting pregnant, that would negatively impact the family's income. Because of that reason, the real estate agent told me that he could get a second mortgage on the house since I did not qualify for an FHA Loan. I asked him how much I would have to put down for a conventional loan. His response was, "About $5,500 or there about." This man did not know me from Adam, yet he assumed that my only source of income was from teaching school; consequently, he apparently thought that was my only source of income.

The truth of the matter, however, was my multiple part-time jobs I had provided twice as much income as my regular teaching salary. I was a

$0.65 an hour part-time clerk at the Circle Food Store's Drug Store after school during the weekdays and on all day on Saturdays and Sundays. Additionally, I was an encyclopedia salesman for Tanglewood Publishing Company, paid on commission basis, and I hanged wallpaper for $25 per room, no matter what size room including ceilings. These three jobs were in addition to my regular home cleaning business.

Now I've got a bigger problem, convincing Gloria the merit of withdrawing most of our savings for a down payment on a brand new home. All day I thought of what strategy I was going to use to convince her that it was in our best interest to take most of our savings to buy our home. Gloria said she wasn't going to take all her money and put it down on a house, no way! At the time we had $7,600.00 in the United Federal Credit Union. Paying $40 a month rent for a two bedroom house can make it difficult to start paying $132.00 a month for twenty-five years. But with some assurances from me that I would work twice as hard to rebuild our savings, Gloria agreed to the conventional loan.

The day I withdrew money from our savings, I called Father to tell him I was going to make a down payment on our new home. Father said, "Son, that's a tremendous accomplishment especially at age twenty-seven; I was sixty-eight when your Mother and I bought our home in 1954, after renting for eight years." Father told me to stop over before going to the real estate office; he had something to give me. When I arrived at the barber shop, Father opened the cedar chest, pulled out a little black box, and opened it. Inside the box were the five one dollar bills and a fifty cent piece that I earned from cleaning Dan's Grocery Store, when I was eleven years old. Inscribed on each of the one dollar bills were this quote: *"This is my Son's Return on His Investments."*

That quote inscribed on the bills was from Father. Additionally, in the little black box were three silver dollar coins, the ones Parraine Cooper gave me when I made three years old. Father took the five one dollar bills and the three silver dollar coins and placed them in my hands and said, "Take this and make sure you include it in your down payment, Son." I stood there for a moment motionless, all of a sudden tears began running down my face. They were tears of joy, admiration, and fulfillment, for there was a very powerful message being conveyed with the exchange of the currency. That message was one of great pride and family accomplishment. There I was standing in the barber shop of my parent's home that they bought in 1954, when Father was sixty-eight years old. I was going to make a down payment on a brand new home at twenty-seven. This was a historic moment in the life of the Poree family. I embraced Father, and I went off to the real estate office to place the down payment on our Providence Place home.

There were ten new homes being built in this newly developed section of Pontchartrain Park. Gloria and I were the youngest couple; the other nine families were older than we were. Several of my new neighbors were college professors at the Southern University at New Orleans, only a block away from our home. Apparently, some of them thought that Gloria and I were too young to purchase a house in that development, especially since we had only been teaching for a mere six years. One of my neighbors even told the security guard working at the construction site that I would be an extremely disappointed young man when I found out that I did not make enough money to qualify for a FHA loan to buy my house.

It's ironic that Gloria and I were the only couple of the new home buyers that acquired a conventional loan. The other nine couples either had a V.A. loan, FHA loan, or some with second mortgages. According to some of my neighbors after reading the real estate official records in the Times Picayune Sunday Newspaper, the Porees had secured a conventional loan with a 20% down-payment on their home, which implied that I must have been in the rackets to afford that type of down payment. It's unfortunate that small minds have a way of thinking small—shame on them. That was just another one of those character-building experiences.

Father's Death

During the construction phase of our new home, I would go over every morning to see what had been done the previous day and what was planned to be done on that day. I always had the building plans with me to make sure that the contractors were doing what the specifications called for. Father's health was declining, and each time that I planned to bring him to see the progress of the house, he was just not strong enough to make the trip. I took pictures so that he could see the progress. In June, Father was hospitalized, and his health was rapidly deteriorating.

The day I was supposed to visit Father, I was watching the NBA Finals, and when the game was over that evening, visiting hours were over; therefore, I did not get to see him. I planned to go to the hospital the next day to see him; however, the next day was too late because Father died during the night of the evening I was looking at the NBA's basketball game. I've never gotten over the fact that I watched the game while there was a chance to spend time with my Father during his last hours. I've had to live with that "heavy" for the rest of my life. Mother as usual tried to console me; however, I would always have a sense of guilt for not visiting Father before his death.

Two months after Father's death, we moved into our new home at 6219 Providence Place in Pontchartrain Park on August 22, 1964. Although it was truly a very wonderful day for Gloria, Deidra, our three-year old daughter, and me, the thought of Father not seeing this blessed and joyful event somehow diminished the luster of this day. As we entered the den, I held Deidra in my arms while embracing Gloria and saying in unison, "Thank you, Heavenly Father our God, for making this Blessing possible, and we know that The Judge, my Father, is up there in your presence, smiling upon us on this day." I didn't have much time to enjoy my stay in our new home because I had to begin packing that night to leave the next morning to begin serving my two week U. S. Army Reserve Training Camp on Ship Island in Mississippi. Betty and Johnny Sneed, our married couple baby sitters, agreed to stay and help Gloria get the house in order during my two week encampment.

When I returned home from training, Gloria and the young couple had transformed the cluttered house into a beautiful home fit for royalty. Fulfilling her commitment that she made as a senior in high school regarding her seamstress career, Gloria said back then, "The day I can spell the word, able will be the very last day I will be seen on a sewing machine!" August 22, 1964 was the day mother was talking about. The day when we moved into our new home, seventeen years and nine months after Gloria declared "The day she could spell able will be the last time you'll see her on a sewing machine." At 6:30 p.m. that evening, when I placed Mrs. Guichard's sewing machine in Deidra's bedroom, that day was the last day Gloria was near any sewing. End of a long and tiring seamstress career.

A New Day, A New Opportunity

With a beautiful baby girl, a brand new home, and a new school year, another wonderful thing happened. After working some three years under a dictatorial principal, the School Board appointed him to a junior high school in the lower Ninth Ward. We got a new principal that was a real gem and gentleman who allowed faculty and staff members to use their individual talents and initiatives in enhancing the learning experiences of the boys and girls. Once again, our school became one big happy family, full of initiatives, full of cooperation, and a new renewed spirit of yes we can. Parent-teacher meetings had full attendance, the school festivals and community drives were most successful, and young and old faculty members supported and respected each other with mutual admiration and dignity.

Catholic Menu and Protestant Students

The elementary school where I taught was located in a predominately Protestant neighborhood. In spite of this, the school system's Friday cafeteria menu was commonly referred to as a Catholic lunch. The lunch consisted of codfish balls, patties, cream potatoes, pees or carrots, a piece of cake, and milk. Many of the students would buy snack food in the morning on the way to school on Fridays rather than eat the "Catholic lunch" in the cafeteria. Even many of the teachers skipped lunch on Fridays, settling for sandwiches purchased at a sweet shop on the corner of the school. One Wednesday I asked my class this question "Tell me what you like most about Fridays?" The class said, "It's the last day of the week to come to school, and we have two days to play on the weekend." Then I asked my class the second question "Tell me what you dislike the most about Friday?" "Codfish balls, cream potatoes, and pees for lunch!" was their response.

Pickle Juice, Moon Pies, and Friday Lunches

Friday public school lunches did not have any meat. As a Protestant, I always thought it was rather unfair for non-Catholics to be forced not to eat meat on Fridays, so I asked my class, "How many of you would like for Mr. Poree to give you a party on Friday for lunch?" Not surprising, every one of my student responded with an enthusiastic "Yes!" Having gotten this resounding approval from all of my students, I decided to challenge each member of my class to invest in "our" party. I went to each student in my class and challenged them: "I bet you can't bring a pack of hot dogs? I bet you can't bring a pack of hot dog buns, some Kool-Aid, potato chips, pickles, or moon pies?" Of course, when you challenge children they always want to prove you wrong, so when I got to the forty-fifth student in my class, I had gotten commitments for more than 40 packs of hot dogs, 40 packs of buns, 10 bottles of pickles, 100 bags of potato chips, 15 cans of chili, jars of mustard, eight boxes of moon pies, dozens of lemons, 20 packs of Kool-Aid, ten pounds of sugar, and 20 bags of cookies. Wow! What a party Mr. Poree was giving his class.

On Friday during our party after giving each student a pickle, I began pouring the pickle juice out of the bottles, several students asked, "Mr. Poree please doesn't throw away that pickle juice?" I stopped immediately, and asked, "How many in class like pickle juice?" To my surprise, most of my students raised their hands and said, "I do!" A large bottle of pickles sold for $0.28 with an average of approximately 14 pickles in them. If you sold pickles for $0.05, that would yield a gross of $0.70, a profit of $0.42. Using a communion size cup, the average amount of pickle juice in a bottle could fill four to five cups of pickle juice. A large pickle bottle at a price of $0.02 a cup would yield an additional $0.08 to $0.10 per bottle. So I began selling pickles for $0.05 and cups of pickle juice for $0.02 on Friday's non-Catholic lunches. The profits from pickles and pickle juice would yield a whopping $0.50 profit.

Well I decided that I would give the students an alternative to eating Friday's school cafeteria's "Catholic lunch" by providing hot dogs, potatoes chips, pickle, and Kool-Aid party meal for $0.15, the same cost of the "Catholic lunch" served in the school cafeteria. Of course, you could get a communion cup of pickle juice for an additional $0.02. Before you knew, my Friday alternative lunch had grown so much that the cafeteria manager complained to the principal that the school's normal Friday's total lunches served had been reduced dramatically. My Friday non-Catholic lunch parties were ordered by the principal to cease.

Rainy Day Raffle Dilemma

Since the principal stopped my Friday non-fasting student lunch sales, I decided to create another fund-raising event that would allow us to purchase games for "rainy day activities" for my students. Raffling a case of Coca-Cola seemed like a good idea. So I made a raffle list for each student in my class. The cost of a case of Coca-Cola was $1.12. Each raffle list had twenty chances. If the student sold all twenty chances that would yield two dollars per raffle list. I always believed in profit sharing so I told my students that if they completely sold all twenty chances on their lists, I would give them fifty cents. One student asked, "Mr. Poree, if I sold all twenty chances on more than one raffle list, would I get another fifty cents for every list that I completely sold out?" I said, "Yes!" The statement that I made about the fifty cents bonus for selling all twenty chances resulted in a phenomenal financial bonanza for the rainy day activities program.

I had planned to have the raffle for one week since I had thirty five students in my class. If all thirty students sold all twenty chances that would generate seventy dollars minus the fifty cent bonuses totaling seventeen dollars, resulting in a profit of fifty-three dollars. Little did I realize, what great salesmen my students were. They were selling-out raffle lists two and three times during the first week. I decided that I would extend the raffle for an additional week, and to my surprise, the students sold more chances that second week than the first one. Since my students were "getting a fifty cent profit-sharing bonus for every raffle list sold, I did not want to deprive them of making some extra money for themselves.

After several weeks of extending the raffle, something happened that I regret to admit was a mistake on my part in judgment. One of my students had a bad habit of coming to school late frequently. I had cautioned her that the next time she came to my class late; I was going to send her to the office, to call her parents to come to school to discuss her tardiness—bad idea. When the secretary called her Mother about the student's excessive tardiness, her Mother told the principal the reason her child was late was because she had not completely sold the twenty chances on the school's raffle list. The principal called me on the classroom speaker phone, and said, "Mr. Poree, come to my office immediately, now!" I was indeed in big trouble.

When I got to the principal's office, he closed the door and immediately began admonishing me about the allegations of the student's Mother. The principal asked, "Mr. Poree, what was the parent talking about a school's raffle list?" I said, "I probably violated a school practice; however, my intentions and motives were good because I was attempting to raise some money to purchase games and competitive activities for my students for rainy days." The principal said emphatically, "Selling or raffling anything for money without authorization and or approval was prohibited by the school district, regardless of good intentions or motives were." The principal demanded I return all of the raffle lists and all of the money that I had received so that the money would be returned to the people who bought chances. I was dumbfounded. The raffle list had generated more than $600 minus the $150 profit-sharing dollars that I had given to my students for selling all their chances.

Fortunately, I had all of the raffle lists and the $450 in a saving account. On the next Monday I brought all of the raffle lists to the principal, and on Tuesday I brought $450 to the principal as per his demands. After determining that it would be difficult to reimburse the hundreds of individuals who took a chance, the principal after conferring with school district officials was granted a waiver that allowed the principal to place the funds in the school general account to purchase games and other development exercises for rainy day activities for students. The $1.25 case of Coca-Cola turns out to be a big gift for buying rainy day games and activities for students after all.

Workaholic

In addition to my primary teaching job, I was still doing my house cleaning service for my old die-hard customers, who claimed that they could not find anyone else to clean their homes. At night you might find me singing at Club Sands on Jefferson Highway or the Conti House on Chef Highway with Danny White's Cavaliers Band or with Edgar Blanchard's Gondoliers Band at Gordon Natal's Lounge. I frequently had singing gigs at Mason's Las Vegas Strip with the Red Tyler's Band and occasional singing gigs with the Royal Dukes of Rhythm Orchestra.

During Carnival Seasons, I sang with the William Houston Orchestra and Clyde Kerr Orchestra at many carnival balls. After school I had a part-time job with the Circle Food Store Pharmacy as a sales clerk six or seven days a week. During Christmas seasons, I worked part-time for the U.S. Post Office at night from 10:00 p.m. until 2:00 a.m. in the morning at the Port of Embarkation Warehouse. Finally, I was a fence salesman for Scott Fencing Company, and I attempted to sell encyclopedias for

Tanglewood Publishing Company—I only sold one set over a three month period. I guess you might attribute that to my "burned-out" condition.

Another Embarrassing Moment

As you might recall, my first major commitments to Gloria was to never disrespect her; however, I qualified that commitment by stating that I couldn't promise I wouldn't embarrass her. Well, just as I had predicted, there were a few embarrassing moments that occurred during this year. Gloria and I were invited to a masquerade dance at the ILA Hall on South Claiborne Avenue, whose theme was "Having a Good Time in Mexico. I got up early Saturday morning, sat at the sewing machine, and began making our ponchos for the dance that night. Gloria asked me where I put the invitations for the dance. I told her I didn't recall where I put the invitations; however, she need not worry because we didn't need invitations since I was the M.C. for the dance. Gloria said, "Edgar, I believe that dance was last night." My response, "I'm the M.C., so I must know when the dance is happening!"

With our beautiful colorful ponchos on and our stylish sombreros hanging down our backs, we were off to the Mexican masquerade dance. After parking down the street from the ILA Hall, as we were walking toward the hall, we didn't see any ponchos or sombreros on any of the people going into the ILA Hall. Instead, everyone had Hawaiian costumes on. Gloria said, "Edgar, I told you that dance was last night." "The dance must be at the Laborers Union Halls on Tchoupitoulas Street, Guich," I said. So off we went to the Laborers Union Hall. Gloria told me that she was not getting out of the car again and be embarrassed.

I parked the car on the corner and began walking toward the dance hall. To my amazement, the closer I got to the hall all the more ladies I saw in hot pants, no ponchos or sombreros. I asked a lady if she knew where the Mexican masquerade dance was. She said, "It was at the ILA last night." When I returned to our car before I could open my mouth, Guich said, "That dance was last night, wasn't it, Mr. Know-it-all, let's go to Dooky's, so tonight won't be a total loss. We will be the only two Mexicans at Dooky's tonight," Needless to say, Guich wasn't very happy to say the least; she was embarrassed!

CHAPTER VII

STRATEGIC TAX PLAN

Sales Tax Campaign

During the summer of 1965, the School District appointed a young visionary school Superintendent that was quite ambitious. The new Superintendent recognized that he would need additional resources in order to improve the physical school facilities, increase teachers' and administrators' salaries and upgrade the academic standards and curriculum to better prepare the students for the rapidly changing world. There was much excitement in the school district about the new Superintendent, and his tenure would dramatically change the fortunes of my family during the new school year.

The new Superintendent's first order of business was to seek an additional source of revenue for the school district. His agenda included a very ambitious and bold initiative to raise revenues. With the support of the School District's Board, the newly appointed Superintendent announced he would seek an increase in the City's sales tax by one cent to help raise the much needed revenues to improve the Public Schools plus increase the pay of the school's personnel. The School District's Board approved the Superintendent's proposal, and an official election would be held in May of 1966. The School District began planning for its One Cent Sales Tax Election during the first quarter of 1966. That initiative motivated me to do something out of the ordinary which would change dramatically my career in the future.

The day that the School District officially announced it was holding an election in May of that year. When I got home from school, I told

Gloria that I was going to develop a strategy that would help the School District to win the One Cent Sales Tax Election. Furthermore, I told her my efforts would eventually take me out of the classroom for another career opportunity. Gloria said, "Yes Edgar, I know you're about to undertake a big project, good luck. That day, that moment would prove to be one of the most significant undertakings in my early career. I was determined to use all of the experiences that I had over the years in working in a wide variety of jobs and being around some of the City's movers and shakers, who were principle owners of some of the most successful business in town.

With a great determination and a willingness to spend countless hours in developing a winning strategy, I began the journey of gathering information regarding past tax issues and elections as well as researching newspapers to get a sense of citizens' attitudes regarding taxing themselves in the interest of improving the quality of public education. In order to develop an appropriate appeal in promoting the One Cent Sales Tax initiative, obtaining accurate and current demographic data on the city, and defining economic benefits to the community from passage of the tax were critical and essential components of a winning strategy.

Fortunately for me, my next door neighbor and a good friend of our family was Dr. Walter Austin, Chairman of the Economics Department at SUNO and one of the nation's leading economists. Dr. Austin was instrumental in helping establish an economic infrastructure for one of Africa's emerging countries. He was a giant of a man, physically and intellectually. More importantly, his expertise in economics and in organizational structure played an invaluable role in assisting me in the development of my One Cent Sales Tax Winning Strategic Plan. His expertise, his insight, and support proved to be my most reliable and most valuable allied and mentor during the entire planning and refining of my proposal. Dr. Austin provided essential economic, demographic, household incomes, social, and educational as well as class differentiation data that were so critical in the development of the plan.

Paul, my Army bunkmate, also played an instrumental role in my developing the sales tax campaign strategy. Since much of the tax related data I needed was in the Legislative Official Records at the State Capitol and in LSU's Library, I did not feel really comfortable or safe about being on the campus since the campus was not fully free of incidents regarding race; therefore, Paul's assistance was invaluable. Paul would not attract much attention researching the data at the Capitol and at LSU. When I needed research data from either the State Capitol or LSU's Library, I would contact Paul, and he would mail the requested data to me.

My multiple working experiences as a beverage truck driver and printing-stationary delivery man during the summers enabled me to be knowledgeable of the neighbors around the City and surrounding areas. This experience was especially helpful in designing appropriate targeted promotional material for distribution according to the different classes of residents residing in those neighborhoods. Our City's unique housing pattern unlike other cities in the country had extremely expensive homes on major streets and two blocks away extremely inexpensive housing. Still there were pockets of the City that housed the more literate residents in the Uptown university section; the Lakefront, emerging LSU-New Orleans, and Dillard University.

Those diverse neighborhoods would require specific tailored messages if we were to be successful in encouraging them to vote yes for the one cent hike in sales tax. That neighborhood which consists of the blue-collar workers and others from the lower socioeconomic level would also require specific targeted messages that would motivate them to support the hike in the sales tax. The mission was clear; we had to have a plan that would reflect the diverse makeup of the neighbors so as to appeal to their senses of community as well as their diverse experiences.

When I came from school, I devoted most of the evening developing the sales tax strategic plan. Guich asked, "Edgar, why are you spending so much time with this project?" "You know how this school system works; it's only the insiders who get to do things and who gets all the attention and the perks," she concluded. I told Guich the "insiders" haven't driven a beverage truck to every neighborhood in the City, delivered to more than 200 businesses in the printing truck, or worked in many of the City's "movers and shakers" businesses and homes. My work at the Circle Food Store's Pharmacy gave me an "insider's look at regular hard working people who made up a significant percentage of our citizen. These experiences enabled me to bring a unique experience to the planning process. It also enabled me to more effectively translate campaign promotional material into real people's lingo language. The School system insiders with only one occupational experience limited their ability to easily "adapt, interpret and transform their everyday language into the working class people's lingo."

After some three months of intensive planning and development of the "winning" tax proposal, along with the assistance of Marion Harris, the school's clerk, the proposal was ready. Marion typed the 72-page document in its entirety and without any errors. The next big step was to get an appointment with the new Superintendent of the School District. Marion also typed my letter for the Superintendent requesting an appointment to meet with him to discuss in detail my plan for winning the One Cent Sales Tax Election. To Gloria's surprise, the Superintendent agreed to an appointment and my fortunes were about to change. After reading the confirmed appointment letter from the Superintendent, Guich said, "Edgar, you are something else; that's why I love you so much."

During the entire time of the development of my proposal, I did not tell my principal what I was doing nor did I tell him about my appointment with the Superintendent. The only persons who knew about what I was doing other than Guich were Dr. Austin, Paul, and Marion, who typed the document. When I arrived for my appointment, I was greeted by Dr. Dolce, the Superintendent, and a Dr. Ed Stump, Associate Superintendent of Pupil Placement. As I presented my proposal, both men were extremely impressed especially with the comprehensive details of the plan. The Superintendent told me that he wanted to let the School District's legal advisor look at the possible legal ramifications of allowing a teacher to actively participate in a political process. He said, "Edgar, I will have the appropriate party get back with you after getting advice from the School District's legal folks."

Politics is Everywhere in Everything

Meanwhile, some two weeks passed, and the Superintendent appointed a political operative who worked for the mayor to head the One Cent Sales Tax Campaign. When I arrived at school one Wednesday morning, Marion, the secretary, told me that I had received some mail from campaign headquarters. The package was addressed to Edgar Poree, School Coordinator One Cent Sales Tax. Marion said, "Poree, this is the same material I typed for you." When I read the instructions in the package to my dismay it was my material with some slight changes in the terminology that I had given to the Superintendent. I was shocked, mad, and really upset because that document took three months of my life to develop, and I was not about to allow anyone else to take advantage of my plan.

I immediately went to the Western Union office to find out how could I send a telegram that only the person that I send it to could sign for it. The Western Union agent told me that I had to send the telegram certified. The reason that I was sending a certified telegram instead of calling the Superintendent's office for an appointment was the possibility of not getting through to the Superintendent himself to request another appointment. When the courier left to bring the Superintendent the certified telegram from me, I followed him. When Western Union arrived in the Superintendent's office, his Secretary attempted to sign the telegram, and the courier told her that only Dr. Dolce could sign it. When Dr. Dolce came out to sign for the telegram he saw me and said, "Mr. Poree, I didn't have an appointment with you today, did I?" I said, "No, but the telegram is from me because I've got to talk to you about my proposal that I left with you two week ago." The Superintendent said, "Mr. Wall, who I appointed to head the sales tax campaign, was supposed to contact you." I told the Superintendent that no one had contacted me and that I received a package from the campaign headquarters today, which just happened to be the same material that that I had developed in my proposal.

After waiting more than an hour, I met with the Superintendent Dolce and Dr. Stump and showed them how my "original" One Cent Sales Tax Proposal was one in the same as the package that came from campaign headquarters. When Dr. Stump saw the documents, he said, "Carl, I don't know what the political ramification fallout will be for allowing a teacher to actively participate in a political campaign' however, anyone who developed such a comprehensive plan as Edgar needs to be a part of the campaign's leadership." The Superintendent agreed with Dr., Stump, and he dictated a letter to my principal, authorizing my "leave of absence" effective the following Monday until the completion of the sales tax campaign. I was somewhat overwhelmed for a few moments; then, I realized that the real test had just begun for I had broken the insider's code of conduct, and I would have to prove my worthiness over and over every day. I called Guich, told her what happened, and she said, "Edgar Poree, you are really something, really special, congratulations."

When word got back to my school, and my coworkers found out that I would be working with the One Cent Sales Tax Campaign Headquarters staff, many of them were excited. They came over to my class to congratulate me and wished me well. I was excited about the opportunity, and I was looking forward to reporting downtown on Monday to be a part of the sales tax campaign.

Backlash from Old Guard

Over the weekend, word spread throughout the public school community about my being selected to work in the School District's campaign office. Little did I realize that my tenure downtown, although not started yet, created an orchestrated backlash from some very disgruntled principals. It was my understanding that a group of about twelve Black principals requested an emergency meeting with the Superintendent to inquire as to why they had not been consulted regarding the selection of a teacher to work in the School District campaign office. They indicated that experience and position in the leadership of the District should have warranted consideration for working in the campaign office.

According to one of the cafeteria managers who brought some refreshments to the Superintendent's meeting with this group of principals, one of the principals referred to me as an arrogant, bullish, egotistical, and somewhat rebellious individual, when it comes to complying with principal dictates and policies. That same principal asked the Superintendent, "How come he selected such a person to work in the campaign headquarters?" The Superintendent told the group that the young man that had been selected presented a very comprehensive plan that seemed to be in accord with a winning strategy. Apparently, the group of twelve left the meeting still not satisfied that they did not have an input in the selection process; therefore, they still appeared to be disgruntled when they left.

My task had just begun, well before I actually started to get orientated to my campaign assignment. It's ironic that my greatest challenge was not with the leadership in the School District's campaign headquarters, instead the obstacle and difficulties that I would encounter throughout the campaign would be with many of the Black principals who were upset about my appointment. In spite of the harsh and sometimes ugly treatment that I received at many of the District's Black schools, I remained focused on the mission of spreading the strategies for winning the election. In the meantime, we were getting close to the countdown period of the campaign and still there was much to be done.

Now, we had reached that part of the campaign where we were preparing for campaigning in the neighborhoods. This task was particularly sensitive because we were about to assign teams of volunteers to canvass neighborhoods throughout the City to help determine the level of support or lack of support for the sales tax hike. Recognizing that the City had become extremely polarized resulting from the imposed integration of the public schools in 1960, selection of volunteers was a critically sensitive undertaking.

I recommended that we assign Black volunteers to work in predominately Black neighborhoods and White volunteers to work in predominately white neighborhoods. A select group of Black and White volunteers will work in targeted neighborhoods near Tulane and Loyola universities and in several other non-blue collar neighborhoods where demographics still contain middle class Black and White residents. Well, this recommendation created such heated furor and outrage among the members of the disgruntled group of principals, who up until that point of the campaign confined their hostility and contempt directly to me during my strategy sessions at their schools. Now they had a cause and a crusade to against meet with the Superintendent to express their opposition to the planned neighborhood canvassing strategy.

Unlike the previously held meeting with the Superintendent, this time the Superintendent invited me to attend the meeting with the Black principals so that I could address their concerns and justify the proposed neighborhood canvassing plan. The unified objection of the Black principals for wanting not to participate in the planned canvassing strategy was because it was against their principles and ethics to take part in a segregated campaign. They felt volunteers should be sent in any neighborhood regardless of their color to encourage the citizens to vote for passage of the tax measure. They stated that sending Blacks only in Black neighborhoods and Whites only in White neighborhoods was sending the wrong message. The Superintendent said, "Mr. Poree, you have heard their objection; now how do you convince them otherwise that your plan is the one needed to win the election."

I told the group that the objective that we had before us was to win new revenues for the School District, and most importantly, the tens of thousands of students of the School District. I emphasized, "To Win!" That being the case, we must seek the most tactful approach in realizing that objective. I also told the group that it had only been a mere six years since the Federal Marshall escorted a few Black children in William Frantz School and McDonogh #19 School in the Lower Ninth Ward. I asked them if they remembered how those unruly Whites, who defied any Whites from allowing their children to enter those two schools and how many "White only" private schools sprang up because of the school integration. I suggested it would be counter-productive to send Black volunteers into those type neighborhoods where there were still very strong sentiments against mixing of the races; therefore, it was better to not awaken sleeping barracudas.

Because it is so critical to the successful passage of the sales tax initiative, it was essential that the selection of our volunteer canvassing teams be reflective of the demographics of the neighborhood that we canvass. The Superintendent asked the group, "Are we in one accord with this strategy and explanation or will it be a strategy of emotions or a strategy of the head?" The Black principals indicated although they did not totally agree with the explanation, in the spirit of cooperation, they would not openly express their dissatisfaction with their faculty and staff. They would comply with the canvassing staffing.

The day before the One-Cent Sales Tax Election, all of the Public Schools were closed and all principals, schools coordinators, and parent coordinators were attending a Sales-Tax Election Day Strategy Rally at McMain High School. At the Rally, Dr. Stump headed the strategy session with the parent coordinators, Bob Walters, Campaign Director, headed the strategy session with the school coordinators, and I served as the Superintendent's consultant with all of the School District's principals.

During the Superintendent's session, many questions were asked by the principals that Dr. Dolce couldn't answer. That's when the ball fell into my hands to respond. That was the moment of truth for me, a critical yet opportune time for me to step up to the challenge or miss a golden opportunity to distinguish myself from the pack. Not only was I able to answer all of the questions, I gave various scenarios and hypothetical situations with appropriate corrective measures and actions. The principals seemed genuinely impressed and satisfied with my presentation. I received a very enthusiastic round of applause. As the election-day strategy session concluded, many of the disgruntled principals who had vigorously opposed my involvement in the leadership team were highly complementary. They came over to me as I stood next to the Superintendent to say they were proud of my leadership and election-day strategies and glad to be a part of a winning team.

The Superintendent asked me, "What you think our winning percentage will be 51% or 52%?" I told the members of the campaign leadership team that I had done a poll of some 82 precincts and findings translated to "a winning margin of approximately 71 % for the One Cent Sales Tax." Many on the leadership team thought I crazy. In fact, one of the Superintendent's closest friends said, "Carl, you said that your sixth grade teacher/One Cent Sales Tax Advisor was extremely talented and smart; well predicting a 71 % yes vote isn't very smart or intelligent either!" At the end of Election Day, the total votes had been counted, and the percentage of "Yes" votes for the one penny tax was a whopping 71.37%. Incredible! Unbelievable! The relatively unknown sixth-grade teacher-Superintendent Sales Tax Advisor Campaign Strategist had predicted in his poll, prior to election day, that the School District was a winner, and the tens of thousands of students of the Public Schools would have a great opportunity for better school and a brighter future.

Well, there was great excitement in the School District, and many of my coworkers and friends anticipated big things for me as result of my involvement and leadership in the winning One-Cent Sales Tax Campaign. I received so many congratulations from so many coworkers, parents and even many of the principals who had opposed me throughout the campaign. There was a "Victory Celebration" banquet held for many of the campaign volunteers, School Board members, and the campaign leadership. The Superintendent acknowledged the campaign director, the public relations team, and several of the community leaders who had supported the sales tax election. Nowhere in the acknowledgement was the name of the Sixth Grade Teacher who had provided the winning strategic plan. My wife, Gloria had tears in her eyes at the affair.

After the election, the director of the One Cent Sales Tax Campaign was promoted and appointed Director of Federal Programs at a salary of $25,000. A Black principal who had just returned from getting an advanced degree from Harvard University was appointed the first Black Associate Superintendent of Special Programs at a salary of $20,000. Although he had an advanced degree from Harvard, his new "boss," the Director of Federal Programs had no college degree at all. He was simply a political crony operative who was a member of Mayor Morrison's PR team.

At the time of the Sales Tax Election, my eight-year teacher's salary was $4,400 and with the scheduled raise from the sales tax, my next-year salary would be $1,100 more or a total salary of $5,500. Although there had been no formal announcement of any promotion for me, as a result of the School District's using my Strategic Sales Tax Plan and my leadership in the One Cent Sales Tax Campaign, there was much anticipation and speculations as to what promotion or appointment I would receive from the School District's Superintendent. My coworkers could hardly wait for what they thought would be a great opportunity for me—a new position, a new job with more money and greater responsibility that was the talk at my school after the successful campaign.

Big Payday or Big Disappointment

Well, the much anticipated big day had arrived, and I had an appointment with the Superintendent. When I arrived, his secretary greeted me with a big hug and congratulations. I was feeling rather good about my prospects. When Dr. Dolce saw me he said, "Young man, the boys and girls of the School District and the citizens of the City have a great debt to you for the tremendous contributions that you made in helping to win the One Cent Sales Tax Election." "You have a great future in the School District, Edgar," concluded the Superintendent.

At that moment, I was extremely excited with anticipation of being advised of a golden new and exciting opportunity for the coming school year. Little did I realize that in an instant I would be brought back to the harsh reality that my contributions to the winning strategy would translate to a mere thank you without any consideration of compensation or elevation of position as a result of my campaign strategy which was the School District's adopted strategic plan. As Dr. Dolce held his hand on my shoulder, he continued saying, "Edgar, you have a bright future in the School District, I want you to get back in school, get your masters, then perhaps a principal-ship, and perhaps one day you'll even become an assistant Superintendent, of course on my leadership team."

I looked at the Superintendent, and I said, "Dr. Dolce, you have helped me make what would have been a very difficult decision for me to make, an easy one now." I told him that twelve weeks ago I walked into his office with a seventy-two page document that took me three months to develop, and I offered it to him as a possible vehicle for winning the One Cent Sales Tax Election. That document eventually became the School District's Blueprint Campaign Strategic Plan, and I was instrumental in providing the winning strategies and recommendations which helped our leadership in successfully directing and coordinating initiatives which resulted in winning the election.

The director of the campaign, who by the way plagiarized my original plan as if he developed it was now rewarded with a $25,000 position, yet I'm being told to get back in school and get a master's degree so that I might become a principal or even one day become an assistant Superintendent. "Thank you very much Dr. Dolce, I'm out of here!" "What do you mean Mr. Poree?" I'm resigning from my teaching career, and I will be devoting the next three summer months in developing a winning strategy for Edgar Poree. If I were good enough to develop a winning strategy to generate $6 to $7 million dollars annually for the School District, then I ought to be good enough to develop a strategy during the next three months that will enhance Gloria and Edgar Poree's future. Dr. Dolce told me to please reconsider my decision regarding resigning from the District.

CHAPTER VIII

NEW OPPORTUNITIES

When I got home, I told Gloria what I had done, and she asked me, "What are you going to do, Edgar?" I said, "Work on getting Edgar and Gloria a brighter future. Three days after my meeting with the school Superintendent, I got a call from Dr. Stump, the person most responsible for getting me out of the classroom and into the One Cent Sales Tax Leadership Team, and my future took a tremendous leap upward during that telephone call. Dr. Stump told me that he had recommended me to the Department of Labor as Director to head up a model ten week youth program that summer. As fate would have it, my weekly salary would be $210 per week for twelve weeks. I would make more than half of my entire new teacher's salary for that new school year in twelve weeks. During the fourth week of the summer model youth program, I developed a full-year-youth-in-school program proposal and submitted it to the U. S. Department of Labor for consideration for funding.

Three weeks after submitting proposal we received an approval by the U.S. Department of Labor and I was appointed Director of the Neighborhood Youth Corps at a Salary of $14,000 Dollars. Yes, Dr. Dolce, Edgar's future was indeed bright, some $10,000 brighter with a much brighter future than the one that he proposed in his office only a few months ago. When I received the letter of approval from the Department of Labor, I immediately left the office and drove home because I wanted to tell Guich about our exciting new future.

When I arrived at home, instead of opening my front door, I rang the doorbell. When Guich opened the door and saw me standing there with the biggest smile on my face, she asked, "Edgar Poree, what have you done now?" I said, "Mrs. Poree, you are looking at the newly appointed Director of the Neighborhood Youth Corps in the City!" For an instant, we both just stood there, wide-eyed and motionless; then all of a sudden, we both screamed jubilantly embracing each other with shouts of joy. After this emotional spectacle in the doorway of our home, I told Guich to get dressed for we were going out to dinner and it wouldn't be a half-chicken with two plates this evening.

Guich smiled, we got dressed, and went to dinner at Dooky's. This time we had a full course meal with all the trimmings. Chef Leah Chase brought two heaping servings of her famous bread pudding she prepared for Gloria and me. Then she and Dooky Chase asked all of the customers present to join them in a special congratulatory toast to Mr. and Mrs. Poree on Edgar Poree's appointment as Director of the Neighborhood Youth Corps. Guich and I were overwhelmed by that very thoughtful gesture of the Chase family and all the customers who individually came over to our table to congratulate us. That was indeed a wonderful evening at our favorite eating place.

A Special Gift

With a brand new career and seemingly a much brighter financial future, I decided to surprise Gloria with a very special gift. The Ford Mustang was the hottest new car on the market. I walked in the Bolton Ford Showroom on Canal Street and purchased a 1966 Ford Mustang Coupe, loaded with power steering, air conditioning, and the very latest radio. It was the most talked-about car of the time. I didn't tell Guich that I was getting her a new car because I wanted to surprise her. I got the dealership to get the Mustang ready for delivery before 2:30 p.m. so I could get the car home before Guich arrived from school that evening.

I parked that beautiful Mustang in our driveway, placed a big red bow on the top, and wrapped the red ribbon around the car. When Guich arrived home, you should have seen her face when she saw that red ribbon wrapped 1966 Mustang. I said, "That's for you for tolerating me and my dreams all these years." Guich, in her ever-present reserved personality, said, "Edgar Poree, you are something else; it's beautiful." Deidra, our five year old didn't waste any time getting in the car with her Mother, and the three of them took a stroll around the park in her brand new toy.

The summer of 1966 was the beginning of many blessings and opportunities that afforded me untold experiences. My job as Director of an in-school youth program made it possible for me to meet and interact with members of the business, political, educational, and religious leadership of the community. I met individually as well as in groups many of the community's movers and shakers during our job development initiative for our program participants. Additionally, my position enabled me to travel to many regional locations of the Federal Government throughout the country while developing programs for youth growth and development. These diverse experiences afforded me numerous opportunities to speak to large audiences across the country, enhancing my public speaking skills as well as affording me greater access to meet with members of the majority community to negotiate and create opportunities for minorities to fill jobs traditionally limited to the majority community.

While sitting in my office gazing out of the window, I couldn't help but think about the message the school Superintendent gave me after the successful One Cent Sales Tax Election. "I want you to go back to school, get your masters, become a principal, and maybe one day, you just might become my assistant." After all that I had contributed to the success of the Sales Tax Campaign, it still wasn't good enough to warrant consideration for a promotion or an appointment in the School District. Well, that experience and those suggestions of the Superintendent at the post-election appointment, though painful and hurtful at the time, made me more committed, courageous, and determined to be more decisive about my future.

Instead of getting angry with the school Superintendent, I felt I owed him a debt of thanks for igniting the fire of self-determination and motivation in fulfilling my dreams and aspirations. With that thought, I decided to treat myself to a new toy. That new toy turned out to be a 1966 white Pontiac Bonneville Coupe with gold interior, loaded with special feature accessories. When I drove the new Bonneville home, my daughter, wife, and next-door neighbor decided to get in the car, and they directed me to drive them around the park and on the Lakefront for a family stroll. I accommodated them, and we enjoyed my new toy.

Youth Development Opportunity

The initial Summer Neighborhood Youth Corp Program was a great success, and we began to plan the newly funded Year-Round In-School Program for the 1966-67 School Year with my staff. I was extremely fortunate to have a tremendously talented and qualified group of individuals who assisted me in the development of the In-School Program. Pete Saunders, Joe Peccarre, and Terrance Duverney were sparkling diamonds, and they all had very special skill-sets and a great ability to communicate and connect with young people. Pete, the elder statesman of the group, was a physical education teacher and coach at a middle school, Terrance was a Ph.D. candidate at Tulane University, and Joe was an elementary teacher.

After the initial summer program was over, Pete and Joe returned to their teaching and coaching jobs in the public schools. Terrance advised me that he was going to defer his doctoral requirements for a semester in order to assist me in launching the full-time NYC In-School Development Program, scheduled for the fall of 1966 School opening. I attempted on numerous occasions to encourage Terrance not to defer completing his doctoral program requirements without any success. He insisted that his participation in the youth development program would be a great asset in completing his doctoral candidacy. He was committed to helping jump start the 1966 NYC In-School Program. With his assistance, we developed a strategic plan that eventually became the prototype "model" for other in-school programs in the region to emulate.

A Breach of Trust

After several months on my new job, Roy, the supply supervisor, extended an invitation to my wife and me to attend his birthday party. I told him that I would check with Gloria and get back with him. Gloria agreed to accept the invitation, and I called Roy to indicate we would attend. The night of the party, Gloria had a terrible sinus headache, and she told me that she did not feel well enough to go to the party. I told her that I would call Roy and tell him that we wouldn't be able to attend because of the circumstances. Gloria said, "Edgar, go to the party; your coworkers are expecting to see you there, and it will be nice to meet, greet, and socialize with them other than the in the daily work routine." I told her that I was going to stay and take care of her and she said, "Edgar, go to the party; I'm going to lie on the sofa and rest, and I'll be fine, now get out here and go enjoy you."

After being admonished and directed by Gloria to go to the party, I reluctantly left home for the party. When I arrived at Roy's house and parked my car across the street from the party, another car pulled next to my car, and a lady got out of the car and began walking toward Roy's house. I arrived at the front door of Roy's house at the same time that the lady who had been dropped off did. I introduced myself to the young lady, and she told me she was the secretary of the Executive Director. I rang the doorbell, and when Roy opened the door, he said mischievously, "Edgar, you have only been working here a few months; buddy what's going on?" I told Roy that my wife Gloria had a terrible headache, and she sent her regrets for not coming." I also told Roy that I was going to stay home, and Gloria insisted that I come. Gloria told me that she would be OK after lying on the sofa, and she said, "Get out of here and go enjoy you."

I must say that I did enjoy myself and the laughter that occurred at the party of Roy's accusations of my being escorted by another woman. When I arrived home from the party, Gloria was still up, and she had apparently gotten over the sinus headache. She asked me how the party was, and I told her I really enjoyed myself. I met some new coworkers and their mates, and Roy was a very gracious and entertaining host. I also told Gloria that when I parked my car across the street from Roy's house, a car stopped next to mine and a lady got out the car and began walking toward Roy's house. We reached the front door of Roy's house at the same time and when Roy opened the door he mischievously inferred that something funny was going on. Roy said, "Excuse me, Mr. Poree; this isn't Mrs. Poree, what's up buddy!" I told Roy you sent your regrets, and I left you lying on the soda with a terrible sinus headache. Roy laughed and that was the joke of the party. Gloria laughed and told me she was glad I had a good time.

Three days later when I got home from work, I said, "How was your day Darling?" Gloria said, "Don't call me Darling; you are just like all those other men, just can't be trusted!" I said, "What are you talking about!" "You know what I'm talking about," she said with tears in her eyes. You come home from the party and tell me this ridiculous story about how you arrived at the same time that this so-called strange woman arrived and coincidentally reached Roy's front door at the same time. I said, "Darling, that's exactly what happened!" Gloria said, "Don't you call me Darling; you're just like those other good men!" I walked toward Gloria in an attempt to console and reassure her that what I told her was the truth, and she said, "Don't touch me. I can't trust you. I can't trust you!"

At that point I got on the telephone and called Roy. I said Roy, "I want you to invite everyone that came to your party for another Roy's birthday II at the same place next weekend, and I'm going to pay for the entire second birthday party. I told Roy that I wanted him to invite one additional person to the second party, the person who dropped off the Executive Director's secretary. Roy asked me whether it was a joke, and I said, "Roy, I'm dead serious because your playful remarks when you opened the door for me and the Executive Director's secretary have gotten me in big, big trouble with my wife." Roy laughed and told me he would call Gloria and tell her that it was just a joke and a way to loosen the party up. Roy told me the fellow who dropped off the secretary was her fiancé, and the reason he did not come to the party was because he had to work the night shift at the post office. I told Roy all that's fine, but someone must have conveyed something other than what really happened at the party to my wife or with one of her coworkers.

After several days of getting the cold shoulder treatment from Gloria, I got a phone call from her one afternoon. She told me not to stay late in the office and come home early she wanted to talk to me. I was not going to be late at all that evening, and when I arrived Gloria was waiting on the porch and as I approached her she embraced me tightly saying, "I'm so sorry, so sorry for doubting you. I love you!" I was relieved and thrilled to hear those words. When I opened the door, the aroma from the kitchen smelled like a steak dinner with all of the delicacies and desserts. Gloria kissed me and again said how sorry she was for doubting me. I told her that I would never disrespect her, and I would always honor that commitment.

She told me that she had received nine telephone calls telling me, "While you were lying on the sofa Mrs. Goodie Two-Shoes with that sinus headache, your husband was out with his woman at the party." Gloria said, "At first, I ignored the calls but after the ninth telephone call, I just could not take it anymore, and I reacted the way that I did, and I am truly sorry, truly sorry. You know I love you so much. These few days have been very difficult for me not talking to you and treating you so badly," she told me. Then, she told me after reacting foolishly and emotionally, these few days allowed her to reflect upon what I had told her was the truth and how we had trusted and treated each other with uncompromising unlimited love. Her trust was restored, and her tears changed to laughter. She told me that never again would she doubt my love, my commitment, and my loyalty. We hugged, kissed, and that was the very best steak dinner that I had ever eaten

Disgruntled Old Guard

With the assistance of a great team of talented individuals, we successfully completed our initial summer program and we now were about to launch the first Full-time NYC In-School Program in the City in September, 1966. One of my former high school teachers became the principal of the school where I began my teaching career upon graduating from college. I thought that it would be an appropriate gesture in expressing my gratitude and appreciation for the nurturing and guidance that he afforded me during my years of development.

Since we were scheduled to have more than 500 part-time jobs for students during the 1966-67 school years, I decided that the first school where I would recruit students for jobs would be at Mr. Walter's brand new Carver Junior High School in the Desire area. I told my staff I wanted to personally go out and recruit our first student employees for the 1966-67 school years. So with a brief case full of applications, a big smile on my face, and a great deal of pride at being able to give back something of value to someone who had contributed to my growth and development, I was off to get my first student employees.

When I arrived at the junior high school where my former principal presided, little did I realize that my welcome would be anything other than pleasant. When I walked into the school's office, the first thing I heard was, "Don't you get sick and tired of seeing these people walking around with a brief case looking important. Yes Prof.," responded one of persons in the office. To my surprise and disappointment, the person making the remarks was my former high school teacher, former principal, and a former coworker at Johnson Lockett Elementary School where I had my first teaching assignment. My former principal and teacher rudely asked, "What do you want?" I told him "I would like to talk to you about some opportunities for student employment during the school year." He told me "You have to wait your turn to see me when I get through with more important things I have on my agenda."

After waiting for more than an hour, the secretary told me I could go in and see the principal. When I entered his office, he told me he did not have much time for any long discussions for he had to get his schedule ready for the opening of school. I told him "Since you have been instrumental in my growth and development, I thought it would be appropriate to show my appreciation by giving the students of your school the first opportunities to be hired."

I opened my brief case and took out several hundred applications for his school's student body. When I gave them to him, he said, "I hope this program won't take up a lot of time because we have enough to do already with the daily routine." I told the principal "I would provide a staff person to come to the school to assist the students with processing their applications, certify the eligible students, and complete orientations for those students were hired for the program." Additionally, I told him "I would personally see to it that all the necessary reporting requirements of the program would be explained in detail to the school coordinator who will be responsible for the documentation of the students' work hours."

The principal advised me under no circumstances would he be available to provide any oversight of the student-work program without being compensated monetarily. Since the work program did not provide any compensation for school personnel supervising student activities, I assured my former principal that I would personally assume the full responsibility for the "oversight" of the student work program during the initial year of operation at his school. With that assurance, Mr. Walter seemingly somewhat reluctant agreed to allow the student work program at his school. In spite of the initial resistance and lack of cooperation by my former principal, the student work program proved to be a great success for the school and the participating students. As a result of those successes, the principal requested an expansion of the program at his school the next school year.

During the preparation for the 1967 Neighborhood Youth Corp. Summer Program, we were extremely fortunate to assemble one of the most talented groups of mentors for our leadership staffing teams. The vitae of the mentors reflected the who's who in youth motivational professionals. Many of the individuals played a significant role in a voluntary capacity in helping coordinated student work activities at schools during the 1966-1967 School year. We hosted an appreciation gathering for several volunteers that played a major role in helping the initial model program meet target performance objectives. Because of the success of the program, funding for the 1967 Summer Program was granted for 1,500 students. The core group of our 1967 Summer Program Leadership Team included, Arthur Age, Principal, Guste Elementary School; Dolores Thompson Aaron, Assistant Superintendent; Walter Mitchell, Elementary Teacher, Richard School; Clifton Davis, Principal, Palmer Elementary School; Milton Coulon, Elementary Teacher; Bertha Aubrey Lee, Counselor; Alfred Collins, Counselor, Clark High School; Turner Thomas, Landry High School Football Coach; Alphonse Pierre, Art Instructor, Green Junior High School; Edgar Blanchard, former Leader of Gondoliers Band; Pete Saunders, Principal Derham Middle School; Joe Peccarea, Teacher Abraham High School; Alfred Liggins, Accountant; and, Terrance Duverney, Assistant Program Director.

Titles and Positions Create Dictators

In the local Anti-Poverty Agency, the bulk of the Agency's program funding was provided by Office of Economic Opportunity (O.E.O.) and the Department of Labor. Salaries, wages, expenses for facilities, supplies, and stipends for program participants as well as support services were all designated "line items" of these two major sources of funding. As Director of the NYC, Neighborhood Youth Corps, my Salary was paid from the Department of Labor. The Deputy Director of the Agency was charged to the O.E.O. funding. Personnel salary standards were established independently by both funding sources since Federal grants were based upon the extent of the prevailing number of family meeting the Poverty Level Eligibility. Although the Deputy Director reported to the Executive Director of the Agency, his primary area of responsibility was in supervising and managing the OEO mandate.

Unfortunately, in a staff meeting where salaries were being prepared for next year's proposed budgets for the Agency, the Deputy Director saw my proposed salary scale under the Department of Labor contract; he decided my salary was too close to what he was making under the O.E.O. Contract. He decided to do something about that situation. Although the

O.E.O. and the Department of Labor had two distinct salary scales, the Deputy Director wrote a letter to the Regional Director, recommending that my proposed salary be decreased by $1,500 so that it would not be comparable to what he was making as the number two executive of the Agency. His reasoning was that he was senior to my position within the Agency; therefore, he should be making much more than I.

What was ironic about this demand was that he did not request an increase of $1,500 in his salary from his funding source, OEO, to make the difference; he also did not provide supporting documentation of his annual performance. Instead, he thought his title and position justified decreasing my compensation. Fortunately, the Department of Labor felt that my job performance warranted the salary treatment that the budget recommended. Titles somehow give some individuals a thirst for power.

Political Influence and the War on Poverty

Politics has a way of life in all phases of life. Its influence is incredible and far reaching, especially in the appointments of leadership positions and awarding of lucrative contracts. That was especially true in the establishment of the local Anti-Poverty Agency in the City. The agency's Executive Director, a former public-relations person and his Deputy Director, a former professor at Tulane, were both well connected with the political powers of the area. The Director of the Head Start Program was a young rising star reporter with the powerful daily newspaper. She had a degree in journalism and no experience whatsoever in child development. She was appointed by the politically connected. My boss, who was the Director of the Department of Labor student training programs at the agency was a seventh grade dropout, who just happens to be the president of one of the area's powerful trade unions, another one of the politically connected appointees to leadership positions.

Politicians weren't the only well connected beneficiaries of government programs during the initial phases of the war on poverty. Owners of large and outdated buildings, especially those located in the downtown areas of the City were prime beneficiaries of lucrative contracts. A prominent large business former headquarters and operations building, located in downtown, would become one of the great cash cows for its owner, as a result of a very lucrative lease that it got from the local Anti-Poverty Agency.

The business was moving its operation to new facilities in mid-city, so this contract was not only a great deal for its owners it was also a very timely one.

According to most of the news stories, this appeared to portray the agreement, between the local Anti-Poverty Agency and the owners of the large business as a model "Community Betterment Partnership?" The downtown building was not a "Class A" building, and the rate the Anti-Poverty Agency received was portrayed as a very generous deal. The going lease rate for the building was estimated at $5 per square-foot, and the owners of the building were also granted a $2.50 per-square-foot tax credit rate for the building. The building had approximately 250,000 square feet, so the war on poverty's agency lease would be $625,000 per year. The owners of the old downtown facility would receive substantial additional monetary benefits from the lease in the form of a $2.50 tax credits for the 250,000 square foot building. It sounded like a great deal for the local Anti-Poverty Agency's War on Poverty.

There was, however, something that unfortunately was missing from most media reports, praising this great commitment of support by the business community for the local Anti-Poverty Agency's efforts in waging war on poverty. The missing information significantly altered who got the best of the "Community Betterment Partnership"—the local Anti-Poverty Agency or the large business owners? Although the building contained 250,000 square feet of space, less than 100,000 square feet could be converted for actual operational usage. Unfortunately, the Anti-Poverty Agency paid substantially more than the $2.50 per square foot rate if you factor in the useable square-footage. It appears that the owners of the old building were the real beneficiary of the "Community Betterment Partnership," so widely praised and portrayed by the political and business leadership of the community.

If you considered the actual useable 100,000 square feet rather than the 250,000 square feet, the owners supposedly and generously discounted the going rate for a less then "Class A" building, the so-called $2.50 per square foot rate, increased tremendously to a whopping $6.25 per square Foot. Adding further insults to this Voodoo economics good-ole-boys patronage and cronyism, the owners also got an additional $2.50 tax credit. That's right, in addition to getting $2.50 for the building's total "250,000 square feet," of which only 40% could be utilized by occupants, the large business owners received a $2.50 tax credit.

That's not philanthropic nor was it a generous deal for the Anti-Poverty Agency, as the business community and the media would have you believe. Imagine getting $625,000 annually for 100,000 square feet of usable space and when it's time to pay the corporate income tax, the prominent large business owners received a$2.50 tax credit. What a taxpayer rip-off.

That's like renting a four bedroom house with two baths for $400 a month. When you move in, you discovered only one and a half bedrooms were available for occupancy; that's less than 40 % of what you paid for. I'm sure the renter would be extremely upset and demand reimbursement of his security deposit as well as the two months advance payments for the deceptive advertisement. Perhaps, the local Anti-Poverty Agency should have consulted a third party to assist in negotiating a more equitable Lease. Unfortunately, the business community had far more influence and connections with the good-ole-boys network. This would be a perfect case study for good-government watch groups to investigate. Corporate corruption in Louisiana from a media perspective was limited to politicians, not prominent business owners.

Major banks were also the beneficiary of sweet-heart deals. The legislation of the War on Poverty mandated that the funds appropriated and granted to the Anti-Poverty Agency could only deposit Federal funds in checking accounts. Those were guaranteed win-fall-profits for the major banks. If the Anti-Poverty Agency would had been allowed to invest large portions of the Federal funds granted in interest bearing accounts, and greater enhanced services would have been available for its clientele. Local major banks made millions of dollars from Federal funds granted for fighting the War on Poverty. Do the math! Let's say the agency received twenty-four million dollars for its summer program. The summer program was funded for three months; that's approximately eight million dollars per month. Since the agency used only a third of the money each month, when they deposited the $24 million in their checking account that meant the banks had to retain only 6%, approximately $1.5 million, for the Federal Reserve. This allowed the banks to invest the remaining $22.5 million in loans, substantially increasing the banks' excessive profits and not expanding or improving the amount of economic and social services for the thousands of individual served by the Anti-Poverty Agency. What a travesty and an extension of the exploitation of the good-ole-boy network.

Insurance brokers were also a beneficiary of the War on Poverty. The anti-poverty agencies had to have workman's compensation coverage, no exceptions. Who were the only sources providing workman's compensation insurance? The insurance brokers! You need not ask the question, "Did they too belong to the good-ole-boys network?" If you compare the dollars that actually flowed directly in servicing the poor constituents of the Anti-Poverty Agency compared with the excessive profits made by the banks, the insurance brokers, and the real estate owners, you must ask this question, "Who did the War on Poverty help?" It certainly wasn't the poor.

Love Affair with '67 Olds

I was an avid admirer of cars from a very early age. From a child I always use to cut out pictures of new model cars, each year when they first came out and pasted them in my Dream Car Tablet. This tradition continued until young adulthood. Unfortunately, when I returned home from my tour of duty in the Army Reserve, I lost my lifelong Dream Car Tablet. When the new model cars became available, I bought a 1967 Oldsmobile Four Door Luxury Sedan for $4,625, including tax, license, and title. I sold my 1966 Bonneville Coupe for $1,800 to one of the finest gentlemen in my old neighborhood. He kept that car for over twenty years, and it still looked like the day I sold it to him. After getting my new Olds on Saturday, Gloria and I with our daughter took a short drive along the Lakefront and returned home shortly thereafter. On Sunday, I received a call from one of my neighbors, requesting the use of our vacuum cleaner. I agreed to drop the vacuum to them during halftime of the NFL football game I was watching.

I drove to my neighbor's house and when I got to the front door to ring the doorbell, all of a sudden I heard a tremendous "collision noise." Then I heard the children shouting, "Oh! They just wrecked that brand new car." I was hesitantly too turned around; however, when I turned to see what had caused that tremendous noise, I saw my brand new car wrecked. My car had only twenty-eight miles on it. A university professor was teaching his teenage daughter how to drive when she plowed into my new two-day old 1967 Oldsmobile Luxury Sedan.

I angrily told the professor that I wanted a new car replacement for my two-day old car. His insurance, however, only agreed to pay for repair of the damage. This was approximately twelve hundred dollars. I tried unsuccessfully to get the dealership to provide me with a new replacement sedan for I was a very frustrated and angry individual. I was so outraged that I parked the car in the garage for over a month, attempting to negotiate a settlement with the professor and his insurance to replace my car. After a month of frustrations and anger, I finally got the car repaired and looking forward to working toward enhancing our dreams.

Birth of Second Daughter, Dana Ann

During my wife's pregnancy I was hoping and praying for a boy to keep the Poree family's name alive. On October 12, 1967, our second daughter was born. Dana Ann was a very beautiful baby, and we were very happy about the new arrival, in spite of the very unpleasant and seemingly discriminatory treatment that we received at this Uptown hospital. My wife's obstetrician was White and did all of his deliveries at this hospital. Elvira and several of Gloria's girl friends had the same obstetrician that she had and had their babies delivered at this Uptown hospital near the river. They warned her that she would probably have to stay in the old section of the hospital during her delivery stay. As a matter of fact, three friends who had their babies delivered within the same year that Dana was born told Gloria that when they asked for semi-private rooms during the admittance processing, they were told all of the rooms reserved for obstetrics patients had been filled, and the only rooms available were private rooms in the old section of the hospital.

Since we were aware of this situation, when we checked in the hospital at the admittance desk, I asked the receptionist for a semi-private room in the new section of the hospital. Her response, "I'm terribly sorry we only have available a private room in the old section of the hospital. I then asked, "Can we get transferred to a semi-private room when one becomes available?" The receptionist indicated that there were limited rooms reserved for the obstetrics ward and that they were filled on a first come-first served basis. With that in mind, I decided to make sure that I would talk to the expectant Fathers, who checked in with their wives at the admittance desk after Gloria had completed our registration.

While we were seated in the waiting-room eagerly awaiting the delivery of our new baby, I introduced myself to all five of the expectant Fathers, who had arrived and registered at the admittance desk after Gloria and I had completed our admittance registration. I asked each of them if this was their "first" child, then I asked each of them what time they checked in. After getting their names and the time they checked in, I asked each of them if they were able to get a semi-private room in the new section of the hospital, and each of them said, "Yes!" As a matter of fact, two of the expectant Fathers were good friends, and their wives were going to share one of the semi-private rooms in the new section of the hospital. Can you imagine how angry I was at that moment; however, I maintained my composure, and I wished each of the Fathers good luck.

Hospital Discrimination

I went straight to the admittance desk and requested a semi-private room, and the receptionist told me I already had a room and that they could not change the accommodations because the room had already been prepared and documented. I asked the receptionist to call her supervisor because I had a serious complaint about my wife's accommodation. When I explained to the supervisor how my wife was denied a semi-private room when we checked-in at the admittance desk, she indicated the rooms for obstetrics were on a first come-first served basis and more than likely at the time that we checked-in the only room that was available was the private room in the older section of the hospital.

I told the supervisor that it appears most unlikely that nine minutes after I had completed our registration at the admittance desk, a White couple was able to get a semi-private room in the new wing of the hospital. The supervisor told me that was possible because perhaps the paper work for the semi-private room probably had not yet been completed at the time of our check-in. I countered her explanation by saying, "Within thirty minutes of our completing our registration four additional semi-private rooms became available for four White couples who checked in within thirty-minutes of our registration."

Furthermore, I told the supervisor I believed that we have been denied access to semi-private accommodations because of our race; that's discrimination. The supervisor vigorously denied that the hospital practiced any bias in its operations. I then told the supervisor I had information that would support my allegations. I had the names and times of the five White couples who arrived shortly after my wife and I checked-in and completed registration. All five of the couples received semi-private rooms shortly after I had been denied semi-private accommodation. Just at that moment, my wife's doctor came out and told me I had a beautiful little girl. My anger turned to excitement and joy, and when two of the expectant Fathers came over and congratulated me, my frustrations and confrontation with the hospital administrator ended. My attention shifted to my new baby girl.

I filed a complaint with the Community Chest regarding the hospital's denial of providing semi-private room accommodation for my wife during her delivery stay for the birth of our daughter, Dana Ann. The Community Chest provided resources and funding for non-profit organizations which included hospital recipients. I met with the Executive Director of the Community Chest and a member of the governing board to discuss the incidents that prevented my wife from getting the same semi-private room accommodations White expectant Mothers received at this hospital. After advising the two individuals, several of my wife's friends who had their babies delivered at the hospital prior to her delivery told her they were unable to get any semi-private room accommodations in the new wing of the hospital, while White expectant Mothers had immediate access to semi-private room accommodations. The Executive Director said that they would investigate my complaint and get back with me. Of course, when they talked to me about a month later, they advised me that they could find no conclusive evidence of the hospital denying anyone admission to semi-private rooms in the obstetrics ward.

Several days after my wife was discharged from the hospital, and we were enjoying the newest member of our family, Dana Ann, Gloria noticed that Dana appeared to have an unusual amount of twitching-like movements in her upper body, especially near the neck and head. At first we thought it was just our imagination, so we attributed it to once again becoming parents of a baby after six years. Our imagination was short-lived because the twitching-like movement continued to occur increasingly. We notified the doctor, and he told us to bring Dana to the hospital the next day. When the doctor completed his examination of Dana, he advised us the twitching-like movement was actual seizers.

We were stunned and rather speechless. Our next question, "What is the cause of this?" The doctor indicated that there were several possible factors that might contribute to the seizers; however, he wanted to try giving her Phenobarbital medication initially to see if would help alleviate the seizers. The doctor said, "Gloria and Edgar, let's see how the medication works before we consider any additional tests at this time. I looked at Gloria, and her eyes were slightly glassy not yet teary. I told her everything would be alright.

Once we began giving Dana the Phenobarbital medication, it appeared to be working and each day Gloria and I observed fewer and fewer twitching seizers. After several weeks, we took Dana for her follow-up appointment with the doctor. We were rather optimistic since it appeared that Dana's seizers were diminishing day by day. When the doctor examined Dana; however, he told us the seizers had not diminished at all; instead the twitching (seizers) had internalized, transformed from being external to internal. He told us he wanted to schedule our baby for a brain scan. Gloria sat motionless with tears flowing down her cheeks, and then she asked the doctor with a trembling voice, "What's wrong with my baby?" The doctor indicated that the seizers could be neurology related and that's why he recommended that we get a brain scan for further diagnosis.

Needless to say, when we left the doctor's office both of us were deeply concerned about the welfare of our Dana Ann. Gloria cried all evening, while holding and rocking Dana until I took Dana and placed her in her crib. I embraced Gloria and reassured her that God would take care of Dana Ann, and she then fell asleep. Two days after visiting the doctor, we went to get the brain scan at the hospital. During the test, I kept my eyes focused on the technician administering the brain scan reading.

Initially during the brain scan, when the right side of Dana's brain was being recorded, the technician's facial expressions remained constant with the same pleasant expressions when she greeted us prior to the administration of the brain scan. However, shortly after the technician began scanning the left side of Dana's brain, her facial expressions changed abruptly and dramatically as if something radically and disturbing was occurring. That's the impression I got from observing an entirely different expression than my initial one. When the technician completed the test, I asked, "Is everything alright?" The technician told us the doctor would consult with us regarding the test.

When we met with the doctor the diagnosis was not very good. The brain scan test revealed that there were some evidence of neurological disorder on the left side of the brain that could adversely impact our little baby girl's ability to function without degrees of impairment. Impairments can include both mental and physical disabilities depending upon the extent of damage attributed to the lack of oxygen in that part of the brain. Both of us sat there with tears running down our cheeks squeezing hands and comforting and re-assuring each other that we were going to make it with the Creator's blessings.

Tragic Day in Our Lives

On November 13, 1967, ten days after Dana had the brain scan, while I was holding and rocking her to sleep, all of a sudden there was a sudden twitch like no other that I had seen, and then Dana's head dropped forward, and I no longer felt a pulse or heartbeat. I placed my hand upon her breast and didn't feel any heartbeat, no breathing, and no sign of life. I woke up Gloria and said, "Dana's not breathing! Dana's not breathing!" Gloria began screaming, and she said, "Give me my baby! Give me my baby!" I placed Dana in her arms and ran across the street to get my neighbor, Dr. Joe Braud, to come to our house to see about our Dana. When he picked Dana up, he said, "I'm so sorry, Dana's gone!" Gloria began screaming incessantly, and I called Lydia LeBlanc, another neighbor who was a registered nurse, to come to the house and help charm Gloria while I notified the coroner's office. When the coroner came to get Dana, Dr. Braud gave Gloria a sedative to help her sleep. That night was the one of the longest and most trying in our lives.

The day before Dana Ann's burial, Gloria placed a beautiful white dress, a tiny white slip, a pair of fancy white socks, and a pair of white footsies, white ribbon, and a gold necklace in a box for me to take to the funeral home. Instead of placing a diaper in the box, Gloria told me to stop at a store on my way to the funeral home and buy the smallest white panties and place them in the box with the other clothing items. I bought the smallest panties I could find, placed it in the box, and then brought the clothing items to the funeral home.

On the day of Dana's burial when we arrived at the funeral home to view our daughter's little body for the final time, Bill and Jane Buchsbaum, our great friends, were there. Gloria initially appeared somewhat hesitant taking steps toward the tiny little casket. With each step she appeared to gain a little more compose as we neared Dana's casket. Holding one of her hands while embracing her with the other, we stood looking down on the remains of our daughter. With tears trickling down her beautiful cheeks, Gloria appeared to be at peace as she placed her hand on Dana's head, slightly adjusting the bow ribbon forward. She then adjusted slightly the tiny gold cross on the gold necklace, and then she adjusted the little ruffles on the bottom of the beautiful white dress. Gloria's facial expression for a moment appeared to be satisfied with the way the funeral home had dressed Dana Ann.

Just before Gloria leaned forward to kiss Dana, she paused and raised the dress of Dana to see the panties that I bought. When Gloria saw those plain cotton panties, she turned around, looked at me, and said, "Edgar, those panties are big enough for a two-year old; you could get Dana's whole body through one of the legs." I told her that was the smallest size that the store had. Gloria shook her head and said, "Edgar, Edgar, two-year old cotton panties for our one-month old baby daughter."

We then leaned over to kiss our Dana for the last time, and when I closed the tiny casket for the last time, it felt like a part of both of us had been taken away. As we rode to the cemetery with the tiny little casket containing the remains of our little Dana Ann resting on my lap, Gloria looked at me saying again, "Edgar, Edgar, two-year old cotton panties for a baby one-month old; you are something else!" As they lowered the tiny casket in the ground at Resthaven Memorial Cemetery on Ole Gentilly Highway, Gloria and I along with Bill and Jane slowly walked back to the limousine for the ride back home. That ride was the loneliest journeys that we had taken during our lives.

Wife's Years of Grief

After the burial of our daughter, Jane and Bill Buchsbaum spent a great deal of time with Gloria and me in an effort to help us cope with the devastating loss of Dana. Jane for weeks devoted much time with Gloria accompanying her at numerous events and outings in an attempt to help Gloria get out of the house and spend time in some of Jane's favorite organizational programs and charities of the National Council of Jewish

Women in which Jane held a leadership position. Jane even convinced Gloria to spend some time at the Buchsbaum's home on Audubon Street for a while immediately after the burial of Dana. Bill and Jane were really incredible pillars of strength, support, and comfort to lean on during those very difficult weeks following Dana's death.

In spite of their noble efforts, for almost two and a half years, Gloria experienced a very difficult time coping with the loss of Dana. Many nights, during that period of time, Gloria woke up during saying, "Edgar, Dana's crying!" That sent chills through me, and I would embrace her saying, "Baby, Dana's gone; she's looking down over us every day from Heaven." We took several trips to Houston and Dallas during that time to help heal the deep sorrow and grief of having lost our daughter. Our daughter, Deidra, played a major role during that healing process. When Gloria appeared down and not having a very good day, Deidra would always say, "Mama, Dana is watching us from Heaven, and she wants you to take me out and enjoy the sunshine today." That would perk Gloria up, and they would go somewhere and enjoy themselves.

California Trip

During the summer of 1968, we decided to take a trip to California so that Deidra could see Disneyland and visit some relatives who had moved there to live. It allowed Gloria and me to spend some healing time with each other after Dana's death. She moved to California when I was twelve, twenty year ago. I told Mother that I would take her to Pasadena; however, when we got there I was going to give her $10 to give to the first young Black man that we saw with a thin mustache dressed with a suit, dress shirt, and necktie who would agree to go with her to Miss Tooseen's house for a visit. I said, "Mother, Miss Tooseen hasn't seen me for twenty years; she wouldn't know the difference between me and any other Black man with a slight mustache dressed up with a suit and necktie." When Miss Tooseen sees that young man, I bet the first thing she'll say is, "Junior, you look just like your Father." Gloria said, "Edgar, you're crazy!" Mother just looked at me, smiled, and said, "That boy is something else." We had a good vacation, and I did take Mother to visit Miss Tooseen. Just like I predicted, when we arrived at her home, and she saw me, she said, "Junior, come over here and give me a big hug; Gertrude, that boy looks just like his daddy!" I should have followed my mind, paid a junior look-a-like impersonator, and let him go with Mother to visit Miss Tooseen and spend those three hours of conversation.

Mother's Nationwide Vacation Tour

Years after our California trip in 1968, Mother traveled across the country extensively. When she traveled to the West Coast, supposedly for a few weeks, she would not return home for several months. Her vacations were extended for a very long period of time. When those former college students, now successful professionals, doctors, lawyer, administrators, judges, and elected municipal officials, who did their research papers with Father's books and ate at Mother's kitchen table, found out that Mother was in town, the mad scramble began. News spread so rapidly across town: *Mama Poree* was in town, and the scrambling and positioning grew like wild fire as to who would be "first" to get Mama Poree" as their special house guest. Who would be first to take her to the finest restaurant or who would be first to take her to some spectacular entertainment or Broadway type musical. As a result, Mother's vacation lasted several months at a time, and she would travel throughout the West Coast as far north as Canada and as far south as Mexico.

Mother's yearly vacations proved to be long extended tours of almost the entire states of America with additional trips to Canada and Mexico. She traveled all over the country until she was eighty-five years old. Mother received monetary gifts from all over the country as well as several countries around the world from those former student members of her extended family, who were welcomed into my parent's home during their stay at Dillard and Xavier Universities many decades ago.

Another Embarrassing Moment

The same week that I gave an inspirational and motivational speech to hundreds of graduates of Carver Senior High School, I had another embarrassing incident. Had I followed Gloria's advice, I probably would have avoided such a moment. Unfortunately, you know how men actually seek or follow their spouse's advice. One of my neighbor's mother died, who I used to visit when I was a teenager. I thought the wake was held at the funeral home on Dumaine Street in Treme. When I entered the funeral home parlor, I began extending my sympathy to everyone that I thought were members of my neighbor's family. After extending sympathy to many of the people I thought were family members, none of them seemed to recognize me nor did I recognize any of them. After all it had been some time since I had visited my old neighborhood.

When I got to the casket to view the body, I didn't recognize the person either. My neighbor's mother was light complexioned with keen features; the person in the casket was extremely dark complexioned with broad features. I should have known something was wrong because I didn't see either my neighbor or his wife at the wake. As I was leaving the funeral home, I recognized one of the funeral directors, who used to live in our neighborhood. I asked him did he know where my neighbor's mother's wake was being held." He told me it was at the Baptist Church around the corner.

I walked around the corner and read the funeral notice at the entrance of the church. At last I was at the right place. This time, as I walked up the isle to view the body, I extended sympathy to quite a few members of the family I recognized. I saw my neighbor and his wife, expressed my sympathy, and sat with them for a few moments of reflections. As I was leaving church I noticed several persons seemed to be looking in my direction, smiling, and chatting with one another. As I left the church building, one of my church's choir members said, "Mr. Poree, that's a might sharp new suit you're wearing." I said "Thanks, how did you know my suit was brand new?" My choir member said while laughing, "Everyone in the church knew it was a brand new suit, Mr. Poree. Everyone saw Inspector #94 Tags on your two side vents!" I turned around and saw what everyone else in the church had seen, Inspector #94 Tags. This of course was another one of those embarrassing moments in Edgar's life.

Cadillac Dealership Boycott

Ten months after an auto accident incident, I broke a two-year boycott of Pontchartrain Motors Cadillac Dealership. For more than twenty-six months I considered purchasing a Cadillac Sedan, the local Cadillac dealership did not have any Black salesmen, only janitors and car prep service workers. For two years I went to the showroom to check out new models, collect new model literature, and most of the times I visited the dealership, I was practically ignored by the salesman. When I approached many of the salesmen to ask questions about the new models, if a White person came into the dealership long after I arrived and approached the salesman, my inquiry became secondary and ignored. The White person's questions or assistance was honored. This situation was not an isolated incident but too often a reoccurrence, especially when I was seriously considering purchasing a new model that year. Because of the bias treatment I received over and over from the dealership's salesmen, I decided not to buy a Cadillac, although it was my favorite car, until the dealership had more inclusive and non-bias accommodating salesmen.

After twenty six months visiting the dealership without getting much attention from the salespersons, one morning after parking my car across from the dealership, I noticed a light complexioned young man in the showroom with a dress shirt and necktie on. I asked myself, "Is it possible this young man is a salesman?" At 9:30 a.m. that morning, I walked into the dealership and asked the young man did he work there and to my surprise, he said, "Yes Sir." "I'm a salesman, and this is my first day on the job." I paused with a broad smile on my face, asked the young man his name, he replied, "Don Matthews." I said, "Mr. Matthews, you are about to sell your very first Cadillac Eldorado this morning."

The young man stood there, speechless and mesmerized. I said, "Don, what are you waiting for; let's go to the third floor; there's a lime-green 1968 Cadillac Eldorado Coupe with a Sticker Price of $10,570." That's the vehicle that you are going to sell me today. I told Don I was going across the street to the parking lot to get my 1967 Olds Mobile Luxury Sedan, so the appraiser could determine the trade-in price toward my purchase of the Eldorado. The faces of some of those old salesmen who had ignored me over the years were very somber as Don was getting the paperwork completed for the sale of the 1968 Cadillac Eldorado Coupe purchased on his first day on the job. It was obvious they were surprised, and some were probably upset for missing out on the sales commission.

Two day after the sale, Don delivered the lime-green 1968 Cadillac Eldorado Coupe to Gloria at school in the Desire Project. On the back seat of the car was a crystal vase containing eighteen long stem red roses with a "Thank You" card signed from Don Matthews. That young man was the talk of the dealership for a very long time. He became the dealership's top salesman, subsequently selling two additional Eldorado vehicles to me before becoming terminally ill in the late seventies. Every time I met Don Matthews any place, he would tell the person or persons who he was with that I was the very first customer to buy a car from him on his first day on the job at the Cadillac dealership.

Avoiding Conflicts

As Director of the Neighborhood Youth Corp, I was privileged to have a Reserve Parking Space for my vehicle in the local Anti-Poverty Agency's Lot. I did, however, avoid parking in the reserve parking space because I was afraid that might cause some catenations and negative impressions from some of the Agency's clientele that we served. Instead of parking free, I decided that it was best to avoid creating any ill will or animosity among the agency's clientele, so I parked around the corner in a two dollar a day parking lot. I did this for over ten months. One Tuesday morning I was scheduled to host a very important Agency meeting in my office 9:00 a.m. We had had an all-night rain and that morning we had a thunder storm in the area. I thought that the circumstances of the very inclement weather would allow me to take advantage of parking in my reserve space in the Agency's parking lot, especially since I had quite a number of charts and other material in the car for the meeting. When I got out of the car in the Agency's lot, the first thing I heard from some of the agency's clientele were, "That's why we can't get any more money because these staff people with their big salaries are buying big luxury cars while the poor people are struggling!" It was on that Tuesday that I decided I would no longer park in the $2 parking lot around the block; instead, I would park in my reserve space at the Agency.

A Very Tragic Summer

During the summer of 1968, the Neighborhood Youth Corps had its largest summer jobs program. There were fifteen hundred part-time jobs for junior and senior high school students, fifteen years and older. Students worked twenty hours per week at $1.25 per hour. Many of the students of the Neighborhood Youth Corps In-School Summer Program were assigned to the work in the Witness Program, sponsored by the Archdiocese. After students completed their orientation and received their work assignments, they were assigned to a work coordinator and a counselor who were responsible for the students' performance, schedule, time sheets, and paycheck distribution. Each student was provided with a handbook which gave the rules and regulations of the summer program. Safety was the prevailing and major issue in the student work program, and all water activities were prohibited in and during the summer student work program. The handbook clearly stated that students will not be allowed to participate in any type of water activities during their official working hours during the entire summer program. All participating agency supervisors and representatives responsible for student participants of the NYC Summer Student Work Program were covered with the rules and regulations of the program.

The Archdiocese wanted to take the students who worked in the NYC summer work program assigned to their Witness Program on a picnic to the Fourth of July Holiday in Waveland, Mississippi. When advised of their plans, I told them that they had a right to sponsor the picnic for their students participants as long as that activity was not during actual NYC sanctioned working hours. Additionally, I advised them since the picnic was not sponsored or sanctioned by the Neighborhood Youth Corps, the Archdiocese must get the consent of the parents of the program participants to attend. I also cautioned the Archdioceses about the potential danger associated with hosting a picnic, especially in Waveland, Mississippi, because of the Gulf waters. My last words to the Archdiocese were, "This is your sponsored event; and therefore, the Archdiocese assumes full responsibility for this event."

I notified all of the Archdiocese' Witness Program student participants that the Fourth of July Picnic planned in Waveland, Mississippi, was sponsored by the Archdiocese exclusively and not in any way sponsored by or supported by the Neighborhood Youth Corp In-School Program.

I also advised the parents that the Archdiocese would be totally responsible for their children's safety. After my family and I return home from an enjoyable Fourth of July at my nephew's home, I called him to extend our appreciation for a wonderful holiday. During our telephone conversation, an operator interrupted our call with an emergency telephone call from Waveland, Mississippi. When I heard the voice of the priest who was the Archdiocese's Witness Program Coordinator, my first question,

"Don't tell me somebody drowned?" The priest, obviously shaken and distraught said, "No, not somebody, three students have drowned!" My greatest fear of this picnic had become a tragic nightmare. Two of the bodies had not been located as of the time of the emergency telephone call. Word of tragedies spread rapidly, and I began getting telephone call from the news media about the drowning. My response, "I have no comments; you need to talk to the Archdiocese; this wasn't a Neighborhood Youth Corps event."

Recognizing that some of the students who attended the picnic had returned home already, I got in my car and drove to the Desire Project to the homes of the missing students to help console the families of this horrific and tragic event. When I rang the doorbell of the first home, the front door opened, and the twelve-year old younger brother of one of the drowning victims took his two fists and struck me in the chest shouting, "You killed my brother! You killed my brother!" With tears running down his cheeks, he continued that outcry. When his Mother came down the stairs to the front door, she said, "Hush, my baby, Mr. Poree didn't kill your brother." With tears flowing and a face of anguish and grief, she took my hands and led me upstairs to see the other members of the family. That moment when that twelve-year old struck me and cried aloud you killed my brother, still resonates with me vividly after five decades.

When the nightly local news came on, each of the news anchors portrayed and characterized me as a non-caring non-consoling individual who refused to comment on the tragic drowning of three young students in his program in Waveland, Mississippi, today. They all quoted me as saying, "I had no comments to the question: What can you tell us about the drowning of the three young people in your program in Waveland, Mississippi, today." What the news anchors didn't tell the viewing audience that night was what I actually told them, "You need to talk to the Archdiocese; this wasn't a Neighborhood Youth Corps event." Strangely, there wasn't any mention of or reference to the Archdiocese in any of the news that night. Reporters from the local press came to my house that same night, and I also gave them the same statement that I gave to the television reporters who questioned me about the drowning. According to the news media, I was this non-caring youth program administrator who showed little compassion and sympathy for the young people who drown who were participants in his youth program.

Ironically, although there was never any mention of the Archdiocese in any of the news media reports throughout this very tragic event, many persons expressed their doubts as to why an unidentified benefactor of the Archdiocese paid the entire expenses associated with the funerals, the repasts, and the burial plots for each of the three young people who drowned while attending the Archdiocese's picnic in Waveland, Mississippi, on the Fourth of July. This tragic experience for these three families and the power of persuasion of the villain, the media, was another one of those characters building moments in my life.

1968 Homecoming Chairman

In 1968, the Sisters of The Blessed Sacrament, the governing Order of Xavier University, the Nation's only Black Catholic University, made a historic decision in selecting its first layperson as its President. Norman C. Francis, an attorney and former graduate and Dean of the University was selected President. This historic appointment of a Black American Layperson to lead the Nation's only Black Catholic University was a most significant event in the life of the University as well as in our City. The news was front page stories of major newspapers across the Nation.

Several members of Xavier's Homecoming Committee asked me to consider serving as the 1968 Chairman. At the time I had several major projects ongoing at the office, so I felt that I could not devote the necessary time to facilitate a grand festivity. Several of my 1958 graduating classmates admonished me for not accepting the chairmanship. One of the more vocal classmates said, "Poree, we are celebrating our Tenth Anniversary at this year's Homecoming, and we are drafting you for Chairman, end of discussion." The next day I called the Homecoming Committee appointment person and volunteered to serve as 1968 Homecoming Chairman. Typically, the University's Homecomings attracted rather modest attendance; however, with the University's appointment of a Black layperson who was a former student and dean, combining the inauguration celebration with the homecoming activities could potentially make Homecoming '68 the largest and grandest ever at Xavier. I envisioned a grand fun-filled, upbeat festive-like celebration in a grand ballroom at a downtown hotel, bigger and more spectacular than ever held on the campus in the Barn.

When I attended the first planning meeting, I did not in any way anticipate what appeared to be, in my opinion, some apparent resentment of my being selected as the 1968 Chairman by some of the committee's more senior members. This was especially evident when I began to discuss what I had envisioned for this year's homecoming in conjunction with the University's Inauguration Ceremonies. Traditionally, our homecomings attracted mostly graduates and their spouses who were mostly from the metro area and from states next to Louisiana. Since graduating in 1958, the largest homecoming event that I had ever attended was a banquet in The Barn that had at most approximately 150 guests in attendance.

With the inauguration celebration of the first Black President of Xavier, this year's homecoming attraction could be enormous if we think-out-the box and strategically plan non-traditional and creative attractions. I told members of the homecoming committee that we were targeting for an attendance of 1,000 guests from all over the country at our banquet in a downtown hotel. Additionally, I told them we were planning a homecoming parade with marching bands, cheer leaders, fraternities, sororities, and new convertibles for the homecoming queen and members of her court to ride in as the parade winds through the surrounding streets of the university.

I said, "Xavier's Inauguration and Homecoming '68 activities will be seen on all local TV stations during the evening and nightly news including the homecoming parade." The expressions on some of the more senior committee members' faces seemed to imply I was dreaming rather than planning. One senior member said, "You were asked to serve as Homecoming Chairman not homecoming planner." Our committee has been planning and coordinating homecomings for more than ten years, and we already know what needs to be done for this year.

I recognized that my task would be extremely challenging because the senior members of the committee simply wanted a puppet-like chairman so that they could do their typical traditional homecoming activities. I had to maintain diplomatic relations with those members while remaining focus on making Homecoming 668 the grandest of all. Instead of revealing all details of Homecoming '68, we gave two separate plans, one for the senior members of the committee and a more detailed explanation of the vision to those members who were supportive of our initiatives.

Many of the committee's senior members expressed doubt in increasing the traditional $5 banquet ticket at The Barn to a $20 banquet ticket at a downtown hotel. We thought otherwise. They also expressed their opposition to spending money for printing expensive invitations and programs for Banquet '68. They felt the cost of printing and mailing invitations was an unnecessary expense since, in the past, they had always gotten the banquet tickets and programs printed free from a Xavier's graduate as a donation.

Instead of engaging in seemingly non-productive debates, I decided to concede and allow them to do whatever they desired, while continuing to execute the envisioned mission for homecoming '68. One of the senior member's husbands even came to a committee meeting to admonish me for not allowing the more experienced members to implement their traditional homecoming plans for 1968. He stated they had been very loyal and dedicated over the years in planning and successfully carrying out the University's homecoming activities; therefore, I should not tamper with success. I concurred with the husband's assertions and acknowledged their years of successful planning and coordinating homecoming activities at Xavier.

Now it was time to execute the envisioned plan. I recognized reaching that very ambitious goal of a thousand guests at Banquet '68 would have to engage and involve undergraduates in the plans. That appeared to be a missing link in previous homecomings. The big question, "What would excite underclassmen to participate in a homecoming banquet with a bunch of old folks, perhaps a fashion show, featuring underclassmen as models and a homecoming parade?" Now that we had a possible formula to attract and involve underclass men and women; our next great challenge was to secure clothing for the models to wear in the fashion show.

Since we were going to depict fashions from the decades ending in eights, we needed to find clothing worn during 1918, 1928, 1938, 1948, 1958, and of course 1968. We went to Saul's, a Black owned costume business and told them what we were planning for Homecoming '68, and they were so excited about the concept and the prospect of getting new customers that they agreed to provide free-of-charge clothing for the event. We then went downtown to talk to the owners of Godchaux and Keller-Zanders Department Stores to solicit some of their 1968 fashions for Homecoming '68. The owners told me the timing was not very good, since most of their models were participating in the Annual Fall Race Track Fashion Show during our planned homecoming activities. I told both owners we didn't need their models since we had some of the most beautiful young college student models, all sizes, shapes, and colors to fashion their clothing in front of the largest captured audience in the history of the University. I told the owners, "The tremendous free publicity and advertisement their store would get from the thousand plus potential customers after seeing their "fashions" from your store at Banquet '68." To my surprise both owners agreed to allow some of their most beautiful 1968 fashions free-of-charge for Homecoming '68.

Our next stop was at Zoller Men's Wear, where I had purchased my first ever hundred dollar suit when I was twenty-seven years old. Herb Zollar, the owner of Zoller's Men's Wear, and I had become personal friends over the years. When I approached him about Homecoming '68 Fashion Show, he personally selected the very latest men's fashions along with the appropriate accessories. He provided free-of-charge the very latest of men fashions for every occasion including the very latest fashions in that year's tuxedoes. Additionally, Herb purchased six banquet tickets for the Homecoming Fashion Show, and he personally helped dress the models for the Fashion Show.

Our next challenge, researching the most popular "hit" tunes during the decades ending in Eighties. After identifying the "hit" tunes during the years ending in the Eighties, we had to find the records. With the help of many classmates as well as of some older graduating classmates, we were able to find most of the hit tune records. One of my old neighborhood buddies had an old Webcor Tape Recorder, and he recorded all of the hit tune records in the appropriate sequence on the tape recorder for the fashion show.

Having secured all of the fashions for the show and tape recording of all of the hit tunes completed, our final chore was to get some beautifully decorated gift boxes large enough to house each year models. I went to Sister Lorraine, Chairman of the Arts Department, to ask her to build and decorate six large eight feet tall gift boxes for the homecoming fashion show. The plan called for the models to come out of large gift wrapped boxes to display their beautiful fashions. Sister Lorraine was so excited about the project she personally supervised and helped build the very first gift wrapped box for the homecoming fashion show. I contacted the local television stations to tell them of the exciting homecoming events planned, and each of the TV's General Managers committed to cover the events. The Inauguration Ceremony of the First African American Layman President of the Nation's only Black Catholic University greatly enhanced the prospects of a bigger and more exciting and spectacular Homecoming Banquet.

Banquet '68: University's Largest and Most Successful

On Saturday afternoon on a beautiful mild day in November, the Homecoming Parade rolled through the surrounding streets of the University's neighborhood. The homecoming queen and her court rode in beautiful 1968 convertibles, the colors and members of the fraternities and sororities marched with pride, and cheerleaders led the viewing crowds with spirited cheers.

The marching bands thrilled the crowds with popular hit tunes as they performed precision formations during Homecoming Parade '68. Television cameramen were on location filming the parade and interviewing spectators along the parade route.

On that fall night in November 1968, in a downtown hotel's grand ballroom, more than one thousand guests were treated to the perhaps the University's grandest and largest ever Homecoming Celebration in the history of the University. The $5 traditional "The Barn" banquet ticket was now a $20 downtown grand ballroom banquet ticket. The 150 guests who attended the largest homecoming banquet ever held in Xavier's Barn had grown to more than 1,000 guests from across the Nation. The previously donated plain banquet tickets and programs were now replaced with black embossed parchment stock with white lettering invitations and the Banquet Program was printed on the finest parchment.

The banquet invitations and programs became collectors' items for hundreds of guests from all over the Nation. After the homecoming banquet celebration was over, Mother walked over to me, embraced me, and with tears of joy in her eyes, said, "Junior, all of the work and difficulty that you endured to make this Grand Celebration such a great success speaks loudly of your tremendous talents and skills." "Son, I'm so blessed and proud of you and what you do for others." All three major television stations featured extended coverage of Xavier University's Inauguration and Homecoming Ceremonies at both their evening and night news. Xavier's University Homecoming '68 was one of New Orleans' most memorable media events.

In addition to my involvement in Xavier's historic Inaugural Homecoming Celebrations, I was quite busy serving on numerous boards and commissions including, Treasurer, Park and Parkway Commission of New Orleans, Advisory Board of State of Louisiana's Humanities, Board of St. Mark Community Center, Board of Social Welfare Planning Council, Board of YMCA, Board of Better Boy's Club, Chairman of Bethany Boosters Association, Fellow of Loyola University's Institute of Politics, Discussion Leader for Tulane University's Southern Assembly's Issues Forum, and Consultant for The Dryades Street YMCA's Membership Drive. I also participated in numerous community events as keynote speaker for Landry Senior High School' Student Government Installation, St. Paul A.M.E. Church's Student Recognition Day, Notre Dame Seminary Ecumenical Day of Theology, Dryades Street YMCA Career Day Conference, John H. Martyn High School's Better Boy's Scholarship Annual Program, St. Paul Lutheran Church's Laymen Seminar, Career Day Conference-Clark Senior High School, and Joseph S. Clark Senior High School All Sports Banquet.

Personnel Director

After serving as Neighborhood Youth Corp In-School Program for two years, the Executive Director of the Agency asked me to take the Personnel Director's position because he wanted to move the Agency in another direction. I recommended Walter J. Mitchell to replace me as Director of the Neighborhood Youth Corp In-School Program, and the Executive Director concurred. After accepting the Personnel Director's position, I immediately initiated a Strategic Skill Set Oriented Development Program which allowed existing employees to acquire more proficient skill sets, through in-house development training. This employee development initiative proved to be a very successful program, enabling existing employees to improve their work performance and skill sets and affording them opportunities to fill agency vacancies with existing workforce. Our Agency was commended for the Workforce Development Training that we implemented, and the morale, proficiency and work performance of our employees contributed significantly to a very favorable work environment.

Executive Assistant

After the successful implementation of the Workforce Development Initiative and the successful transitioning of existing employees filling vacancies at the Anti-Poverty Agency, the Executive Director once again came to my office and said that there were more challenges ahead of our agency that needed special attention because of the agency's tremendous growth. He said, "Edgar, since you have established a very strong and proficient Personnel Office and staff, we need to again call upon your skill sets to help us work on the Agency's Strategic Plan for the Future, the Five Year Plan." "In that capacity, I want someone who can work with little or no supervision, who thinks-outside the box, and who's willing to take risks; that person is you," said the Executive Director. So on a late Friday evening, I arrived home and told Guich that Dan asked me to become his Executive Assistant. Gloria said, "Edgar, are you getting any more money and how many different jobs are you going to have at that Agency? My response, "I'm continuing to build my skill sets and resume' for that big opportunity." Gloria's response, "Yes, Edgar, how many time I have heard that before."

Graduation Speaker for Pay

I was the commencement speaker for one of the City's newest and largest high schools. Many of the high school graduates attended the elementary school where I taught for eight years; therefore, I knew many parents of the graduates. Every seat in the high school auditorium was filled to capacity with proud parents, relatives, and friends. When I arrived at the school, members of the faculty and staff greeted me warmly and lead me to the room where the graduates were lining up for the procession. The principal indicated he was thrilled to have me as the speaker for the graduation because they received such a great ovation from the students when we told them who was going to be their commencement speaker. The principal also told me he had something for me that he would present after the graduation.

The graduation was a great success, and apparently my speech was well received from the standing ovation that I received. I was presented with a Certificate of Appreciation for my participation as the Commencement

Speaker. When the graduation ceremony was over, many of the graduates and their parents expressed their thanks and appreciation for making the graduation a tremendous celebration. Several of the graduates asked me if I got paid a hundred dollars for every graduation ceremony that I spoke for. Initially, I just smiled and said "Not really." However, one of my former students, who was a graduate said, "Mr. Poree, we are so proud and happy you were our speaker that our class donated a hundred dollar to give you as our appreciation."

Since I had not yet received their generous appreciation gift, I said, "That's very commendable what their class had done." I thought to myself, that's what the principal must have been referring to before the graduation ceremony, when he told me he had something for me after the ceremony. I saw the principal while leaving the ceremony and he said, "Mr. Poree, thank you very much for a beautiful message." Unfortunately, to this date, I did not get the hundred dollar donation the graduating class raised. I assumed the principal must have forgotten about his offer of providing me with something after the ceremony. Guess that was another one of those character building experiences.

In addition to my non-paid graduate class budgeted appreciation gift, I had plenty other wonderful speaking engagements at Bethel A.M. E. Church's Men's Day, American Education Week at Helen S. Edwards School, Counselor Training Seminar at the U.S. Naval Support Activity Personnel Department, Founder's Day at Phillips Junior High. and Orleans Parish Public School's Counselor's Workshop, Career Day at Eleanor McMain Jr. High School, L.B. Landry Sr. Hi Achievement Day, and The Junior League of Greater New Orleans.

CHAPTER IX

BUSINESS INTEREST

Pee Vee's Meat Market

During our work on the Agency's Strategic Five Year Plan, one of the things that got our attention early during the initial phase of our neighborhood needs assessment was the limited number of markets in the Lower Ninth Ward. Dan and I took a driving tour of the Lower Ninth Ward, and the only markets serving that area was Puglia's on St. Claude and Caffin Avenue, a market on Caffin Avenue and North Johnson Street, a corner grocery on Tennessee and North Galvez Street, and another corner grocery on Gordon and Tupelo Street. The only major market in the area located on the Upper Ninth Ward side of the Industrial Canal was Canal Villere located on Almonaster and North Robinson Street at the foot of the Industrial Canal Bridge. Since many resident of the Lower Ninth Ward depended upon public transportation, making groceries was not the easiest chore, especially for many senior citizens.

Persons living on the north side of North Claiborne Street had a long walk to get to the St. Claude Street market, and those persons who lived below Caffin Avenue had an even longer walk if they wanted to go to Canal Villere Super Market on the other side of the Industrial Canal bridge. Since going to the market was not an easy chore either because buses were not always on regular schedules due to Industrial Canal bridge's opening-and-closing for boat traffic or the locations of the few markets in areas made it even more difficult for the elderly residents. These conditions plus the un-regulated on-the-books credit practice by corner grocers/

markets owners contributed significantly to possible "financial abuse" of area customers, especially for members of the elderly community.

Many corner grocery/markets extended credit to regular customers throughout the city, and the owners of the Lower Ninth Ward corner grocery/markets extended their "Owner's Book Credits" of purchases made during the weeks or months, depending on when the customers, who received credit, got paid. Typically the owner's book's credit practice worked this way: regular customers would make purchase of groceries and/or meat from grocery/market, and the owner would record in his books, log the date, and the amount of the customer's purchase. The customer may or may not be told by the owner of the amount of credit extended for the purchase at that time nor would the owner give the customer any statement or record for future reference of the credit extended.

When the customer would get his check or got paid, he would bring his check or money to pay the owner for the week's or month's credit. If the on-the-credit customer brought cash, the owner simply told the customer how much they owed. If the customer brought a check, the owner deducted the amount of credit he extended, according to his books giving the customer his balance in cash. Since the on-the-book-credit customers didn't get any statement from the owner when he made his purchases on credit, the possibility of the customer getting short-changed on cash-checking day was highly possible. This unregulated on-the-books credit extension practice, in our opinion, contributed significantly to financial abuse of many area residents, especially the elderly.

After our driving tour of the area, we decided that we would invest in developing a meat market/grocery that was conveniently located for walking residents that would sell a good quality and grade of affordable meat and grocery items for residences of that area, especially the elderly. We also wanted to provide helpful information for area residents about safeguards in protecting themselves from possibly financial abuse and being "short-changed" from on-the-books credit practice. After looking for a facility to rent for the market, we settled on the lower floor building located on the corner of North Johnson and Caffin Avenue. The building was owned by the political organization, S.O.U.L. It was located across the street from the Caffin Avenue Market which had the widely practiced on-the-books credit practice. Our motives were honorable. Perhaps our mission was more from our "Hearts" and not of the "Heads," and this endeavor would prove to be a most challenging and frustrating debacle full of miscalculations and blunders.

Driven by our passion to make the Lower Ninth Ward residents have an affordable, quality, and convenient market/grocery in their neighborhood, especially the senior citizens and those residents who depended heavily on public transportation. Dan and I began the journey of putting all the pieces together. Since we were going to be the investors, we needed assistance and counsel of those who had actually been in the meat market business. We were very fortunate to know one of the city's legendary meat market owners who gave us many of the dos and don'ts of the business plus he also gave us the name of one of the finest butchers who just returned home from a stint in prison. We were willing to take a chance on this individual, since he had been highly recommended by an experienced business owner. We met with the young man and explained what we were attempting to do, and he made a commitment to work in concert with us in making this goal a successful one.

Our next task was hiring essential tradesmen to do the physical modifications of the rented space. We hired an electrician, my former next door neighbor when we lived on Marigny Street, to provide the necessary building code requirements for the meat market. We then hired one of the agency's part-time maintenance workers who were an exceptional carpenter to do the building modifications, necessary in meeting regulating and building codes. The last essential piece in preparing and transforming the building into a meat-market-grocery was hiring a plumber. Dan had a very close friendship with one of the area's top plumbing firms, and the owner agreed to provide complete plumbing services, free of charge because he felt what we were planning to do was quite commendable.

Now that we had all of the essential tradesmen to modify the building to market specifications, we had to get a vendor to get market equipment. Sonny, who had given us the dos and don'ts of operating a meat market, recommended an equipment vendor to us. We met with the owner of the equipment who gave us a good price that was affordable for our facility. With everything seemingly in place, Dan and I began working on a time-table for opening date. Since my last name started with the letter "P" and Dan's with the letter "V," we decided to name the meat market Pee Vee's.

Banking Bias

Our next task was to borrow some startup capital. Since both of us were gainfully employed, married, home owners, had established good credit, and were free of any unlawful charges, securing a loan would be easy. Additionally, I had $7,500 savings in United Federal Credit Union, so I anticipated borrowing $3,500 would be a cinch. My partner, an executive with the Anti-Poverty Agency also, had savings in the United Federal Credit Union. Well, what I thought would be a cinch getting a $3,500 loan turned out to be a very rude awakening of the White banking establishment's bias toward Blacks seeking money for capital for business ventures.

After completing my loan application, the banking officer told me that they would be willing to loan me the $3,500, subject to my surrendering my United Federal Credit Union Saving Passbook, as Collateral for nine month. "Excuse me, you want to loan me my own money and charge me interest on it?" I said. The loan officer told me surrendering my savings passbook simply was a way of allowing me an opportunity to demonstrate and establish a good faith relationship with the bank. He further stated that after nine months the bank would relinquish holding my savings passbook because I would have established by then a good relationship with the bank.

I told the banking officer that my integrity had been questioned, and the practice imposed upon me was a very biased one, based upon my race not my credit-worthiness. Of course the banking officer denied that. I also told the banking officer if I had come to the bank to get a loan to buy a car or a boat, it wouldn't have been a problem because the bank could always confiscate the car or boat for non-payment. After leaving First NBC, I got a shared-loan from United Federal Credit Union, where I had a saving account. My partner had no problem getting his loan at FNBC because of the large banking activity account of the agency which he controlled.

After acquiring limited start-up capital, a series of miscalculations and blunders occurred. First, we had to provide upfront money for the electrician to get parts and begin working. Next, we also provided money for the carpenter to get material needed for construction. The carpenter began changing the looks of the building on schedule, the plumber completed his work in one week, and there was very little evidence of any electrical work being done. We contacted the electrician who said he was waiting for the carpenter to finish the rough-in walls so that he could begin installing wire, outlets, and switches. He said that it would not take much time to get his work done.

The equipment vendor delivered the meat cases and began constructing the walk-in freezer and that work was completed in two weeks. The vendor's equipment was tested on existing electrical outlets, none of the electrical outlets met City's building code specifications. When the Italian equipment vendor completed his work he said, "You guys are making this place too good, too fancy to succeed; you won't last six months in business." Dan and I were rather perplexed by his remarks, which seemed to imply that we were making the place to good for Black people, how disturbing and demeaning. We resented that statement, and it only strengthened and galvanized our commitment of proving the contrary.

The electrician would come over once in a while and provide temporary service for the equipment testing; however, he had not done sufficient work for the electric inspection yet. Our opening date was three weeks late, and we began to exhaust most of our start-up capital. We were now operating on out-of-pocket money to facilitate the preparation. We demanded that the electrician stop doing other side jobs and complete our project. We had to give him additional money over and above his original price, so we had no other choice, at that time, in order to get opened to generate some capital.

The night before our first day opening, we asked the electrician to let us hold $500 of his final payment for a week to allow us to generate some cash, especially since he was responsible for the three and a half week delayed opening. He told me he needed the money to pay his workers. This was the same person who took our upfront money, supposedly to buy parts and began work immediately; instead, he worked other jobs and delayed our opening for more than three and a half weeks. We gave him $500 cash, and he left the market.

The butcher, Dan and I began preparing the meat case for tomorrow's opening. The freezer was full of meat and poultry, the grocery shelves had basic foods, and some household items and the knives. The meat saw and chopping block were spotless, the floors were cleaned, and all we needed were customer in the morning. After checking our things-to-do list, I noticed that we did not have a second large bucket and mop. I went to Canal Villere Super Market across the Industrial Canal to buy an additional mop and large bucket. Guess who I saw with a basket full of meats, chickens, and groceries—our electrician. When he saw me his eyes opened as wide as a coconut. I said, "Alvin, we hired you to do our work. You took our money, delayed our opening three weeks, and had an opportunity to be our very first customer, yet you went to someone else who never gave you a dime and patronized them!" He said, "My wife gave me a market list to bring home tonight, and I knew that your market wasn't opening until tomorrow." That was just the beginning of multi-blunders to follow.

The next thing I did was to hire one of my neighbor's daughters who had just graduated from high school and had not yet determined whether she wanted to go to college. The young lady was rather stout, but she had a great personality and a willingness to become a great sales clerk at Pee Vee's Meat Market. After interviewing the young lady, my business partner agreed that she had the perfect personality to greet and serve our customers. After a brief orientation of how we wanted to welcome and serve our customers, maintain a spotless facility, and make sure that every customer received a sales receipt, we were ready for opening our doors to residents of the Lower Ninth Ward.

After several weeks of initial operations, we were getting ready for our Grand Opening. We distributed hundreds of flyers in the neighborhood announcing our Grand Opening date, our location, and the many special meat sales for our Opening Celebration. We were all excited with great anticipation. The meat packing company convinced us that bacon would be a good opening day sale item, so we bought several hundred pounds of bacon. We also planned to sell chickens five cents less a pound than Schwegmann's plus other reduced prices on neck-bones, pigtails, stew meat, and pork chops. After finishing our things to do list for opening week, we left the market at 1:30 a.m. Saturday morning. Grand Opening was scheduled for eight o'clock, and we were all scheduled to report to work at 6 o'clock in the morning.

Grand Opening

Dan and I along with my neighbor's daughter, our sales-clerk, arrived at 6:00 a. m. Saturday morning. The butcher had not arrived as of yet. At 6:30 a.m., still no butcher. I called the butcher's telephone number and got a recording stating the number was no longer in service. Since the butcher lived on the other side of the canal, we thought that the bridge might have been stuck, delaying traffic coming to the Lower Ninth Ward. We called Sonny to see if he had another telephone number for the butcher, and he told us that was the only number he had. We were beginning to panic because neither one of us knew how to cut meat, other than slicing turkey or roast for dinner. At 7:00 a.m. I drove to the butcher's apartment where he was living, knocked on the door, and got no answer so I returned to the market. He had still not arrived.

I called Sonny again and asked him if he could loan one of his butcher's for a few hours this morning until our butcher showed up. He said that Saturday is our busiest day, and he just could not send one of his butchers for they were preparing the cuts for today, this morning. He said he would send one of his apprentice butchers to help us; however, he did not have a car, and he would have to take the bus. It was 7:45 a.m.; we did not have the luxury to leave and go and pick up the apprentice butcher. So Dan and I became instant butchers for opening day.

Needless to say our instant butchering experiences did not go over very smoothly, since our only major previous experiences took place carving Thanksgiving turkeys or small veal roast for Sunday dinners. Since we had extremely limited carving experiences, we were cutting most of the meat with the cutting saw. Professional butchers use sharp knives for most of their cuts, because it provides the greatest amount of meat with very little losses. The meat cutting saw was mostly used by the professional butcher for cutting the boney portion of the meat to be cut. Unfortunately, we did not know that, nor did we know for every pound of meat cut with the saw, you lose approximately an eighth of a pound. So for every 8 pounds of meat that Dan and I cut on opening day, we lost a pound of meat and a pound of revenues.

To further make our opening day a rather chaotic one, because we were selling chickens five-cents a pound less than the largest supermarket in the city, we did not put a limit on the amount of pounds a customer could buy. So customers were buying tens of pounds of chickens which required Dan and me to rotate throughout the day, and we were cutting meat on the saw or leaving the market to buy additional crates of chickens from the poultry company all day long. Customers were buying three times more chickens than meat. In one aspect that meant that we were not loosing as many eighths of pounds of meat from cutting with the saw, but Dan and I were so tired from going back and forth all day to the poultry company buying crates of chickens. Profits were dwindling from the sales. Our cars smelled like a chicken factory, and we felt like chicken factory workers at the end of the day. We didn't sell much bacon opening day, but we made it through the entire day without the butcher. Gross sales exceeded our projections for the first day; however, the disproportionate amount of chicken sales plunged our profit margin to a negative level. The butcher never showed up on opening day.

Two days later the butcher showed up. He told us he had a family emergency in the country, and he did not have an opportunity to contact us because he didn't have a telephone. We told him how disappointed and dissatisfied we were with his actions; however, we were going to give him another opportunity to demonstrate his willingness to make the market a success. The butcher said that he was grateful to us for allowing him another chance. During the next few weeks the butcher demonstrated his commitment and ability of providing good quality customer services. During the first month of operation, it appeared the market was experiencing some degree of walk-in customer traffic, which was slightly less than we originally projected.

During those initials weeks, we knew we would have to subsidize operational expenses out of pocket, since we were the new kids in the neighborhood. Little did we realize that there were numerous underlying factors and factions negatively impacting customer traffic? Our major targeted market, senior citizens who traditionally did not have private transportation to get to the more distant supermarkets serving the Lower Ninth Ward; one located on St. Claude the other across the Industrial Canal. Secondly, we thought by providing a superior quality grade of meat along with traditional and frequently prepared food items, we would gradually attract senior citizen walking customers. Thirdly, we were of the opinion the many hundreds of individuals that we were instrumental in assisting in getting meaningful educational and social activity opportunities over the years could possibly translate into a greater customer base. However, the customer base we anticipated did not materialize.

We met with area pastors introducing ourselves and the new market in an effort to encourage them to let their congregation know there was an affordable quality meat market in the neighborhood. We walked the streets in surrounding neighborhoods, personally introduced ourselves to the neighbors, distributing Pee Vee Market Flyers encouraging them to come and do business with us. We were encouraged by the warm and friendly response of many of the neighbors. Unfortunately, what we did not know was that there was a faction going on in the Lower Ninth Ward politically between long-time older community activists and members of the younger adult, highly influential Black political organization that owned the building we leased for the meat market. Although my partner was extremely politically astute, neither he nor I were aware of the magnitude of this deep rooted resentment. Consequently, our efforts of attracting senior citizens were greatly compromised. In spite of all the seemingly warm reception we received during our canvassing of the neighborhoods and promoting Pee Vee's Meat Market, many of the senior residents apparently thought the political organization owned the market.

The other potential customer base we thought would be available for shopping with us was the very large number of individuals that my partner and I had been instrumental in getting them meaning employment. Unfortunately, that anticipated segment did not materialize and when asked, "Have you been in to shop at Pee Vee's?" The most frequent responses were "Oh! My wife just bought a half cow for our freezer!" or "Man, it's just too far to shop for meat!" We did not become discouraged because we knew it would be a very challenging proposition, and we were determining to stay and make it work.

During the fifth week of operation, I received a call from the butcher advising me the young lady that we had hired had apparently taken ill, and they had to get an ambulance and rush her to the hospital. He said, "You better get over to the hospital because the young lady seems to be in serious pain, and she looked very pale!" I asked what hospital, and he said, "Charity Hospital." I rushed over to the hospital to see about getting information on our employee. When I reached the admitting desk in the emergency room, I asked the nurse, "Did the young lady that arrived in an ambulance a few minutes ago have a heart attack?" The nurse said, "No!" with a little smile on her face, "The young lady just delivered a nine pound ten ounce baby boy!" I was shocked; I did not know the young lady was pregnant. When her Mother arrived at the hospital, apparently she didn't know her daughter was pregnant either. What a way to run a business.

Needless to say, both of our wives were extremely sick and fed up with Pee Vee's and its two owners. Our prospects for success weren't very promising, and our weekly out-of-pocket expenses continued to increase.

In spite of this difficult situation, we were committed to stick it out in hope that things would turn around and word of mouth from those satisfied customers would help generate additional sales. Dan and I continued to walk the neighborhood, greeting and introducing ourselves to hundreds of residents, inviting them to come and shop with us. We were once again encouraged by what appeared to be a favorable response from many of the residents, especially the senior residents, so we were a bit more optimistic about a possible new source of customers.

Unfortunately, as fate would have it, it was time for my wife's car to be serviced at the dealership. At that time, she had a three year old Ford Mustang, and that was the car that I always used to go back and forth to the market. I never used my 1968 Cadillac Eldorado to go to the market because I knew that it might discourage some potential customers from shopping with us. My intention was to park my car down the street from the market so that it would not be a distraction. I had several very heavy supplies in the trunk of the car so, I decided to back the car into the parking space, remove the supplies, and then move the car down the street from the market. As I was removing supplies from the trunk and bringing them into the market, I hear one of the elderly men in the market asked, "Who's that big "Hog" for?" (Nickname for Cadillac) An elderly lady said, "I think it belongs to one of the young men who own the market." The old gentleman, who asked the question, said, "I ain't spending my money buying no gas for nobody's Hog! He walked out of the market, and his two older buddies followed him. I suppose they agreed with him.

During the following weeks, things were not showing any improvement, our wives weren't talking to us, our out-of-pocket expenses were continuing to increase, and prospects were dim. I went in early one Sunday morning to post sale items of the day on our outside sales board. While I was posting sale items, a teenager was passing the market. I asked, "Young man have you ever shopped with us?" He said, "No!" Then I told him to come in, we've got some great sales today. The young man said, "No, you might not have what my Mama wants." I stood there motionless for a moment, and then it hit me. This teenager was sending me a message that was so profound that I could no longer ignore the reality. The market was dead not even on life support.

The teenager didn't even give us an opportunity to see if we had what his Mother sent him to get from a market. Instead he ignored our invitation and walked across the street to the market that had much higher prices and ungraded meat. I decided then; it was time to move on and cease operation at Pee Vee's. I called Dan, told him it was time to cut our losses, and devote our efforts in being more accessible and attentive husbands and Fathers. The Italian vendor was right after all, for we lasted less than five months.

When we put out the going out of business sales' sign, many of the people who did not shop with us came in, bought sales items and some asked us not to close the market. Even the elderly gentlemen who walked out because he wasn't going to buy any gas for my Cadillac Eldorado came in a bought some sale items. Finally, the young teenager who didn't think we had what his mama wanted came in and bought many sale items on our last day opened. We donated the use of the market facility to a senior community group for the remainder of time we had on our nine month lease option. We also donated some equipment to a non-profit organization in the Lower Ninth Ward.

In spite of all the challenges and headaches associated with the disastrous market experience, I had great satisfaction participating as keynote speaker for the Council of Jewish Women's Program of Greater New Orleans Section-National Council Christian and Jews, Men's Day at Phillip Memorial United Methodist Church, World of Work Assembly, Carter G. Woodson Jr. High School, LSUNO's Graduate Class Counseling and Guidance Seminar, Men's Day at Grace United Methodist Church, All Sports Banquet Cohen Senior High, Father's Son Day at St. John Institutional Baptist Church, Men's Day at Mount Zion Baptist Church, LSUNO's Urban Studies, Bethany United Methodist Church, Trinity United Methodist Church, Presbyterian Institute of Industrial Relations Seminar, and Edward H. Phillips Jr. High School's Achievement Day.

An Incredible Gift

Shortly after the closing of our disastrous business partnership, Pee Vee's Market, a blessing occurred on August 4, 1970. Our long awaited, name-bearing baby boy was born. Edgar Francis Poree, III. Oh, what a moment that was and the sequence of events leading up to his birth. On the date of delivery, Gloria went to the hair salon to get her hair done in anticipation of her possible trip to the hospital during that night. While the hair dresser was styling her hair, Gloria's water bag burst. The hair dresser said, "Guich, you better get out of here and get to the hospital." Gloria said, "You better finish styling my hair." The hair stylist finished Gloria's hair, and Gloria drove home.

While Gloria was at the hair salon, I began getting ready by placing my shoes on my side of the bed and putting my clothing on the chair next to the bed in anticipation and preparation of Gloria's call, "It's Time!" Normally, I parked the car facing the house in the driveway. This time I backed the car up so when the time came to get to the hospital, there would be no delay in speeding off. When Gloria arrived at home, she didn't tell me her water bag had already burst; instead, she finished packing her clothing and toiletries and lay down next to me in bed.

I fell asleep, and all of a sudden Gloria whispered in my ear, "Edgar, it time!" I jumped up, put on my cloths, and as fate would have it, I couldn't find my shoes. I looked all over the bedroom, but I couldn't locate my shoes that I placed on my side of the bed earlier. Apparently, when I jumped up to put on my clothes, I must have accidentally kicked my shoes under the bed. Gloria said, "Edgar, your shoes are right next to your feet." I looked down and amazingly both shoes were looking at me. With shoes on and Gloria at my side, we got into the car, and off to the hospital we went. At 8:40 p.m. a handsome seven pound fifteen ounce baby boy was born. When the doctor came to advise me that I had a son, I let out a scream of joy so loud the hospital must have been placed on an emergency alert. At last, the Poree name would be carried on. I called Mother and Mrs. Guichard, Gloria's Mother, advising them they had a handsome grandson.

CHAPTER X

CAREER LADDER TO CORPORATE AMERICA

Associate Director

Another wonderful happening occurred after the disastrous meat market business venture. A career changing opportunity occurred in September of 1970. Citizen groups from business, higher education, industry, and local government from Orleans, Jefferson, and St. Bernard parishes convened meetings to discuss initiatives that could foster greater communication, cooperation, and sharing resources among the parishes. This group coupled with the area's Chamber of Commerce formed a Goals Foundation Committee to develop plans and processes to bring about a regional cooperative endeavor for the area. The Foundation selected the Theme "Goals to Grow" as it marquee marketing strategy. Dr. James Bobo, Dean of LSUNO Business School was selected as the Executive Director of the Goals to Grow. After an extensive selection process, Joe Walker, a Political Professor Strategist was appointed Associate Director of the program.

Many of my coworkers and some members of the Chamber encouraged me to submit my resume for consideration for the other Associate Director's vacancy. I discussed the opportunity with Gloria, and she said, "Edgar, you love new challenges, don't you?" I said, "Yes, my love." Shortly thereafter I submitted my application for the vacancy. I had a very lengthy and gratifying interview with Dr. Bobo. He told me he had received more than sixty applications for the Associate Director's position from across the spectrum of the community's leadership. He said, "Edgar, I received so many very favorable recommendations of your candidacy for the Associate Director's position from numerous community leaders. I'm prepared to offer you the position of Associate Director of Goals Foundation today. I paused for a moment then said, "Dr. Bobo, I accept your offer graciously." I called Gloria told her she was talking to the newly appointed Associate Director of Goals to Grow. She said, "Does that mean we are going to Dooky's for dinner?" "Yep, no half-chicken with two plates dinner either." We both laughed, and that evening, once again we had dinner at Dooky's. Leah Chase extended her congratulations to us while serving her famous bread pudding, complimentary of the house.

During my tenure as Associate Director of Goals Foundation, a think tank organization in the early seventies, I met a professor from a local university who had completed a study of the need and justification of a minority bank in New Orleans. His findings helped initiate an interest in the Black community to begin formulating and developing plans for creating a minority owned bank in New Orleans. After many years of hard work and planning the groundwork for a minority bank, I was extended an invitation to become a founding member of Republic National Bank, a minority owned bank in New Orleans. After consulting with my wife, I agreed to become a founding member of the newly organized banking institution.

Little did I realize; this new venture would be an awesome responsibility, time-consuming endeavor, and seemingly impossible challenge. There were numerous factions and powers that were not pleased to see a minority banking institution established in a rapidly growing minority population in the City. Those factions and powers were determined to minimize the financial impact and success of the nationally chartered minority bank. The factions even included the regional federal regulating administrator, who in his initial meeting with the minority board told us he was not excited about our bank being assigned to his jurisdiction. His closing remarks at that meeting, "Don't expect any favors from this office!" Our corresponding bank's principal senior banking officers, responsible for providing guidance and oversight during our initial operations, did not do so with much enthusiasm or diligence. Further complicating matters, the mandated downtown located initial lease, originally negotiated for twenty thousand dollars mushroomed to over a hundred thousand dollars annually.

While we were awaiting authorization and certification to become eligible to begin seeking investors for capitalization of Republic National Bank, we experienced numerous bureaucratic red tape impediments which delayed significantly our opening. In the meantime, the formation of a State-chartered bank, owned by one of the State's most powerful senators and a former roofing company/loan shark, was rapidly completing its application for a State-chartered banking. Because of the numerous delays in acquiring authorization to operate, Republic's opening was delayed several years after the State-chartered bank was operating.

In February of 1971, I was the featured speaker for New Orleans Public Library's Inaugural Black Opportunities Lecture Series. My opening statement got immediate attention of the Times Picayune reporter covering the event, evident by The Times Picayune's Thursday morning newspaper headlines "Housing-Employment Bias Cycles Said to Injure City." Unfairness in the Black housing market and unfairness in Black employment opportunities are linked in a cycle that keeps New Orleans from realizing the full potential of its citizens" Twenty four percent of the housing in New Orleans was substandard, and Blacks occupied 90% of the dilapidated housing. The real estate man was the chief culprit in perpetuating this condition and preys upon the emotions of Whites instilling a fear for their neighborhood with the entrance of a Black family. This undermining, fear-mongering scheme frightened White neighbors so convincingly that it resulted in a massive exodus of Whites from the inner City, taking with them the very foundation of the City's middle income economics.

Even though Whites left City in masses, they continued working in the City, leaving the job market unchanged for Blacks. This unfairness in employment was the root of unfairness in the housing market because it takes capital to make home improvements. Unfortunately, Blacks were denied access to middle and higher income jobs essential for earning capital. In the Black employment market, Orleans Parish School Board was the largest single employer that provided the greatest amount of middle income jobs for Blacks. Unfortunately, only three Blacks in the entire school system were in positions of authority. This disproportionate lack of Blacks in leadership positions in the School District had an adverse impact on Black youth, forcing many of them to seek less desirable "heroes" to emulate. This was a major factor in the rapidly increasing school dropout rate and subsequent increase in crime.

Although, the Federal government offered employment opportunities to Blacks in a notable amount; the majority of those non-White jobs were in the Post Office with very few Blacks working for the government in the higher salary brackets. The conditions were even worse within city government with the Civil Service System acting like the unscrupulous real estate "culprit" serving as a mechanism for protecting incompetence and nepotism. That system was in need of revamping to include ongoing job evaluation and employee's evaluation, making certain that both progress with changing conditions and skill sets.

Louisiana State government was one of the most medieval agencies in the New Orleans area in regards to hiring Blacks, especially in supervisory categories. As bad as Louisiana State government was, it wasn't nearly as bleak as the picture in the private sector. Perhaps that was a major reason why the City couldn't develop a strong Black middle class, essential to and critical for a robust economy. If New Orleans was to prosper and become a leading community to invest in the future, Blacks must be allowed to compete fairly for jobs. Banks and labor unions must afford Blacks a fair share of employment opportunities so that there can be a significant flow of Blacks not only found in entry level positions but also in middle and higher income positions, if human resources are to be used to their fullest in the community.

Black youth must accept the challenges and responsibilities even in entry level jobs. They must develop a competitive spirit in which they can use the entry level job to prove their ability to handle the job successfully, competently, productively, and efficiently. If given an opportunity to prove their worth in handling job responsibilities with great resolve, Black youth will demonstrate their competence in moving into jobs at a higher level of employment. Before that can become a reality, the City's educational, housing, and economic bias must cease and be replaced with a dynamic and innovative deployment of the City's greatest assets, its diverse citizens.

On Thursday evening February 4, 1971, I received a long distance call from the State's Personnel Director, regarding my remarks of State government's being the most medieval agency in the City, according to Times Picayune newspaper article. The most memorable comment that the Personnel Director made was that even though we had differences of opinions as to the State's lack of supervisory opportunities for Blacks, the mere fact we were talking on the telephone was surely a sign of progress! My response to the State's Personnel Director, "Does it mean on Friday,

February 5, 1971, that a new Personnel Policy will be implemented that will significantly improve opportunities for Blacks in supervisory and management positions in State government!" His response, "Mr. Poree, it was nice talking to you." The Times-Picayune article written by Mary Lou Atkinson regarding my address of how housing and employment bias prevented New Orleans from realizing the full potential of its citizens was accurate, and it generated tremendous interest even up river in Baton Rouge at the State Capitol.

Graduation Cancellation

In May of 1971, I was the Commencement Speaker for John McDonogh Senior High School. This was the first graduating class for one of the City's first integrated senior high school graduations. At the time of the scheduled graduation, there was some apparent racial unrest and antagonists among some of faculty members who were not satisfied with the extent of their participation in the planning of the commencement exercise. It had been rumored a faculty member had encouraged students to engage in a "Black Power" demonstration during the graduation ceremony. When members of the school board were made aware of the potential protest, several members considered canceling the scheduled graduation ceremony, simply issuing diplomas to graduates on the last official day of the school year.

Mr. Abraham, Principal of McDonogh, pleaded with the school board not to cancel the graduation ceremony. He told them how important the 1971 John McDonogh Graduation Exercise was for the parents, faculty, graduates, and students who overcame tremendous odds and challenges facing John Mac's integrated student environment. Dr. Edward McKnight, physician and the most honorable and highly respected school board member who had been very instrumental and supportive of Mr. Abraham in creating a wholesome environment at John Mac, enabling students to focus on their academic achievement rather than their differences and bias, help prevent the cancellation of the graduation ceremony. Dr. McKnight, because of his impeccable integrity and ardent dedication as a champion of public education, was able to convince the other members of the school board to allow the graduation exercise to take place as scheduled with some additional security assigned. Dr. McKnight's intervention did indeed save the 1971 John McDonogh High School Graduation.

I visited John Mac the week of graduation, so as to get an appreciation of the apparent racial unrest and so that I could possibly mitigate any potential disruptions that might adversely impact the graduating seniors' historic event. I discovered the valedictorian of the class, upon completion of her address was going to take off her cap and gown, raise her right arm, giving a "Black Power" sign, and denounce White people. This student had been encouraged by a faculty member to initiate the protest demonstration during the graduation ceremony.

The night of the graduation, when the valedictorian completed her speech, she took off her cap and gown, raised her arm giving the "Black Power" sign, and denounced Whites. Many band members and non-graduating students rose to their feet giving "Black Power" sign and applauding the valedictorian's antics. The atmosphere in the Municipal Auditorium was extremely tense, and many parents and relatives of the graduates were extremely upset. One of the school board members wanted to suspend the graduating exercise, and Mr. Abrahams pleaded, "Please don't stop the ceremony, our Commencement Speaker will restore order." Dr. McKnight concurred and convinced the other board member to allow the ceremony to continue.

After being introduced by Mr. Abraham, I walked up to the podium, and said, "Tonight, young lady, you told us just how you feel in your own special way. Many of your friends stood up, cheered, shouted their approval, and applauded your Declaration of Independence, your "Black Power" pact. Tonight you might be seen as a heroine for the words you had to say, but tomorrow when you wake, young lady, will those words make your life's dreams come true in a very special way? In other words, young lady, ask yourself this question. Will my Black Power speech and demonstration tonight be my big payback tomorrow when I wake up in the morning? Will tomorrow be my big payback? Wake up, young Lady, wake up! That's the really big question that you must be able to answer. Will Tomorrow Be Your Big Payback?"

All of a sudden a silence and calm overcame the shouting and disruptive behavior that threatened cancellation of the graduating ceremony. Band members and many of their classmates and friends sat in their seats and the once hostile environment became tranquil, attentive, and focused on the accomplishments and achievements of the honorees, the graduates. The 1971 Graduation Ceremony of John McDonogh Senior High School was a tremendous event, and the honorees, their parents, guardians, relatives, friends, faculty staff, and School Board members all were extremely complimentary of the tone and the outcome of the first integrated graduating exercise.

In addition to participating in McDonogh's most eventful experience, I had the pleasure of participating as a featured speaker/lecturer for LSUNO's Urban Studies Graduate Class, Judah P. Benjamin School, Velena S. Jones School, and Eleanor McMain Junior High School, Carver Community School, Haven United Methodist Church, and Lawless Junior High School. Additionally I was the featured speaker at Landry Senior High, Warren Easton Senior High School, American Business Women's Association Audubon Chapter, and The Future Leaders of America Six Parishes Conference.

After successfully conducting community task force summits and developing the Foundation's Framework for the Future events, funding for the implementation phase of the Foundation became very difficult. The Foundation sought many creative initiatives in an effort to fund its implementation phase of the program. Mr. Murray Fincher, President of the Foundation's Board and Vice President of the Telephone Company' statewide operations, encouraged other local corporations to help underwrite essential expenses of the implementation phase of the Foundation.

Expenses such as communications, utilities, reproduction, and salaries were under consideration. Fortunately, during time of this dilemma, the Telephone Company had a Staff Manager's vacancy in the New Orleans area. The Vice President, during a conversation with me, advised me that the company was looking for a good candidate to fill a staff manager's position in the New Orleans area. He said, "Edgar, I am confident you have the skills and qualifications to become an outstanding manager, and I encourage you seriously to consider this career opportunity." Gloria and I were already scheduled to leave for New York the very next day to celebrate our twelfth wedding anniversary. I asked Mr. Fincher if I could have a few days to discuss his offer with Gloria, and he said, "Yes!"

While in New York, Gloria and I had an opportunity to talk about the manager's position. At that time, my salary at the Foundation was more than the staff manager's yearly salary. Unfortunately, if the Foundation did not generate additional operating funds, my salary would become non-existent. Gloria said, "I know you like what you're doing, and the job has been very gratifying; however, you'll have an opportunity to demonstrate your worth which will mean more money in the future. Take the job, Edgar." I called Mr. Fincher and told him I accepted his offer and he said, "Edgar, you won't regret this decision."

Loan Executive

When I returned from New York, I went to the corporation to fill out the documentations required as a new employee. After completing all of the paper work, the Vice President introduced me to several of his executive staff members, and he had lunch brought to his office for me. I asked him when was I scheduled to report to work and how would I be able to complete the Foundation's Implementation Phase assignment. The Vice President told me I would continue working on my assignment as a Loaned Executive of the Company for the Foundation for the next eleven months until the project was completed. Once the project was completed, my staff-manager's tenure at the corporation would begin. I officially became an employee of the Telephone Company on September 1, 1971.

As the Loaned Executive of the Company, the Foundation was freed of paying my salary during my eleven month assignment. I got a call from the department where I had been appointed every two weeks telling me my check was in the office. I always told them to mail my check. After working for ten months, I got a call from the General Manager of the Company inviting me to lunch with some of the company's senior executives. This would be my very first opportunity to meet with some of the senior leadership of my department. Of course, I accepted the invitation and expressed my eagerness to begin my assignment at the Company.

Meeting Company Executives

The Goals Foundation office was only three blocks from the Telephone Company on Poydras Street, across from LePavillon Hotel where we were scheduled to have lunch. Lunch was scheduled for noon so I left my office at 11:30 a.m. to make sure I would be on time for my first official meeting with company executives. When I arrived at the phone company's Poydras Street entrance, there were six very distinguished looking southern gentlemen, waiting to greet me. "Good afternoon, Edgar Poree, welcome aboard," said the executives. We've heard so much about you, and we are looking forward to having you on our team. I shook hands with each executive and thanked them individually for inviting me to lunch.

As we began walking toward the hotel, something very strange occurred as we were passing a parking lot. One of the executives said, "Edgar, I understand you drive an extremely expensive luxury car." I thought that was a rather unusual statement, particularly since this was my first meeting with them. I did not respond initially, attempting to focus my excitement of beginning my new career. Another one of the executives pointed to several automobiles parked next to one another in the parking lot saying, "These are our vehicles, they are over six years old, and you can see they are not considered luxury cars." Still another executive said, "We understand you drive the top of the line luxury model." At that point, I said "I'm glad you knew what kind of car I had before joining the company, and perhaps you won't be able to accuse me of spending all of my phone company paychecks on expensive automobiles." I must admit that my response didn't garner any favorable impressions from those six southern gentlemen.

During lunch, I was questioned extensively about my background, my work experiences, and how I met the company's vice president. After giving them rather extensive details of my work experience, my educational background, and my community service, the executives seemed to be somewhat relieved. I arrived at this conclusion from some of the comments of the executives, noticeably, "I see why the Vice President spoke so very highly of you." The luncheon was very cordial and when we parted company, I'm sure the real impression among the executives might not have been as complimentary as expressed during our luncheon.

My First Company Boss

As fate would have it, one of the six executives that I attended the luncheon became my first boss. I'm sure he didn't relish the fact that of all of the departments in the company, he would be the one who had the distinction of having the first Black middle manager in his group, especially since he had no say-so in the hiring or the assignment. To help you understand the dilemma I faced, let's look at our diverse backgrounds. My boss was the President of the Audubon Golf Association, which did not allow Blacks or other minority members, nor use of the Audubon Golf Course. The car he drove was seven years old, and he was the southern gentleman executive who first mentioned I drove an expensive luxury car during the initial luncheon. His office was responsible for processing my payroll check every two weeks for eleven months without ever seeing me during that period. Each time my checks were issued, his office called me to pick my check up, and my response was always, "Put it in the mail."

Now that I had finally reported to his office for work after being on his payroll for eleven months, it was very obvious I was not much of a favorite team member. Fortunately, the office had some very young employees that extended a very warm welcome, and they made my initial days very pleasant ones. During my first few weeks, I underwent a series of intelligence and skills assessment tests at the company's headquarters on Prytania. Street. One evening after completing several intelligence tests, one of the instructors said, "You must have taken a lot of tests and mastered the art of test taking." I asked, "Why?" The instructor replied, "You had pretty impressive test scores. I said, "Perhaps it's due to my intelligence instead of test taking skills." The instructor said, "Oh, no I didn't mean to imply your test scores were simply due to your test taking skills, I was impressed with the consistency of your test performance."

Needless to say my boss did very little in providing an adequate orientation and insight in the operation of the department. He simply introduced me to the supervisory team of the department and briefly discussed some of the office performance standards by which I would be measured to determine whether the office was meeting department performance objectives. My assignment was to make sure the five offices for which I was responsible met all of the performance standards. I did not get much assistance from other supervisory personnel, especially when I attended department and inter-departmental meetings. Most of the discussions during those meetings were full of telephone acronyms that were foreign and certainly unfamiliar to me. I realized I would have to quick-start my very own development plan if I were to become successful in meeting the performance standards.

An Invaluable Resource

Recognizing that I would not get very much assistance from my boss, I discovered an invaluable knowledgeable resource in the district office. Margaret, the district clerk and a thirty-year employee who had worked extensively in every phase of operator services as well as numerous assignments in the plant department, was the person who actually handled most of the district's daily coordination and record keeping of our department's performance objectives. She was really an operation's staff expert. My boss' daily routine did not include being in the office very much, apparently visiting the offices located across the city or conducting meetings on the golf course.

Margaret, in my opinion, rarely got credit or recognition for her efficient coordination of the district office from my boss. In contrast, the young attractive supervisors in the district were frequently praised and recognized for far less performance by the district manager. When he would return to the office from his daily visits, he usually gave Margaret work to complete that required staying in the office after normal work hours. I saw this as an opportunity to befriend Margaret. Since she had the knowledge and tremendous work experience I needed to learn the business and I had administrative and time management experiences, these could enable both of us to achieve mutual benefits.

Whenever Margaret had to stay after normal work hour to complete assignments given to her by my boss, I would remain in the office reviewing performance measured items and reviewing personnel manuals to familiarize myself with the district's operation. I would always strike up a conversation with Margaret during our stay in an effort to develop a closer working relationship. During our conversations, I would ask Margaret what assignments she was working on so as to better acquaint myself with the various operational recordkeeping and performance requirements of our department. When Margaret would explain what she was doing, I would always ask, "Have you ever tried identifying the most important and pressing issues that had to be completed first in your assignment?"

If Margaret's answer were no, I would look over her assignment then ask her to select the three most important items she thought had to be completed first. After she identified the three, I asked her to rank them as the one that was the most important, the second most important, and the third most important. Then I suggested that she complete the items in the order she ranked them, and she did. By prioritizing the most important issues and resolving them first, Margaret's afterhours work assignments began to take far less time to complete, and she began to develop a relationship of trust with me as we shared experiences during those after-hour late assignments.

Those after-hour sessions with Margaret provided an invaluable orientation of the inner-workings of the operator's services department. Additionally, she would interpret and explain the specific identifications of and the relationships of the numerous telephone acronyms that were discussed at departmental meetings. Margaret was my subject-matter expert in quick-starting and enhancing my knowledge of the business. She was my developmental mentor who enabled me to manage more effectively my departmental responsibilities. The after-hours sessions were beneficial to both Margaret and me. She taught me the business operations, and I assisted her in more effectively completing after-work assignments enabling her to spend more leisure at doing those things that made her happy.

Black Dialect Class

During my initial tenure with the company, I attended a class designed to help better familiarize company employees with Black dialect and colloquialism. This was the most obnoxious and ridiculous class that I had ever encountered at the company. The class was taught by a twenty eight year old Tupelo, Mississippi, native supervisor, who apparently hadn't experienced living near or with any Black community. His assignment was to help supervisory employees to understand better Black dialect and colloquialism. When I walked into the classroom where the training was held, the young training supervisor's facial expression seemed to convey a sense of embarrassment, questioning what was I doing here. None the less, he had a mission to accomplish during that class, and I did not want to convey my personal frustration for attending such an obscurity.

Initially, I sat quietly through the instructor's initial introduction of the class. However, when he began to describe what he characterized as typical Black colloquialism and Black dialect, I told him I had never heard those expressions in my entire life, and I was more than thirty years old. The young instructor appeared quite embarrassed, and he indicated those expressions had been found in some books used in developing the course. My response was, "Wendell, it would have been helpful to talk with some of the Black employees about some lingo and colloquialism they might have used or heard during their early childhood years, instead of solely depending on some books which were obviously based on hearsay rather than facts."

Most of the class attendees seemed uncomfortable during the presentation and relieved at the class' conclusion. After the class, Wendell asked me if I would convey my observations with personnel, and I agreed to do so. After several meetings and discussions with members of the personnel staff and subsequently meeting with the Personnel Director, the training class was suspended, pending further assessment of its merit.

With a new career, new responsibilities, and increased demands for speaking engagements, 1971 kept me plenty busy participating in community activities across the spectrum. I was the featured or keynote speaker for Parent Workshop, Carver Middle School; Career Day, McMain Junior High School; Honors Banquet, Helen Edwards School; Honors Banquet, Lawless Senior High School; Annual Achievement Day, Valena C. Jones Elementary School; Achievement Day, Judah P. Benjamin School; Presbyterian Institute of Industrial Relations Seminar, First Presbyterian Church; Student Day, Haven United Methodist Church; Urban Studies Graduate Class Seminar, LSUNO; Student Recognition Day, Bethany United Methodist Church; Men's Day, Trinity United Methodist Church; and, the Institute of Human Relations, Loyola University.

Military Type Administration

During my initial employment with the Telephone Company, a new General Manager, from Mississippi was appointed head of Operator Services' department. He was a former Colonel in the Army, and he immediately transformed our department into a military type operation. My boss could no longer spend a lot of time on the golf course or on Kiwanis activities as he did prior to Big Al's administration. The General Manager had "red" telephones installed in each District Manager's office in the department, and the District manager had to answer the red telephone within three rings. If the District Manager did not answer the GM's red telephone within the three rings, he better have a very good reason for justifying his late response.

Prior to the appointment of the new general manager, the Chief Clerk of the department gave the previous day's office performance totals to the general manager's Chief Clerk on the telephone. When the red telephone rang at 8:30 a.m., the District Manager would personally give the previous day's office performance to the General Manager over the telephone. The only exception to that morning routine report would be either hospitalization or death of the District Manager. The General Manager ran a very tight military-type operation. He set the rules, he made the rules, and he expected everyone to abide by his rules.

Here's an example of just how the General Manager exercised his authority. Company policy allowed supervisory personnel to use their personal cars, especially when motor pool cars were not available. Since my assignment required frequent visits to offices outside my downtown office location, I frequently used my personal car. I frequently park my car down stairs from the office on the corner of Crondelet and Poydras Streets. Parking was not permitted after 4:30 p.m. in the evening during the five day work week. One evening after 4:30 p.m., the General Manager's car was parked immediately behind my car in the "No Parking after 4:30 p.m. Zone."

When the General Manager came down to his car after meeting with the District Manager, he found a traffic ticket on his windshield. He noticed that there was not any traffic ticket on my windshield so he came back up to the District office and asked me if I had removed a traffic ticket from my car. I said, "No Sir." He left hastily. The next morning when the red telephone rang, apparently the district's office normal previous day's performance reporting was not the topic, instead the General Manager advised the District Manager that supervisory personnel's use of personal vehicles on official company business must be authorized in writing by the General Manager in all cases, no exceptions. I believe the General Manager became quite upset and outraged when he discovered his car was ticketed and my car was not when both cars were in the No Parking Zone.

First Controversial Decision

I was responsible for five operator services offices in the metropolitan area including the company's twenty-four hour operator offices in the main downtown building. This office was rather unique because it had female and male operators. Most of the five offices had mostly female employees.

The twenty-four hour office was rather unique because it had male and female operators. Most of the male operators were recently hired veterans. I received a call early one morning at 2:00 a.m. from a supervisor advising me a major conflict occurred between two employees that required some restraining to curtail it. I told the supervisor I would be there within a half hour.

When I arrived at the office, I noticed an employee seated in the supervisor's office. I asked the supervisor who was involved in the conflict? She identified the employee sitting in her office as one of the participants, and she said she sent the other employee home. I asked the supervisor, "Why didn't she send both employees home." She told me the employee in her office was so upset she thought it would allow her an opportunity to calm down. I told the supervisor send the employee in the office home. The employee who was sent home initially by the group manager was Black, and the employee who was allowed to remain on the job was White.

During my investigation, after talking with employees on duty at the time of the incident, it appeared the conflict had racial implications, which could have escalated into a major altercation. Because of the potential negative impact upon working relationships and morale in the office, I decided to research personnel cases that occurred, which had been sanctioned and upheld as appropriate discipline for behavior detrimental to the company's polices governing conduct in the workplace. After spending several hours reviewing cases arbitrated, I decided to suspend both employees for five days.

Little did I realize how this decision would create such furor and outrage among the management and the union? The husband of the White female employee I suspended was my District Manager's personal friend and golf partner. Three of the senior executives I had lunch with expressed dissatisfaction with the five-day suspension and vowed to have the suspension decision overturned. The General Manager scheduled a hearing for the purpose of determining whether the suspensions were justified. I was in a very precarious position, having been galvanized by superiors' opposition to my first managerial decision as a newly appointed manager.

During the hearing, my boss and three of the luncheon executives expressed their dissatisfaction with my five-day suspension. One of them said, "In my twenty-eight years with the company, I never heard of any five-day suspension, even for employees who actual had physical fights." My boss said the employee that the supervisor did not send home was a good employee that didn't deserve such an excessive discipline. What he didn't say was that the employee's husband was an Audubon Golf Association member and his golf partner. After being criticized and admonished by the senior managers including my boss, the General Manager said, "Edgar, let's hear what you have to say about the issue and upon what basis you arrived at your decision."

I opened my briefcase and removed three documents obtained from personnel's arbitrated suspension cases having similar circumstances of the conflict, as well as the accepted suspension decision reached. After articulating the findings of my research to justify the 5-day suspension of the employees, I gave the documents to the General Manager for his review. When the General Manager read the three arbitrated briefs he said, "Edgar, it looks like you have been doing some really serious research in arriving at your decision." The General Manager then asked the senior executives if they had any documented evidence to challenge or refute the arbitrated suspension cases that Edgar provided, and they acknowledged they did not. The General Manager said, "Based upon the arbitrated cases Edgar presented and his explanation of the potential adverse work relations consequences, he has proved his case; the 5-day suspension is sustained." The senior executives appeared stunned and obviously disappointed in the decision. When word of the General Manager's decision reached the offices, it appeared I had hit a grand slam home run with employees. Unfortunately it did not enhance my relationship with my boss or the senior executives who vigorously opposed the five-day suspension.

Big Surprise

Shortly thereafter, I got a new boss, who was quite a fresh air of decency, fairness, and rather color blind. One morning when I reported to work, my new boss came over to my desk and told me he had a package for me in his office. I said, "A package for me, what kind of package is it?" I walked into his office anticipating seeing a box; instead, there was an envelope on his desk addressed to Edgar F. Poree, Jr. When I opened the envelop, to my surprise it was a check for nearly two thousand dollars as a result of a "Class Action Discrimination Suit" against the Company of the hiring of Blacks. With a smile on his face my boss said, "Mr. Poree,

I never got any such check for working for the company for over thirty years, congratulations." I called Gloria to tell her we were going to Dooky Chase for a "non-half-chicken-two-plates dinner. Gloria laughed and said, "Edgar, what have you done this time?"

One of the ongoing developmental projects included the assessment of company employees as candidates for consideration for supervisory and management positions. Management employees served on a Personnel Assessment Team that critiqued and assessed potential supervisory candidates so as to maintain a dynamic pool of candidates ready to fill supervisory and management positions promptly when vacancies occurred. Because of my background having served as Personnel Director for the Anti-Poverty Agency and my work in supervising five operator services offices in the District, I was selected to serve on the Company's Personnel Assessment Team. We were instrumental in identifying numerous craft employees who became outstanding supervisory and managerial personnel in the company.

Chamber of Commerce Prevents Publishing Article

The New Orleans Magazine commissioned me to write a position paper on the state of New Orleans from a Black perspective for its publication. The magazine was an economic development initiative promoting New Orleans as a hub for commerce and tourist attractions. I agreed to provide a very candid article as seen from a Black perspective of the City's pros and cons. The magazine's editor assured me that candor was exactly what they were looking for and he was awaiting with great anticipation the article. After completing the article, entitled *"The State of Black New Orleans,"* I presented it to the New Orleans Magazine's Editor, and he expressed extreme adulations and congratulations upon reading the article. He told me the article would be published in the next issue.

When the next issue of the New Orleans Magazine came out, I went to the newspaper stand downtown to get my copy. When I looked through the magazine for my *"The State of Black New Orleans"* article, it was nowhere to be found in the publication. I was shocked and extremely disappointed because I was eager to see my work in print. I called the magazine's editor to find out what happened, and he told me that some members of the Chamber were rather uncomfortable about the implication of the article, particularly the candor of the article. The magazine paid me twice as much as the original commission promised. The editor apologized for not publishing the article, citing the financial support of the Chamber for the publication.

Apparently during those initial years of my employment with the company, I was not aware that our department had apparently been providing semi-annual updates of the diversity profile (makeup) of our operation to Headquarters Personnel Office. Since employee ethnic identity was described numerically in the employees' personnel files, rather than specifically by race, compiling a department diversity head count profile was rather cumbersome. Our department was one of the largest operations in the company with more than eight hundred operator employees working in three offices in downtown New Orleans and two offices in Jefferson Parish.

Late one Friday evening, our district office got a call from headquarters requesting that we provide them with a diversity head count profile of the district by Monday. This would require working unanticipated overtime to compile the data plus the weekend workforce was drastically reduced from the five-day work week, so compiling the data would be a great challenge. The District Clerk looked at me and asked, "Mr. Poree, how are we going to get this report compiled when it requires labor intensive work?" I told Margaret that we were going to get the diversity profile together on time and without much overtime. I called Gloria and told her that I was going to be late, so don't wait for me for dinner.

Margaret asked, "How are we going to get this done?" I told Margaret that we were going to depend on my home beverage consignment delivery service and office supplies delivery service experiences to help identify the racial make-up of our department. Margaret looked at me with an expression that conveyed what I had up his sleeves this time. I told Margaret I use to deliver home beverages to more than seventy five different residencies all over the city and in Jefferson Parish. During the summer time, I delivered office supplies to more than a hundred and fifty businesses per day to locations in Orleans, St. Bernard, Jefferson, and Plaquemines Parishes, so I knew where many of the different racial natives lived in those four parishes. Let's go through our office files and look at the home addresses of our employees. I'm going to identify most of them by race.

Margaret said, "Edgar, we have to compare the employee's numeric code with the race classification sheet in order to identify the employees' ethnic classification. I said, "Margaret, trust me, you and the two office clerks just give me the address of each employee, and I'll tell you to which racial group she belongs." Margaret shook her head, and she and the other two office clerks who agreed to work overtime began calling names and addresses of the employees as I identified their race. Margaret and the two clerks would stroke one short line under the appropriate race category, as I identified them. For example, Margaret identified the employee's residential address as 1025 Henry Clay Avenue, I said, "White." The district clerk would stroke a short line under the "White" category column. The next addressed identified was 3501 Republic Street, and I said, "Black." The Black category column was stroked with one short line.

After some three and a half hours, we finished the process and compiled the diversity profile of the office. Margaret wanted to make sure our report we had compiled using my method was consistent with the numerical classification listed in the employees' personnel files. Since the District Manager was on vacation, I authorized overtime for Margaret and the two clerks to work on Saturday to verify our totals. The three of them reviewed all employee files and verified and compared Friday's preliminary totals with the actual employee numerical ethnic classification found in the individual personnel records. Margaret and the two clerks were amazed that our Friday evening street address process was more than 85% accurate compared to the actual numerical classification designation in the employees files. The report was finished in half the time of previous updates, and the amount of overtime was slashed dramatically. Headquarters got its report on time on Monday.

Honorable Intentions, Disastrous Outcomes

When an employee sought a transfer to another department or one similar to hers in a different geographic location, she had to file an official request with her existing department and with the company's personnel office. Many factors were taken into consideration for every transfer request. Factors such as existing vacancies in desired departments, skill-set expertise requirements, and whether the department can afford releasing a person with critical skill sets were considered. In keeping with the company's commitment of providing employment opportunities for a more diverse workforce, an additional factor that could impact one's transfer request was whether or not the department or location had a certain employee deficiency classification in its workforce.

One of my subordinate supervisors, a native of a small town north of Birmingham, Alabama, requested a lateral transfer to a vacancy supervisor's job in Birmingham. The supervisor had been a highly rated performer year after year. Since she was requesting a lateral job in her home town, one would assume her transfer would be easy. Unfortunately, the supervisor married a person of Latin decent; therefore, she had a Spanish surname which placed her in a different category than that of being a north Alabama native. The supervisor submitted her request for the transfer when a vacancy in the same job in Alabama was posted after her divorce. Although she had the critical skill-sets for the position in Alabama and had consistently been rated a high performer, unfortunately, the location where the vacancy occurred did not have an opening for a Spanish surname employee. Although she was divorced from her, her married name was the one of record; therefore, she was ineligible for the transfer because the vacancy did not call for a Spanish surname employee. This was a perfect example of how honorable intentions, unfortunately, can have disastrous consequences, and outcomes such as my subordinate supervisor experienced

Confrontation with Mayor

The Seventies brought a brand new type of political administration to City of New Orleans. For the very first time Black citizens played a major role in the election of a young White, moderate Democratic lawyer. Black political organizations actively participated in concert with the Moon's political organization, canvassing, holding neighborhood meetings, mailing ballots, and working the streets and polls on Election Day. Many of the Blacks were first-time participants in political campaigning, and their efforts were extremely instrumental in the young lawyer becoming the Mayor of the City of New Orleans.

When the newly elected Mayor began appointing members of his administration team, he appointed a number of Blacks in positions previously held exclusively by White males. The Mayor even selected two Blacks as Department Heads in his Administration. During an interview with the Times-Picayune, the State's largest newspaper, the

Mayor was asked whether he planned to appoint any additional Blacks as Department Heads in his administration. The Mayor indicated he had reviewed numerous résumés of Blacks, and he was satisfied he had appointed all of the qualified Blacks as Department Head. When I read the Mayor's statement, I was rather bewildered because I knew numerous highly qualified Blacks who would have been excellent candidates for department heads. Apparently the Mayor did not have any of the résumés of those highly qualified Blacks.

My first inclination was to send a letter of exception to the newly elected Mayor; however, Loyola University's Institute of Politics' (IOP) Quarterly Meeting had as its special quest the new Mayor of the City of New Orleans. This afforded me an opportunity to question the Mayor about having appointed all of the qualified Blacks as Department Heads. At the IOP Meeting, after the Mayor completed his presentation of how he won the election and during the questions and answers session, I asked the Mayor if the newspaper misquoted his statement regarding having already hired all of the qualified Blacks as department heads in his administration. The Mayor said, "The newspaper was accurate."

At that point I responded, "Mr. Mayor, the problem I have with your statement is that it gave the impression there were only two Blacks in the City of New Orleans who had qualifications for department head positions in your administration." The IOP's Director sarcastically said, "Mr. Mayor, Edgar wanted one of those department head jobs." I responded, "I'm not interested in a politically appointed job." If the Mayor had stated he appointed two qualified Blacks who had been instrumental in his successful mayoral campaign, this would not be an issue at all. However, I knew many highly qualified Blacks in the City who did not submit their résumés for consideration because they felt the appointments would be based upon patronage not qualifications. At that point, the IOP Director called a recess for refreshment, since it appeared the Mayor had become rather perturbed. For some time I was not one of the Mayor's favorite citizens

Minority Bank?

During the time Republic National Bank was awaiting certification for operation in the City, a State-chartered bank was already opened and targeting Blacks in New Orleans. The State bank was owned by one of the

State's most powerful senators and a former roofing company owner, who was also the Black public schools personnel loan shark. The principal owners were extremely well connected politically as well as with "special-interest groups" in the City and State. Their connection with the State Banking Commission and state and local political operatives afforded immediate access to getting business locally and from the State.

When the State-chartered bank opened in Mid-City, it was promoted as a minority bank by its owners, yet there was little known evidence of minority investors at the time of its inaugural operations. It was speculated and rumored the bank's executive officer was selected a few days before the bank's opening. Media and other public relations efforts were designed to give the impression that the State-chartered bank was owned by these two well positioned individuals and that it was a minority institution.

A defining moment for the State-chartered bank to seize an opportunity to promote its minority affiliations came after the assignation of Dr. Martin Luther King, Jr. in Memphis. The bank sponsored a televised "Tribute to the late Dr. Martin Luther King, Jr." The "Tribute" was televised on the City's top television affiliate with a viewing audience in the television studio during the telecast. The viewing audience in the studio consisted of some of New Orleans' most prominent minority citizens. Each time a commercial break occurred during the telecast, a live shot of the studio audience was shown as the *voiceover commercial* said, "This Tribute to Dr. Martin Luther King, Jr. is brought to you by the Board of Bank."

What an effective public relations coup. After seeing those prominent Blacks in the studio during the telecast, many Blacks in New Orleans apparently thought the bank that sponsored the Tribute to Dr. Martin Luther King, Jr. was a minority bank. Unfortunately and cleverly not mentioned in the voice-over commercial, the prominent Blacks seen in the television studio were members of an advisory group of the bank not investors or owners of the sponsoring bank. Perception can be a very powerful influence and after seeing all of those prominent Blacks in the studio and hearing that slick promotional voiceover commercials, many Black citizens accepted the notion that this bank was a minority one.

The State-chartered bank did not become a minority bank until many years later when the Federal government began an initiative, promoting minority vendors in the maritime industry. A Black Catholic Priest in Lafayette, Louisiana, was given a multi-million dollars grant to initiate and develop a minority vendors program for the maritime industry in

Louisiana. The Priest selected the State-chartered bank as its depository of the multimillion dollars operational funds grant. That deposit coupled with the total investments of the minority members on the board of directors of the State-chartered bank enabled that institution to reach the qualifying 51% minority ownership requirements to qualify for being certified to receive the 10% of Federal Funds allocated to municipalities.

After a long and exhaustive process and involvement in getting authorization and certification to begin banking operations, Republic National Bank was finally opened at its downtown Barron Street location. I continued being involved in community activities. I was the commencement speaker for John McDonogh High School, keynote speaker for LSU-New Orleans' Urban Studies Graduate Class, McMain's Career Day, Carver Middle School's Parent Workshop, Edwards School's Honors Day, Jones School's Achievement Day, Benjamin School's Achievement Day, Haven Memorial Church's Student Day, Trinity Church's Men's Day, Bethany Methodist Church's Student Recognition Day, Presbyterian Institute of Industrial Relations' Seminar, and New Orleans Public Library's Kaleidoscope Forum.

Public Relations Coup or Bust

Republic National Bank, a certified minority National Bank, was capitalized at a million dollars. The maximum loan the bank could make would be equal to 10 % of the existing capital. This requirement, coupled with the minority bank's decision to take advantage of television and front-page newspaper headlines during its initial operations, resulted in a public relations dilemma that hindered the bank's image and its ability to attract potential major business customers that were essential for the viability and growth.

An African-American Corporation, whose principal owners were major contributors and participants in the successful election of the State's governor, was awarded a no-bid multi-million dollar contract to service the State's largest sports arena. The newly established corporation needed a million dollar capitalization loan to start-up its operation; therefore, it sought funding from the established banks in the city. Because of the obvious political ramifications of the no-bid contract to a corporation with no known experience or expertise in maintaining such a tremendous facility, none of the area's established banks wanted to be perceived as being a part of this politically inspired no-bid contract.

After being turned down by the established banks in the area, the owners of the newly established corporation turned to the minority owned bank for a capitalization start-up loan. Since members of the leadership of the minority bank thought this would be a great public relations coup to fund this corporation. There was one major obstacle. At the time of the request, the minority bank's capital because of the banks "start-up" expense was $910,000, meaning the maximize loan that the bank could make was $91,000. Since the corporation sought a million dollar loan, it would require an additional $909,000 to satisfy the million dollar loan.

This is where ethics and integrity seem to place a blindfold on the eyes of the senior executives of the established banking institutions. Remember, none of the established banks in the area wanted to be seen as partners in this no-bid politically inspired deal. The key word in this outrage was *seen*. The State's no-bid contract, according to the some of the leading legal minds and contractual experts, indicated that even if the minority firm defaulted on the contract, the State was obligated to pay in "full" the balance of the capitalization loan. By law, only the lead bank's name was required to be divulged publically; therefore, any other participating banks supplementing the loan were not required to be mentioned. This loophole enabled the outraged established banks to hide behind cover in the politically inspired no-bid contract capitalization loan.

With that opening behind the scenes, one of New Orleans largest established banks provided the additional $909,000 dollars as the participating bank in the one million dollar capitalization loan for the politically inspired no-bid-contract. The evening news and daily newspaper's lead story was, "Minority National Bank makes Million Dollar Loan for No-Bid Contract Principals." Some of the minority bank's senior leadership thought that would give the minority bank instant great public relations. However and unfortunately, those headlines were a short-term bonus because it proved to be an emotional feeling public relations coup in some parts of the minority community; however, it was a nightmare in attracting clients and large business customers because of the association with this politically inspired no-bid contract. It was ironic that the participating bank for the million dollar loan did not receive any negative publicity or customer flight because it was done behind closed doors—no ethical or integrity violations, just good-ole-boy business.

Another Confrontation with Mayor

During the years of operations, under a Federal edit, cities receiving Federal grants were encouraged to invest ten percent of Federal Funds in minority banking institutions in the area. As a member of the board of Republic National Bank, I met with the Finance Director of the City to inquire when the city would begin depositing some of the mandated Federal Funds in our bank. The Finance Director advised me that the City had already invested Federal Funds in a minority bank. I told him that the Republic National bank was the only minority bank in the City, and I wanted to meet with the Mayor to provide the supportive documents substantiating our credentials as a minority bank. The Finance Director again advised me the City had already satisfied the Federal edit by depositing its share of Federal Funds in the City's other minority bank. The Director told me I had to get an appointment with the Mayor, since he had already fulfilled the City's responsibility for depositing funds in another minority bank.

After several weeks attempting to get an appointment, we finally got a meeting with him. I was accompanied by one of our bank's officer to discuss the Federal Depositing Program for minority banks. The Mayor listened and after a rather brief meeting, he told us he was confident and satisfied his Finance Director had met the Federal edit's depository program for minority banks; therefore, the matter was closed. "Mr. Mayor, I respectfully disagree with you because Republic National Bank was the only certified minority bank eligible and qualified for the Federal depository program at that time." The Mayor, however, once again told us the City had satisfied its obligations under the guidelines of the Federal depository program so the matter was closed. It was apparent the alleged minority bank with its political connections had usurped the process and prevented our banking institution from receiving mandated deposits.

We met with the top administrator for the Archdiocese of New Orleans to seek deposits for our bank, and the administrator told us they had already deposited in the other alleged minority bank. When I told the administrator that our bank was the only minority-owned bank in the City, he told me they were convinced the other bank was a minority bank because he knew one of the City's leading citizens who was affiliated with that bank. I told the administrator that the other bank was not owned by minorities and that the principal owners of the bank were two politically connected individuals who promoted the bank as a minority bank. Our appeal to the Archdiocese like that to the City proved to be without any success.

In spite of my difficulties with the Mayor and increased responsibilities of my management job, I continued to get numerous requests for speaking engagements from the metropolitan community. I received a telephone call from the Director of The Institute of Human Relations of Loyola University inviting me to participate as one of four featured contributing authors in a Symposium on Urban Values and Clergymen in America, a joint collaboration with the Department of Continuing Education of Notre Dame Seminary. I was indeed quite flattered with this very prodigious offer, especially when I was advised of the other three contributing participants, Dr. Daniel C. Thompson, nationally known sociologist and author of several highly acclaimed publications and books on race, Anthony "Toney" Gagliano, a leading urban planner, and Father Edward F. Heenan, S.J. and former President of University. That was quite an awesome association with which to be affiliated. Of course, I was thrilled to be a part of such a unique and highly respected group of Americans. Without any hesitation, I accepted the invitation.

I met with Father David Boileaux, Director of The Institute of Human Relations, to discuss the topic he wanted me to focus on. He said, "Your impressions and assessment of the state of our urban centers, our cities." Without any hesitation, I said, "The rapidly declining quality of life in our cities creates an opportunity to develop comparative analyses of the cities declining health to its ultimate demise to that of the human body's declining health to its eventual death." Father Boileaux told me that was exactly what he wanted as the premise for the position paper. "The Coroner's Report of the Deceased Urban Center" was the metaphor for my presentation. Orchestrating themes of sickness and disease, I conducted a dirge of death inflicting illnesses that contributed to the decline of the quality of life in urban America. However, I recommended possible corrective measures that could remediate and resurrect vitality and vigor into an ailing and lethargic dying city.

On Wednesday, June 21, 1972, I presented my "Coroner's Report of the Deceased Urban Center" position paper to a packed auditorium at St. Joseph's Hall of Notre Dame Seminary. When I completed my presentation, the audience gave me a standing ovation. My presentation along with Dr. Daniel C. Thompson's "The Role of the Church in Urban Affairs," Anthony Gagliano's "The Contemporary Urban Center," and Edward F. Heenan's "The New Religion of the Age of Aquarius," was published in the Symposium on Urban Values and Clergymen in American Publication found in Catholic Libraries. The editor of *The Louisiana Weekly* newspaper was so impressed with my "Coroner's Report of the Deceased Urban Center" presentation that he printed the entire presentation in two weekly newspapers.

In addition to this incredible opportunity of participating with some of the City's most respected leaders, I served as principal lecturer or keynote speaker for The Future Business Leaders of America Seminar, Louisiana Education Association Convention; Southern University in New Orleans; Institute of Human Relations, Leadership Forum, Loyola University; Boyinton United Methodist Church' Men's Day; Junior Chamber of Commerce Recognition Day; New Orleans Chapter, International Association of Business Communicators; St. Mary's Academy Commencement; Carver Community School's Awards Ceremony; Kappa Delta Pi Honor Society, Tulane University; Joseph S. Clark High School Honor's Day; and, the District Conference of Future Business Leaders of America.

Years of Discriminatory Salary Treatment

While the City was welcoming its newly elected Mayor, our department was getting its third District Manager in five years. My new boss was a native of a tiny town in Tennessee. He was an Air Force veteran, a two-time prisoner of war, and an active member of the Air Force Reserve. It was apparent he did not relinquish his good-old-boy hometown description of Negroes. When speaking about People of Color, Negroes, my new boss always referred to them as "Niggress."

I will never forget the morning after an NBC TV Nightly News Special, featuring Martha Collins, the owner of the Martha Collins' Academy where Negro children from the housing projects of Chicago were being taught great Shakespearean works. My boss came in my office so excited and asked, "Edgar, did you see that Niggress teacher in Chicago, teaching all those little Niggress children about Shakespeare last night on television?" I said, "Yes." My boss said how shocked he was seeing how well behaved those little Niggress children were when that Niggress teacher was quoting from some of the great works of Shakespeare. "I know that must have made you some proud, Edgar, to see that amazing story last night. I said, "The Martha Collin story was a great story for all Americans to be proud of."

Well, it was obvious, a boss still referring to Negro people as Niggress would, in my opinion, never accept the premises that the level of intelligence, ability, or competence of Negroes could be equal to that of Whites. My observation proved to be incredibly accurate over the years. As a second level staff manager, I was responsible for five offices in the Greater New Orleans metropolitan area, three offices in Downtown, and two offices in Jefferson. During five consecutive years, all five of the offices had the best overall service performance in the Company's five states jurisdiction. Since my performance was supposedly measured on the overall composite performance of all five offices, one would assume that my performance raise would be a significant one.

All of my direct-report subordinate office supervisors annually received the maximum allowable percentage pay raise for outstanding service performance each year. Their average raise was approximately 110% of their pay scale level. Unfortunately, during those same five years, my annual performance raises, averaged slightly more than 92% of the newly established Manager's Base Salary Classification. Although my salary scale was significantly greater than my subordinates, the tremendous disparity of their five-year performance raises and mine resulted in my salary being less than all five of my subordinates in the fifth year.

Fortunately, because of the numerous paid professional speaking and singing engagements that I had during that five-year period; I was able to offset much of the losses associated with the pay raise disparity. Consequently, I did not address the pay raise disparity issue with my boss during that time. However, because of the tremendous expansion of management responsibilities, opportunities for my professional engagements were significantly curtailed; therefore, I decided to address the compensation disparity with my boss. That was quite an adventure, to say the least. When I asked my boss for a meeting to discuss what I considered a disparity of compensation issue, he seems rather perplexed and shocked. He hesitated for a moment and then agreed to see me the next evening after working hours.

The next evening, after all district office personnel had left work, my boss called me to his office. He asked what I wanted to talk about because he didn't have any clue of compensation disparity. I told him during the past five years my five operating offices had the top performance among comparable offices in the company. He agreed. I also told him that during the last five years, my subordinates received maximum annual performance raises each year, while I only received a raise slightly higher than the newly established base of my management salary classification. As a result of these five years of disparities in annual raises, all of my subordinates' current salaries exceeded my new salary, in spite of the significant difference in my management salary scale compared with my subordinates.

My boss told me my subordinates had a direct impact upon the overall operating performance of their offices and that I had only an indirect impact on their overall performance outcome. I responded, "When any of my five operating offices were not meeting Company's benchmark performance standards, the first thing that you asked me was, what are you going to do to get the problem fixed and when will it is accomplished?" In my opinion, that's certainly much more than a mere indirect influence or indirect impact on results. My boss said, "When I look at your contributions to the team, I compare you with a typical middle manager of the Bell System. A typical middle manager in the Bell System wears his hair differently than yours." At the time I had a neat short well groomed bush, which was a popular style of young Blacks.

My boss continued comparing me with what he perceived as being a typical Bell System middle manager. "Edgar, you are unquestionably the best dressed staff manager in the District; however, a typical middle manager in the Bell System wears more conservative suits, polyester ties, blazers, slacks, and loafers." My wardrobe included designer suits with silk neckties, pastel shirts, and fashionable shoes. My boss continued his comparison, saying that "I was a tremendous speaker, evident by the numerous requests from across the community; however, my subordinates had difficulty understanding me because I used hundred dollar words in communicating with them." Finally, my boss told me that "unlike the typical middle managers in the Bell System, I appear a bit more defensive and involved in Niggress complaints and issues."

After concluding his comparisons, I told my boss in my opinion his assessment of my performance appeared to be more of an assessment of morays rather than measurements of achievements and accomplishments of mission and goals. I felt my influence and leadership in assisting my subordinates in meeting and exceeding company performance standards successfully and resolving and restoring unsatisfactory performance to levels of excellence should have warranted more favorable salary increases. My boss did not respond to my observations and the meeting concluded at that point.

Home Boys' Revolt

After my meeting with my boss, I knew I would have to adjust my personal strategic performance plan to make sure morays would no longer be the prevailing obstacle negatively impacting my evaluation and salary increases in the future. My personal strategic performance plan included getting my bush trimmed slightly more, purchasing some more conservative suits, polyester neckties, and traditional black and dark brown shoes, and modifying my hundred dollar words, converting them to fifty-cent words when communicating with subordinates. Finally, I would be more tactful and diplomatically balanced when dealing with sensitive issues and complaints of African-American employees.

When I told my home boys of my personal strategic performance plan, they were extremely disappointed and adamantly outraged because they thought I had sold out my ethnicity and masculinity to Whitey. I asked my home boys, to give my plan an opportunity to work, before labeling me a sellout to Whitey! I said, "What will my boss tell me next year when my five offices maintain the best performance?" "He will no longer be able to use the excuse that my hair, my dress, my communication, and my reactions in Niggress issues and complaints are unlike the typical Bell System middle managers." My boss will no longer be able to use morays as the defining criteria for assessment of my performance and salary treatment. My home boys agreed to postpone their sell-out opinion until the next appraisal period.

During the tenure of my Tennessee native boss, I experienced repeatedly the most discouraging and demeaning feeling every time that I submitted a written document to my boss. It didn't matter what the correspondence addressed; my boss always made changes to my correspondences? After numerous occasions, I asked him whether he found any grammatical or content errors or omissions in the correspondences, and he always responded, "No it's just a matter of style." This was extremely frustrating because I had always been a rather good writer.

I decided to bring some of my original correspondences that I had submitted to my boss to one of my Tulane University's A.B. Freeman Business Council meeting. I asked several of my council comrades to look at some of my correspondences that my boss changed to see if they could find any deficiencies warranting corrections or changes. They seemed rather amused while commenting: "Edgar, can't you recognize that this is obviously a person who made the changes simply because he has a superiority intelligence complex. It had nothing to do with any grammatical or content deficiencies." Their assessment somehow mirrored my impression of my boss's actions.

I decided to become more proactive in resolving and vindicating my impression. When I prepared subsequent correspondence for the District, I would always get from the District files a correspondence written by my boss with comparable topic and subject matter contents. When I drafted my correspondence, I would copy verbatim word for word from by boss prepared correspondence that I got from the files. When I submitted my correspondence to my boss, like always, he changed those documents also. At last, I was finally vindicated and convinced that it was my boss' superiority complex, rather than any deficiencies in my writing skills that triggered his changes in all of my submitted correspondences.

Big Trouble with Mrs. P

Shortly after being vindicated of being less than competent in my writing skills, I accidently and regrettably did something far more egregious and serious than being perceived as a poor writer. One evening, I got home before Gloria and I took the mail out of the mailbox and began to sort through the mail. I placed all of Gloria's mail on the table next to her "sales coupons," and I placed all of the junk mail in a special AD basket. Without really looking at the addressee on what I thought was our bank's checking account monthly statement, I opened the envelope and immediately recognized that there was no way we could have had that much money in our checking, especially since I had just made a withdrawal a week ago. All of a sudden I noticed the statement was not a checking account balance, but a savings account balance. I thought the bank must have made a serious mistake until I noticed the name of the person whose account it was, Gloria G. Poree. Needless to say, I was shocked by these revelations, but more importantly I was frightened about the prospects and consequences of opening Gloria's mail.

When Gloria arrived at home from the hair salon, I said, "Darling I made a big mistake today." She said, "What's new? What did you do Edgar that's any different from the other thousands you've already done?" I told her I accidently opened her mail today. She looked at me with fiery eyes and bluntly said, "You opened my mail; how dare you!" "I'm sorry; I thought it was our checking account monthly statement without looking at the name on the envelope." Then I began to asking a series of dumb questions. "Darling, I didn't know you had a secret account." Gloria said authoritatively, "It's a mighty poor rat that's got only one hole to get through!" The second dumb question I asked, "How long have you had this account?" She said, "Before I married your poor ass!" The third dumb question I asked, "How much money did you have when we got married?" "More than fifteen hundred dollars," she said sarcastically.

I stood there speechless with my mouth wide open. For I had broken a commitment and solemn promise we each made when we first married: our personal belongings were just that, "personal." Prior to that incident, neither one of us had broken that promise. I never went into her purse nor did she ever go into my wallet. If we wanted something that may have been in either Gloria's purse or in my wallet, we never opened the other one's personal property. Instead, Gloria opened her purse, and I would open my wallet and probe for the requested item or items. Eighteen years after our marriage, I had broken what had been a solemn promise up until that time. I apologized for my actions; however, Gloria was not so forgiving at that moment. I was surprised she had a secret that lasted eighteen years. Gloria always felt I was rather slow when it came to rather simple things.

I was selected by the President of the Chamber of Commerce to be one of three persons to be featured spokespersons in Television Commercials for the Chamber of Commerce. After several months of the Chamber's commercial being televised, a public opinion poll taken for The Chamber indicated that my Chamber commercial was rated the most favorable of the Chamber series.

Another Embarrassing Moment

During the carnival season leading up to Mardi Gras, the City's merriment and festive celebrations were at a feverish level, virtually around-the-lock events. Every night there were dances, masquerades, and elaborate debutante balls taking place throughout the region? I really enjoyed attending the more fun-filled socials such as the semi-formal dances and masquerades because I love to dance. However, I was not a fan of the more formal carnival debutante balls. Gloria was in a social club that held their annual semi-formal dance during the carnival season. Many of Gloria's club members' husbands belonged to some of the City's most prominent social clubs that held their annual formal debutante balls during the carnival season. Unfortunately for me, we received invitations to many of the formal debutante balls from Gloria's club members' husbands. As a matter of courtesy we accepted some invitations, and I had to put on my pleasant-face for this rather painful event. Gloria would always remind me to please refrain from any remarks reflecting my displeasure of having to attend this event.

The debutante balls showcased young ladies making their formal entrance into society, wearing beautifully beaded evening gowns and being introduced by an articulate Master of Ceremony befitting royalty. This particular evening, I really did not feel up to going to the debutante ball because this social club had so many debs making their debut that it was going to be a really long evening. Another reason for my reluctance to attend, the MC for this social club's ball relished showcasing himself in the spotlight with his very proper articulation and extremely lengthy introductions and descriptions of each debutante. In spite of my reluctance, I escorted my wife to the ball.

We were seated in the first balcony which had the best seats in the auditorium for viewing the debutants during the formal presentation. After seeing and hearing about some twenty debutantes, I was growing weary of the lengthy presentations, and I began to express my opinion of some of the descriptions of the debs. Several guests seated near us who apparently had been attending debutante balls for decades, based upon the style and colors of their tuxedos, became rather annoyed with my comments. Gloria told me to take a walk or go to the restroom, and those couples seemed quite delighted with my departure.

When I returned to my seat, the next debutante who was about to be introduce was a very portly young lady. As the Master of Ceremony began to introduce the debutante, I said quietly, "Wow, that's a really big young lady." After introducing the young debutante, the Master of Ceremony then began describing her many talents. He said, "Ladies and Gentlemen, our beautiful and lovely debutante is a member of the honor society, the school newspaper staff, and a member of the debate team." The MC then said, "Her hobbies include reading, sewing, camping, cooking," "And eating," I said. Unfortunately, where we were sitting, the resonance of my voice carried, and many guests heard my outburst; some chuckled; others laughed; and, others appeared quite annoyed. Gloria told me to get up and get out, now! I left and sat in the lobby until Gloria came moments later and marched me out of the auditorium. Needless to say that was one of those embarrassing moments I alluded to during my pre-marital commitment declaration.

Honor Graduate Cheated

In May, our daughter Deidra was an honor graduate at St. Mary's Academy High School. Deidra was ranked third in her graduating class, and the grade points separating the first place, second place, and third place were less than a half point. We were extremely proud parents when the announcement was made during the Honors Day Ceremony held at the school. Deidra had been on the school's honor roll since her initial year which was quite an accomplishment.

During the Ceremony, it was announced that the top ten graduates were all recipients of scholarships to colleges. We were extremely happy to hear about the scholarships because Deidra had earned that reward through hard work and merit.

As the school's principal announced each recipient's scholarship award, Gloria and I were waiting with great anticipation for Deidra's scholarship award. After the ninth student's scholarship award was announced, we were anticipating Deidra's announcement. Holding our breath and our jubilation, the principal identified the final four-year scholarship being awarded to someone one else, not Deidra. We were shocked, we were in a state of disbelief, and there must be a mistake. Our daughter was number three in the graduating class, and the top ten honor students were awarded scholarships. Obviously, a great mistake had been made, and we were going to inquire about this apparent error. When we looked; Deidra appeared to be in a state of shock with tears streaming down her cheeks.

Gloria went over to Deidra, embraced her, and told her how proud we were of her accomplishments and that everything was going to be alright. This was a very difficult moment in Deidra's life for what she had earned by hard work and dedicated scarifies for five years of academic achievement was somehow stolen from her. I was outraged and determined to get to the bottom of this injustice. I requested an appointment with the school's administrator to get an explanation as to why Deidra, having earned honors academically throughout her entire five years at the school, yet she did not receive a scholarship as one of the top ten honor students of this year's graduating class.

When we met with the school's administrator and were told of what had transpired, we were understandable angry and extremely upset. We were advised when the selections were being made for the top ten graduating honor students who had earned the distinction of being academically qualified for scholarship awards, a nun on the faculty told the scholarship committee that Deidra's parents could afford sending their daughter to college. That nun was Gloria's sister's sister-in-law. So rather than awarding the four-year scholarship to Deidra, which she had earned through merit, the four year scholarship was given to a student who was not in the top ten graduates. What an egregious decision by a person of the cloth denying Deidra what she had earned meritoriously and substituting financial consideration over merit. What an injustice and a travesty.

Another Class Clown

While Deidra was headed to college, our son, Edgar, III, was a carbon copy of his Father based upon his school antics. I received so many calls from Edgar's third grade teacher that it was like déjà vu all over again, reminiscent of my third grade years at Craig School. According to little Edgar's third grade teacher, he was distracting his classmates from doing their work with his clowning. I could anticipate at least one call a week from his teacher. I would schedule my contact visits in locations of the City in close proximity to Edgar's school, just in case I got my alert call from his teacher. When I showed up at school, little girls would greet me with, "Mr. Poree, Little Edgar won't stop teasing us or pulling our hair or calling us funny names!" Each time I entered his classroom, preparing to spank him, his teacher always said, "Mr. Poree, don't spank him; your presence will make him behave." This was the usual story line of Edgar's third grade teacher. Whenever I arrived to take some disciplinary action, she intervened to prevent his spanking.

Some of the older and more experienced teachers at the school told me Edgar's teacher had a crush on me, and that's the reason she uses his miss-behaving stories just to get me to come to her class. That's the same thing Gloria had been telling me about little Edgar's teacher. I just laughed and brushed that off as typical female talk. I can't tell you how many dry runs I made to that third grade teacher's room during the school year.

Unfortunately, Little Edgar's antics didn't stop at third grade, they continued through the remaining years at Mary Coghill Elementary School. Since I had been summoned so frequently, I decided it was in my best interest to transform those disciplinary visits into more meaningful and productive ones so I reluctantly agreed to serve as president of the PTA. I didn't realize I would be the PTA president for most of the years that Little Edgar spent at Coghill. I was extremely happy when the sixth grade promotional exercise concluded at Coghill; it meant my reign as PTA president was over. Edgar was promoted to seventh grade, and he was scheduled to attend Francis Gregory Junior High School in the fall.

One of the things Edgar love doing was playing baseball. He started playing biddy ball at five years old at Pontchartrain Park, and he continued improving his baseball skills under the guidance and direction of Coach James Wagner, a former professional baseball player, and Coach Ebanks. Pontchartrain Park had a tremendous football and baseball program under the leadership of Coach Mac Knox. There were teams for every age group, and the dedication of the volunteer coaches was exceptional. When Little Edgar began attending Gregory School, his attention-getting antics dwindled, and his focus on class work and behavior improved. I believe his behavioral change was influenced by the prospects of him playing baseball on Gregory School's team.

Mr. Broyard, Principal of Gregory Junior High School, frequently visited Pontchartrain Park's playgrounds during football and baseball practices and games held there. Students who lived in Pontchartrain Park were feeder students for Gregory Junior High School. Mr. Broyard always complimented little Edgar about his play after baseball practice or games. Baseball was a major influence in Edgar, III's growth and development during his days at Gregory. He was an outstanding player on the baseball team and good student in the classroom.

Still Another Case of Bias

During the summer of 1984, Edgar, III had a terrific year as a member of Pontchartrain Park Patriot's Baseball Team in NORD's Fourteen-Year-Old Division League. He finished with a .350 batting average and a .875 pitching percentage, winning seven out of eight games, and he played three different positions—pitcher, catcher, and left field. When the selection of candidates for the fourteen year olds All Star Team was made, Edgar was not a candidate. This was a gross injustice and a very biased decision made by NORD's Athletic Director, who over the years had a pattern of only selecting a very few Black candidates for NORD's All Star Teams.

Although parents in our community complained among themselves about this yearly biased and discriminatory selection process, they never pursued the issue with NORD. I attempted to get an appointment with the Athletic Director to discuss the specific criteria used in determining eligibility for selection of candidates for NORD's All Star Teams without any success. I had all of Edgar's actual performance statistics taken from the official box scores of all games that summer, and his record far exceeded many of the candidates selected for the 1984 All Star Team.

After several unsuccessful attempts getting a meeting with the Athletic Director, I contacted Mrs. Dolores Aaron, Director of NORD, regarding my request, and she immediately scheduled a meeting with the Athletic Director. He really didn't have specific criteria or plan for selecting candidates other than his personal assessment of the team's needs, the sons of his friends, the sons of sponsors, or his coaching friends' sons. He wielded more power than most NORD Directors. He had been allowed to singularly and exclusively select anyone he wanted for "his" All Star Teams without suffering any consequences.

National Minority Bank Declared Insolvent

After only a few years of operation and just when Republic National Bank was beginning to turn-around making a profit, the Feds came in and declared the bank to be insolvent. It's ironic that the corporation that bought the minority bank's assets included a former Comptroller of the Currency who reviewed our bank's assets and the Regional Supervisory Director's hand-picked, designated corresponding bank's vice president who assessed and analyzed the assets and financial portfolio of our bank. Unfortunately, we could not overcome the robust opposition and anti-sentiments efforts collectively orchestrated by the politically well-connected and powerful special interest power-brokers. Republic National Bank, our minority banking effort, was short circuited, eliminating a promising banking alternative for minorities in the region.

Sickle Cell Foundation Telethon

The Sickle Cell Foundation had conducted radio-telethons, in the City for several years, and support of the foundation's efforts was increasing. Members of Sickle-Cell Foundation were successful in getting a commitment from Kim Fields, television and motion picture artist, to participate in this year's telethon. This commitment inspired the Foundation to move from the usual radio telethon format to a more ambitious television telethon. This new format was a major challenge for the Foundation, yet it was also a tremendous opportunity to expand its appeal to a much larger audience through the television network.

I received a call from the Executive Director of the Foundation requesting corporate sponsorship in support of the Foundation's efforts to televise this year's Sickle Cell Foundation's Community Appeal. The Director indicated they had a firm commitment from Kim Fields to play a major role in this year community appeal. I had been an active supporter of the Foundation for several years, and I had already agreed to serve as one of the hourly master of ceremony participants for this year's appeal. The Director asked me to serve as a Co-Host with Kim Fields for this year's Sickle Cell Community Appeal.

I felt that Kim Fields' popularity, her rapidly expanding household appeal, and her active involvement in Sickle Cell's Educational Initiatives were attractive enough for sponsorship considerations. When I advised my boss I had been asked to Co-Host with Kim Fields the very popular TV star for this year's Sickle Cell Foundation's Community Appeal, he was excited. I told him the Foundation was seeking sponsorships for a televised broadcast instead of the usual radio broadcast for the first time. My boss immediately approved it, and we were the first major company to come on board as a major sponsor for Sickle Cell Foundation's initial televised Community Appeal Telethon.

When Kim Fields arrived in the City early that afternoon, a legion of her fans was waiting at the airport for the motorcade ride into the City. Fields had several television appearances to make before heading to the hospital to visit with some sickle cell patients. I met Kim at the hospital and accompanied her as she visited several very young sickle cell patients. When Kim walked into the room, you could somehow feel the joy and excitement of her presence on the faces of the patients. She spoke with each patient and gave them each an autographed photograph, a Kim Fields notebook, pencil, and a big hug. Tears, big smiles, and warm embraces from parents of the sickle cell patients were gratifying expression of Thank You.

Kim's Mother had already made arrangements with Gloria to allow Kim and her to take a brief rest and shower at our home before getting ready for Saturday Night's Telethon. You should have seen my daughter and son's faces as Kim's motorcade pulled up in our driveway and the TV star was at the Poree's. Our block was full of neighbors and their children waving and cheering Kim Fields' arrival as well as her departure. The Telethon was the most successful one from a financial and audience penetration standpoint. Thanks to our Company's leadership and sponsorship, the Foundation was successful in attracting numerous additional sponsorships for next year's telethon.

Another Sales Tax Campaign—Public Schools

The Public Schools of New Orleans, facing increased student population, declining revenues, over-crowded schools, and outdated buildings, decided to once again seek public support for additional funding of the school system. The Board of the Public Schools launched a "One Half Cent Sales Tax Campaign" in an effort to raise the needed capital. The School Board then authorized a budget of $110,000 to secure the services of a local public relations firm to promote and coordinate the overall Sales Tax Campaign. Dr. Mack Spears, the only Black on the School Board, questioned the wisdom of spending such a large amount of funds for a public relations firm, especially in light of the financial condition of the school system. He felt the 1966 One Cent Sales Tax Campaign was a valuable resource after which the school system could model its campaign strategy, minimizing the need for such an expensive capital outlay for a public relations firm. Unfortunately, Dr. Spears was outnumbered by board members, who sided with the Board's President to hire the PR firm to promote and direct the One Half Cent Sales Tax Campaign.

Once the PR firm was hired, Dr. Spears at a subsequent School Board meeting recommended the Board should seek the professional services of the person who many in the school system felt was the major architect and "key" strategist of the successful 1966 One Cent Sales Tax Campaign for the 1980 Campaign. The President of the Board stated the PR firm hired had the necessary expertise; therefore, acquiring any additional assistance was unnecessary. Dr. Spears insisted we needed all of the resources available if we were going to be successful in this campaign. A majority of the Board agreed with his observation, and the President reluctantly agreed to allow Dr. Spears to inquire about my availability to assist and participate in the 1980 One Half Cent Sales Tax Campaign.

When Dr. Spears contacted me about the possibility of my participating, I told him I had to assess the extent of my involvement because of my full-time position with the Telephone Company. Additionally, I had to check with my superiors to see if there were any restrictions regarding my participation in a political process, even though it was in the interest of helping to improve the educational opportunities for the City's students. Fortunately, my superiors agreed to allow me to participate in the campaign process as long it was done only on my own time, not company time. The other stipulation was that my participation was strictly as a citizen supporter of public education, not as a representative of the company. I knew I would have to walk a very thin line of not being seen in any promotional material during my participation in the campaign. After conferring with my superiors, I contacted Dr. Spears to advise him I would be available to assist in the school system's campaign.

I was extended an invitation to attend a meeting with the Board to discuss and define the scope and extent of my involvement in the campaign as well as what restrictions I had as it related to my employer. The President of the Board indicated they had very limited funds available for additional professional services since a PR firm had already been contracted. She asked, "What was my fee and how did I intend to provide the services, since I was a full-time employee of the telephone company?" I told the members of the Board that because of my commitment to quality education for students of the public schools, I would commit to working in a duel capacity, a non-fee volunteer for unspecified hours and approximately fifteen hours of professional service hours at $100 per hour for specific initiatives and strategies.

Recognizing the lack of enthusiasm by the Board's President regarding my participation in the campaign process since she was most influential in the hiring of PR firm, I realized I had to be extremely careful and diplomatic in my approach and orchestration of strategies, so as not to be perceived as usurping the PR firm's initiatives. Ultimately, I knew my participation in this endeavor would afford me a tremendous opportunity for enhancing and expanding my skill sets and expertise in revenue generation campaigns. This was a major consideration which outweighed the limited monetary professional fees for my participation in the campaign.

After completing my daily company responsibilities, I reported to the school board office, to work on the strategic plan. With tremendous assistance of Dr. Alice Geoffrey, we would work until the wee hours in the mornings, sometimes as late as 2:30 a.m. formulating campaign strategy for the next day. Each workday produced an additional phase and activity for the campaign school coordinators for disseminating information to their coordinates and volunteers. After many long hours of volunteering in which we developed strategies for the campaign, the day of reckoning, Election Day, was here. In spite of the numerous roadblocks by the board's president who became more and more hostile toward me because school personnel more readily embraced the campaign initiatives Dr. Geoffrey and I had formulated, Election Day appeared a turf battle. The School Superintendent did not generate any brownie points with the Board President either because he followed our Election Day Agenda to the limit. At the close of the day, the Half Cent Sales Tax campaign was a great success, and like in 1966 our strategic plan worked to perfection.

The President of the Board, in spite of our tremendous contribution to the success of the campaign, prevented me from getting the full amount of compensation for the numerous requested initiatives and specialties associated with the revised plan Dr. Geoffrey and I developed over and above the original scope of my participation. Unfortunately, I had to wait an additional thirteen months to get the compensation for what I was entitled for the extra strategy initiatives that were essential in the passage of the Half Cent Sales Tax. Once again like in 1966, my contributions to the success of the School Board's 1980 Half Cent Sales Tax Campaign were not readily acknowledged by the School's Board leadership. The PR firm utilizing my strategic plan got credit for the victory and the $110,000.

Telephone Company Strike

My tenure as a second-level supervisor was full of unexpected experiences. When the Company's contract with the union expired and no agreement had been reached, it resulted in a strike. I was assigned to the Security Department to provide security at one of my assigned operator services offices in Jefferson Parish. Most of the operator personnel in that office were White females. The Western Electric employees on strike were White males, and they targeted that office as their primary outpost. Their pickets were the most vocal and aggressive. Adding to the problems was the availability of alcoholic beverages across the street from the office.

Our responsibility as Security Staff was to escort the non-striking employees and temporary workers, who were not regular employees, into the parking area when reporting to work and out of the parking lot when they were leaving work. Additionally, we were responsible for monitoring actions of striking employees to ensure that they were not engaging in behavior or actions which violated the safety of the non-striking temporary personnel. We were stationed among the striking employees during the entrance and exiting of working personnel throughout the day. As the day turned to nightfall, many of the striking protestors, especially the male protestors who had been drinking most of the evening, assembled near the parking lot entrance to confront and heckle non-striking employees and temporary workers arriving for work or leaving from work. The protesters became extremely boisterous and aggressive, making the tension level rise to very heated and hostile level.

Numerous temporary workers were Black, and most of the regular workers in the Jefferson Parish office were White, plus most of the striking protesters were White which created a boiling pot environment. I remember quite vividly standing among the striking employees of that office who were vigorously protesting and hear the ugly remarks, as the temporary worker came to work. When the non-striking employees arrived for work, the protesters shouted, "Go home, you no good-for-nothing scabs." When the Black temporary workers arrived for work, the shouts were much uglier, "Go home Niggers; you low down nappy head Niggers; get out of here!" Recognizing my presence among them, the striking employees after shouting their racial outburst, turned to me immediately saying, "Mr. Poree, we don't mean that for you; that's just for those Nigger scabs." "You know, Mr. Poree, we respect you highly; it's those no good Nigger scabs who are trying to take our jobs." Those chants and shouts continued throughout the strike.

When the strike was over, many of the returning striking employees who did not participate in the ugly racial taunting came to me and apologized for their coworkers' behavior during the strike. Many of the protesting strikers, who participated in the ugly and hated taunting, subsequently requested a meeting with me to express their apologies for their behavior during the strike. The unpleasant experiences of the strike were overcome by the outpouring of regrets and sincere dedication of demonstrating genuine comradeship for many newly hired Black employees in the suburban office.

SCB'S United Way Campaign Coordinator

After spending almost six years with my Tennessee native boss in Operator Services Department, I was loaned to the Company's Corporate and Community Affairs Staff to assist in the Coordination of the Company's United Way Annual Campaign. This was a great opportunity for me to showcase my organizational skills which I had demonstrated during the successful 1966 One Cent Sales Campaign for Orleans Parish Public Schools. I was assigned as one of the Coordinators of the Company's United Way Campaign. My primary responsibility was to develop a plan that would generate new dollars, increase the number of "Fair Share" gifts, and increase the average gifts from supervisory and management employees of the Company. A Company Union Stewart was selected as Coordinator for non-management employees, and her mission was to coordinate activities, meetings, and campaign events among all non-supervisory and management employees.

The largest Company's United Way contributions, prior to the year I served as Coordinator, were $396, 000. After conferring with my Co-Coordinator Flo Corcoran, who represented the Communicators Workers of America, I recommended we set a goal of $500,000 for our Company's United Way Campaign. That was really a lofty goal, for no company had ever reached that level in the City's United Way history. My experience in developing the 1966 and 1980 School System successful sales tax campaigns afforded me greater insight in formulating a United Way strategy that would mobilize and inspire more of our Company employees to actively participate in the Company's Annual United Way Campaign. Our plan resulted in the Company's exceeding the Half Million Dollar Goal, and the final total for our United Way Campaign was $596,000, two hundred thousand dollars more than the previous highest giving level. Additionally, our Company was recognized as the Number One United Way Major Contributor of the Year as well as the very first company to reach and exceed a half million dollars United Way Campaign Donor Status.

Liaison with City Government

After a very successful United Way Campaign in which I played a major role in coordinating the company's "First-ever Corporate Half Million Dollar Giving," I was appointed Staff Manager, Corporate and Community Affairs Department, which was responsible for governmental, educational, and community relations. In that assignment, I became the Company's chief liaison with the City of New Orleans and the Parish Councils of St Bernard and Plaquemine. Additionally, I was the Company's liaison with the local universities, the school districts, and the press, including newspapers, radio, and television. In my assignment, I was expected to present the company's legislative positions, maintain a positive corporate image, and minimize negative or adverse press.

Fortunately, my participation and involvement over the years in diverse community initiatives enabled me to become a dependable resource for my

Department's District Manager, who was not a native of the State. I was instrumental in familiarizing the District Manager with the community's culture, its politics, and the major power brokers, both obvious and those behind the scenes. Additionally, I was instrumental in introducing the District Manager to some of the area's most influential business, educational, political, civic, social, and community leaders—many who could become allies during issues important to our company's interests. The combination of getting the District Manager out the office into the community and meeting allies and foes in their environment enabled our department to manage our corporate strategies successfully and to meet company standards and expectations.

Chauffeur, Bus Drive, Musician, Preacher, Undertaker?

The company sponsored a Special Complementary Long-Distance Calling Program for elderly Mothers on Mother's Day. The program allowed senior citizen Mothers to make long distance calls anywhere in the world to family members free of charge. Elderly Mothers or their relatives could register them to participate in the free long-distance calling program on Mother's Day. The first hundred Mothers registered would be eligible to make free long distance calls anywhere in the world to family members. Each Mother would be allowed to make as many free calls within a fifteen minute period. Because of the tremendous number of senior Mothers registered during the registration period, the program was expanded to two hundred Mothers. Several banks and financial brokerage firms who were closed on the weekends allowed us to utilize their facilities to conduct the free calling program. Company supervisors and management personnel were assigned to groups of senior Mothers to assist them in making the calls to their family members all over the world.

I was a member of the management team assigned to assist the Mothers in helping them make their free long distance calls. Many of the Mothers had poor vision, and others had physical disabilities which limited their abilities to actually make the calls, so we would assist them in making their calls. One of the Mothers assigned to me, whose family lived in Germany and Austria, kept her eyes focused on me during the entire time that I assisted her and another Mother who was making calls to Rome. I was wearing a dark blue suit with a light blue shirt and a paisley blue necktie.

I was curious as to why this senior Mother kept looking at me with such focus. As I assisted her in making her calls to Berlin and even when she was talking to members of her family on the telephone, her eyes were still very much focused directly on me.

When she completed her last call, that senior Mother said, "I know what you are young man; you must be a chauffeur." I said, "No!" She said, "You are a bus driver." I said, "No." "You play music." I said, "No." Then she paused and said, "You must be a preacher." "No, I'm not." Finally, she said, "You must be an undertaker." I told her I was a manager at the Telephone Company helping to assist persons to talk to family members across the world. The elderly Mother seemed shocked that I was a manager and not one of those persons she thought I was. Perhaps it was my dark blue suit. Although I had provided a valuable service to enable her to reach her relatives across the world, perhaps her life experiences limited her perception of what I was capable of being. This was just another character building experience.

United Way Loan Executive

Because of the tremendous success of our Company's Half Million Dollar Campaign, the President of the United Way requested that I be allowed to serve as a Loan Executive with the United Way for next year's campaign. Our State Vice President agreed to allow me participate in the United Way Campaign as a SCB Loan Executive. One of the major categories that did not have much success in past United Way campaigns was the shipping industry. Year after year, the shipping industry's division generated very little contributions during the annual United Way campaigns.

Because of our successes during the Half Million Dollar United Way Campaign, I was asked to assist in the development of strategic initiatives that could enable our volunteers to more effectively articulate our appeal to the employees of the shipping industry to support the United Way Campaign. I was assigned to work with Jim, a Senior Vice President of a Large Petroleum Offshore Company, who was the Chairman of the Shipping Industry Division. During my first meeting with Jim, he told me that he was most impressed with my leadership and strategic planning skills demonstrated during South Central Bell's Half Million Dollar

Campaign, and he was counting on me to help him jump-start a very spirited and successful Shipping Division Campaign.

Jim and I boarded his company's helicopter to visit what he declared would be our first shipping industry test case. While flying over the City, Jim said, "Edgar, the United Way has been trying to get this company to conduct a United Way Campaign without any success at all." Our job will be to get them to participate this year. When we arrived at the shipping company in St. Bernard Parish, we met with the company's young president and some of his foremen to talk about the prospects of conducting a United Way Campaign there. We had a very good meeting, and the company's president agreed to allow the United Way to conduct an appeal to its employees.

On our flight back to the City, Jim told me that his company had done over a million dollars of business with this shipping company this year and that there was a possibility of awarding an additional two and a half million dollar contract next year to build some lift-boats. When I heard that I had a trump card to use during my appeal. My assignment was to convince the employees that it was in their best interest to give their "Fair Share" to the United Way Campaign. As we arrived at Jim office, he said, "Edgar, if we could get $6,000 from that lift-boat shipping company, we would be off to a great start."

On the date that I was to conduct the United Way appeal, I arrived at the lift-boat company approximately two hours before the scheduled meeting time. When I arrived, I met the company foreman in the trailer where the meeting was to be held. A Parcel Service truck had just delivered two large boxes that the foreman was opening. To my surprise, the boxes contained company T-shirts for its employees. I asked the foreman could I have a company T-shirt, and he gave me one. I took off my shirt and tie and put the company T-shirt on. I put my shirt and tie back on, and I began setting up the equipment to show a short United Way movie for the company employees.

The meeting location and time were not the most desirable for a typical United Way appeal. The parish where the company was located did not have many Black folks, and I saw only one Black worker during my first visit there. When I drove into the parking lot, I did not see a car or a motorcycle that did not have a Rebel flag and some other type Rebel accessories on them. The foremen appeared to be characters from the movie On the Waterfront, clad in T-shirts, coveralls, cowboy boots, bandanas, and tattoos all over. Further complicating matters, most of the employees attending the meeting had been at work since six thirty in the morning. I knew they would not be too happy listening to some tear-jerking stories at four thirty in the evening, especially why they should give their hard earned dollars to someone else.

As the employees began coming into the trailer, I began showing the United Way Movie. Beer and sandwiches were being served through the windows of the trailer. There I stood, in front of the room waiting to begin my appeal. At first, I began undressing; that's right. First, I removed my coat and my necktie and began to un-button my shirt. When I completed unbuttoning my shirt, I popped open my shirt and all of a sudden the company's T-shirt appeared, and the employees jumped up cheering, "Blue Streak, Blue Streak, Blue Streak!" I got their attention big time! I told the employees I wasn't going to bore them with the typical United Way appeal. No tear-jerking stories, no sad movies, or any examples of people who got help from the United Way. Instead, I was going to tell them about something that might encourage them to consider giving their "Fair Share" to this year's United Way Campaign.

I told them the gentleman that they saw the other day when we arrived in the Offshore Oil Company Helicopter to meet with their president told me his Offshore Oil Company did more than a million dollars of business with your company this year, and his company was considering getting Blue Streak to build more than two and a half million dollars of lift-boats next year. That gentleman is the Shipping Industry Volunteer for this year's United Way Campaign. Wouldn't it be nice to show Jim just how much you appreciate what he and his company are doing for the shipping industry and United Way? I asked them to consider giving their "Fair Share" for this year's United Way Campaign. I gave them instructions as to how to fill out their United Way Pledge Cards, and I encouraged them to get their coworkers to join with them in making Blue Streak one of the leading "Fair Share" Companies for this year's United Way Campaign. I thanked them for their time and their possible participation.

When Jim and I flew back to Blue Streak several days after my appeal to get the preliminary totals for the company, we were shocked at the totals, an unbelievable Sixty-Five Thousand Dollars United Way Gift. We could not believe the first tabulations so we carefully and thoroughly recounted all of the cash and pledges of the company and its employees. The total was a whopping $65,000 United Way Gift. When Jim and

I flew back with the President of Blue Streak Company to attend the United Way's Pace Setters Luncheon at a downtown hotel, we were so awe struck that we just looked at each other and smiled from ear to ear. Jim's Six Thousand Dollar Dream had exploded to an unbelievable $65,000 contribution.

When we walked into the downtown hotel's grand ballroom and announced the totals, the audience jumped up and began a sustained thunderous applause that lasted seemingly for several minutes. Jim said to our State President, "Bob, I'm not going to allow Edgar to return to your company; I'm making him an offer he can't refuse"!

CHAPTER XI

BREAKUP OF BELL SYSTEM

The Seven Baby Bell Telephone Systems were mandated to divest (give up) their long-distance part of the business, as a result of an antitrust lawsuit filed by the U.S. Justice Department, which cited the Baby Bell Telephone Companies as a monopoly. The lawsuit directed the Bells to sever its long distance business by 1984 in order that citizens would have greater choices in selecting providers for their telecommunication requirements. The Seven Baby Bells would be restricted to providing local telephone service, and the newly established telephone companies would provide long-distance services. With the newly mandated regulatory authority, governing local service providers like South Central Bell, much more oversight and greater restrictions were imposed than under the old monopoly environment era.

The separation of the company into two independent companies created great anxieties and uncertainty among the thousands of our employees. Once the staffing matrix was developed and essential personnel with special skill sets were assigned, remaining employees were given an opportunity to select which company they preferred to work for. That proved to be a very agonizing decision for most employees because they did not know which one of the companies would have the greatest chance to survive. I opted to stay with the local service company because I felt that my skill sets were better suited for administratively and diplomatically managing the more closely scrutinized and regulated company initiatives. Fortunately, my loan status changed. I was assigned to the Company's Corporate and Community Affairs Department. My new boss was a breath of fresh air and a marked improvement from my previous supervisors.

Because of the newly imposed regulations, coupled with the numerous municipalities seeking to generate revenue by demanding franchise agreements from competitive telephone company providers, it was obvious that we needed to re-vamp and re-tool the way we interacted with the State's political establishment. I asked my District Manager to allow me an opportunity to develop a strategic legislative action plan that would help us develop greater numbers of company allies and more effectively mitigate and neutralize those adversaries who traditionally opposed our agenda. My District Manager, R.E., agreed to release me to work full time on The Strategic Legislative Action Plan.

The first thing that I had to secure in conjunction with developing the Action Plan was to secure the company's employee roster from personnel. Additionally, I secured all State spending from the procurement office, identified the one hundred and forty-four legislators and their jurisdictions, identified the governing political leadership of the State's largest municipalities and their jurisdictions, and secured the company's educational as well as charitable contributions. I also secured from our office, all media accounts of our company's voluntary efforts throughout the State. With all of this data, I had to convert its impact into very easily understandable language that the least intelligent could understand. What are the two most important things that all politicians understand most? Votes and money!

My action plan would require my developing a Corporate Matrix that would easily convince even our most staunch adversaries why we were an important economic driver in their communities. To realize this mission, I converted all of the data into a Financial Statement Profile for two hundred and ninety political jurisdictions in the State. I identified the number of voters, the amount of spending, and the amount of taxes generated by our company annually. After approximately three months of manually converting the data into 290 individual Financial Statement Profiles, I made a formal presentation to the Company's senior management. The senior management officials were extremely impressed, and the Strategic Action Plan was taken under advisement for consideration for implementation in other states where the corporation operated.

A testament to the measurement of the potential success of the action plan was clearly demonstrated by its use with a very adversarial state Senator. This metro Senator always made unreasonable demands on the company, yet never extended any opportunities to allow the company to engage in reasonable dialog. I asked my District Manager if he would allow me to leave a copy of the Senator's Economic Financial Statement Profile Record during my regular legislative visit with the Senator. After a brief hesitation, R.E. said, "Edgar, nothing we have done seems to satisfy him; so let's give it a try." When I arrived at the Senator's office, as usual he did not have much time to give me other than his usual greetings, "Here comes that telephone man, good afternoon or good evening; unfortunately I've got another appointment." Usually my response would be, "Thank you, Senator, I understand." However, this time I said, "Senator, I'd like to leave you with something that I thought you might have an interest in." The Senator took the document and said, "Goodbye." and returned to his office.

Two days later, I received a telephone call from the Senator inviting me to come to his office if my schedule would allow that evening. I told him I would happy to do so. When I arrived at his office, for the very first time he greeted me at the door, offered me coffee or a cold drink, and told me he was rather impressed with the information I left for him. He told me he had no idea that nine hundred plus employees of South Central Bell lived in his district. He also stated that the forty-five plus million dollars in salaries, purchases, and taxes had a tremendous economic impact upon the citizens of his district and the City.

From that day on this once staunch adversary became one of the company's leading advocates and allies. Whenever we visited a legislative or municipal political leader, we always left a copy of his Economic Financial Statement Profile Record with him, and former allies became stronger supporters of our company and former adversaries became at least less hostile and in many cases joined our allies' ranks. The action plan was adopted and used statewide very effectively and successfully.

Another New Boss

Just when my District Manager J.R. and I were enjoying a tremendous working relationship, another abrupt change occurred. J.R. had an opportunity to transfer to his home state, and the next thing I knew was that I had to start all over with a fifth boss. I thought to myself, what a disaster! Just when I finally got a supervisor who had my interest at heart who trusted my ability and respected my judgment and decision-making, all of a sudden he's gone. Once again, I was faced with the prospect of getting a boss from the good-old-boys era. My greatest apprehensions were certainly not relieved when this stocky, red headed, heavy mustached Italian looking man walked into my office, introduced himself as Bill, extended his hand of welcome, and said, "Edgar, I've heard so many good things about you, and I'm really looking forward to working with you." At that moment I did not know just what to expect of this new beginning for I had just begun to get accustomed to working with someone who valued my talents and skills and who had acknowledged them openly and in compensation.

Well that day of transition proved to be one of the great turning points in my career. Working with Bill Cangelosi turned out to be one of the most promising and rewarding experiences that I had ever had during my tenure at the Company. Even though his title was district manager and my title was staff manager, we worked as a team of equals, not as a supervisor and a subordinate. We were known as the company's metro brothers. Because of Bill's accounting background and expertise, he was the budget expert of the Corporate and Community Affairs Department. Consequently, he was out of our office often working with the general management team in budgetary matters. His absence afforded me numerous opportunities to administer district responsibilities successfully. Bill's trust and confidence in my ability to handle district matters successfully in his absence enabled me tremendous opportunities to demonstrate to the department's general manager my capacity and ability to maintain a high degree of competence in administering the duties and responsibilities of the district manager. This would be very beneficial to my career in the future.

Citizen of the Year

Working with Bill Cangelosi allowed me numerous opportunities to participate and volunteer with community organizations, especially the United Negro College Fund (UNCF). Under the Company's matching program which matched an employee's contributions dollar-for-dollar for a certified charitable organization, I decided to encourage employees to support the United Negro College Program to take advantage of the matching gift program. When I requested two hundred matching gift applications from the Company's Personnel Office, I was shocked to find out that they had only ten applications available. Apparently, even though the Company's Matching Gift Program had been available for quite some time, few employees took advantage of that program.

When Company Headquarters were notified of our request for two hundred Matching Gifts Program Applications, they seemed mystified as to the numbers requested because they apparently had never distributed anywhere near that number of applications for any states. Bill was contacted by Headquarters to verify the two hundred applications request. Headquarters had never experienced such a tremendous number requested from any state before. Bill told the Headquarters representative that the 200 applications request was correct and that we needed them soon. Taking advantage of the Company Matching Gift Program proved to be a tremendous financial success for the United Negro College Fund Campaign that year. It was the largest ever Company employee contribution to the UNCF.

Audrey Turnquest, Assistant National Director of the UNCF's Southern Region, told the attendees at the UNCF Campaign Celebration that Edgar Poree's success in generating support for the UNCF among South Central Bell employees was truly incredible and tremendous, and his leadership made it possible for our campaign to exceed its goal. She said, "Because of his visionary leadership and commitment to the UNCF, I am appointing him Chairman of Community Development, a position that entailed gathering funds from within the community.

Additionally, Turnquest recommended to the Board that I be the nominee for The Lou Rawl's Parade of Star's UNCF Distinguished Leadership Award which was presented at a special UNCF reception.

On the front cover of *The Spectator News Journal*, published by the Samlincin Publishing Company of New Orleans, was the photograph of *The Spectator's* 1983 recipient of its Citizen of the Year Award, Edgar Poree, Jr. According to Paul Beaulieu, Publisher and Chief Spokesman of *The Spectator*, he stated that *The Spectator News Journal* asked the general public to submit their recommendations of local citizens who had made outstanding contributions to our City. When all of the recommendations were reviewed by the Selection Committee of *The Spectator*, Beaulieu said, "Edgar Poree emerged as the captain among those battling to make New Orleans a better community." Beaulieu stated that Poree's numerous contributions for the betterment of the City and his tremendous leadership in spear-heading and generating tremendous support and financial contributions for the United Negro College Fund Campaign were major factors in his selection as *The Spectator's* 1983 Citizen of the Year Award Recipient. Valencia Hawkins, staff writer, did an extensive story appearing in the December edition of *The Spectator News Journal* of the many contributions that the honoree had made for the community's betterment. A reception was held at the Touch of Class in recognition and honor of Poree's prestigious Award.

Edgar, III's High School

In the fall of 1984, Edgar, III became a Purple Knight Freshman at St. Augustine High School. This was a beginning of his maturation and development. His old antics and playfulness during his junior high days at Gregory Junior High School were over, and his growing up phase had begun in earnest. He really began concentrating more on his academic as well as his individual responsibility and behavior. St. Augustine's discipline as well as its regimentation of academics first required greater commitment to improving study habits as well as appropriate allocation of quality time in concentrating on individual responsibility and development. Edgar's antics of the early years in elementary and junior high school disappeared during his initial semester at St. Augustine.

Edgar successfully completed his freshman and sophomore years at St. Aug both academically and athletically. He was the starting left fielder on St. Aug's baseball team, having made the first team in his freshman year, and he excelled in both seasons. His maturation and his development as a disciplined responsible young man were evident by his walk, his talk, and his mannerism exemplifying what a Purple Knight stood for.

During Edgar's junior year at St. Aug, he received a "D" in Father's McCarthy's religion class. It was the first and only non-satisfactory grade that he had during his three years at St. Aug. When baseball practice began, Edgar was advised that he could not play because he had a "D" in religion. He was distraught, and when he called to tell me what happened, I wasn't distraught, I was mad as hell. I asked for and got an appointment to meet with Father Verrett, the principal, to discuss what I considered to be an extraordinary penalty for not "passing" a religion class.

When I met with Father Verrett I told him we were quite concerned about the possible ramifications that could adversely impact my son's distinction of what was fair and what was just as consequences for one's actions. I told him that we sent Edgar to St. Augustine to get a quality education and a character building regiment to become a self-sustaining citizen. As a Methodist, I didn't object at all to students attending a religion class; however, I had a problem with mandating a "passing" grade for a religion class. I asked Father Verret, "How does one fail religion?" He didn't have an answer other than that Edgar received a "D" for the class.

I attempted to explain to Father Verret how difficult it had been for my son to achieve successes of his own outside his Father's shadows. I was a pretty good football and basketball player, a good student, an outstanding vocalist, etc. My son always asked his Mother, "Why did I have to have daddy's same name? I'll never be able to have a name of my own." To make my point, I told Father the one distinguishable achievement that my son accomplished by himself without my influence or help were his baseball skills and prowess. He was a terrific baseball player. That was his signature card that was his individual identity which separated him from his Father's shadow. I said, "Father, a baseball player's greatest maturation and development period occurs during the junior year of school." To prohibit Edgar from playing on the varsity baseball team as a consequence of getting a "D" in religion is a penalty that's too sever, too harsh, and exceeds any level of justification. Father Verret told me that my son would be OK, since he will be allowed to be an official score keeper for the team this year. Next year he will be eligible to play. I guess that was his way of telling me to take a hike.

Acting District Manager

After working very closely with Bill as a tandem team for several years, we were successful in maintaining our department and company standards as well as meeting our customers' expectations, both external and internal customers. In addition, we were successful in meeting and in many instances exceeding departmental objectives and goals enabling a sustained growth in both customer retention and earnings. One of the great assets of our office successes was the tremendous resource that we had in the person of our District Clerk, Edith Kernan.

Edith knew the City's and the company's inner workings, relationships, and powerbrokers as well as State and municipal legislative leaders in which she had interacted with over more than thirty years. Edith provided such a wealth of knowledge about our external and internal key contacts along with invaluable information for Bill and me as to the company's allies and adversaries. Edith's grasp of the department's mission plus her expertise in handling customer complaints without much assistance from us or outside intervention enabled Bill and me greater opportunities in building stronger relations with our allies as well as fostering more civil relations with adversaries.

As Bill assumed more and more responsibilities in the company's budgetary matters, I began handling most of the District's overall operation. When Bill was assigned to Company Headquarters to serve on the Chairman's Financial Team, I was appointed Acting District Manager of Corporate and External Affairs in 1985. In that capacity, Edith Kernan was my trusted advisor, my counsel, and my most trusted protector. She knew most of the company secrets and where most of the company's skeletons were hidden. Edith was an expert in reading and analyzing management as well as union officials, their egos, their turf, and their biases. I knew when I left the office to interact with our external customers that the District was in good hands. Edith also helped tremendously in identifying some "hot button" issues that some of the older and more resentful managers of my new assignment might use in hope that it would negatively impact my effectiveness as leader of the area's Department Operational Council. Her insight and counsel helped me to counter more diplomatically and effectively potential confrontational backlashes from some of the older, more reactionary and biased managers. My tenure as the acting District Manager was tremendously less stressful because of Edith Kernan's support, dedication, fierce protection, and finally an uncompromising love.

Another Casualty of Integration

Milton Batiste, Assistant Band Director of Dejan's Olympia Brass Band, and I devoted many months to reviewing videos, promotional pamphlets, programs, photographs, and newspaper accounts of the Olympia Band's worldwide performances. In addition, we produced "Back-a-Town," a jazz, dance musical comedy that I wrote. Batiste, known as "Bat," was a tremendous trumpet player, musical arranger, and a jazz historian, and he possessed one of the most extensive musical library ever assembled. In a backyard garage at his home, thousands and thousands of albums, 45 records, photographs, videos, sheet music, pamphlets, magazines, concert programs, newspapers, and artifacts from all over the world were housed, in what I called Bat's Garage Musical Library Museum Studio. That's the only way you could accurately describe this hidden treasure of diverse music from Bach to blues, from gospel to pop, from jazz to second-line. Whatever your musical persuasion was, you could find one of your favorite artist's renditions at Bat's Place.

After putting all the pieces together for Back-a-Town and recruiting performers, we had an opportunity to perform at the American Legion Hall on Old Metairie Road. Alan Jeffery, Booking Agent for the Olympia Brass Band, scheduled a concert for the band for 300 seniors from Florida. Bat told me, "Let's do a dress rehearsal of Back-a-Town instead just a band concert." I said, "Bat we've never had a rehearsal of Back-a-Town, how in the hell are we going to pull that off?" Bat said, "We've played for most of the second lines for funerals, social and pleasure clubs, St. Joseph Indians parades, and jazz funerals so we don't have to have a rehearsal. Back-a-Town is a living thing. All we got to do is introduce those acts along the way and end the musical with a jazz funeral and second line. The audience will join in, and it will be an experience they will never forget." Bat concluded that we could pull it off in a big way.

I said, "Bat, we haven't gotten anyone to play Mr. Con, the main character in Back-a-Town, so how are we going to orchestrate the story?" Bat turned to me saying, "You wrote it; you know the script by heart; you're Mr. Con." I said, "Bat you're crazy. I'm a corporate manager. Those folks will begin second-guessing and questioning their decision." Bat said, "You are already an actor, if you work for Corporate America, so this time you'll be acting as a conman that's no different from working on Corporate America's stage, end of debate!" Just like Bat predicted, without any rehearsals, we successfully thrilled those 500 plus seniors from Florida, and Back-a-Town became a hit jazz, musical comedy performed before large audiences at downtown hotels and school auditoriums.

The booking agent for the Olympia Brass Band arranged with a major television station to film Back-a-Town for its PM Magazine Series. Potentially, this could be the "breakthrough" for Back-a-Town on a major entertainment scale. One of the station's personalities and the star of the PM's Series was actually going have a part in Back-a-Town for the production.

Everything was in place for the filming of Back-a-Town, scheduled at Derham Middle School's Auditorium for an evening performance, when an impasse occurred that drastically changed the fortunes and possibilities of Back-a-Town. The problem was the integrated (merged) Black and White musician union's position that the musicians and TV personnel as well as all other participating persons in the production must be paid prevailing union wages. Olympia Jazz Band's members, who were all members of the integrated musician's union plus all of the other participants in the cast, opted to waive the prevailing union wages for the production. However, the union rejected that and stated that they would sanction the band and the TV station if it filmed the production. Because of the union's position, the scheduled filming of the Back-a-Town production was withdrawn by the TV station one hour and a half before the starting time of the production. This was another one of the casualties of integration.

District Manager Assessment Class Candidate

During my tenure as Acting District Manager of the Company's Corporate and External Affairs, there were very few days that I did not have to prove over and over that my last successful accomplishment was not just a lucky one. There was always that "What if this or that happens, can he handle it?" Can he really be the "Face and Voice of the company?" How will he be accepted by the power brokers and the political powers of the city? Those were daily questions from the good-old-boys network. In spite of the naysayers, I continued to work twice as hard, be twice as tactful, and even more determined to prove my worthiness and competence to enhance the image, prestige, and company profitability as its Face and Voice.

Headquarters scheduled a District Level Management Assessment Class for Second Level Managers considered as candidates for promotion. I was scheduled to participate in the Assessment Class held in Atlanta, the Company's Headquarters. The candidates scheduled for that Assessment Class were from some of the nation's most prestigious universities, including, Georgia Tech, MIT, Penn, Stanford, Boston College, University of Florida, Princeton, Vanderbilt, and yes, little Xavier University in New Orleans. There were fourteen second-level management candidates in the class, and we underwent four and a half days of vigorous and intense intelligence and problem-solving exercises where we had to develop strategies, debate and justify our decisions, and formulate courses of action to better position the company in a more competitive environment.

After completing this highly competitive assessment, each candidate had to personally select the candidate in their opinion that finished "First" in the Assessment Class. Then each candidate must rate himself as to how he assessed his performance during the Class. Of course, if they rated themselves as the number one candidate in the Class, they would name the Second Best performer in the Class. The official result of the each District Level Assessment Class Candidate would be given on a specific date via telephone within two weeks. I rated the candidate from Penn as the Number One performer in my opinion, and I rated myself as "Second" in the Assessment.

As I waited with much anticipation for the telephone call from Headquarters, I started the Webcor Tape Recorder about a minute before my scheduled call to make sure that I had evidence, just in case something unfortunate happened to the person giving me the results of the assessment. When the instructor greeted me with a very spirited, "Good Morning, Edgar Poree, how are you doing down there in New Orleans?" I responded, "I'm just waiting to get the results of the assessment." The instructor said, "Edgar you rated yourself as second in the class, and your peers rated you as the number one performer in the class." I was breathless, but not yet totally satisfied because about how my peers rated me. The official rating and the one that counts is how the instructors rated you; theirs was the official assessment. The instructor said, "The Assessment Staff concurred with your peers, and you were rated the "top" candidate of the District Level Assessment Class, congratulations!" I was silent for a brief moment, and then I yell, "Yes! Yes, thank you so much!" The instructor indicated my superiors would get the results in a few days and again congratulated me for a tremendous performance.

I put my coat on and immediately hopped into the elevator to go to the thirtieth floor to break the good news to my boss. When I arrived in his office his secretary said, "Edgar, they are behind closed door in a meeting." Without hesitation, when I opened the door, the facial expressions of Dick Sharp, Company State Vice President, and Fred Nodier, Assistant Vice President and my boss, weren't very pleasant. "This better be critically important, Edgar!" said the State Vice President. I said enthusiastically, "U-no, U-no, number one in the Assessment Class. The strained faces of Dick Sharp and Fred Nodier turned into jubilation, and each of them congratulated me with a big hug and healthy handshakes. Fred asked, "Edgar, did you call Gloria yet with the news?" "No, she's at work." "What are you waiting for Edgar? Get out of here; go and tell Gloria the great news," said Dick Sharp. I returned to my office, told Edith and my staff, and then I ran down to the parking garage, jumped into my car, sped over to Mouton School to tell Gloria my good news. No half-chicken-two-plate dinner at Dooky's tonight. Instead, we had a beautiful candle-light dinner with all of the amenities associated with fine dining at Dooky's, of course.

District Manager

Once the celebration of my District Manager appointment was over, my major assignment in my new capacity was to do something that my previous predecessors never accomplished. My priority mission was to get a favorable editorial from one of the most influential power brokers in the region, the CBS local affiliated television station's editorialist. For almost two decades, the company was unsuccessful in getting a favorable editorial from the CBS Chief Editorialist. My objective, get one! The second priority was to secure a more manageable and equitable relief in the City's administration of its parking enforcement mandates imposed by the City Council.

These two priorities were extremely critical to the company's financial stability as well as its cost-control administration. The annual fines and penalties imposed on company vehicles by the City's Parking Enforcement exceeded $200,000. It was the company's contention that the parking fines and penalty expenses associated with servicing its customers in downtown high rise building was a legitimate operating expense. Unfortunately, since the City's imposed expenses were parking fines and penalties, those expenses could not be classified as operating expenses under the mandates of accounting practices. It would be my job to get the City to agree to some plausible alternative parking agreement that would convert potential parking fines to parking permits agreeable to both parties.

Although the mandated mission of getting a favorable editorial was top priority, something had to be done with the present rapidly increase in expenses in servicing major customers in downtown. I met with the City's Department of Streets Enforcement Deputy Director to discuss an alternative parking permit program in conjunction with possibly amending and converting some of the language in the existing city ordinance governing parking enforcement to include a "Pay-in Advance Permit Fee" option for anticipated requirements for parking in downtown to service customers. This Pay-in Advance Permit Fee Program would be based on analyses of previous documented parking violations in downtown as well as non-downtown and would be used as the new matrix model of re-designating and classifying previously identified parking violations.

After numerous meetings and negotiations with the Street Department leadership and influential members of the City Council, the City agreed to accept my Pay-in-Advance Permit Program. This change significantly reduced the company's actual parking fines and penalties to less than $25,000 annually and more significantly allowed for the company to charge parking permit expense as a legitimate operational expense of doing business. Mission two had been accomplished!

In 1988, Edith, my right arm, my trusted and devoted Administrative Assistant, confident, operational expert, chief liaison of political contacts, and overall glue of our office, retired. Edith was like the Guru of Corporate and Community Affairs because of her many years of vast experiences in numerous operating departments of the company. Whenever anyone wanted information about company operations, all they had to do was call Edith. She was a company historian and operational manual. Edith's retirement would create a huge void in our operation.

New Administrative Assistant

On September 15, 1988, Dian Kent, my new Administrative Assistant and Edith's replacement, arrived in my office to begin a journey that had tremendously large shoes to fill. Dian was half the age of Edith, and she certainly did not have the years of multiple departmental experiences; however, her resume was most impressive and her skills and formal education could be utilized immediately in the company's conversion from paper to electronic administration and processing. Dian's task was to accelerate the learning phase, establish internal and external contacts, maintain the department's operational mandates, and make sure that I'm in the right place at the right time to protect the company's image and reputation at all times. Like my immediate mandates articulated by my superiors, after the congratulatory phase of my promotion, I gave Dian her marching orders during that September morning.

From that moment on, Dian Kent immediately took charge, transforming our office from paper to electronics; she accelerated the administrative processes such that our operations were functioning at its highest level of performance at all times. Additionally, because of her administrative skills and overall competence plus her obvious high level of intelligence and analytical skills, I would never have to worry about being blinded-sided whenever I would be away from our office. Most importantly, her commitment of making our office the number one operation in the company coupled with her promise of trust in maintaining ethical behavior made my assignment and mission much easier to attain. Like with Dian's predecessor, Edith, I was confident that I would never have to worry about watching my back. Dian made it clear that she was going to maintain that trusted bond. What a blessing!

Editorial Strategic Mission

Now it was time to deal with the daunting task of completely making a three hundred sixty degree turn around with the metropolitan most powerful Editorialist, Phil Johnson. I requested an appointment with him and received an invitation from this giant of a power broker. Our meeting was cordial and all of a sudden, Phil Johnson said, "How in the hell did you get to be a part of this behemoth giant that gets everything it wants, when it comes to making more money? My response, "Perhaps it was fate and being in the right place at the right time and having a highly respected business leader vouch for my competence and qualifications."

When I told Phil Johnson how many jobs I had during high school, college, and my teaching career, he offered me a cup of coffee, then a cold drink. He said, "Tell me more about Edgar Poree, District Manager of South Central Bell Telephone Company." When I told him that I had the leading role in Clarence Cameron White's Opera, "Ouanga," depicting the rise and fall of Haiti's Emperor Toussaint L'Ouverture at Xavier University as a freshman in 1955, he said, "Edgar Poree and classical music, what a coincidence!" Phil Johnson told his secretary to hold all his telephone calls until he finished his meeting with me. He told me that he was a member of the New Orleans Civic Orchestra that had performed with Loyola University and Xavier University during the early fifties. He said that he had the pleasure of performing with one of the most talented sopranos at Xavier University, Miss Emma Goldman, and that she challenged the Metropolitan Opera Company's preeminent "Aida's." He told me Emma Goldman was one of the finest talents that he had ever seen and heard. A bright light went straight to my head! Emma Goldman could be the key in my conversion plan to re-ignite the passion of winning over favorably this powerful opponent to our side.

I knew that I would have to find Emma Goldman, convince her to come to New Orleans, and arrange an appointment or lunch with Phil Johnson, her avid admirer. I went to Xavier University to visit the Music Department to look through all of the old yearbooks to see if there were some photographs of Emma Goldman, the most admired soloist of one of the Greater New Orleans Metropolitan Area's most influential and powerful voices, Phil Johnson. Bingo, I found several photographs of her performance as "Aida" in an early 1950 yearbook. The next thing I had to do was to inquire if she was still alive and if so where she was living, since it was some forty plus years since she had performed at Xavier. After getting some leads from some of the music teachers, I found out Emma Goldman had an aunt who lived in Lafon Home, a residence for the elderly, she visited.

I went to Lafon Home the next day, and I met Emma's aunt. She was a strikingly beautiful, spunky, and alert individual. When I introduced myself as a former Xavier Concert Choir member and graduate of Xavier that was all I needed to say. When Emma's aunt heard the words, music and Xavier University, her cheeks perked up, and she began to talk about her wonderful musical niece, Emma Goldman. I told her that there were many persons in the City that still remembered how wonderful her niece performed as "Aida" in the Opera at Xavier University in 1951. Her Aunt said, "I was there, and she was spectacular, and the audience gave her a standing ovation!" She told me with a big smile that she had the pleasure of presenting Emma with a dozen red roses after the performance. Then she showed me the picture presenting the roses to Emma at the 1951 opera performance.

I asked Emma's aunt, "When was the last time she spoke with her niece or saw her? She told me she talks with Emma every month and

Emma visits her every Thanksgiving. I asked her if she would give me Emma's telephone number, and she agreed to do so. Her Aunt told me that her niece was working at a college in North Carolina. She gave me four telephone numbers. After calling several numbers unsuccessfully, the avidly admired "Aida" soloist answered the telephone. I was almost speechless for a moment. That's pretty hard to believe of me; however, I began introducing myself as a Xavier alumnus and how I met an extremely influential television personality that was an avid admirer of her, especially her "Aida" performance. Emma asked "Are you serious?" I told her that he had played in the New Orleans Civic Orchestra when Loyola and Xavier Universities performed a joint concert in which she performed some scenes from "Aida" that he described as incredible. He compared your performance with those great Metropolitan Opera "Aida's," that's a tremendous tribute!

Miss Goldman told me she would be in New Orleans during the Thanksgiving Holidays visiting her aunt in the Lafon Home. I asked her would she mind having lunch with Phil Johnson, if I could arrange it during her visit. She said that she would be happy to do so. What happened after that invitation can only be described as the beginning of the conversion process. When I called Phil Johnson and asked him if he would have lunch with his most admired soprano during the Thanksgiving week. He responded, "Edgar Poree, I thought you were different from your telephone contemporaries promising things that you could not deliver!" I told him I was serious, and he said he would be delighted to do so. Well, the beginning of the conversion strategy was in its second phase. On Tuesday, the week of Thanksgiving, we had lunch reservations for eleven-thirty a.m. at Commander's Palace. At four-thirty p.m. after discussing their musical experiences of almost fifty years, our lunch date concluded. Emma Goldman autographed a picture that Phil Johnson had of her some forty plus years ago, and he gave her a draft of an editorial that he was going to do in conjunction with his appreciation of her talent. That luncheon was indeed the catalyst for possible endeavors that just might reverse the tendencies of his appreciation about the possible merits of future plans addressing our company's need for Rate Consideration in the future; only time would tell.

Decline in Mother's Health

During the late nineteen eighties, Mother's health began declining, particularly after Mother found out that Julia's health was imperiled. Mother, like so many Mothers, has an incredible extraordinary visual sense. Mother called me early one morning to tell me she had a terrible dream last night. She said, "Edgar, I dreamt that Julia had cancer!" I told Mother, it was only a dream. Ironically that same day, Julia was scheduled to go to her doctor to get the results and diagnosis of her test. Unfortunately, Mother's dream was not just a dream but a very devastating reality. Julia had been diagnosed with bone cancer. This discovery had an immediate impact on Mother's physic and her apparent desire not to face losing a child before her own death. Because of Mother's health condition, it was becoming obvious that we had to make a major decision that would dramatically alter her independence of living alone.

That decision was not going to be an easy one for it would require getting a consensus from all of my sisters as to how we would address this situation. Mother had been diagnosed with having acute emphysema, which adversely impaired her heart's functioning. It also significantly impaired her strength, stamina, and ability to function independently. These factors severely and adversely affected Mother because she always relished the fact that she could take care of herself and maintain her home impeccably and independently. However, the doctors had advised that Mother should not be left alone because of the severity of the emphysema.

Since we all had homes and family obligations, we had to make arrangements to make sure that Mother would not be alone. Initially, each of us committed to providing someone from our family to stay with Mother. We made a schedule for each of our families to make sure that Mother had someone with her throughout the entire days and nights. Dolores Aaron, our non-biological sister, also pledged and provided additional help in being with Mother. It appeared that we had a good plan that would ensure that Mother would always have someone with her around the clock.

Unfortunately, after several weeks passed, more and more family members were unable to fulfill their commitments which prevented them from being with Mother during their scheduled times. Consequently, Edna Floe, my oldest sister, and I revised our schedules to make sure that someone would be with Mother at all times. Dolores, our surrogate sister, provided a paid helper to be with Mother. Unfortunately, it became apparent that our plan though admirable would not be the long-term solution of providing someone around the clock with Mother. Dolores indicated Mother could live with her at her home. That gracious offer, however, was vehemently opposed by some siblings. We were certainly facing a major dilemma.

Floe and I recalled that the doctor, who diagnosed Mother's aliment and advised that she should not be left alone, indicated his willingness of getting her in the New Orleans Rehabilitation Center with which he was affiliated. We recalled how the doctor spoke of Mother's bubbling personality, innate intelligence, and wit which made him conclude, that he wanted to make sure he remained her attending physician. That's the reason he indicated he would make provisions to cut through the red tape of getting her in the Center. Floe and I contacted the doctor to see if his offer still stood since we were unable of providing around-the-clock presence for Mother. Fortunately, the doctor was thrilled to get Mother into the Center. We spoke with our three sisters about placing Mother into the Center, and they agreed to do so.

The difficult part of this solution was convincing Mother to go to the Center. Edna Floe and I again contacted the doctor who arranged the residence for Mother to ask him if he could arrange a personal tour of the Center. He told us that instead of bringing Mother to the hospital for her next scheduled appointment, he would arrange for her next appointment to be in the New Orleans Rehabilitation Center. That turned out to be a winning formula. When the doctor completed Mother's examination he personally pushed her around in a wheelchair on a tour of the entire facility of the Center, especially the cafeteria where they both enjoyed eating a delicious lunch. Mother was quite happy with her day at the Center and particularly with the time she spent with the doctor. Our very difficult decision was made less stressful by the intervention and the compassionate commitment of Mother's attending doctor. All of my sisters and Dolores visited the Center and agreed that it was indeed the best place for Mother.

Once Mother checked into the Center, like her doctor's admiration the Center's personnel also fell in love with her, and they treated her like a queen, everyday around the clock. After dropping out of college in her junior year eight years earlier, Deidra, our daughter, resumed her college education. Deidra made her decision after years of continued encouragement from Mother, and Deidra's decision seemed to strengthen and enhance Mother's physic as well as her acceptance of her new home.

Obtaining Sponsorship for Bayou Classic

In the summer of 1989, Dr. Joe Johnson, President of Grambling State University and Dr. Eric Green, his Executive Assistant, visited my office to discuss the possibility of securing support for the annual Bayou Classic Football Game and associated activities. The corporate annual donation for Southern University and Grambling State University had only been twenty-five hundred dollar per year. Dr. Johnson had been visiting cities across the state seeking support from businesses for the Bayou Classic. He and Dr. Green were making a concerted effort, especially in the Black community encouraging businesses and Black organizations to begin supporting the Bayou Classic. Increased support from the business community would strengthen the universities' position during contract negotiations for broadcasting rights with NBC Television Company. As more sponsorships of the Classic were secured, the greater leverage the universities would have in securing greater financial benefits in its negotiations with NBC Television Company.

Dr. Johnson asked if I could appeal to the Company for at least a $10,000 sponsorship for this year's Bayou Classic. He indicated that Alden McDonald, President Liberty Bank and Trust, and Preston Edwards, Publisher of Black Collegiate, had made substantial commitments in support of the Classic, and it would be great if BellSouth would join in the New Orleans connection of support for the Classic. I made an appeal to my boss, and he concurred that it was an opportunity to demonstrate our commitment in support of the Bayou Classic. So we joined other businesses and individual supporters in the New Orleans community bolstering the universities' negotiating position in their contract with NBC Television Company.

Our commitment along with others businesses in New Orleans helped Dr. Johnson and members of his negotiating team to successfully negotiate a long-term contract agreement with NBC to televise The Grambling State-Southern University Annual Bayou Classic Football Game.

Bayou Classic Souvenir Program—University Benefit or Hoax

In conjunction, with the Bayou Classic, I received a call from the AD/Publishing Company of the Bayou Classic Souvenir Program. The caller identified himself as the Vice President of Marketing for the Company. He said he was calling to get BellSouth's Corporate Ad in the Nation's number one Black event of the year. He said the Bayou Classic Souvenir Program will be read by more than 70,000 individuals, and he knew our company wouldn't pass up an opportunity to be a major sponsor of the Souvenir Program. I advised the representative that we weren't planning to take an ad in the souvenir program. The representative said, "You mean, your corporation is not going to take advantage of being read by over seventy thousand persons." I responded, "No!" He said, "Mr. Poree, are you telling me your company does not support the greatest Black Entertainment Event of the year." "No, I did not imply we would not support the number one Black event of the year; I said we would not take an ad in the souvenir program."

The Vice President told me Grambling State and Southern Universities both received significant financial benefits from the sales of the Bayou Classic Souvenir Programs so he could not understand why my company wasn't planning to take an ad in a 70,000 copies publication. My response, "We have over three million copies of our BellSouth Directories distributed throughout the State of Louisiana, so our Brand is obviously recognized." As far as your assertions that the universities received significant financial benefits from the sales of the souvenir programs, there appears to be little evidence supporting those claims. I told the Vice President I had completed a cost analysis of last year's dollars generated to his agency by computing the pricing of the color and black and white printed ads, coupled with the cost of the front and back covers, times the number of pages in last year's Classic Souvenir Program. Based upon my findings, the ads generated approximately a half million dollars of revenue. Additionally, I told him according to our sources, his company provided about twenty-thousand complimentary copies of the souvenir programs to be equally divided between Grambling and Southern to be sold as their financial benefit from the sales of the souvenir programs.

Based upon the cost of the program, that's approximately $60,000 divided between the two universities, $30,000 each, minus shipping expenses and commissions paid to salespersons. The other 50,000 copies sold generated an additional $150,000 for his company, minus shipping expenses and commissions paid to salespersons. I said, "Mr. Vice President, your company was the real winner in the Bayou Classic Souvenir Program yielding more than $600,000 in revenue, while Grambling State and Southern Universities only received a little less than $30,000 each, approximately 5% of the generated revenues. That's hardly a significant financial benefit for the universities." I concluded my conversation with the Vice President of the ad/publishing company by advising him we declined his invitation to purchase any ad in this year's souvenir program.

Gloria Featured in Times Picayune News Article and Editorial

Henderson H. Dunn Elementary School in the Desire housing community, where Gloria taught for over twenty-years had been described by community leaders as a gloomy and prison-like facility. The enrollment had plunged from over a thousand students in 1981 to only 325 at the beginning of the 1988-89 school years. Second floor classrooms had been closed because chunks of cancer-causing asbestos insulation were falling from the ceiling. There were additional problems such as extensive cracks in the foundation, restrooms without heat and ventilation, missing fixtures, and leaks in the roof. Dunn also had serious security shortcomings, yet a security guard was assigned only once a week.

The school had so many major problems and serious deterioration deficiencies that community leaders as well as the press, both television and printed media, were highly critical of the run-down school and its danger to the students, faculty, and staff. The Times Picayune had a series of stories depicting the numerous problems at Dunn School. Rhonda McKendall, Staff Writer for the *Times Picayune*, visited Dunn school on numerous occasions during the school year documenting the many problems occurring at the school. In an article appearing in the *Times Picayune* on Sunday edition, January 22, 1989, entitled, "Desire Area Grade School Falling Apart," McKendall described how on a rainy day, it meant mopping the principal's office and switching students to drier classrooms. When a sewer backup occurred in the cafeteria, it forced the children to eat bag lunches in their classrooms for months. She indicated that the school's security was a nightmare. To curb vandalism, sliding glass doors in the classrooms had been replaced with plywood.

McKendall interviewed Gloria who had been a second grade teacher for twenty years at Dunn. Gloria's classroom had been vandalized too numerous times to count, and three windows of her classroom were boarded up with plywood after repeated break-ins. The one remaining glass window of her classroom had a large bullet hole in it. Gloria's classroom was located at the front entrance of the school. She had two purses snatched by intruders in her classroom, hub caps were stolen from my car, and her Buick Riviera vanished from the school's parking lot in May. McKendall asked Gloria, "Mrs. Poree, why did you stay here all those years with all of the problems and the security risk?" Gloria said, "I stayed here because the children needed me; they are deprived and needed someone who cares." McKendall told Gloria that she was not only a courageous teacher but a truly incredibly dedicated one. The *Times Picayune* editorial on Wednesday, February 25, 1989, entitled, "Run-Down School Unfit for Kids," included Gloria's encounters of vandalism, purse snatchings, and stolen car security breaches. The article also contained her reason for remaining at Dunn School, "I stay here because the children needed me!" Mr. Wilbert Dunn, School Principal, told Ms. McKendall that Gloria Poree was a Master Teacher with an enormous compassionate and caring heart.

CHAPTER XII

1990: Year of Highs and Lows

The year of 1990 brought unusual weather conditions to our city in May, especially on Mother's day. Most major streets of the City were almost impassable, making travel extremely difficult. I was determined to visit Mother at the Rehabilitation Center on Mother's Day in spite of the flooding. Gloria, Deidra, little Edgar, and I left home to pick up Fadge Flowers, one of our friends in route to the Center. We had to use streets that we didn't usually travel to get to the Center because of the flooding. It took us three times longer than the normal travel time to reach the Center. I decided to bring my camcorder to record our visit with Mother, since we probably would be Mother's only visitors due to the flooding.

When we arrived, Mother was surprised to see us because of the flooding. Gloria told Mother, "You know your son wasn't going to let the flood keep us from being with you, especially on Mother's Day." Mother said, "That's my Edgar." We brought Mother our gifts and some personalized cards to cheer her on this special day. I told Mother I brought my camcorder to record our visit so that other family members, who couldn't get here because of the flood, would be able to see her. Mother said most emphatically, "You got here!"

I then asked Mother to talk about her grandchildren so that they could see what she thought about each of them on this Mother's Day. At first Mother seemed hesitant to do so, and then she began to talk about each of her grandchildren accordingly by age. I began recording Mother's personal assessment of each of her grandchildren and what she thought each of them and what they thought of her. This request resulted in an eye-opening and very compelling analysis of Mother's assessment of each of her grandchildren in her opinion and from her perspective. It certainly was an incredible revelation from the heart. I hope one day each of Mother's grandchildren will get an opportunity to see and reflect on Mother's very candid opinion and viewpoint as to their personal relationship with her. As of the date of this publication, only my daughter, Deidra and son, Edgar, III, who were present during the recording on Mother's Day, have seen Mother's individual assessment of each grandchild.

Daughter's Graduation

After the Mother's Day flood, something very special occurred in the Poree family in May. Deidra graduated Magna Cum Laude from Southern University at New Orleans after being out of school for eight years. That was certainly quite an accomplishment, particularly working a full-time job and carrying a 21 semester hours schedule at the same time. Gloria and I were proud parents. It was indeed a tremendous accomplishment, especially in the eyes of Mother who over the years and in every encounter with Deidra stressed the importance of her fulfilling her dream of finishing college. That May day was one of the most fulfilling and gratifying days of our lives.

I recorded the entire Graduation Ceremony with my brand new camcorder, anticipating the possibility of Mother not being strong enough to attend the ceremony. Capturing her granddaughter walking across the stage to receive that long awaited diploma would indeed be a memorable occasion for Mother. As soon as the Graduation Ceremony was over, we went immediately to the Center so Mother could see and actually hold Deidra's diploma, cap, gown, and her Magna Cum Laude shoal in her hands. Mother kissed and hugged Deidra with all her strength and told her how very proud she was for completing her mission. They again embraced one another and tears of adulation and fulfillment flowed down their cheeks freely. When I looked around, everyone in Mother's room had tears flowing abundantly. That was truly a blessed moment in lives of the Poree family.

Mother's 90th Birthday Celebration

On May 31, 1990, we were all getting ready for the grandest and most exciting celebration—Mother's ninetieth birthday. My nephew and his wife, Alverez and Dorselyn Chapital, hosted the celebration in their lovely home in eastern New Orleans. We got permission from the City to re-name the street Gertrude Poree's Birthday Lane for the day of the celebration. When I arrived early that morning of May 31, 1990, the preparation for Mother's 90th birthday celebration was feverishly and enthusiastically in action. Mother's great grandchildren, Dana, Adrian, and Chris were helping their Father, Alverez, hang the huge "Welcome to Gertrude Poree's 90th Birthday Celebration Banner." The banner covered almost the entire front of the house. We changed the street name on the corner, from Dogwood Drive to Gertrude Poree's Birthday Lane, and Dorselyn along with other family members and friends began decorating and preparing the food and desserts for the celebration.

As the welcoming party began gathering on the front lawn in anticipation of Mother's arrival, all of a sudden loud cheers began filling the air as a long white stretch limousine turned onto Gertrude Poree's Birthday Lane. Atlas, a white, stretch limo stopped in front of the cheering crowd. When the door opened, Mother began waving and nodding approval of the cheering crowd's welcoming. When the limo driver gave Mother's walker to her, apparently Mother's adrenalin was so feverously high that she pushed the walker aside and began walking toward the cheering crowd. The crowd released a deafening "Welcome Gertrude!' "Welcome Gertrude!" "Welcome Gertrude!" As the welcoming party continued its chant, one of Mother's granddaughters escorted her inside. The 90th Birthday Celebration of Gertrude Boyd Poree started with a resounding beginning. Eighty-nine friends and family members attended the six-hour plus celebration. Mother did not use her oxygen dispenser during the entire six hours plus 90th Birthday Celebration.

We recorded the entire six hours plus celebration with my new camcorder. When we first viewed Mother's birthday's celebration, we noted that Mother seemed to be eating on four different segments during the recording playback. Initially, we thought that it was perhaps the same plate of red beans and rice she apparently did not finish eating, while welcoming her guests. However, when we re-winded the tape to see if it was the same plate, we noticed one plate had meatballs and spaghetti. When we re-winded the tape again, we saw Mother eating a plate full of veal roast, macaroni, and string beans that time. Finally, during the last hour of the celebration, we saw Mother eating a plate full of smothered okra, candy yams, and baked chicken.

We couldn't believe our eyes, after seeing the playbacks because it indeed substantiated that Mother actually ate four super serving plates during her 90th Birthday Celebration. Oh! I forgot to include the two servings of ice cream and birthday cake she ate during the closing of her 90th Birthday Celebration. What an incredibly, fascinating, and spectacular event was Gertrude Boyd Poree's 90th Birthday Celebration. That was the consensus of the eighty-nine family members, friends, and guests who showered her with gifts and expressions of appreciation and most of all their love and respect for this compassionate humanitarian and great Matriarch.

Mother's Death

Four months after Mother's fantastic 90th Birthday Celebration, her health began deteriorating and in October of 1990, Mother's devoted attending physician called to tell us that Mother was dying. All five of us rushed to the Center, and we were there in prayer during Mother's last moments of life. Even in death Mother's sense was as clear as her compassion and wisdom, always timely and candid. As we were all singing her favorite gospel songs, one of my sisters who couldn't hold an in-tune note at all was a bit off key. Although Mother's life was rapidly fading, she still recognized her daughter's out-of-tune monotone singing. Mother, whispered, "Baby, I know you want to sing Mother to sleep to go home to Glory, but please for the sake of me getting to Glory on a good note just remain silent and say a prayer while your sisters and brothers sing." Mother smiled, Natalie, a practical nurse placed her hand on Mother's neck and shoulder said, "Mother's gone!" The glue of our family and extended families was dead. This century's most compassionate and generous Matriarch was laid to Rest in Peace.

I was the spokesperson for our family's Celebration of Life Home Going Service for Mother. I spoke of how Mother had such an incredible influence and positive impact on so many lives. If you added all of numbers of students that sat at her dinner table doing research papers with Father's books, getting inspiration and guidance from Mother's spirituality messages, and eating those delicious meals, plus the numerous church members, family members, friends, and neighbors who ate at Mother's table as well as received those delivered take-home meals that Edna Floe and I delivered to their homes and those who received those beautiful decorated, tasty cakes, plus all of the suppers and Sunday dinners that Edna Floe and I delivered over the years, you would have a population the size of a small city. Edna Floe and I delivered more cakes than McKenzie's Bakery drivers did each year, and we delivered as many suppers and dinners as the Home Beverage Company delivered soft drinks and beer to all those weekend suppers all over the City. Most of the congregation nodded their heads in agreement for most had received and eaten Gertrude's finger licking suppers, dinners, or delicious cakes, or had been the recipient of her generosity and spiritual counsel. At that point I was full with emotions, yet retained my composure to share with Mother's extended family, our congregation, My Special Tribute to Gertrude Boyd Poree, entitled *"Mother, What Are Friends Really For?*

Mother, What Are Friends Really For?
When we need someone to share our inner thoughts,
When there are special needs, to satisfy our human heart.

Mother, What Are Friends Really For?
To hear not merely words we speak.
Try to understand our deeper feelings, for which there are no words.
To know the worth of silence, and listen without judging the merit of what we may have said.

Mother, What Are Friends Really For?
To provide sometimes that needed relief, from the frantic pace of competitive living
Someone with whom we can drop all pretence
Someone who will care for us, not for what we may one day become,
But will care for us for what we are today.

Mother, What Are Friends Really For?
To close their eyes to our human frailties, seeing only
which is good in us.
To know there is someone who cares
Someone to share our burdens
Someone we can trust.

Mother, What Are Friends Really For?
Someone who knows just when to speak, when to stand silently by,
Giving us strength and comfort by simply being near,
that's one thing very hard to do.
True friends are deeply concern of what happens to you!

Mother, What Are Friends Really For?
For those time when you become tired, discouraged and even despair,
To know that there's someone to give encouragement,
someone who really cares.

Mother, What Are Friends Really For?
To cheer you on and bring you face to face, with your better self to
endure the pain,
To restore the faith in you that will conquer fear
To know that's someone who cares who's also very near.

Mother, What Are Friends Really For?
For those times when we stumble and fall
Someone reaches out to clutch our hands
Someone helps us, pick ourselves back up over and over again.

Mother, What Are Friends Really For?
To help us laugh at our own mistakes and smiles even when there is pain,
To help give us support because of our convictions,
To stand beside us when there are complex questions to be answered
To give us wisdom in our decision-making
Sacrificing our selfish ambitions for what's best for you
not what's best for me!

Mother, What Are Friends Really For?
To be honest above all and to share what they feel
No matter how childish or silly it might seem
For a true friend is expressed through their dreams and deeds
Perhaps, sometimes it may appears that your true friend can't match-up
With all of the many qualities described, a true friend
will do their very best.

To pass this most rigid test, to prove that they are worthy
a true friend indeed,
Someone you can count on, whenever there is need.
Above all, a true friend will want you to know
Whatever impression you might have of them, just give
them a chance to show,
Just one opportunity to live up to their genuine and
sincere concern for thee
That's what friends are really for,
A Love, a Bond, a Trust in You, Until Eternity!

Mother, What Are Friends Really For?

Please Tell Me Mother What Are Friends Really For?

"Jr. you remembered all my answers to that question,
so beautifully articulated above,

Respectively,
Gertrude Boyd Poree
With Everlasting LOVE!

Gloria's Non-Ceremonial Career Exit

Gloria decided she would make a decision during the Christmas Holidays as to whether she would join the ranks of the unemployed after this school year. The unemployed she was talking about was retirement. She indicated that when she began her teaching career, thirty years was her targeted number for retirement. So if she was going to fulfill that goal, it would have to occur at the end of that school year. Christmas Holidays passed and still no word of retirement. I asked Guich if she had changed her mind, and she told me that she would tell me at the appropriate time, when and if she was going to retire. As the school year was nearing its last few months, Guich told me that this was going to be her last few months of employment. I asked her why she didn't notify the principal earlier during the year about her plans. She said, "Because I wanted to end my teaching career just like I started it, un-ceremonially.

Well as fate would have it, Guich's desire to simply walk away from a thirty year teaching career quietly and unnoticed failed miserably. When I got up early Saturday morning, May 31, 1991, the day after school closed to get the daily newspaper. On the front page of the *Times Picayune* was picture of Gloria in living color. There she was embracing one of her students, who had big crocodile tears rolling down his cheek, the caption read, "I don't want you to go!" Unnoticed and un-ceremonial like Gloria's teaching career started. No such happening, in stark contrast, Gloria's planned quiet exit was witnessed and read by more than two hundred thousand *Times Picayune* subscribers on May 31, 1991.

Well after literally receiving hundreds of congratulatory calls that weekend from well-wishers, Gloria was asked over and over, "Why didn't you tell us you were retiring?" We would have given you a grand retirement celebration? Gloria's response, "I appreciate that, but I did not think my decision to retire warranted any special considerations or recognition." That was Gloria's persona, her personality, and her willingness to perform without the need of recognition. My son, however, was not satisfied with his Mother not having a grand celebration ceremony for her thirty years of proving the highest quality teaching and development for more than a thousand young people and hundreds of families. He made it very clear to me seven days of the week.

After complaining about my not doing something special for his Mother's retirement, I told little Edgar that I was going to take care of business, trust me. Little Edgar said, "Daddy, you've been saying that for months, and you haven't done anything yet for Mama yet. One evening, when I got home from work, I asked Guich, "What do you want for your retirement?" She told me that she was going to buy a new Legend car. I said, "A new Legend, that's not good enough for your retirement Darling, I'm going to buy you a brand new Lexus 400 Four-Door Luxury Sedan!" Guich said, "I don't have Lexus money." I asked her to loan me $20,000 for fifteen days, until I cashed a CD. Guich said, "I'm going to charge you 15% interest on the sixteenth day if you don't repay me on the fifteenth day of the loan." I said, "Guich, did you hear me ask you to loan me twenty thousand dollars?" I'm the fellow who had only $246.23 to my name, when I married you. You think God hasn't blessed us, tremendously! I didn't have to go to a bank or a loan company to borrow the money to get the retirement gift. Instead I came to my lifelong dream girl, my sweetheart, my wife. What an awesome blessing.

Well, when my son heard I was buying a new Lexus for his Mother, he stopped bugging me about not doing anything for her retirement. One Saturday, there was a really big sale of fur coats at a fur salon that was going out of business in Canal Place. Gloria and I decided to go and see what was on sale at the closing. You might recall, I bought Gloria a mink coat for our sixteenth anniversary, and she returned the mink coat to the salon because she felt that there were other things more important than the mink at that time.

Age and maturity, however, change what's important. After Gloria tried on several mink coats without selecting any of them, the saleslady brought a gorgeous full-length, swing mink coat for her to try on. The coat was awesome! When Gloria tried on the swing mink coat, it was incredibly stunning; however, its length was a bit too long, nearly to the floor. The saleslady told us that they could alter the mink to the desired length Gloria wanted. However, when Guich saw the price tag of the mink coat, she said, "I think it's a bit long for me." So she began trying on additional mink coats to see if she could find one of her choice.

After unsuccessfully finding one she really liked, the saleslady said, "Mrs. Poree, swing mink coat is for you; it's the perfect coat for you." When our furrier alters the coat to your length satisfactorily, you'll have the most incredible and beautiful mink coat, period!" It wasn't that Gloria didn't like the swing mink coat; it was the twelve thousand dollar price tag that prompted her to say it was too long. I said, "Darling, the saleslady is right; that coat looks like you—stunningly beautiful." Guich looked me straight in the eye, and said, "Edgar, you must be joking, aren't you?" I said, "You've earned every dollar of it, putting up with me for all these years. I told the saleslady, "You've got a deal."

When we got home, I told little Edgar and Deidra to be sure to be at the house at three o'clock on Valentine Day for Mother's big retirement celebration. I bought the 1992 Lexus LS400 Four-Door Luxury Sedan from a dealership in Dallas, Texas, that was owned by the Sewell Cadillac Dealership in New Orleans. The car was shipped in an eighteen wheeler and prepped at the Sewell Cadillac Dealership. I brought the mink coat to the dealership, placed it in the trunk of the car, and, Charles Jones, the salesman that arranged my purchase of the car, secured the car and the mink until it was ready for delivery for the three-thirty arrival at our home at 6219 Providence Place in Pontchartrain Park.

When I arrived at home, Edgar, III, his buddies, Deidra, and her six classmates were all in front of the house when I pulled up. At 3:15 p.m. on Valentine day, when the 1992 Lexus 400 Four-Door Luxury Sedan pulled up in the driveway, my son, daughter, and my extended family daughters began celebrating the arrival of Gloria's retirement gift. Edgar, III said, "Mama, Mama, come outside right now; my Daddy is about to throw down something big for you!" There was a big bright red ribbon tied around the car with a very large bow setting on top of the car. The cheers got louder and louder as the driver demonstrated all of the special features of the car to Guich. When the driver pressed a button and the trunk opened, I told my extended family daughters to look in the trunk of the car. When they saw that beautiful full-length swing mink coat, bedlam broke out as the cheering reach a peak!

Edgar, III repeatedly shouted, "I told you my Daddy was gonna throw down for Mother's retirement; I told you!" The long awaited retirement celebration was a huge success; just ask Edgar, III and the Little Mr. Throw Down!"

Employee Corporate Direction Conference

One constant in corporate America is training, training, and more training. I would not be stretching to say that we were in some type of training every quarter of the year. We attended classes or training sessions introducing new technology, new Federal regulations, new accounting mandates, competition, employee information, and corporate mission and values. The Company scheduled an Employee Corporate Direction Conference Seminar for all State employees in New Orleans. I was one of several District Managers serving as Host for the Corporate Conference. As Host, we had a dual role of introducing Seminar Session Presenters as well as making sure that sessions were completed as scheduled. Each District Manager was provided a binder containing the entire resumes of Conference Seminar Presenters. Most of the seminar presenters were company management personnel except for guest speakers from the political, business, and university leadership.

As a Staff Manager, I served on the Company's Personnel Assessment Team for a considerable time. The Assessment Team was responsible for assessing and identifying non-supervisory employees as potential candidates for promotional considerations. As a part of the assessment process, we had to review the candidates' resume to determine what areas they might be better suited for if deemed promotable. We noted that there was a distinct difference in the number of college graduate and non-college graduates candidates.

Most of the assessment candidates who were college graduates were African-Americans and most of the non-college candidates were White. I guess you might be wondering why this is relevant to the Corporate Direction Conference. After reviewing the resumes of all the management personnel seminar presenters, it somehow validated my assertion and assumptions that there existed a tremendous disparity in qualification requirements for promotion considerations. Most of the management personnel, who were presenters, were non-college graduates; instead their resumes contained similar language and did studies at some colleges or universities. Perhaps, attending Company-sponsored three summer sessions and two-week executive programs at state universities, like I attended, was considered college graduate equivalent.

Corporate Mixed Messages

Because of the rapidly changing telecommunication landscape, the company had to configure its operational strategy as well as strengthen its customer focus initiatives. Headquarters scheduled a Senior Management Conference in Atlanta for all District level and above personnel to discuss newly mandated Federal regulations, the Corporate Mission and Values, and new sources of revenues. The Chairman of the Corporation opened the Conference with a very impelling and candid discussion of the State of Company's Strategic Initiatives for Becoming the Industry's Leading Telecommunication Company. State Presidents, Group Presidents, and Financial Officers were conference presenters, and attendance at all sessions was mandatory.

The Company devoted nearly four hours during the morning session articulating the absolute ethical practices that remained the core value of the Corporation. The overall theme throughout the morning session emphasized the Corporation's Core Values, its principles of operational integrity, and its commitment to never compromise its values during negotiations to acquire business or financial gains! When it was revealed that a company official had lunch with a former associate and friend whose daughter just happened to be an employee of the Federal General Accounting Office, the Company immediately suspended its half billion dollar government contract that was awarded through the bid process. Even though the luncheon between friends had nothing to do with the government awarded contract, the corporation did not want in any way to have even an appearance or perception of any impropriety. That was certainly a most exemplary illustration of not compromising the company's core values and ethical operational principles. After that extraordinary session, it was lunch time.

The afternoon session was devoted to a new and extremely exciting revenue generating business, Tiers Service. That's right; Tiers Service as in prisons. Law enforcement agencies across the Nation have been exploring opportunities for generating revenue sources to help supplement their operational budgets. The Tier Service telephone service for prisoners can be an extremely robust revenue generating mechanism for the company and at the same time help the law enforcement establishment to generate a new source of revenues for operating budgets. The VP presenter was extremely excited about the tremendous revenue generating possibilities of forming a partnership with the law enforcement community. He stated that the potential of Tier Services were unlimited. The company would provide the network facilities for the Tier Services, and the prisons would receive a percentage of the revenues generated.

At that point of the discussion, I raised my hand and the presenter acknowledged me. I asked, "How will the billing of prisoner generating calls be handled?" The VP said that the calls would be charged to the responsible party authorizing the Tier Service. I said, "Such as the prisoner's Mother, Grandmother, wife, or some other relative that may feel compelled to provide some type of relief for their kin." The VP responded, all of the parties you mentioned. I then said, "I am rather confused, this afternoon, regarding our apparent pursuit of establishing a partnership with law enforcement in providing Tier Service, especially in light of the lengthy discussion this morning about our not ever compromising our core values of integrity and practices of ethical behavior in exchange for generating revenues. The audience was deadly silent at that point. "My concern is that the authorized responsible parties, whose sympathy and empathy for their incarcerated sons, grandsons, or siblings, may be placed in an unsustainable financial position, jeopardizing their ability to pay for their bare necessities."

At that that point, a recess was called, and as I began walking out of the auditorium, my peers took the most distant route to the refreshment area. When I reached the refreshment area to get some of the most irresistible variety of disserts and pastries, apparently I was the only one who wanted any of the goodies. All of my peers assembled far and away from the refreshment area, so I had a good time sampling all of the goodies. Just before the recess was nearing a close, a brave young company executive walked over to me and said, "Edgar, you sure got guts, to say perhaps what others may have been thinking, but wouldn't dare comment. "Your former boss, Bill, said that you are driven by strong ethical behavior at all times. That was evident by your remarks. My boss told me someone told him it was refreshing to see someone brave enough to ask tough questions. I sat quietly throughout the remainder of that session.

First and Only Favorable TV Editorial

As you may recall, when I was given my top priority as District Manager, it was to get a favorable editorial from the metropolitan leading editorialist when we would go before the Louisiana Public Service Commission in Rate Consideration Cases. That mission had never been accomplished by any District Managers preceding my tenure. As a matter of fact, we had never gotten a favorable anything from this leading Television Editorial Department in almost two decades. Every week, especially those weeks nearing the hearings scheduled before the Louisiana Public Service Commission regarding the Company's Rate Case, I was asked this question over and over, "Edgar, what's our chances of getting a positive editorial?" I responded, "I remain rather confident." You see I never told them of my strategic musical related conversion plan that I had been successfully developing with the editorialist. This time I felt that we just might pull off a miracle and get a positive editorial from one of the company's most staunch adversary. I knew that the old-timers thought that things would be the same since none of their good-old-boys had gotten any positive results over the years.

The day before the Public Service Commissioners' meeting, everyone was tense as usual awaiting the evening editorialist's rendering. The Senior

Officers of the Company were assembled in the President's Conference Room, and I was there also. Each of the Senior Management Team asked, "Edgar, what's your take on this?" I still believe that this will be a "First" for the company!" With the VCR Recorder on ready for the taping of the editorial, all members of the Senior Management Team were focused on the television. When the editorialist appeared, the conference room was dead silent and all eyes and ears were at attention.

The editorialist said, "A Company that had thousands of employees, who contributed hundreds of millions of dollars in economic development to our City as well as communities all over the State plus donated thousands of volunteer hours of assisting community worthwhile projects as well as contributed hundreds of thousands of dollars to the United Way, deserves considerations of relief from the Louisiana Public Service Commission in its Rate Case Hearing on tomorrow." The dead silence broke into cheers of excitement, adulation, and congratulations. "Edgar Poree, you're the Man," exclaimed the President! I was immediately surrounded by the Officers, and each individually bear hugged me and gave me a heavy congratulatory hand shake. A courier was waiting for the taped editorial to bring to the corporate jet so that the Official Taped Editorial Message could be flown to the Chairman of the Corporation in Atlanta. Mission Accomplished.

First African American Keynote Speaker

Terry Brooks, High School Principal of Jefferson County's Public Schools District, was the featured speaker at Tulane University's Educational Development Foundation's School Leadership Seminar. Terry Brook's High School had the greatest ethnic, by-racial student body in the School District and was one of the highest academic achievement performance schools in the entire Nation. The Jefferson County Public School District in Louisville, Kentucky, at that time was rated the Third Best School District in the Nation. The Seminar's participants were public school principals and administrators from surrounding metropolitan parishes. Dr. King, Chairman of the Foundation, asked me to give pep-talks to begin the Seminar to engage the audience in welcoming Terry Brooks to our City.

When I completed my brief pep-talk and after Dr. King's introduction of Terry Brooks, the keynote speaker, his very first comments, "How in the hell can you follow such a dynamic and incredibly inspiring message!" "Edgar Poree, you are going to give that message to the Jefferson County Public School District at its School Year's Administrators Conference in Louisville Kentucky this August," said Terry Brooks. "That's a certainty, I can promise," concluded Brooks. I thought that was just a compliment by the guest speaker as he began to address the audience. After Brook's presentation, he met with Dr. King and me to get my contact information so that he could make the necessary accommodation reservations for my trip to Louisville for the School District's Administrators Conference. I was indeed elated of the prospect of participating in such an elite School District in the country.

When I notified my boss of the invitation to participate in the Jefferson County Public School District's Administrators Conference in Louisville, Kentucky, he did not hesitate to authorize my travel and hotel accommodations for the trip. He also notified his counterpart in the Louisville Corporate and External Affairs Office of my participation so they may have a presence at the Conference. The Gheens Foundation, the sponsoring organization of the Administrators Conference and one of the Nation's leading developmental catalysts for transforming schools in Jefferson County and other school districts across the country, contacted me to get my fee for professional service. Since I did not have an established fee for professional service, I asked Dr. King to recommend a possible fee that would be appropriate for my participation in the conference. She suggested $ 700. I notified the Gheens Foundation of my fee of $700, and they sent me a letter of confirmation covering all expenses for my participation in the 1919-92 Jefferson County Public School District's Administrators Conference.

When I arrived at the airport in Louisville, Kentucky, Tom Johnson a consulting administrator of the Gheens Foundation greeted and welcomed me to Louisville. Tom said, "Brother, you must be able to walk and talk on water, according to Terry Brooks." Tom told me that the Gheens Foundation had never experienced such raving from any of its top associates like that of Terry Brooks about your dynamic and inspiring speech at Tulane University. Johnson said, "Edgar Poree, you are the very first African-American Keynote Speaker in the history of the Jefferson County Public School District's Administrators Conference; that's certainly quite an accomplishment." As much as the raving and complimentary reviews of your oratory skills were articulated, by Terry Brooks, I must tell you

I was extremely disappointed, while processing your fee for professional services. Your seven hundred dollar fee was at the very least, a thousand dollars short of the norm for your scheduled presentation. We are going to make up for that in the future, you can count on that.

After my "No More Excuses" keynote address to the more than seven hundred administrators of the Jefferson County Public School District's 1991 School Year Conference, I received a standing ovation. Several senior management officials of Bellsouth, including the Vice President of Corporate and External Affairs, who were present, expressed their congratulations most enthusiastically. The Vice President told me that Bellsouth's stature as a Good Corporate Citizen was greatly enhanced by my presence and presentation. Officials of the Jefferson County Public Schools expressed interest in my participating in their Leadership Training Seminar, sponsored by the Annie B. Casey Foundation. Since this was a great opportunity for me professionally, I would have to take some vacation time to schedule my participation in the Annie B. Casey Foundation's Leadership Seminar. All expenses would be covered by the Foundation. My professional fee this time will not be "less" than the going rate, you can count on that.

Annie B. Casey Foundation Seminar Leadership Consultant

The Annie B. Casey Foundation's Leadership Seminar for School Superintendents and Deputy Superintendents was held in Louisville, Kentucky. The three-day Leadership Seminar focused on the role, duties, responsibilities, and the delegation of authority of School's Leadership Cadre. I served as a Consultant Leadership Trainer for the Seminar workshops addressing Parental Involvement Initiatives, Establishing Greater School, Neighborhood, and Business Partnerships, and Developing School's Economic Development Impact on Community Initiative. The Seminar participants were extremely complimentary of my presentations, and many inquired as to my availability to conduct similar leadership training in their school districts.

The Deputy Superintendent of Buffalo, New York, Public School District told me that her three-day experience in my leadership training classes warranted establishing a Leadership Training Seminar in the Buffalo School District. She wanted the Buffalo Public School District to be the very "first" district on my schedule. Since the Leadership Training ended on Thursday evening, I decided to spend Friday and Saturday in Louisville with Tom Johnson's family. Gloria told me that the Deputy Superintendent from Buffalo called her five times about sending my resume to her office so she could begin preparing the paperwork required in setting up the training.

When I returned home, I sent my resume to the Buffalo's Deputy Superintendent's office. Unfortunately, although she was most impressed with her three days of leadership training in my classes, apparently my Bachelor of Arts Degree in Education, which qualified my participation as a Consulting Leadership Trainer for the Annie B. Casey Foundation, was not prestigious enough for Buffalo's School District. It's ironic that after being in my class for three days of leadership training in which she championed my skill sets, my multiple parent, neighborhood, and business partnership initiatives, the Deputy Superintendent of The Buffalo School District felt that my resume did not justify such a financial commitment. Unfortunately, "Title Consciousness" for some is the only validation of competence. I wonder if the Deputy Superintendent knew anything about Bill Gates.

Death of Juli Rose, Second Oldest Sister

During the spring of 1993, the corporation committed a team of employees to participate in Habitat Humanity 20/20,000 House Project in Americus, Georgia, that summer. I was selected along with two other employees from Louisiana to be a part of BellSouth's Corporate Team. It was a great honor to be one of the State's representatives for this historic events, and I was eagerly waiting with great anticipation this exciting opportunity. Unfortunately, my exuberance turned to grief on May 11, 1993, at the death of my second oldest sister, Juli Rose, who had battled bone cancer for years. Juli, the physically beautiful, talented, quiet no-none-sense teacher and avid gardener, no longer would be seen manicuring her flower beds on Press Drive in Pontchartrain Park. No longer would we see those beautifully embroiderer needle works of art Juli created. Nor would we see those very stylish hairdos, fashioned by this artistic cosmologist. Finally, no longer would I be able to sit down and enjoy eating her famous stewed bananas sandwich. Juli's death was certainly painful to us; however, her suffering was finally over.

Habitat for Humanity 20/20,000 House Project

In the summer of 1993, Habitat for Humanity began its most ambitious projects in Americus, Georgia. The project's mission was to build 20 houses in one week in conjunction with its celebration of reaching 20,000 housing built since its beginning. Corporations in the Gulf South Region were encouraged to provide volunteers to participate in the building of the twenty homes. BellSouth provided forty-two employees from our nine operating state territory. Our Louisiana team consisted of two men and one woman.

As we arrived in Americus, Georgia, on Sunday afternoon, there were hundreds of volunteers from all over the country congregating in this huge open field in the middle of nowhere. The volunteers were young, old, men, women, tall, short, stocky, Black, White, Asian, Native Americans, crippled, and even some who were blind and some who were getting around in wheelchairs. I had never seen such a widely diverse group of volunteer workers, as I saw that Sunday. It had been raining most of the day, and the field was quite soggy, but the spirits of the volunteers were not dampened in the least. There were signs designating were the volunteer meeting tent was located; where toilet and shower facilities were located; where tools sheds were located; where safety equipment was located; and, where the sleeping quarter tents for male and female volunteers were located.

There were huge army-type tents scattered around this huge open field which housed the assembly hall, the cafeteria, the shower stalls and toilets, and our sleeping quarters. At five o'clock that evening, we had dinner and briefings from the Director of Habitat and the project manager who gave us our assignments. We were all in awe when the Director introduced the number one and two volunteers in the project, President Jimmy Carter and his wife, Roslyn. Every volunteer stood up, cheered, and followed with thunderous applause. After the Director concluded our assignment, there were photo-ops with the President and his wife, and then we were off to the tool shed to get our equipment and safety items for tomorrow's building work. As we left the meeting, we saw huge stacks of straw bundles

Dreamer Who's Been Extremely Blessed

near the construction site of each of the twenty houses for use in the event of rain during the construction.

Monday morning, we had breakfast at 5 a.m. and after an opening prayer and construction assignment, we were off to our construction site to begin our day's assignment. When we arrived at our construction site, the slab had been completed and the lumber, plywood sheeting, siding nails, roofing tussles, rolls of felt, and ladders were provided. Day One's objective was to complete the framing with roof covered with felt. That was a tall order, considering the tremendous overcast weather conditions. In spite of the challenge, we were all ready to complete Day One assignment. Our company had forty-two volunteers scheduled to work during the week; however, only about half that total was present for day one. We were fortunate to have volunteers who had worked on Habitat projects in their communities so they were skillful in building. As we began lining up to start work that morning, a tremendously dark cloud appeared, and all of a sudden loud thunder and lightning lit up the sky. It looked like we would not have a chance to complete the Day One assignment of having completely finished the framing and roofing for our house.

The week's mission of building twenty homes in five days appeared to be in great jeopardy that morning. As the clouds grew darker and the lighting and thunder roared louder and more intently, something unlike I had ever experienced occurred. The open field where the twenty construction sites were scheduled for building twenty homes miraculously escaped the thunderous and lightening-striking rainy weather which surrounded the open field all day long. It had to be an act of Devine Intervention that occurred which allowed most of the volunteers to complete their assignments of finishing the framing and roofing of their homes on Day One. Because many of our company volunteers were very skillful, we completed framing and roofing our assigned home, and we provided assistance to two other construction crews in completing their framing and roofing before nightfall.

In spite of the heavy winds and storm-like rain throughout the day around the open field where the twenty homes were being constructed, not one rain drop fell on any of the construction sites until the very last roof was completely finished on the twentieth home. Many volunteers expressed openly about their feelings and belief that this day's experience had to be on very sacred and blessed grounds. At that night's dinner, many volunteers expressed their gratitude of having witnessed and experienced visual evidence of the enormity, grandeur, and unlimited power of the Creator.

As more and more of our company volunteers reported back home during the week, we were ahead of schedule, and we finished building our home in four days. Jane Fonda, the controversial actress and activist worked on our home on Wednesday, as we were hanging the roofing shingles. While I was on the roof at the time she was taking photo-ops nailing shingles, I asked Fonda to say a few words to my wife Gloria for me. She asked, "How am I going to say a few words to your wife Gloria, when she's not here?" I said, "She's not here, but my tape recorded is in my pocket." Jane Fonda laughed and began saying, "Hello Gloria, I just want to tell you while other volunteers were working on the roof nailing shingles, your husband, Edgar, was getting interviews from other working volunteers for his wife, Gloria." "I had to stop working on the Habitat project to comply with his request, so Hello, Gloria, bet you got your hands full with Edgar, goodbye and much happiness, Jane Fonda."

Since we completed our home site on Thursday, I volunteered to design the garden for our BellSouth home site. Since we had two crape myrtle trees, I designed two bell shaped gardens for the front lawn of the house for the two trees. Company officials stood on the roof of homes across the street of our home site to take photographs of the bell-shaped gardens that I constructed for distribution among the company volunteers. Our company volunteers raised enough money to purchase a refrigerator for the family scheduled to own the home. We were fortunate to take pictures with President Carter and his wife for our Habitat for Humanity experience. We met a lot of wonderful new associates and new friends in Americus, Georgia.

Burkenroad Institute's Seminar with Dr. Cornell West

As a member of the Business Council of Tulane University's A. B. Freeman School of Business, I was extremely pleased to hear that Professor Art Brief had been successful in getting Dr. Cornel West, author of "Race Matters," to be The 1994 Burkenroad Institute's Seminar Speaker. Dr. West was one of the Nation's premier leaders in the field of social science. The Burkenroad Institute, in addition to hosting the seminar planned a luncheon with Dr. West and some of the community's leadership following

Dreamer Who's Been Extremely Blessed

the seminar. Because of the tremendous interest in Dr. West's appearance, accommodating such a luncheon on Tulane's campus posed some logistical problems, especially the limited parking. Professor Brief also felt that hosting both the seminar and luncheon on Tulane's campus might not afford an optimum opportunity of getting a more diverse reflection of the community's leadership to interface with Dr. West.

In conjunction with that concern, Dr. Brief contacted me to inquire about alternative facilities that would be a good prospect for hosting the Burkenroad Institute's Community Leadership Luncheon with Dr. Cornel West. I suggested Xavier University. Dr. Brief said, "Edgar, that's a great idea; do you think we can pull that off?" I contacted Sybil Morial, Director of Xavier's Drexel's Center for Extended Learning, to discuss the possibility of utilizing Xavier University's Student Center as the place to hold Tulane University's Burkenroad Institute's Community Leadership Luncheon with Dr. Cornel West. I told Director Morial that the institute would be responsible for the financing and staffing for the luncheon. Sybil seemed pleased about the prospects of such a unique partnership. She indicated that she would check the Student Center's availability plus the food service provider as to their capability of providing both the students' normal luncheon service plus the expanded services for the luncheon. She told me that she would get back with me after talking with the Dr. Norman Francis, Xavier's President.

I received a call from the Sybil advising me that Dr. Francis agreed to allow Tulane to use Xavier's Student Center to host the Burkenroad Institute's Community Leadership Luncheon with Dr. Cornel West. Sybil did an incredible job of coordinating and facilitating the entire behind the scene essential components of hosting a successful event. She was also instrumental in developing a cross-section listing of our community's leadership. The enhanced and incredible representation of our City's diverse leadership at the Tulane University and Xavier University Partnership Luncheon with the, distinguished guest, Dr. Cornel West, were the real winners in this Community Leadership Luncheon.

After Dr. Cornel West's dynamic and inspirational presentation in the standing-room only audience in Dixon Hall, cheers of Bravo, Bravo, Bravo, echoed the auditorium followed by thunderous applauds by the enthusiastic guests. The Community Leadership Luncheon concluded a day that can only be described as a banner day for Tulane University and Xavier University Partnership.

University's Economic Impact Matrix

As a Founding member of the University of New Orleans' Higher Education Council, I had an opportunity to discuss the possibility of developing a Comprehensive Economic Profile, similar to the one that I had developed for my corporation. Members of the Council and Chancellor O'Brian were very receptive of my offer and they indicated that we should proceed in exploring how best to commence initiating development of the profile. After several discussions with Chancellor O'Brian and members of his staff, I began the process by identifying key informational data need to develop the University's Economic Impact Profile.

The university's registration office and the procurement office were vital components in developing the profile. Political and business leaders understood two very essentials components in marketing, voters and dollars. Identification of the student, faculty and staff residential locations, coupled with the dollars spent by the university's family translates into tremendous influence exercised by the university. Once we obtained the numbers from the registration office and the dollar figures from the comptroller's and procurement office, we than began to develop the university's Economic Impact Profile. UNO's extended family, including current faculty, staff and student body and graduating alumnus exceeded forty-nine thousand.

That figure alone exceeds many communities' population totals. When you include the salaries and wages of the current faculty and staff of the university plus the university's annual procurement spending, the university's becomes a major participant in helping shape policy making and funding appropriations of the state's one hundred and forty-four (144) legislators. When the University's Economic Impact Profile was completed, a Financial Profile was developed for each of the 144 legislators as well as elected officials in the largest metropolitan cities in the state. As results, the university had greater access and influence with decision makers enhancing tremendously, funding for university initiatives.

The University's Economic Impact Profile Initiative, also enabled Chancellor O'Brian and his legislative team to more effectively negotiate and acquire funding resources, at the national level by our congressional delegation. It proved to be a tremendous resource in generating much needed resources for UNO.

Death of Big Sister

On August 17, 1995, Edna Floe Poree-Harrington, our oldest of the Poree's children died. Like Mother, the matriarch and spiritual backbone and family curator, Edna Floe was the source and inspiration of family support, the provider of spiritual reinforcement, the mediator of conflict and the most unselfish, caring and loving person that exemplified goodness and decency at all times. When Edna Floe became aware of the situation, no matter how difficult or how seemingly impossible to resolve, her dignified diplomacy, her lady-like persuasion and her ability to mediate and transform conflicts and confrontations into amicable resolution, made her the "healer" and patron saint of our family. Edna Floe, my big sister was my champion and protector throughout my development. When I should have been punished and even spanked for my misbehavior, in school, she would always find something good that I did on the day of my misbehaving, to lessen my punishment.

Edna Floe made it possible for our family to purchase our home by providing seventy percent of the down payment. Edna Floe did the groceries, paid the bills drove Mother most places and provided assistance for decades for nieces and a nephew until they were grown. Everyone who had the good fortune of being in the company of Edna Floe, during their lives, experienced goodness, graciousness, warmth, kindness as because of her, they experienced and became a better person as a result of her.

At Edna Floe Poree Harrington's Home Going Celebration of Life Service at Grace United Methodist Church, our family's Church, I spoke on behalf of the Poree family. After summarizing the many acts of love, kindness and unselfish assistances rendered to so many lives throughout her lifetime, I concluded my reflection saying, "Words along cannot express the tremendous loss, that all who had been fortunate of being in Edna's presence, those who had been touched and influenced by her spirituality and uncompromising and unwavering ethical and moral discipline of Edna Floe Poree Harrington, by my big sister: we were all made stronger, wiser, more tolerant and more loving because we all were extremely blessed for being in the presence of and touching shoulders with Edna Floe Poree Harrington during our lifetime." The entire church congregation stood up responded in unison, "Yes, we've been touched, blessed and made better because of having been loved by Edna Floe Poree Harrington."

I wrote a letter Rev. Robert Harrington, my brother-in-law a year after Edna Floe's death to express how all of us had grown, because we had been touched, we had been made more understanding because we all had been blessed by her presence. (See Appendix A: Letter to Rev. Robert Harrington.)

Secured Much Needed Resources for University

As the company began transferring operational offices from downtown headquarters to New Orleans East complex, much of the existing furniture and audio-visual equipment housed at headquarters was being replaced. I inquired as to the status of the surplus furniture and audio equipment and discovered that no claim had been made as of yet. I immediately requested considerations of donating the furniture and audio-visual equipment be donated to Xavier University, once those resources were declared surplus. I was advised to draft a proposal justifying the donation and it was approved.

As a result of the Company's approval the university received a significant number of Steelcase desks, credenzas, open service modules, executive desk chairs, clerical chairs, side chairs and conference tables. Additionally, the university received a complete computer-controlled image projection system. The university's president indicated that the image projection system would be an excellent addition to the Center's resources. He envisioned the Art Department getting invaluable usage from portfolio slides presentations while the Development Office could get great use in its presentations for capital campaign. The university expressed its sincere thanks and appreciation for the company's tremendous generosity.

Bayou Classic Sponsorship

Year after year Southern University and Grambling State University's Bayou Classic Weekend Experience in New Orleans became the visitors' Mecca location for the Thanksgiving weekend. The Bayou Classic was a tremendous economic engine, pumping tens of millions in the New Orleans area and bringing tens of thousands of visitors to the city, especially during what was once a traditionally slow tourist's time of the year. With that tremendous growth and national appeal, the Bayou Classic became a much sought after marketing attraction for corporate sponsors.

Southern and Grambling State Universities sought a $50,000 level Bayou Classic Corporate Sponsorship from BellSouth, ten times the amount of the initial two twenty-five hundred dollar checks that I delivered to the two universities. This would require some major justification initiatives. After researching the corporation's South Eastern Conference Sponsorships (SEC), I developed a strong case, from a marketing prospective and appeal, with the growth and brand association with the Bayou Classic that resulted in our corporation being one of the first Fifty Thousand Dollar Sponsors of the Bayou Classic. This was quite an accomplishment, especially in light of the initial levels of support of the Southern University and Grambling State University's annual Football Game.

Closed Door Meeting with Company President

After returning from a meeting that I attended on behalf of the Company's President, I met three young men, while entering Canal Place, One of the young men was Gregory Smith a former sixth grade student that I taught at Johnson Lockett School. Gregory was one student that I could never forget, because he was always getting in trouble meddling little girls, pulling their pony tails and calling them funny names. I spanked Gregory more times than all of the other boys in my class that year. He wasn't a bad little boy, just mischievous like his teacher, when I was in elementary school.

Gregory was now a very successful electrical engineer for an elevator company. He was married, owned his home, and had three lovely children, two college graduates, and one technical school graduate, not bad for a little mischievous sixth grader. Gregory said, "That's the man who spanked me more than my parents, and the man who's responsible for me being able to buy a house, send my kids to college and make it possible for my family to take vacations." We embraced each other and Gregory said, "Mr. Poree, I still have my original five dollar savings account receipt and Savings Account Book from the credit union that you made us open a savings account as a condition of employment in the summer program that you were the Director."

At that point, we exchanged information about our families, than Gregory asked, "Mr. Poree, what's on your agenda this afternoon?" I told Gregory that I was going to meet with the company's president when I got to the office, then I was going to do something that just might make today, my last day on the job! Gregory and the two young men looked rather perplexed at my statement and one of the two young men asked, "What you mean today might be your last day on the job?" I told the young men that after I finished my report, of the meeting I attended for the president, I was going to ask, if I could speak with him behind closed door, candidly and frankly about things that others would not have the courage to share with him. Gregory said, "That's why we always had great respect for you, even though you whipped our behinds, more than anyone else at school, you were always honest and willing to tell it like it was, rather than sugar coat it make it to appear to be something else. We parted our ways and I proceeded to the president's office to give my report.

After giving the president a synopsis of what had taken place at the meeting that I had attended on his behalf I asked him if I could speak with him a few moments, behind closed doors? He said, "Certainly you may." I began by saying, "I must admit what I'm about to say might result in my not being looked upon as a very promising future in the company." However, since I'm almost ten years your senior in age, I felt compelled to share with you some observations. Because of your tremendous commitment to the success of the corporation's missions and values, coupled with the enormous pressure manifested in fulfilling your leadership responsibilities, perhaps it didn't allow for getting candid feedback of your approach in fulfilling your responsibilities. At that point, the president sat up in his chair, began patting the back of his manicured hair, then I knew my observations were immediately under intense scrutiny.

I began telling the president about the perception of the employees' regarding his morning routine pattern of selecting which elevator to take to his thirtieth floor office. The employees indicated you either wait until the elevator was almost full, before you stepped in, or you would wait until another elevator arrives, immediately entering and closing the door before anyone else arrived to take a solo trip to the thirtieth floor. Their impression of the reason for your selection process was not perceived as an eagerness getting to work immediately, but to make sure you were avoiding any opportunity of engaging in any dialogue with them. The expression, on the president's face was not very pleasant.

I continued my observations, with my perception of the manner in which he addressed the questioning of some of the members of the senior leadership team about the questioning addressed to them my subordinates. I told the president the questions raised by some members of the leadership team were the same questions raised by our non-manage and management employees, as to why and what happened to change drastically previous commitments that appeared to be somewhat misleading. I told the president that a very chilling and intimidating feeling occurred at that meeting, when you admonished a member of the leadership team when he asked if you would come to his department and help explain our position in the matter being questioned. The silent response was deafening. I then said, "Sometimes, the end results aren't appreciated by the masses, at the time when critical decisions must be made to save the majority of the masses." The president's facial expression was not very pleasant however he continued listening.

Then I turned my focus to the company's OJT reduction process. I said, "When you were responsible for the OJT job reduction process, you were not the favorite person on the employees' list. Numerous employees perceived you as the bad person who caused their long time coworkers to lose their jobs and wreck havoc on their families. At that point, when I said, "Mr. President, you and I have a lot in common." His facial expression abruptly changed from one of tolerance to one of distain. I continued, "Many years ago, I found myself in the same type of predicament, that you may be perceived today; when I had to make a decision that would negatively impact one of my supervisor's employment. The case had similar circumstances but not in the magnitude that you had in the company's employee reduction process. The supervisor that I had to make a decision whether or not to terminate him was not an easy one because he had a wife and six children to support.

When I got home I mentioned to my wife that I had to make a tough decision as to whether I should keep one of my supervisors, who was a nice guy, but I just didn't feel that he was the right person, at that time to fulfill his commitments or developing those two hundred teenage student assignees. My wife told me that my employee was responsible for taking care of eight people, and I should consider the hardships that I would cause by terminating that person. That was a heavy burden placed on my plate. That night, as I pondered my decision, I took into consideration, "Would those 200 teenagers be better off with someone else's leadership for their development or was it more responsible and considerate on my part to continue providing a source of income to support his family of eight persons?"

Finally, I decided to compare the numbers affected. I subtracted the numbers of the eight family members that would be adversely affected by my decision of terminating the supervisor against the 192 teenagers whose critical development might be impaired by retaining the supervisor. I concluded that there were 192 reasons justifying my decision to terminate the supervisor. I did seek an opportunity for the supervisor to get another assignment in the agency that he was better suited. I changed his termination to resignation, and he was gainfully employed within two weeks of his separation from my program without losing any loss of income with his two week severance pay.

Before finishing my comparison of what we had in common, I said, "Mr. President, all of those employees that targeted you as the really bad person, responsible for terminating their long time coworkers and friends, did not realize that if you had not fulfill your responsibility to trim the size of the employee base, at that time prevented the corporation's demise in the rapidly evolving telecommunication environment." Unfortunately, the thousands of employees whose employment was saved were unaware of those extremely stressful nights and days that you painfully deliberated options of salvaging their jobs. The retention of their jobs was only made possible because of your leadership and willingness to make the tough decisions during the job elimination process. When you are not completely knowledgeable of all of the facts and circumstances impacting a decision, your absence from the deliberations process sometimes taint and lessen the full ramification of the decision.

When I completed, my observations and comparisons, the president said, "Edgar, if you had told me that I was not totally committed to the corporate goals and mission, then you might have been in a questionable position." He further told me he appreciated my candor and the frank manner in which I had express some observations that perhaps in his delineations, deliberations and commitments associated with administering the corporate mandate, perception and appearance had not been a priority. In closing the president stated he would began paying more attention to many of the observations that I had shared with him that day. The president stood up, walked around his desk, gave me a hardy hand shake and thanks.

When my boss heard I had a meeting with the president, behind closed doors for more than an hour, he asked, "Edgar what were you talking about?" When I told him what I discussed, he was astonished saying, "You told the president all of those things, are you still employed?" My boss said "That's unbelievable Edgar," with a smile. After my closed door meeting with the president, I got direct telephone calls from him from time to time, inquiring about my impressions and assessments of some of the observations and traits I had discussed with him. Subsequent to our closed door meeting, I felt comfortable in calling the president in instances I thought appropriate.

Edgar, III's Honors, Disappointment and Graduation

After a very successful and profitable job opportunity during the summer, Edgar, III told me before the beginning of his junior year at Southern University at New Orleans that he was getting a 4.0 Grade Point Average this semester. Like most Father's I was rather skeptical about this declaration since I had never seen multiple A's in any courses or semester reports. Edgar, III was rather emphatic about his intentions. He told me I would be the first one to see his 4.0 mid-term grades. One thing for sure, whenever Edgar, III made up his mind to do something he usually did it. However, when it came to concentrating on completing college, or competing in auto car and truck shows, or being an awesome billiard competitor, college appeared to be third. My response to his declaration was, "I'll be looking forward to mid-term."

Well, when mid-term came, Edgar was true to his word and I was the first to see his 4.0 mid-term grades. I was speechless, motionless, mesmerized yet proud as I could be. He said, "Daddy, didn't I tell you what I was going to do, do me!" I looked up toward heaven and said, "Father, is the big one coming?" Meaning my departure! When Gloria saw her baby she embraced him and as usual said, "That's my baby, that's my baby, I knew he could do it, I didn't have any doubt in my mind that he couldn't do it!" There was no doubt among us that this was truly an incredible accomplishment and we were extremely proud of Edgar, III. After congratulating Edgar, like a typical Father, I told him the real challenge now was to retain that 4.0 Grade Point Average at the end of the semester. Edgar, III said with great confidence, "You can bank on it, Father!"

At the end of the semester, Edgar, III's maintained his 4.0 Grade Point Average, just as he promised at the beginning of the year. What was at first a truly challenging and extremely ambitious goal, turn out to be an incredibly awesome accomplishment. Well done my son well done. On April 13, 1994, Southern University at New Orleans held its Honors and Awards Day Ceremony in the Multi-Purpose Auditorium. We were all awaiting with great this event. We were very excited with great anticipation, of witnessing our son's recognition for achieving an incredible 4.0 Grade Point Average. As Edgar, III approached the stage, the Dean of the College of Arts and Social Sciences said, "I am extremely proud to present, recognize and acknowledge the extraordinary academic achievement of excellence of having attained a perfect 4.0 Grade Point Average in Criminal Justice, Mr. Edgar Francis Poree, Jr." Edgar's facial expression was rather somber, not jubilant. Because the name announced, the name listed in the Program and the name on the Honor's Certificate was not that of Edgar Francis Poree, III, unfortunately it was his Father's name, Edgar Francis Poree, Jr.

At that moment I recalled that evening, many years ago when little Edgar asked his Mother, "Momma why didn't I have my own name instead of Daddy's name, I'll never be able to have my own identity or recognized for my own accomplishments." SUNO's Honors Ceremony confirmed little Edgar's fears. When Edgar, III came over to our seats, after the ceremony, you could see the disappointment in his eyes, having been called Edgar Francis Poree, Jr. The first thing he said, "Daddy, you never had a 4.0 Grade Point Average and I worked so hard for my 4.0 and who got the credit and recognition, you did." He continued, "I love you Daddy and I've always been proud of what you did and what you accomplished, but having the same name hinders my identity, I'm always, Edgar's son. The Dean apologized for the error in the program and the acknowledgment. Unfortunately, the official program was official, Edgar, III won't have a document with his Official Name listed in it. That was a bitter sweet event, filled with great accomplishments, and unfortunate improper acknowledgments.

On Saturday May 11, 1996, during an Eleven O'clock Ceremony, at Nat G. Kiefer's Lakefront Arena, Edgar Francis Poree, III received his Bachelor of Science Degree in Criminal Justice from Southern University at New Orleans. This time the official invitation, the official program, and the Dean's official announcement and recognition of Edgar Francis Poree,

III's graduation from SUNO clearly identified with great clarity and distinction, Edgar Francis Poree, III. This was truly a wonderful occasion for the Poree family. That evening, Edgar Francis Poree, III had a fantastic Graduation Celebration in his honor at the Alpha Plaza, Suite 123 at 9701 Lake Forest Boulevard. The disappointment of the Honors Ceremony was in the past and Edgar Francis Poree, III told me he was so very proud of being my son, and hearing his name called during Graduation, meant "Victory, Mission Accomplished." We embraced, touched fists, gave "thumbs-up and high fives!

Company's Reorganization—Pluses and Minuses

During the Corporation's Reorganization, our former General Counsel and the Corporation's Associate General Counsel was appointed President of Louisiana Operations on July 1, 1996. The announcement of the new president's appointment brought immediate very favorable response from the business, educational, and community leadership. The new president was a local highly respected and well known community leader who had actively participated in the business, educational and social services initiatives in leadership capacities for decades. Additionally, his political savvy coupled with his senior affiliations with one of the region's largest and most prestigious legal firm positioned the company like never before, in a dynamic get things done mode.

Management personnel, especially members of the senior management team, who had working experiences with the newly appointed president, when he was Company's General Counsel were extremely enthusiastic about his inclusion management philosophy and style. Non-management employees, who had worked on numerous community projects, with the new president, were quite complimentary of him, especially his obvious genuine caring of others, and his no-none sense title consciousness. They indicated that they felt comfortable in communicating with him, never intimated by him because he always treated them with respect. What a change!

From a personal standpoint, my participation and direct involvement in resolving numerous critical issues facing the company, during the newly appointed president's tenure as General Counsel, afforded many forthcoming opportunities that I had previously been omitted. This became obvious; a few days after the new president began his administration. I received a telephone call from the new president inviting me to his office for some coffee. When I arrived, he gave me a hardy hand shake and a bear hug, saying, "Edgar, it's great to have you on the team and I look forward to your insight, your candor and willingness to think outside the box in addressing evolving issues." After articulating some of the initiatives and challenges that were facing us, he asked, "What's Gloria and your vacationing plans for next month?" You noticed how knowledgeable he was about the senior leadership of the Poree family by acknowledging Gloria than me in his inquiry. My response, "I've got to check with Gloria about our vacation plans." We laughed and he said, "Tell Gloria that if her plans were open for late August, he and his wife were extending an invitation to join them for a week in Chicago, to attend the Democratic National Convention."

I called Gloria and told her of the president's invitation, and then I asked "What were our vacation plans for late August?" She said, "Chicago!" My immediate boss and his wife were also a part of our company contingent for the August convention trip. That was quite a new beginning for Gloria and I and the start of numerous opportunities that heretofore were not afforded. The Chicago Democratic National Convention trip was an incredible experience. We stayed in a four star hotel, ate in the finest restaurants, shopped in many of the Nation's finest stores and toured many of the city's most notable landmarks as well as enjoying one of the funniest and entertaining musical at the theatre.

Unfortunately, the more invitations that Gloria and I received from the president and the more inclusion of my participation in the resolution of critical issues and matters confronting the company, further exuberating resentment from my immediate boss. Consequently, I had to be quite diplomatic in accepting certain invitations, especially social ones, so as to not further fuel my superior's resentment. My concern about the possible negative ramifications and consequences of my being included in so many events and activities, previously not afforded me, were legitimate, particularly as it related to my performance assessment.

Inclusion, is certainly desirable, however, it does have its consequences and potential adverse impacts, particularly on those who felt that their title alone entitled them to special considerations and perks, exclusively. Unfortunately, individual performance evaluations somehow became inter-twined with and secondary to the personal morays of the superior, rather than objective assessment of their subordinate's actual performance. This became most apparent with individuals who felt threatened by their superior's inclusion of subordinates in matters important to the company. Inclusion, of Gloria and I in the Chicago trip was the beginning of a series of events and activities that adversely contributed to a deteriorating of objective assessment of my performance by, my superior.

Factors Impacting My Superior's Relationship with Me

The initial months of the new president's tenure afforded me numerous opportunities to participate in company perks: trips on corporate jets to the Nation's capital for a senator's fundraiser, early arrival for the Washing Mardi Gras festivities and invitations to socials that I had not attended under previous senior officials. These inclusions, did not grant me much favor with my superior, nor did it make me one of our department's revered insider. One event in particular that, according to numerous coworkers, that attended my daughter's wedding and reception, indicated that when my superior entered the university grand ballroom, his facial expressions told it all. He could not camouflage, his curiosity and seemingly befuddled feelings of wondering how in the hell could I afford such an elaborate reception, particularly since he knew what my corporate compensation was. To further complicate matters, when the live entertainment began and when the food was served in china and the drinks in crystal, his silence was broken. One of my guests over heard him saying to one of the staff members, "I wonder where in the hell he's gotten this kind of money to pay for this lavished bash?"

During the Washington Mardi Gras festivities in D.C., traditionally district managers hosted a hospitality reception for the company's guests. Prior to leaving, I told my superior I had never prepared a mixed drink; therefore, I would need someone to handle the bar during my date to host the reception. I would graciously provide assistance to any of my peers in any capacity, other than working the bar during their assigned hospitality schedule. My superior response, "Every district manager, that he has known knew how to mix drinks; therefore, he suggested that I take an accelerated mixologist course before coming to Washington."

When it was my turn to host the hospitality reception, I once again reminded my superior of my non-experience of mixing drinks. His response, "District managers always manned the bar during their hospitality assignment; therefore, I see no need in changing that requirement for you." Once again I said, "You were told by many of my coworkers that they had never seen me drinking nor mixing any alcoholic drinks at any functions, at anytime. Furthermore, I told my superior that I didn't even sip an ounce of champagne during our wedding toast. Instead, I got the waiter to replace my glass of champagne with a glass of 7-Up beverage for our wedding toast. My superior said, "Edgar, when it's your turn to work the bar, we expect you to do just that."

At that point, it was obvious that any effort on my part to get any considerations from what I had proposed to my superior regarding working the bar was futile; therefore, I said, "I wasn't hired or promoted because of my bartender skills." Well my stock further plummeted, to say the least. I knew that I would not get any of my peers to assist me during my host assignment so I had to establish a strategic Plan B, immediately. I called one of my invited guests who was an expert mixologist who always worked the bars with great distinction and praise to see if he would serve as my celebrity bartender during my host assignment, and he indicated he would be delighted to do so. The Celebrity Bartender was the Star of the hospitality night, and the success of my assigned host night was incredible. The President and the other guests that night raved about the best tasting drinks that were prepared by my very good friend. They even took turns in making special toasts for the guest celebrity bartender. Once again, I got praise from the new President and more resentment from my superior. What a dilemma.

Assisting UNCF in Securing New Regional Office

When we returned home from the Chicago trip, I attended a United Negro College Fund Advisory Board meeting that discussed the need to acquire a larger facility that could house the increasing demands for servicing the region's colleges and universities better. The current facility's lease was expiring at the end of the year, and the owner indicated that the space in which the UNCF office occupied would no longer be available. One of the larger tenants in the building decided to exercise its option in acquiring the UNCF office for its expansion.

This was not very good news because there was not much time in locating another facility to accommodate the expanding needs of the UNCF, and of course, limited availability of funds certainly increased the challenge facing the organization.

I spoke with the Area Director after the meeting about possibly getting a facility at the company headquarters. One of the company's departments currently housed at headquarters was moving its operation to our eastern facility, and that entire floor would be completely vacant before the end of the year. Additionally, since headquarters had a long-term lease with no immediate plans for occupying that space, I thought that it would be a win-win situation for the company and the UNCF. I decided to talk with the new President about the prospects of exercising our good corporate image and at the same time afford the UNCF an opportunity to secure much needed facilities downtown at a price that their limited budget could afford.

From a financial point, it would give the company a tax write-off for the donated facility as well as greatly enhance its good corporate citizen image among thousands of its customers. It would afford the UNCF to fulfill its most pressing need of acquiring adequate office facilities as well as furniture and furnishings made available from the departing department locating to the eastern facility. After conferring with the new President, he thought that it was an excellent idea, and he suggested that I develop a proposal and submit it to my boss for consideration and submission to the facility management department for implementation. I drafted a proposal and submitted it to my superior, and he concurred that it had mutual benefits for the company and the UNCF. At the beginning of the New Year, the UNCF Regional Office became a reality.

Gertrude's Place

After two years and three months of agonizing and painful negotiations of acquiring the home of my deceased parents, coupled with the over burdening city's building outdated permit requirements, finally and at last, 2115 Bienville Street residence was about to get new life and revitalization. I got a substantial working capital loan from Liberty Bank and Trust to begin renovation of my deceased parents' home. After purchasing the blighted double house next door to my deceased parents' house and incorporating the two individual properties into one parcel, I began to get unreasonable demands by the city's building permit office. After acquiring a building permit, we started construction. When we began converting the two existing old galvanized tin roofs connecting shades into a single triple garage, a building inspector from the City came to the house and issued a Stop Construction Order. The inspector issued the stop-work order after the entire new structure had been completely framed.

Unfortunately, when the stop-work order was issued, we were in the midst of a rainy summer, and the twenty foot-long 2 by 12 pine roofing joists were extremely expensive plus the contractor was forced to take another job until the Cease Order was lifted. The other problem, The Board of Zoning docket was so extensive that I was not scheduled to appear until the end of September, three month away. I had to replace all of the pine roofing joists plus replace a tremendous amount of plywood and other wooden items damaged in the weather.

When I appeared before the Board of Zoning to appeal the Stop-Work Order, the sinister like grueling that I got from two of the board members was relentless. One was a former coworker of mine at the Telephone Company. I showed her and her husband with Company "perks" over the years, and the other was the mother of one of the City Councilmen's staff members, whose son I had to prevent interruption of his monthly telephone service for non-payment during most of the time he served on the staff. The two of them attempted to impose requirements that exceeded the mandates of the building code; however, their proposals were defeated by the board. After providing the proof of all of the so-called items that triggered the Stop-Work Order, my appeal was granted after 120 days and an additional $12,000 in construction costs due to delay and replacement of damaged material.

In spite of those setbacks, the construction and renovation of the Poree family's historic home and newly acquired addition was worth the pain. Our home had so much history and great memories that I was compelled to revive the tremendous history and renew the occasions of fellowship that took place over forty-four years at that location. Most of all, I wanted to recognize and to pay respect and tribute to my parents for the awesome sacrifices and commitment of providing spiritual, moral, and ethical leadership in helping to mold and develop my four sisters and me in becoming self-sustaining good citizens. From the time that my Father and Mother moved to 2115 Bienville Street in the summer of 1946 and until Father's death in May of 1964 and Mother's death in October of 1990, 2115 Bienville for more than forty-four years was a home with rich history and incredible tradition.

My Father's 500 plus books that once helped hundreds of students from the two historical Black colleges were almost completely destroyed from Hurricane Katrina in August of 2005. However, those few books salvaged remain as evidence of the off-campus library that once provided an invaluable resource for hundreds of college students that studied and ate at the Poree's over forty plus years. Additionally, I preserved my Father's Letter of Commendations from the Commanding Officer of the 805th Pioneer Infantry, signed on June 24, 1919, commending faithfulness, dependability, and primary qualities of leadership and judgment, during the Meuse-Argonne offensive of the First American Army, which culminated in the Armistice on November 11, 1918. Father received the letter on the shores of Normandy, France, in 1919. Today, the original letter can be seen on the wall of the Pavillion Room along with Father's war helmet and the 1865 Civil War issued Canteen at 2115 Bienville Street.

Since Father and Mother played such a significant role in the lives of hundreds of individuals over more than forty-four years, it was important to make sure that our house at 2115 Bienville Street, which had been an incubator of good citizens, be restored and maintained as an enrichment center for future generations. Gertrude Boyd Poree and 2115 Bienville Street provided such an oasis of love, of hospitality, and of growth and development for so many people, both locally and across our Nation. It was in recognition of and in conjunction with keeping Mother's incredible legacy alive that Gloria and I renovated and dedicated our home in Mother's honor. We changed the name of 2115 Bienville Street to Gertrude's Place, a home with rich history, tradition, and a place for all people.

Each year when most people get Hallmark Cards for special occasions, like anniversaries, birthdays and congratulatory accomplishments, I prefer to express my appreciation for my wife in my own words. As the first year of the twenty-first century I decided to substitute the traditional hallmark birthday card with a Special Tribute to my wife on her birthday. (See Appendix B: A Special Tribute to My Wife.)

CHAPTER XIII

COMPANY REORGANIZATION, PLUSES AND MINUSES, AND RETIREMENT

The Company reorganization in 2001 made retirement consideration most attractive because of the financial package options being offered at that time. When our President discussed the reorganization plan for our department and the available financial packages being offered, I did not hesitate one moment before saying, "Hershel, I'm ready for retirement." He responded, "Edgar, we haven't gotten all of the specifics of the full value of the package options yet, so there's no need for any premature decisions, especially retirement decisions. One thing that I learned over the years, especially in Corporate America, there's a time to know when it's time to go.

I was eight months shy of being sixty-five and to be able to retire before sixty-five was quite appealing, especially with an extremely good financial benefit package available. I had already calculated the difference between a thirty-year employee allotment package compared to a twenty-nine year allotment package, and the dollar difference was not significant enough to defer for the full allotment financial benefit. Retirement was my answer, and the timing was right. After our meeting, the President once again asked me not to make a retirement decision until I had some time to seek it out. My response, "Herschel, I've had a tremendous journey and opportunity to experience a fine career with the company. I'm grateful for all of the benefits and the rewards; however, I'm still full of energy, and there are things that I like to do, that retirement will allow me to do—spend more quality time with Gloria, my family, and of course Troy and Alexis, my two incredible grandchildren.

When I got home that evening, I told Gloria that you are looking at a retired executive! Her response was just like the President's, "What? When did you make that decision, Edgar?" I said, "Today during a reorganization meeting." Gloria's facial expression changed abruptly from curiosity to that of great concern. I suspect the prospect of having me at home around the clock all day long was overwhelming and a bit too much for her to contemplate at that time.

After all, Gloria had been enjoying the luxury of having her very own space for more than ten years since retirement, and the shock of having me around all day had earth shattering shock waves. Gloria's final utterance, "Edgar, are you sure you are ready to retire now?" Recognizing how painful and agonizing my revelations had on her, I said, "Darling, when I get the specifics of the financial benefits that we could get from retiring now, I'll bring the retirement package home for you to see and discuss so that you will be comfortable with the decision. In the meantime that will afford you time to begin working on your personal strategic plan to establish provisions of including me, so that I won't be crowding your space." Gloria reluctantly agreed to my suggestion. When I received the retirement benefit package, she agreed that it was the right decision.

The official date of my retirement was March 31, 2001; five months shy of thirty years of service. When I received my retirement package, I was pleasantly surprised to discover that I would receive the full amount of the thirty-year service value award. The timing was right, and the beginning was set in motion by Dian, Keith, and Mary Ann for one of the most incredible retirement receptions ever held in Louisiana. In spite of a limited amount allocated for a Regional Director's retirement reception, I recognized that the number of potential guests would require substantial more dollars than the company's allotment. Consequently, I contacted the company President to tell him that I would probably have to pay the difference of the expense to underwrite the full cost of the reception. The President told me that his office would be responsible for making up the difference of the reception expenses.

Dian and Keith worked around the clock in making every detail closely monitored to ensure that my retirement would be the very best ever that the company ever had. My superior, called Keith attempting to get details of the reception, since he had not discussed nor mentioned any plans in conjunction with my announced retirement. During his call, my superior told Keith that he had been bombarded with requests for invitations for Edgar's retirement. He advised Keith that he would be scrutinizing all vouchers submitted by him, especially anything that had to do with a reception. He cautioned Keith that any voucher that he submitted that exceeded the department's reception allowance, he, Keith, would be responsible for personally paying that bill.

Apparently, my superior had not yet been made aware of the President's intentions to underwrite any expenses that exceeded the reception allowance budget. The President expressed confidence that my retirement reception would attract many of the community's major leadership stakeholders, which more than justified an expanded reception allowance. After the President's meeting with my superior, neither Keith nor Dian ever received another call from my superior regarding the retirement reception. On the evening of my reception, one of my coworkers who was leaving at the same time that my superior and another VP were leaving to attend my retirement reception, overheard my boss saying, "I don't know what to expect when we get there."

Retirement Reception

On Wednesday, April 11, 2001, hundreds of guests filled the University Center's Royal/Bourbon Room at the University of New Orleans to celebrate the retirement of Edgar F. Poree, Jr., commemorating 29 years and 7 months of service at BellSouth Telecommunications, Inc. That gathering was the largest and probably had the most distinguished guests across the entire community leadership. The guests included Mayor Marc Morial, whose tardiness was legendary throughout his tenure. Guests were amazed to see the Mayor's car parked in front of the University Center's thirty-five minutes before the start of the retirement reception.

The guest list included the community leadership across the business, political, educational, legal, religious, and social strata and the major TV network affiliates' anchors. The guests included my mentor and the person responsible for my employment at the company, Mr. Murray Fincher, Vice President and one of the Company's most respected and admired statesmen and community leaders. When Mr. Fincher took the mike, he said, "When I heard that Edgar was retiring after almost thirty years, I knew that I had gotten old." Edgar and I go back a long way when we were associated together with Dr. Jim Bobo and Professor Joe Walker at

Goals Foundation. "He was a hard worker, and he knew exactly what to do and how to get it done." I opened the door, "Edgar made the record and performed, and I'm so very proud of him and his accomplishments."

Also present were Dick Sharp, former Vice President who appointed me District Manager; Fred Nodier, former General Manager and former boss, truly one of the great gentlemen in Corporate America; my boss, Vice President Bill Oliver; my favorite General Counsel, Vicky McHenry; our President, Hershel Abbott; and, of course my devoted and loyal staff that kept me out of trouble and protected my back twenty-four hours a day—Dian Kent, my exceptionally talented and competent Administrative Assistant and Keith Hitchen, my learned and devoted Staff Manager who effectively communicated the company's message as well as demonstrated at all time that good corporate image, internally and externally. Mary Ann Francois, Staff Manager of Corporate and External Affairs, who reported to another District, always maintained a high level of support for my wellbeing and did considerable work in protecting my back and keeping me abreast of events and activities that I needed to be aware of or participate in. Collectively, this core group of professionals did an incredible planning and coordination of my retirement reception.

The Saga of Edgar Poree

One of the highlights and certainly a most memorable moment during the retirement celebration occurred when the once most outspoken and influential company critic stepped up to the podium to deliver a non-traditional "editorial" entitled *The Saga of Edgar Poree*. Phil Johnson, the former Vice President and News Director of WWL-TV who for over two decades opposed the company's rate relief efforts continuously with negative editorials. This influential giant was about to pay tribute to a member of that nearly twenty-year apparent anti-company discourse. Johnson, an impressive looking physical stature with a distinguishable beard and a powerful resonating voice, commanded attention without saying a word. With his ever present opening, "Good Evening," Johnson began delivering his *The Saga of Edgar Poree*. His presentation was so captivating and so well received by all present I decided to include his entire presentation in Appendix C: *The Saga of Edgar Poree*.

After the guests heard extremely complementary tributes and reflections from twenty community leaders, including a very special and memorable tribute by the incomparable and distinguished Phil Johnson, former Vice President, General Manger, and Editorialist Extraordinaire of WWL-TV, Hershel Abbott, President of BellSouth walked up to the podium to express his remarks. He looked over the audience and his opening words were, "What an impressive and distinguished audience gathered here paying tribute to you, Edgar Poree, for a career of tremendous achievements and accomplishments and most of all of service to this community. We have the current Mayor, a former Mayor, four members of the City Council, three university presidents, a former university president, the chancellor of the community college, former Lieutenant Governor, two major bank presidents, several judges, and even a former king of Zulu and former King of Rex; that in itself is quite a fete. And, of course, Phil Johnson's enlightened tribute.

Edgar and I have had the good times and the bad. We had extremely good times at the Democratic National Convention. I won't talk about the bad times. When I called him, he would always come and willing to give advice and counsel with his vision. He's had a vision a very long time, and he's blessed with the ability to articulate his vision, and I treasure his advice. And he's always prepared to give his advice and counsel. I have sought his advice and counsel, and I welcome his advice with great confidence. I have expressed that, although he's retired, I will seek his advice and counsel from time to time for he's only a telephone away.

Finally, Hershel said, "I want to pay tribute to Gloria, his lovely wife for her support, over the years for allowing Edgar to spend countless hours away from home in conjunction with fostering the company's mission. Hershel then quoted portions of the Thirty-First Chapter of Proverbs—*The Virtuous Wife,* to describe Gloria's incredible support, her worth which far exceeded the value of rubies, her dependability and willingness to sacrifice her time to ensure Edgar's safety, his fulfillment of his vision, his community betterment initiatives, and his legacy as a truly dedicated community servant. "Gloria thanks for your generosity in allowing all of us who were fortunate to share an incredible journey with our Honoree, Edgar F. Poree." Hershel concluded his observations saying, "Congratulations, my adviser, my counselor, and most importantly, my friend."

The reception guests were most generous as they showered me with hundreds of lavish gifts and well wishes. Dan Packer, President of Entergy, provided an evening of incredible musical treats by the very talented Herb Taylor's Trio. Dian Kent along with Mary Ann Francois' assistance spent many hours assembling all of the reception photographs, congratulatory letters, expressions, signed guests rosters, photographs of my South Central Bell-BellSouth events and activities for my Retirement Memoirs. As usual, the final product was an awesome "memento" capturing that most memorable and gratifying event. Alden McDonald, President Liberty Bank and Trust Company and an avid photographer, worked feverishly capturing memorable moments taking numerous photographs of me and the hundreds of guests during the reception. He later presented to me in a beautifully embossed album of photographs capturing the spirit and the excitement of my retirement. That was a tremendous memento gift that will always be cherished by me and my family.

My April 11, 2001, Retirement Reception has been described as BellSouth's best and biggest ever. And all those present will attest to that. For a person who has never been at a loss for words, my Retirement Reception was so spectacular and awesome that when I got up to respond after the last tribute was given by Greg O'Brian, Chancellor, University of New Orleans, ironically the video camera's battery stopped functioning just before I reached the podium so apparently that was an omen for me to K.I.S.S., Keep It Simply Short. All of the presenters' congratulatory messages were captured on the video; unfortunately; the video stopped the minute I reached the podium. I thanked my guests and encouraged them to begin eating. That was the first occasion where I had only a very few words, and my guests appeared surprised and at the same time relieved. Gloria and I, along with our children, grandchildren, and family enjoyed meeting and sharing stories among friends.

Several weeks after my retirement, Hershel and I had lunch at The Palace Canal Restaurant, where we talked about that fantastic retirement reception and all of the highly complementary calls that he and I had received from numerous guests. Hershel indicated that he had never witnessed anything like it at BellSouth at any level. He told me that it was reflective of the tremendous respect and admiration that this community felt for me and my numerous contributions over the years. They are still talking about that impressive and distinguished guests assembled to pay tribute to you and your good works; that's super and most deserving for one that I'm proud to call my friend.

As we were finishing our lunch, the President said, "Edgar, we will have plenty time to renew our working relations at the end of your ninety day furlough after retirement." "So take advantage of those remaining furlough days, remember your retirement is simply an interlude before getting my telephone call for advice and counsel," he concluded. The ninety days that he referred to was that required period of time that an individual must be off the company's payroll before becoming eligible to serve in a contractual professional service capacity. Ironically, just as the battery stopped functioning when I reached the podium at my retirement reception to give my remarks, my ninety day furlough lasted indefinitely because on the eighty-second day of my furlough, the President was promoted and guess who got his job? If you guessed my superior, my boss, you're right, and my professional service contract became null in void.

Adjunct Instructor Stints

After being home for a while, relaxing and crowding Gloria's once paradise space, I received numerous telephone calls from the Director of Continuing Education at Delgado Community College attempting to recruit me as an Adjunct Instructor for Delgado's Work Force Training Initiative. I had previously served as a visiting Adjunct Instructor for The University of New Orleans Downtown Metropolitan College, when the Director served in the same capacity there earlier. After the sixth call, I agreed to assist in the development of more comprehensive conflict resolution training, customer service training, and professional development training and communicating and working with people training packages for the Work Force Training Initiative. Additionally, I agreed to serve as an Adjunct Instructor for four different courses, including Excelling as a First-Time Supervisor, Effective Communications, Conflict Resolution, and Customer Services. I did extensive management and non-management training for the Regional Transit Authority, the hotel, culinary, hospitality and automotive industries until Hurricane Katrina devastated our City.

CHAPTER XIV

Hurricane Katrina and the Aftermath

Like always, when a hurricane alert appears, we usually pack a few things and wait until the winds began to blow with authority before really getting gearing up for possibly heading out of the City for a brief furlough. We pay close attention to the meteorologist's updates and make sure that we have the necessary supplies and batteries in the event that the electricity is knocked out. Unlike most of the previous hurricane alerts, the weather deteriorated rapidly, and the alert changed to a warning. Still residents hesitated to begin the exodus from the City. My family, like so many other natives, decided to wait a little longer before starting our exodus from the City. As the night grew more questionable and the winds and the warnings to get out the City reached a fervent level, I called our daughter to get Troy and Alexis, our grandchildren, to get out of the house immediately, and to pick us up for our trip out of the City.

At 5:30 a.m. Sunday morning, Deidra arrived at our home, and we jumped in her SUV along with a few clothes and started what turned out to be the longest most nerve racking gridlock journey to Baton Rouge, Louisiana. That trip, which normally took about an hour and a quarter during normal circumstances, took almost eight hours. Since we lived only one mile from the Lakefront, I told my daughter to take Lakeshore Drive because I-10 Interstate Highway was gridlocked near our home. I thought we could avoid the gridlock taking the route along the Lakefront and West Esplanade Avenue to the mall in Kenner, approximately eighteen miles from our home. Gloria normally took this route to go to the mall for shopping. Unfortunately, other motorists took the same route that we took, and what would have been a twenty minute drive took two hours.

Once we reached the shopping center, we proceeded along Loyola Drive to I-10 West for the next leg of our journey, LaPlace in St. John's Parish 14 miles away. That trip across the Bonnet Carre Spillway took an additional two hours. Although State Police Troopers supervised the westward contraflow traffic flow, there were just too many vehicles on the highways to accommodate a normal flow of traffic. Because of the traffic gridlock, hundreds of cars were seen disabled with hoods up; many out of gas; still others with flat tires. Further complicating our trip there weren't any places to stop for our five and six year old grandchildren to use the toilet. Gas stations either had block-long lines with gas rationing or no gas at all, further eroding the situation. After eight and a half hours, we finally arrived at Jeanetta's home in the northern part of Baton Rouge. Jeanetta and Gloria had been really close friends for more than forty-four years, since they met during the birth of their children. We thought we would probably be at Jeanetta's home for a few days, the usual "turnaround" time for evacuating for potential hurricane's warning routine. Little did we realize that our stay would exceed a few days at the most. We had no idea what the future held; consequently, we thought that in a few days we would be back in New Orleans, once again following our usual hurricane routine.

Oh! How wrong we were. When we watched the news and saw the devastation and the massive destruction from the flooding of the City of New Orleans, we could not believe what we were seeing. There was a deafening silence in the room as we saw our City under water. There was crying, there was disbelief, and there was a sense of numbness in all of us, as we watched our lives and our situations drastically changed in a matter of seconds right before our eyes. This was certainly a rude awakening for all of us. Yesterday, we had the best of good times, a home, cars, many amenities, and many material things. Today, we had only those things that we have on our backs and a few clothing that we packed as our only processions. How were we going to cope with this enormous challenge? Would we be able to overcome this overwhelming crisis and at the same time maintain our faith during these uncertain circumstances?

The true test of character is when uncertainty and doubt appear to be inevitable, and circumstances seem impossible to overcome. That's the true test of character, of having faith in God, the Creator, and oneself to be able to maintain focus, stamina, and determination to withstand whatever unfortunate circumstances that confront you and to overcome those conditions or circumstances with strategic plans of success. First and foremost for our plan was transportation. We left both cars in the driveway when we evacuated New Orleans; consequently, we were without any vehicle to get around other than our Deidra's SUV. I contacted our AARP Insurance carrier for our cars to get on the waiting list to get our allotted rental vehicles. We were advised to go to Enterprise to get our rental vehicles. This was the beginning of the immense challenges we were going to face during this catastrophically uncertain time.

When we arrived at Enterprise in conjunction with securing our rental car, we were advised that we were entitled to two rental vehicles. Because of the uncertainty of our future during that time, we felt that we did not need two rental vehicles. When we advised the rental representative that we only wanted to get only one of the two rentals allowed under the terms of our insurance contract, the representative told me that I would have to contact my insurance company about that exception. When I asked the representative, why I had to contact my insurance company regarding my request for only one rental, the representative advised me that I only had a thirty-day rental allowance period from the time the disaster was officially declared. I said, "That makes no sense, I have two vehicles with two separate thirty-day rental allowance provisions; therefore, I should determine when I need the second vehicle!" The Enterprise representative told me that the insurance company advised them that their eligible period for the thirty-day allowable rental expires from the declared official date of the disaster.

I called the Hartfort Company, the insurer of my two Lexus 400 vehicles, resting under ten feet of flooded waters in New Orleans, to clarify what I was told by the Enterprise representative regarding my request for only one rental at the time. The Hartfort Insurance representative advised me that even though I was entitled to two separate rental vehicles under the terms of the insurance policy, like an accident, eligibility for the rental commences thirty-days from the date of the claim. I told the representative that the flooding displacement disaster was unlike no other natural occurrence; therefore, there should be some flexibility under these circumstances.

The representatives told me that the company would pay for two rental vehicles for me until the thirty-day window allowance expires from the date of the claim. My response, "I'm filing only one of my insurance policies for one rental vehicle at this time." Furthermore, technically, I have two thirty-days allowable rental vehicles periods; therefore, I'm only requesting half of my eligible allotment, based on my interpretation of my vehicular insurance policy. At that point, I asked the Hartfort representative to let me speak with a supervisor who simply repeated what others told me. I advised the supervisor that I was going to contact the Louisiana Insurance Commission to file a claim of "misrepresentation" by Hartfort, especially under the dire circumstances that Louisianans found themselves.

When I returned to Enterprise to get my rental, they had two vehicles ready for me, along with two separate Rental Documentation Records. I signed one of the Rental Documents, and I specifically wrote "Void, Rejected, and Refused to Accept" on the other Rental Document. After numerous discussions with the AARP-Hartfort Insurance Company, I was allowed to get the second thirty-day allowable vehicle rental when I exhausted the thirty days initial eligibility. In the end, I got my sixty days of allowable rental, after all.

The second pressing challenge was access to savings. Our bank like others was flooded; consequently, financial records were simply non-accessible making withdrawals impossible. Additionally, our federal credit union like the banks was also under water; therefore, access to them was not readily available. Since our credit union was federally chartered, we were able to withdraw a maximum of $500 from the federally chartered credit union in Baton Rouge. Fortunately, we brought along with us twelve hundred dollars in cash to handle a few days of anticipated displacement, not permanent displacement. When we attempted to withdraw funds from our bank, we were told that because the entire computer system was dysfunctional at that time, withdrawal was limited to two hundred dollars. Unanticipated circumstances require immediate moderations and adjustments, so we began enacting our austerity survival reliance plan.

The third and most pressing challenge was housing. Initially, our daughter and our two grandchildren, plus Gloria and I stayed at Jeanetta's home in north Baton Rouge for two weeks. Deidra and her two children began living with Mada, whose parents had been lifelong friends of the Poree's family. Mada's home was located in mid-city, approximately eight miles from where we lived. Consequently, we were constantly traveling numerous times between the two living locations daily in conjunction with attempting to get those essential household and personal items necessary in bringing some normalcy to our lives.

Deidra's was notified she had to report to work at the Bluebonnet Post Office, two weeks after Hurricane Katrina. This required immediate adjustment in our daily schedule because it meant keeping our grandchildren during the week. Our daily routine included traveling to Mada's home five days a week to care for our grandchildren, while Deidra worked. Gloria prepared dinner each day and after having dinner with Deidra, Mada and our two grandchildren, we returned to Jeanetta's home for the night. Deidra was successful in getting Troy and Alexis enrolled at St. Francis Xavier Catholic School for the 2006-2007 school year. This of course expanded our daily routine when the school year began.

In October, Deidra was able to get an apartment on College Drive, much closer to Troy and Alexis's school and much closer to her work location. This allowed more time in preparing her morning routine in getting the children to school and getting to work on time. This, however, increased dramatically our daily routine of picking up our grandchildren from school, helping with homework, preparing food, giving them a bath, and doing any other task associated with child care. We lived approximately seventeen miles from our grandchildren's school, and because of the seeming daily traffic gridlock, we would leave no later than forty minutes before the end of school day to pick up the children.

On Tuesday and Thursday, Alexis attended McMain Child Development Center for speech therapy after school at four o'clock so those two days required additional child care time. After some of the daily routines, we would sleep at Deidra's apartment instead of returning to Jeanetta's home. Because we only had one rental car at the time, both Gloria and I had to perform the chores together. As the allowable rental period approached expiration, I decided to purchase a 2006 Lexus GS 300 four door sedan. We recognized that returning to live in New Orleans was not a viable option; therefore, we began to seek possible relocation alternatives in the Baton Rouge metro-area.

Since Gertrude's Place, our second home in mid-city New Orleans, had sustained damages that could be renovated at a reasonable cost; we wanted to retain that property. In addition, Edgar, III had gotten a job at a Delta Petroleum Plant on Airline Highway in Jefferson Parish. After an extensive search for our relocated home, I found a model home in Prairieville in Ascension Parish that had tremendous possibilities. Gloria and I were most impressed with the many amenities and beautiful features in Bert Prater Builder's Mimosa Model home in Old Dutchtown Subdivision. For three months, I visited the Mimosa model home hoping to convince Gloria that this would be an ideal location for our new home. In spite of Gloria's appreciation of the beauty and amenities of the Mimosa's model home, her position remained the same. "You are not getting me to live in the country, period." No matter what favorable features or amenities that Gloria liked in the house or the lake location that she really loved, I could not change her mind regarding relocating in the country.

After, three long months of attempting to get her to reconsider her adamant rejection of living in the country, I decided to take one more attempt to convince her to select the Mimosa model home in Old Dutchtown Subdivision in Ascension Parish. I got Edgar to come to the model home in Old Dutchtown, after exactly three months and two days of unsuccessful attempts, on my part in getting Gloria to consider living in the country. When Edgar, III arrived at the model home, fifteen minutes before closing on that Sunday evening, his eyes lit up like a two thousand watts spotlight and after completing his tour of the model he said, "Mother, this house is the Bomb; this house is off the Chart!"

On Monday, the next day, three months and three days of futile attempts of convincing Gloria to consider living in the country, Edgar, III's recommendations of getting the Mimosa as the Poree's new residence became a reality. When Gloria got up that Monday morning, she said, "Go buy the damn house, Edgar." What a relief. As husband I could not get a single "yes" from Gloria; however, Edgar, III without hardly any effort was able to reverse her decision within fifteen-minutes. You can bet in the future before I suggest anything, I'm going to get my chief lobbyist's, Edgar, III's, advise.

When we signed the contract to purchase the Mimosa Model home, the builder told us that we would be able to celebrate our Thanksgiving dinner in our new home. The weather favorably allowed for timely construction in spite of the tremendous number of work-order changes that we initiated in enhancing "our foot prints" on the final product. I was at the construction site every day during construction, and my camera took literally thousands of pictures of every phase of the building. After expanding the house living area's square footage, building a cosmetic fire place, converting garage into a theater, increasing the open living area twofold, redesigning master bath, and changing most of the lighting fixtures and the appliances, the Mimosa house began to reflect the Poree's contemporary foot print.

One Friday evening, Bert Prater asked Gloria and me if October 24th would be a good day for us to go to closing. Gloria, let out a lady-like scream at Prater's question, and he asked, "Mrs. Poree, is there anything wrong?" "No, that's my birthday." On, October 24, 2006, Gloria and I received the keys to our newly constructed Mimosa home in Old Dutchtown Subdivision in Prairieville. That evening, we celebrated Gloria's birthday in the empty home with our daughter, Deidra, our grandchildren, Troy and Alexis, our son Edgar, III, our friend Jeannetta and her daughter, Cathy, and Keith, my former BellSouth associate. Traditionally, we had ice cream and cake for all family birthday celebrations; however, in the excitement of the day's historic closing, I forgot to get the ice cream. This is another one of those embarrassing moments in the life of Edgar Poree, one more character building opportunity.

Hurricane Katrina's Impact on African American Community

Hurricane Katrina exposed some of the most sinister and devious scamming practices used in pilfering and stealing from citizens during their most venerable times. One of the untold tragedies of Hurricane Katrina was the unscrupulous fleecing of homeowners, especially African-American homeowners by the insurance industry. For decades homeowners paid premiums for coverage, dictated by the insurance industry without much oversight. Whatever the insurance company charged for "available coverage for us," we paid. Homeowners in Pontchartrain Park and Gentilly Woods thought that their homeowners and flood insurance coverage that was available to them was one in the same that every other homeowner in comparable neighborhoods with comparable real estate values in New Orleans had. When Hurricane Katrina struck, homeowners especially Africa-American faced their worst nightmare. Residences of Pontchartrain Park and Gentilly Woods discovered that they were grossly underinsured in homeowners and flood coverage, both structure and contents.

In speaking too many of my White friends and associates, living in comparable neighborhoods in homes of comparable real estate values, we discovered something very disturbing and repulsive. Our White friends and associates "paid significantly lower premiums for their homeowners' policies and flood insurance with significantly higher structure and content coverage." It appeared that our community to be victims of "Red Lining." For years my parents had been paying outrageous flood insurance premiums for their home without ever questioning the insurance company that provided their flood insurance for decades. After the death of my parents, I asked Bill, one of my closest White friends, whose parents' home was of similar size and value, located on the same street only twelve blocks away, how much did his parents pay for flood insurance? When he told me his parents paid approximately 60% less than what my parents had been paying, I was shocked! I asked him about the coverage of his parents' home, and he told me that their coverage was 50% greater than my parents. Bill said his parents' home was not in a flood zone, and he couldn't understand why my parents were paying so much more for coverage.

Bill suggested I get a Flood Elevation Survey of my parent's home to determine if it's not in the flood zone. I told Bill that the insurance company never told my parents about such a survey. I got a Flood Elevation Survey at a cost of $375. I asked several other insurance companies to give me quotes for comparable coverage that Bill's parents had, and I got coverage for flood insurance with one of the major insurance companies for my deceased parents' home with a premium 60% lower than what my parents paid for more than a decade. The new flood coverage of the policy was 45% more than what my parents paid over a decade. You noticed that I hadn't mentioned The Road Home Program—my reason, that agency was as unscrupulous as the sinister insurance industry.

Hurricane Katrina also exposed another sinister plot by the political forces and chief architects of the State and City whose initial assault on our community began during the 1960's. Prior to integration, Black principals, administrators, teachers, and faculty were the real "role models" of the Black community. They along with our parents and guardians were totally dedicated and committed to providing the best of educational excellence and development of their students. Students all looked forward to going to school because the Black leadership provided such a wholesome experience each and every day.

Hurricane Katrina provided the sinister forces plan to eliminate the Black middle class of New Orleans. The State of Louisiana's so-called intervention, more readily assault and seizure of Orleans Parish Public Schools in the best interest of students' academic opportunities was an all-out gigantic lie! The assault and seizure was based on stealing control of the half billion dollar annual budget that the predominantly Black School Board had for its yearly operations. After they seized control and governance of the Public Schools of New Orleans, the State of Louisiana fired all of its personnel without any *due process,* replacing them with so-called recovery schools (corporate cash cows), inexperienced administrators, and inexperienced teachers, practically eliminating the Black middle class of New Orleans. What an egregious and injustice act of by the State of Louisiana's and City's political forces.

An Incredible Commitment

After moving from Deidra's College Drive apartment to our Prairieville home, Gloria's daily routine of caring for our grandchildren increased tenfold. The round trip requirement of picking up the kids from school was fifty-four miles. Two days a week required additional time and miles because Alexis had to be taken for speech therapy, plus Troy and Alexis had to be taken to their regular schedule doctor and dentist appointments. This incredible commitment of caring for our grandchildren during and traveling fifty-four miles for five days a week lasted for two years. That's approximately 13,608 miles of child care. Since Gloria needed to leave home approximately an hour before school closing to get our grandchildren, that's five hours a week travel, or approximately seven and a half days of travel time associated with her trip to school. After two years, we discovered an incredible alternative, school after-care.

Daughter's Prayers Answered

After living in an apartment in Baton Rouge for three years, our daughter Deidra located a lovely ranch-style house in Brookhollow Glen Subdivision off Perkins Road in South Baton Rouge in June of 2009. The house was located only one exit from ours, and the distance was exactly ten miles from our home in Prairieville. That alone significantly reduced the round-trip distance from her apartment to our house, approximately 18 miles, and considerably reduced the time to travel between our home and her apartment. The house had three bedrooms, a large living-dining room, kitchen, two bathrooms, a laundry room, large storage room, and a covered two car carport. Troy and Alexis could have their own bedroom, and they could share a bath. Additionally, the ranch-style house had a huge yard, containing gym-swing equipment plus a very large utility room with A/C, affording our grandchildren a play area option other than their bedrooms and out of inclement weather.

On July 15, 2008, Deidra was successful in becoming a homeowner once again, after the devastating destruction of her home in New Orleans from the flood after Hurricane Katrina. Just as I did when Deidra bought her first house in New Orleans, immediately after the closing, I began renovating Deidra's newly purchased home. Within two weeks, the kitchen, two bedrooms, two bathrooms and hallway were painted. The kitchen cabinets had newly installed custom knobs and a brand new dishwasher, the two bathrooms had newly installed toilets, and several lighting fixtures had been replaced. Additionally, the window shutters and exterior doors were painter. I made curtains and valences for the kitchen, dining room and floor length curtains for the living room. Additionally, I made floor length multi-color curtains for Alexis' bedroom and floor length curtains for Troy's bedroom. I also made custom design curtains for Deidra's bathroom.

Both Troy and Alexis had their individual bedrooms. Once I finished the tasks of painting and making curtains for their rooms, I then began looking for furniture that I could modify to blend with the décor of their bedrooms. Since they already had their bed frames and mattresses, I had to find headboards that I could modify or re-design to compliment the bedroom décor. After several weeks of looking I found a damaged Hanna Montana headboard, at a major furniture thrift store for a fraction (89%) less than the original price of a new headboard. I removed the damaged section and I replicated a template to replace the damaged portion. I replaced the woodened sculptured portion of the center with a two inch form and covered the template and form with pink satin fabric, one of the two colors of Alexis' curtains. Before inserting the newly custom insert, I covered the recessed mirrors, partially surrounding the template boundaries with mastic tape so that I could spray paint the refurbished headboard. Once the paint dried, I installed the pink satin upholstered insert into the headboard and Alexi's bed was more fashionable and beautiful than the original headboard version. Alexis said, Poppee, my bedroom looks like a castle.

Now I was faced with locating a headboard for Troy. Since his theme bedding ensemble was Cars, I decided to purchase two sheets of plywood and replicate Cars theme headboard. Unfortunately, I could not locate my electric jig-saw; therefore my task had been delayed. Two weeks past and I went back to the furniture store to look for a headboard that I could possibly modify for Troy' bed and I saw a computer hutch, approximately the same width as his single bed. The hatch had an attractive masculine look with an enclosed two shelf cabinet located on each front side of the hatch. There was an open display shelf in the center of the enclosed cabinets. The hutch had sufficient space under the cabinets to allow both the mattress and bed frame to dock underneath. The hatch was white so I painted red to match the Cars motif. I purchased the slightly damaged hutch for Forty-nine dollars, $49.00 (79%) less than the original price, new. After sanding the nicks and scratches, on the hutch I then sprayed bright red paint replicating the color of Cars décor.

When I attempted to place Troy's bed frame and extremely tall mattress under the display shelf enclosure, the mattress was too tall to fit under the hutch. It was approximately six inches too short to accommodate the bedding. I built an eight inches tall platform to be placed under the original hutch to correct this problem. I used the plywood that I originally planned to use to build a Cars décor headboard. I sprayed the newly constructed platform bright red and when it dried I attached the base with drywall screws to the hutch. The hutch headboard was rather unique. Troy was excited with his custom designer hutch headboard. He used the top shelf to display his many trophies and awards.

Finally, I located two damaged six drawers/one enclosed cabinet/bunk bed chest units. The chest units supported the top bunk beds while the other end of the bunk beds was supported by posts. Both units had large openings at the top of the chest, which allowed the stabilization of the top bunk bed when inserted in the opening. To cover the opening, I used additional pieces of plywood as an insert, in the opening to give the top a smooth finish. For Alexis' chest of drawers, instead of simply finishing the top plywood insert and painting it, I covered the top insert with the same pink satin fabric that I used to cover the center insert for her Hanna Montana Headboard. I sprayed the chest of draws a bright white, matching her headboard. The combination gave her room a touch of elegance. Troy's top insert was inlaid into the opening and sprayed bright red to match his Hutch Headboard. He was thrilled to get his newly refurbished Chest of

Drawers for his Cars Theme room. Oh! By the way I got the two bunk bed chest of drawers support base for a fraction of the original price. I believe that some thrift stores damaged items can be transformed, or refurbished into treasures. Just visit Deidra's home and see the evidence.

CHAPTER XV

A Year of Festive Family Celebrations

The year of 2009 was marked with two milestones and festive celebrations for our family. The first half of the year of 2009 marked a significant moment in our lives, especially my life. However, you would have to talk to Gloria to get her opinion on that subject matter to get the candid whole story, or her appreciation of the significance moments. Fifty years ago on Valentine Day on February 14, 1959, the first significant moment took place, at Fort Chaffee, Arkansas during my six-month Army Reserve tour of duty. The lines to use the public telephone were so very long on Valentine Day that your wait could exceed a few hours, depending how far back you were. While waiting in line, for over an hour to use the Army Base public telephone to make the most ambitious long-distance telephone call to the girl of my dreams; finally I reached the public telephone. I must confess I was nervous dialing Gloria's number because I didn't know what answer I would get.

When the telephone began ringing, my pulse began beating very rapidly and when Gloria answered, the moment of truth was about to become a reality. Would I be able to successfully and succinctly persuade a positive response for my proposal or will my quest be short circuited from a negative response? I looked at my watch, it was twenty-nine minutes after three, no longer could I wait to ask, if she would marry me. With a conciliatory tone of voice I asked, "Will you marry me?" There was a moment of silence, and then she said, "Yes." Oh, what joy and relief, the girl of my dreams, agreed to marry me? I was overjoyed; excited as can be from the answer I got at thirty minutes after three. The way I reacted at the public telephone, one would have thought I had won a million dollar jackpot, I did. Fifty years ago on that cold winter day in Fort Chaffee, Arkansas, was the confirmation and realization of the first phase of my ambitious dream.

In keeping with my tradition of personally scripting messages of admiration and congratulations on special occasions, on February 14, 2009, instead of buying a Hallmark Card, to express my feelings, I wrote a poem, entitled: *"It Seem As If It Was Only A Moment Ago"* for our 50th Engagement Anniversary on Valentine Day, 2009. I presented my message in a Gold Frame to my sweet-heart wife along with an extremely generous monetary gift. (See Appendix D: *It Seem As If It Was Only a Moment Ago*.)

Son's Wedding

The second event during the first half of the year was pre-emptied by the planning, preparation and hosting of our son, Edgar, III and his fiancée Tyra Mitchell's wedding scheduled for May 15, 2009. I must confess, Gloria and I contributed very little to their internet planning celebrations, however, we must tell you that the end results were simply spectacular. Gloria and I had long since experienced the planning of a traditional bridal shower, and rehearsal dinner associated with a wedding. When Edgar, III told us that they had planned a pre-wedding celebration at Gertrude's Place in April, we didn't have the slightest clue of what a pre-wedding celebration consisted of. He told us they were handling all the details for the pre-wedding celebration, so all we had to do was relax and enjoy. We simply planned to be curious observers at the event.

The Saturday, of the pre-wedding event was full of brisk activities. Early that morning, Edgar's friends began arriving with food items and drinks for the celebration. During the afternoon, a crew arrived with three huge commercial grills, butane tanks and three giant size pots along with sacks containing hundreds of pounds of mudbugs (crawfish). After setting up their operating space in the Gloria's Courtyard, a gentleman arrived with two giant deep-fryers, butane tanks and multiple trays of freshly caught catfish. Two ladies arrived and began setting up their chocolate covering strawberry operation in the Pavillion Room. Another crew arrived and began setting up giant picnic back-drops along with a male and female mannequin props, depicting a barbeque setting for guest's photographs shooting. Finally, a D.J. arrived began setting up his equipment for the musical entertainment and a delivery man brought two of the most artistically decorated cakes depicting a huge hamburger and a basket full of crawfish. I watched with amazement the comprehensive staging of an event that we had no clue of.

That evening, over a 150 guests experienced a celebration fit for a king and queen. They enjoyed the most extensive variety of food that you would get in a five star restaurant: barbeque ribs, chicken, sausage and steaks from the grill. There was boiled shrimp, crawfish spicy new potatoes, corn on the cobs, fried catfish, baked fish, fried chicken, baked chicken, barbeque chicken, jambalaya, red beans and rice, poor-boy sandwiches multiple desserts, including chocolate covered strawberries, cakes and pralines, beer, and wine coolers.

The celebration, reached its peak, when Edgar, III performed his "Wipe It Down" dance which brought everyone to their feet, clapping and chanting, "Go, Edgar, Go, Edgar, Wipe It Down! Man, did that boy wiped it down, I stood there shaking my head; acknowledging that Edgar, III, most definitely did, "Wipe It Down! The pre-wedding celebration was an incredible evening and all guests were tremendously impressed with the variety of choices of food, the music and the individual favors that each guest received, especially the individual photograph of each quest. Each guest was given a Tyra and Edgar, III Pre-Wedding Celebration DVD, depicting the couple's storied relations leading to their planned marriage on May 15, 2009.

Well, if you thought that the pre-wedding celebration was incredible, then you were only scratching the surface. Saturday, May 15, 2009 event could only be described as an elegant classy spectacular happening. When you arrived at the wedding facility and entered the beautifully decorated courtyard adorned with white chairs, a steel Domed Gazebo, the candle risers along the carpeted aisles, you were serenaded by a symphony orchestra cellist while being escorted to your seat. You were also entertained by a professional sextet and soloists prior to and during the wedding ceremony. The wedding ceremony was administered by the Tyra's Godfather, Bishop Paul Morton and inspirational orations were delivered by members of her family.

Minnie Raby, who was matron of honor in our wedding, sang during the ceremony and also during the reception. Vernon Ward, one of our many surrogate family members also sang during the wedding ceremony.

The reception facility was beautifully and elegantly decorated and the food was superb. After the wedding celebration, Edgar, III and Tyra spent their honeymoon in Hawaii. When they returned from their honeymoon in Hawaii they moved into their newly constructed beautiful home in Laplace, Louisiana. My, my how times have changed from one generation to another.

Unlike Edgar, III and Tyra, Gloria and I spent our honeymoon at our newly acquired rental home on North Dorgenoir Street in the Ninth Ward, the week before Thanksgiving in 1959. We purchased our very first newly constructed home in May of 1964, four years and six months after our marriage in November 21, 1959. We moved into our new home in Pontchartrain Park on August 22, 1964, on day before I reported to Ship Island in Mississippi for U.S. Army Reserve Training. My Father and Mother bought their home at 2115 Bienville Street in 1957, fifty years after they were married on Christmas Day, December 25, 1917. My parents rented their 2115 Bienville Street home ten years before purchasing the home in 1957.

50th-Golden Wedding Anniversary

Fifty years ago in November of 1959, the most important and significant phase of my ambitious dream occurred on a Saturday afternoon on the Twenty-first of November at Corpus Christi Catholic Church, my sweetheart and girl of my dreams, were solemnly married as Mr. and Mrs. Poree. What a blessing and what an incredible journey that concluded victoriously. Just as the first phase of my eventful journey resulted in a most rewarding gift, Saturday, November 21, 1959, at approximately, and ironically at the same time of the day of my historic engagement, thirty minutes after three, I was rewarded the ultimate gift, the gift of life with the most beautiful person in the world, my dream girl. I'm so glad that I had the good fortune of maintaining the courage, the tenacity, the persistence, and the perseverance in persuading my dream girl to partner with me for a life long journey.

Fifty years of marriage is quite an accomplishment and blessing and one must realize that it was only through the grace and compassion of God that this milestone could be possible. Needless to say, I began planning for anniversary celebrations in earnest. When I looked at the month of November on the 2009 Calendar, I noticed that November 21, 2009 was a Saturday, the same day that we were married, fifty years ago accordingly, we scheduled our Fiftieth Wedding Anniversary Celebration for Saturday, November 21, 2009 in Gloria's Courtyard at Gertrude Place in New Orleans.

Gertrude's Place, my deceased parents' home since 1946 had had three wedding receptions held in the yard. My three older sisters, Edna Floe, Juli Rose and Natalie all had their wedding reception celebration in the yard. I suspect there would have been a fourth wedding reception held there if my sister, Anna Lea had not been married in Michigan. In keeping with my family's tradition, we felt that it would be most appropriate to celebrate our fiftieth anniversary at Gertrude's Place, 2115 Bienville Street the place where most gathering took place over a period of sixty plus years. I began the preparation of the celebration by renovating the Pavillion Room of Gertrude's Place.

Since we no longer used the facility for vehicles, we removed the overhead door tracks and installed wider crown molding and baseboards throughout the entire facility. We replaced most of the lighting and we painted the ceilings and walls complementing colors. At the entrance of the Pavillion Room we built a Pergola, a word derived from the Latin "pergula" a term referring to projecting eaves. The Pergola structure consist of a series of large pillars supporting a roof made of cross beams and open lattice which provides unique, dancing light patterns at the entrance of the Pavilion Room.

I personally built a lectern/podium, guest registration desk, a circular display table (for wedding cake or trophies) and pillar risers for the floral displays. In addition, I made all the drapes, the table clothes and the silk floral arrangements for the celebration. Gloria began developing the guest list and selecting the invitations. Deidra began coordinating programs, favors, photographers, cinematographers, and D. J. for the celebration. Edgar, III always kept the courtyard beautifully manicured. The count-down had begun in earnest.

The Pavillion Room was completely renovated, Gloria's Courtyard was quite impressive, and the newly constructed Pergola added a certain charm and elegance to the courtyard. According, to the Almanac, Saturday, November 21, 2009 appeared to be a mild sunny day, so we planned our 50th Anniversary Celebration to be held in Gloria's Courtyard with the reception to be held in the Pavillion Room. The next order of business was securing invitations, and planning the menu. Gloria insisted that her participation in the 50th celebration would be highly dependent, upon my ensuring that she would not be involved in any way in the preparation of food, or participation in any work requirement for the celebration. I promised her she would not have to do anything but look for her dress and accessories, review and approve the menu, select the cake, and select the guests.

After, Gloria approved the guest's listings and we secured the invitations, the following Invitation was sent to one hundred and twenty guests:

> *In Honor of our parents*
> *Gloria and Edgar Poree's*
> *Fiftieth Wedding Anniversary*
> *We request the pleasure of your presence*
> *At the renewal of their wedding vows and reception*
> *On Saturday, twenty-first of November*
> *Two Thousand and nine*
> *At three-thirty in the afternoon*
> *Gloria's Courtyard at Gertrude's Place*
> *2115 Bienville Street*
> *New Orleans, Louisiana*
> *Regrets only 504-451-0219*

Once, the invitations were sent out, I took one of our 8 by 11 inch, black and white wedding photographs to Signs Now, a Black owned reproduction company specializing in blowing up photos and signs. The company transformed the 1959 wedding photograph of Gloria and me embracing each other into a two foot by three foot poster. We also had our wedding photographs with our parents, our wedding party, and Gloria and me cutting our cake enlarged and framed to be displayed prominently at the Anniversary Celebration.

The next 50th anniversary agenda item was looking for that special anniversary outfit for Gloria which proved to be an extremely difficult challenge. I began looking in the Baton Rouge and New Orleans Telephone Directories to identify all bridal and formals stores locations in the area so that I could visit each to look at potential outfits for Gloria. I took my digital camera to photograph those outfits that I thought would be Gloria's taste. Since I had purchased most of Gloria's high end fashion clothing for over thirty-five years, I pretty much knew what would satisfy her taste. This search proved to be an exhaustive one and time was of essence. Several weeks before our 50th Anniversary Celebration after visiting more than twenty formals establishments, we finally found a beautiful three piece formal at The Treasure Chest, Boutique in the Seventh Ward, on the corner behind, my son's former high school, St Augustine High School. The proprietor, of the boutique was a former coworker of mine during my stint with the local poverty agency, TCA, Total Community Action, Inc.

Once Gloria's anniversary outfit was acquired, I began purchasing the food items for the menu in advance to make sure we had the quantity necessary to serve the number of guests. Everything was going quite well until three weeks before our planned 50th anniversary celebration, my son Edgar, III created, and a big, big problem. He told his Mother that I was planning on doing most of the cooking for the anniversary, and all hell broke out. I wanted to make sure the anniversary would be a successful on in the Poree tradition. Oh! How I goofed on this well intentions. When I arrive home, from the market with food items for the celebration, Gloria confronted me at the front door saying most emphatically, "Edgar, if after fifty years of marriage, you can't afford to have our anniversary catered, then Gloria's not showing up for any celebration!" In other words, I was in a deep dilemma, to say the least. When Gloria speaks, it's like E.F. Hutton, you can believe it; more importantly, when and if she says it, you better believe it.

I had already purchased a hundred pounds of shrimp, for the pasta, hundreds of pounds chicken wings and drumsticks, the pasta, dozen gallon cans of corn and string beans, thirty pounds of okra, and other items associated with preparing the planned menu. Time was critical and I knew that it would be extremely difficult to get the food catered at this late date especially since all Poree-sponsored functions were always accustomed of being served the finest of foods. Where could I turn, to salvage our anniversary and avoid Gloria's absence? Leah Chase was my only hope. I drove over to Dooky Chase Restaurant, where I use to get my half-chicken, two plate's dinners for $1.39 and split a fifteen cents bottle of Barq's with Gloria, when I was courting her during our college days.

When I entered the restaurant's kitchen, I suspect my expression told Leah that I had a problem. Before I said anything, Leah Chase, asked, "Mr. Poree how can I help you?" "Leah I'm in deep deep trouble and the trouble is even more complicated because of the limited time to resolving my problem." Gloria and I will be celebrating our fiftieth marriage anniversary on Saturday, November 21, 2009. I had planned to prepare most of the food for the celebration, un-be-known to Gloria. Unfortunately, when little Edgar told her of my plans, Gloria admonished me adamantly, saying, "If I couldn't afford getting the food catered after 50 years being married to her, then she wasn't showing up for our celebration!" "Leah, you know Gloria really well, when she says something, believe it because she's always candid." I also told Leah that I had already purchased most of the food and the perishable items were stored in refrigerator—freezer. After reviewing her catering schedule, Leah told me she had a big party scheduled on the 21st of November. However, she said she would make an adjustment and prepare the food for our anniversary. With a sigh of relief, I said, "Thank you, thank you, Leah, from the bottom of my heart." She told me to bring the food items to her several days before the celebration and she would prepare all the food for the 50th celebration. Wow! What a relief, Lear Chase New Orleans' most celebrated and revered Culinary Chef afforded me an opportunity to press forward with our planned celebration.

    I told Guich that Leah agreed to cater all of the food for our anniversary. I asked her if I could still prepare my special smothered okra and sautéed fried corn specialties and she said, "Ok, Edgar I realize how much that means to you." We embraced, kissed and she said, "You are such a pest, but I love you just the same." I felt like ten million dollars at that point. The 50th anniversary celebration was in high gear, jetting toward the big date. Countdown was on a fast track. I had over 100 pounds of beheaded shrimp that had to be thawed and peeled; the only person available for that chore was me. Time was fast approaching D-Day and I had to begin peeling and removing veins from a hundred pounds of frozen shrimp, cut seasoning for a dozen gallons of string beans and kernels of corn? Well mission accomplished, in record time, however my fingers and hands were immobilized for quite some time during the process.

    The week before our anniversary, I watched all of the local daily weather forecasts to see what the weather would be on November 21st. We planned to renew our wedding vows in Gloria's Courtyard, at Gertrude's Place. All week, the forecast appeared to be favorable and the afternoon temperatures, appeared to be mild. Things were looking very favorable and Friday, November 20th was a beautiful day. Unfortunately, the Five o'clock local news meteorologist, spotted a western front, with scattered showers headed for New Orleans and surrounding areas, throughout the weekend.

This certainly dampened our prospects, for an outdoor ceremony. Friday night the sky was covered with thick dark clouds. We were still optimistic that we might be able to have the ceremony in the courtyard before the scattered showers occurred.

Saturday morning, the 21st of November, the sky was overcast yet occasional sunlight appeared giving us hope that the outside ceremony was possible. We experienced light rainfall and the clouds disappear and sunlight appeared. All the chairs in the courtyard were covered with plastic, hoping for favorable weather to allow us to renew our wedding vows outdoor. An hour and a half before the scheduled celebration, the sun was shining brightly and we began removing the plastic covering from the chairs, preparing for the outdoor event. Gloria, in her infinite wisdom, suggested that we abandon our outdoor plans and start bringing the chairs into the Pavillion Room. She felt that it was in the best interest of our guests, if the weather changed during the ceremony.

As usual, she was right because forty-five minutes before the scheduled event was to began, it started to rain again. We were able to implement Plan B, which was our inclement weather arrangement, switching the renewal of vows ceremony from the courtyard into the Pavillion Room. This necessitated breaking down reception table setups in The Pavillion Room and re-arranges the configuration into a church style setting. Even the best of plans sometimes require modification to satisfy extenuating circumstances, such as rainy conditions. We made the necessary adjustment just in time and the 50th Wedding Anniversary Celebration was about to begin.

I asked Dian Kent, my former Administrative Assistant and Mary Ann Francois, a former associated at BellSouth to assist welcoming and registering our guests. My granddaughter Alexis, Miss Personality Plus, without any coasting at all, began welcoming each guest as they arrived. Mary Ann noticed the Official 50th Anniversary Guests Registration Book was missing from the Registration Desk. When she entered the Pavillion Room, looking for the Register, she noticed Troy, our grandson circulating among some of the early arrival guests getting their signatures in the Official Register. After getting signatures from several early arrival guests, Troy returned the Official Register to the Registration Desk.

Mary Ann told Troy she was looking for the Guest Register. Troy said, "Ms. Francois some of the guests got here early before you got here, so I wanted to make sure everybody signed Meme and Poppee's Anniversary

Book." Mary Ann shook her head saying, "Thank you Master Pierre for helping Ms. Kent and I do our job." Dian and Mary Ann with assistance of Troy and Alexis began fulfilling their assignment with great professionalism. Alexis and Troy began distributing the 50th Anniversary Programs to each guest. (See Appendix E: 50th Anniversary Celebration Program.)

In keeping with those Three-thirty events of our journey, Our 50th Anniversary Celebration officially began. Reverend Hadley S. Edwards, Pastor of my church, Bethany United Methodist Church was the Presiding Official Master of Ceremony. He opened the Celebration with this observation: "It is good to be here this afternoon for the celebration that we are called together. Realizing that it's a time that we live, when nothing last forever, we are glad that for 50 years Edgar and Gloria have made a life together in holy matrimony and that is to be celebrated. There are so many people now that think this marriage contract today, this marriage thing is a short term thing, but it is forever; so we came to celebrate today two who have made a forever commitment to each other. He then paused and began a solemn prayer.

Our daughter-in-law Tyra Mitchell Poree rendered the Welcome address. "We came to the Golden Era of Edgar and Gloria" We have gathered here today to salute five decades of marriage. "Did you hear?" She continued, "Fifty years, including love, life, commitment, honor, respect, empowerment, support, friendship, caring, sharing, memory, time, challenges, understanding, wisdom, value, tradition, achievement, partnership, trust, dedication, history, communication, strength, commonality and family." Tyra concluded her welcoming by saying,

"We celebrate now, those 50 years, we honor and share what Edgar and Gloria; two partners in life in both work or in play." "It is our pleasure to have all of you here on this Golden Day." The audience responded, with great and enthusiastic applauds.

Minnie Raby, our matron of honor, 50 years ago, took the microphone and began electrifying the audience with her scintillating rendition of the melodic and soulful song, *You are so Beautiful*. I began proceeding up the aisle to await the arrival of the most beautiful girl in the world, my wife of 50 years, Gloria Mildred Theresa Guichard Poree. As I began my entrance, Sterling Henry, my college classmate, former H & W Drug Store employer and husband of Elvira, my daughter's God Mother and bride's maid in our wedding, began shouting "Edgar Poree, Edgar Poree," and the audience began to cheerfully get into the festive mood. Minnie's soaring and moving You Are So Beautiful reached frenzy peak as Gloria, escorted by our son Edgar, III entered the Pavillion Room, thunderous applauds continued throughout her journey up the aisle, by the standing audience.

As we began the Renewal of Our Vows Ceremony, unlike 50 year ago, when dictates of the Church prohibited free expressions during the solemn ceremony, this was a more festive jovial and keeping it real and expressive, Ceremony. Fifty years ago when Gloria and I were making our vows, it was "too business like", in my opinion not festive enough. Although, our wedding was the thrill of my long awaited dream, that of marrying my Dream Girl, my Queen, the ceremony itself was rather mundane. The presiding Priest did not have any knowledge of me and I don't believe he had much contact personally with Gloria, other than the weekly services that she attended, therefore the ceremony, in my opinion the priest was simply performing his duty as head of the parish. There was no personal connection with the couple entering a lifelong partnership.

Rev. Edwards had been my pastor and friend and he knew and loved my wife and children dearly, therefore the renewal of our vows ceremony, during our 50th anniversary was a 360 degree difference, from our original responses 50 years ago. This time it was much more festive and jovial during our responses. When I reached the ending of my vow response, saying enthusiastically, most emphatically and with much gusto, the audience responded with loud boisterous chants and applauds. When it was time for Gloria's response to her vows, initially, she was extremely gracious; articulate with a pleasant smile that was contagious. However, when Rev. Edwards reached the part of the vows which dealt with being richer or poorer, especially poorer, Gloria's expression changed drastically and response was rather questionable. The audience erupted into uncontrollable laughter and joyous discourse. The renewal of our vows was quite a fun filled and gratifying experience.

Rev. Edwards concluded this portion of our anniversary with a very solemn prayer for this occasion. He said, "Let us pray together. Holy God we come this afternoon to say thank you for a journey that you have established long ago, fifty years. And Lord, we thank you for all of the mountains and all the valleys, all the smooth places over 50 years that you have made for them. We thank you, oh God, for the love that you have given Gloria and Edgar. They have walked together and traveled together.

Oh God, you have been there. You know all about their uprising, and you know about their down falling, but Lord, we just thank you for 50 years they lived out their commitment from one to another. Continue, oh God, to let your light shine on them. Let the rest of their days be the best of their days in the name of God the Father, God the Son, and the Holy Spirit, Amen!" Finally, Rev. Edwards said, "Mr. Poree, I know those 50 years ago, a preacher (priest) stood before you, after pre-announcing you husband and wife and said to a younger Edgar and younger Gloria, that you may kiss your wife." My reaction was just like 50 years ago, eager, thrilled, enthusiastically anticipating that great electrifying sensation, still exhilarating after 50 years. With a triumphant thumbs up and a big smile, after that kiss, the audience once again lost their composure and reacted with thunderous applauds.

Vernon Ward, another one of our extended family members then serenaded Gloria and I and our guests with his stylistic, contemporary rendition of the classic song, *Winds beneath My Wings*. Vernon wooded and mesmerized everyone with his romantic syncopated rhythmic vocal delivery, capitalizing on his expressive alluring gestures as he carefully and fluidly crafted a musical portrait. Our guests, Gloria and I were once again treated to a masterful performance on this our 50th anniversary celebration.

The next performer on the program was my ten-year old grandson, Troy Dion Pierre, II. Troy read so very eloquently, the poem that I wrote entitled: *It Seems As If It Was Only A Moment Ago*. That was my very own Hallmark Signature Card for Our 50th Engagement Anniversary which took place on February 14, 1959, Valentine Day 50 years ago. Troy's facial expressions and voice inflections, during his readings were priceless. Everyone in the audience responded joyfully to Troy captivating delivery. Troy was the orchestra's director his facial expressions was his baton and his voice inflections changed the pitch from mere witty, laughter to just going wild, especially when Troy read this part of the poem:

I asked Gloria Guichard, would you marry me?
There was a moment of silence,
Then she said "Yes" at thirty after three.
Man, I was so excited, emotional as can be
Cause the girl of my dreams would forever be with me!
So on Valentine Day, in the year of 1959

I was rewarded the most beautiful lady that anyone could find.
Fifty years later, I still feel the same,
This lady of mine's is at the top of the game.

When Troy finished his priceless rendition of *It Seems As If It Was Only a Moment Ago*, the audience, Gloria and I gave him a standing ovation.

(See Appendix B: *It Seems As If It Was Only A Moment Ago*.)

Not to be over shadowed by her older brother, Alexis Kirsten Pierre, our nine-year old grand-daughter took the mike and the center of the stage and declared to Meme and Poppee that she was going to sing a song for us. Alex's began singing the melodic and beautiful, *I believe I can Fly,"* hit song. In spite of the malfunctioning microphone, she never lost her cool or her beat during her stellar performance. Rev. Edwards could be heard saying, "sing pretty, sing pretty," throughout Alexis' performance. When she completed her beautiful rendition of *I believe I Can Fly*, every one of our guests believed that she did indeed fly high soaring in praise for her stellar performance. When Alexis completed her song, she looked toward Gloria and me, blowing a kiss then turning toward the audience her gracefully and artistically curtsied. The audience showered her with applause.

Edgar, III, our son and newly married husband, took the stage and declared that he's not much of a speaker. However, when he began asking the question "Did you know? The audience dispelled the myth of his declaration of not being a good speaker within minutes. After unfolding his notes and wearing a smirk expression on his face, he said:

"Did You Know?" My Father set his eyes on his dream girl in the schoolyard of Joseph A. Craig Elementary School in the fall of 1945.

"Did You Know?" A nine-year old third grader could have such a dream, hoping that one day she would be his Queen.

"Did You Know?" My Father after nine years chasing his dream girl got his very first date in April of 1954. Three week later, his second date at the Claiborne Show.

"Did You Know?" My Father kept his eyes on the Prize in spite of my Mother's Mother not letting my Father be the only guy that she could date during four years of college.

"Did You Know?" That when my Father talks about that restriction he still gets upset, but he kept on trying his best to successfully pass the test, no matter how much stress.

"Did You Know?" On Valentine's Day in 1959 at 2:29 p.m., my Father popped the question on a public telephone in Fort Chaffee Army Base, "Would you marry me?" There was a moment of silence, she said "Yes" at 3:30, and my Father started beating his chest; his dream was close to victory.

"Did You Know?" On Saturday, November 21, 1959, in Corpus Christi Catholic Church, when Mother said "I do," at 3:30 p.m. my Father's Dream Girl was his at last. Today, Fifty years later, I'm so proud to say that Father's Dream Girl is still his Queen. I'm sure that third grader had vision beyond dreams.

"Did You Know?" My Father was a work-alcoholic during his pursuit of his dreams. I still don't know how he got and still gets the energy on this 50th Wedding Anniversary.

"Did You Know?" That my Father was a newspaper boy for *The States Item*, a grocery boy at Dan's Grocery, a shoe shine boy at Poree's Barber Shop, a domestic worker for more than fifty customers, specializing in floors and furniture polishing, and grass cutting service, a drug store clerk at Circle Food Store and H and W Drug Store, a longshoremen at J. Smith Company, a salesman/truck driver for Dot's Home Beverage, a parcel service driver for O'Donnell Brothers Stationary Company, a janitor for Sears and Roebucks, and a pickup and delivery man for Broad Street Laundry.

"Did You Know?" He was a summer camp director for Bethany Methodist Church, a fence salesman for Scott Fence Company, and a landscape designer for Poree's Exterior Design.

"Did You Know?" He was a featured vocalist for William Houston and Clyde Kerr Orchestras, Edgar Blanchard's Gondoliers, Danny White and the Cavaliers' bands, an interior designer specializing in custom curtains and draperies, an educational material salesman for Tanglewood Inc., a laborer for a construction company, and recreation supervisor for NORD.

"Did You Know?" He was **a** U.S. Army Reservist, a 6th grade teacher at Johnson Lockett Elementary School, a U.S. Postal Service Warehouseman, Poree's Wallpapering, sewing and tailoring service specializing in men and women clothing alterations, a strategic planner and tax consultant for Orleans Parish Public Schools.

"Did You Know?" He was an actor on the CBS TV-Tracer Series, an actor in a Coca-Cola Commercial, Projector Director-NYC Total Community Action, Personnel Director-TCA, Executive Assistant to Executor Director-TCA, Associate Director-Goals Foundation, Traffic Manager-South Central Bell Telephone, Co-Owner-Pee Vee's Meat Market, Administrative Manager-South Central Bell Telephone, Staff Manager-External Affairs South Central Bell Telephone, District Manager and Chief Spokesman-BellSouth, Adjunct Instructor-University of New Orleans Metropolitan College, Delgado Community College, and Baton Rouge Community College, Chamber of Commerce Television Commercial Spokesperson, and Author and Producer-Back-A-Town Jazz Dance Musical, featuring the International Famous Dejan's Olympia Brass Band.

Finally, when Edgar, III reached the end of his *Did You Know Inquiry*, he began choking up with teary eyes saying, "For a man who had only $246.23 when he married my Mother, his Dream Girl Queen, I must admit this Brother is like no other." "I'm so proud to say we love you so much Father; you did it your way and in a very Blessed and Special Way!" "Love you Daddy!" Our guests, Gloria and I jumped to our feed with resounding applauses.

My daughter, Deidra walked up to the podium and announced that she had been working on this, referring to her part in the program for a week and a half. She then said, "Where do I begin, my Dad, Glo and Ed, Edgar and Gloria, the Porees? They have touched all who passed their lives, but this is for me and Edgar." Ephesians Chapter 6, Verse 1, "Honor your Father and Mother, which is the first commandment with promise that it may be well with you and you may live long on this earth." Deidra then presented a very detailed Floor Chart of Daddy and Mother describing Glo's and Edgar's traits. (See Appendix F.)

After completing her floor chart explanation, Deidra paused for a moment and said, "What I witnessed as a child was love and friendship." There was always love in the house, even when Glo's Laffite came out. When Mother was fussing, Daddy would begin singing how much he loved her, and she'd forget what she was fussing about. But, when coming over to our house, everybody knew they were going to be entertained—be it food, singing, storytelling; just raw fun. You didn't have to bring anything. Back to me and my brother: <u>Proverbs 22 Chapter Verse 6:</u> Train ups a child in the way he should go and when he is old, he will not depart from it.

Ma always let Daddy shine. For years I thought they were smothering us from the real world, but when I experienced it for myself, WOW!" What our parents had is priceless! True love, some people never acquire it in their lifetime, but Mom, Daddy, Edgar III, and I had the privilege and honor to be created by God, just for them. What a fine intricate masterpiece of tapestry to follow, we still enjoy the dream!" Deidra said, "Last but not least, Matthews 7-16 conclusion: You can tell what they are by what they do. My parents have a serving heart and they still have it!" <u>Matthew 25-23:</u> Well down my good and faithful servant. Mom and Daddy, I'm everything I am because you loved me!"

Deidra walked away from the podium, looked at us, and then turned facing the audience, saying I'm going to do something that Mom and Daddy always used to ask me to do, I'm going to sing. What a shocker, Deidra hadn't sung for us in over twenty years. "Put it on Cousin, our D.J. ; all of a sudden the music began and to everyone's amazement, Deidra began singing Aletta Adams' soulful classic, *Get There If You Can*. The guests in the game room came rushing into the Pavillion Room, and The 50th Anniversary Celebration erupted into a boisterous screaming, applauding throng as Deidra thrilled and mesmerized everyone with her soulful rendition of *Get There If You Can*. What an awesome Celebration. With deafening applause, everyone in the Pavillion was standing on their feet, as Deidra finished her rendition that song. Deidra came over, embraced Gloria and me, and we gave her a big kiss, and as usual, tears of joy were flowing from my eyes.

Minnie exclaimed, "That was simply wonderful, simply wonderful," as she walked over to us and when she reached us, she said, "Now Woman, they don't understand when I call you Woman, that's because it's been over fifty years we've been the best of friends". Then she began singing *Oh! My Love, My Darling, I Hunger for Your Touch* over fifty years ago. Every guest and Gloria and I began responding in unison like a well-practiced chorus. Her powerful soulful rendition of *Unchained Melody* kept the entire audience spellbound. When she concluded her song not one person was seated, they were all standing and shouting and applauding.

Rev. Edwards returned to the Center and said, "Ladies and Gentlemen we have feasted our eyes, our ears, and our hearts on one of the jewels of New Orleans. We are rewriting the headlines of the tomorrow's newspaper". There was laughter by the audience, then Rev. Edwards said, "Rewriting the headlines of tomorrow's paper about the celebration of fifty years of happy marriage rather than the growing number of divorces in our city." He continued, "We have been able to sit this evening, underneath the tree." Before we came in, we didn't know what kind of tree it was, but we knew and we know now what kind of tree it is because we've seen the fruit, on the tree. This evening we have sat underneath a golden delicious apple tree, and we have seen the fruits of that tree come and parade before us, two generations. Not one of the apples had been spotted, not one of the apples tainted, not one of the apples had been messed up! Every one of those came representing a strong tree."

Rev. Edwards turned, looked at Gloria and said, "Sister Poree, I don't know very many others today that would marry a man with less than three hundred dollars." The audience went wild with laughter and applause. He continued, "Mrs. Poree, you must have faith in God. Mr. Poree, you are a strong man, sir, and we thank God for your leadership in the church and in the community. We thank God for the leadership that you represent for African-American men!" A standing ovation with thunderous applause followed. "For all that has been said about you tonight, you started out knowing where you wanted to go; you got there by every means that you knew. Step by step you got there; step by step you knew what you wanted as your prize and thanks are to God, thanks are to God, you'll get one another!" The audience responded with applause.

Rev. turned toward the audience, and said, "Ladies and gentlemen when we leave here tonight, we had a life lesson lived out before us." "Some people have put their life lessons between covers in a book that became best sellers." "We sat here tonight and read the best seller, on marriage, belief in oneself, self-motivation. We have witnessed that, and we have read that tonight, authored by none other than Gloria and Edgar Poree. It is on the best sellers list. Mr. and Mrs. Poree, if by God's help and God's blessings, I hope you can do it for another fifty years "But, if God doesn't say do it in the body, what you have done in this community, what you have done in your children and now your grandchildren, it will live on." Rev. Edwards concluded, "Your book the life you lived, the life you leave, the legacy that you leave here will be read by them and embraced by them, and we thank God for your life being a best seller." "Fifty years a bestselling book for the whole world to view and to read, we thank you for that."

"Ladies and gentleman, it is my privilege today, it is a honor today for me to present, somebody you already know, somebody whose children have told you everything about them, but to present you somebody who is walking a journey together, Mr. and Mrs. Edgar Poree. I want them to walk down the aisle so you can acknowledge their presence. Our guests cheered and applauded loudly and we strolled down the aisle.

When we returned to the front of the Pavillion Room, Gloria asked me to announce that she wanted Alexis to sing one of our favorite's songs, *A Night with the King*, an inspiring Gospel. When Alexis began singing, Rev. Edwards could not restrain himself from frequent outburst, "Sing pretty, sing pretty Baby! Sing pretty darling. Alright! Alright!" The audience joined in his choral-like response throughout her very inspirational rendition. When she completed singing, Alexis received a standing ovation with shouts of Bravo! Bravo! Alexis walked over to us, and we gave her a big bear hug embrace and big, big kisses.

It was our time to respond and Gloria as usual, gave the nod to me to speak first. As I looked over the audience and saw who was there, I felt humble and blessed. My opening remarks were rather uncharacteristic mellowed. "I just want to say that this has been an incredible celebration. The rain came; we were planning to do this outside in Gloria's Courtyard, as late as two o'clock, and unfortunately the rain came. We were fiddling with the chairs in and out trying to fulfill what the invitation stated. In spite of this inconvenience, we weren't going to let the weather, or storm, or hurricane in anyway minimize the incredible experience that we had today." I then looked at Deidra and said, "I knew you could sing as a little girl, today you sang like a superstar, you're on the way to stardom." When I saw little Edgar, Troy, and Alex, I knew that God had granted his blessings upon the Poree and the Pierre family.

During my initial remarks, Gloria was standing along my side smiling and occasionally nodding her consent. Then I decided to say something that I was probably going to get a rather different response from Gloria. I then said, "One of the things that my son didn't say, was eighteen years after I married Gloria I discovered something I did not know was a secret." Gloria's expression was still rather pleasant at that point so I continued to discuss the subject of secrecy. "One of the things that we never did was to go in one another's personal property, like her purse or my wallet at any time. At that moment, Gloria's facial expression was beginning to reflect a slight change, as if she was anticipating a change of heart.

Continuing my story I said, "I got home early one day, took out the mail, and opened an envelope with the return address of the Bank of New Orleans. I assumed it was our checking account billing statement. When I opened the envelope and I saw the amount in the account, I was shocked and mind blown. I had never seen such a large amount of money in my eighteen years of marriage!" The audience went wild again and the laughter broke the decibel meter. "That was the second observation." Gloria was still smiling and even laughing with the audience. "The third observation when I looked was that it wasn't addressed to Edgar and Gloria Poree, it was addressed to Mrs. Gloria G. Poree. I was shocked!" The audience erupted into a loud boisterous laughter.

Now, I would have to prepare myself to be able to explain how I had violated a sacred rule. So when she came home, I said, "Darling, I made a mistake today!" She said, "Tell me something different Edgar; you are all the time making mistakes, clarify then!" Gloria and the audience were still laughing at that point. Then I said, "I accidently opened your mail; that's when the Tyson came out!" Gloria said emphatically, "You opened my mail!" Surprisingly, Gloria was still in a very jovial mood while I was relating my story of secrecy.

Then I began asking three dumb questions, "I didn't know you had a secret account." Gloria said, "It's a mighty poor rat that got one hole!" The audience went ballistic with laughter and Gloria still seems to enjoy the story. The second dumb question I asked was, "How long have you had this account?" She then cautioned the audience by saying, "Excuse the expression, she said, before I married your poor ass!" At that point all hell broke out, the audience went crazy again. Because of the frenzied-like behavior of our guests at that point, I lost my concentration and repeated asking the same question previously asked. My third question, "How much did you have when we got married?" Gloria said, "Over fifteen hundred dollars!" I then responded saying, "All those times, do you remember when we were paying fifty-two dollars a month for rent, and Dot Home Beverage told us that we could move in a house for forty dollars a month, and we jumped at it, and you had fifteen hundred dollars." Our guests continued to enjoy the conservation with laughter.

Finally, I said, "I'm not going to spoil this evening; I have to tell you something that I'm going to get in big trouble for. You heard the story of how long I chased the girl. Well my first date you knew about we went to the football banquet, my second date you knew about because we went to the movie, where I placed my arm around her chair. You noticed that I said I placed my arm around her chair. Gloria politely lifted my arm up and removed it from the back of her chair and placed it where it belongs. Then I asked Gloria could we go out on a graduation date". I'm going to get in trouble, but I got to tell, I got to tell it. At that point, Gloria's facial expression was no longer jovial or hospitable. She placed her right hand on my shoulder encouraging me to sit down. After a pleasant exchange, Gloria decided to sit down. I then declared, "This was one night that had never occurred in the world."

After the graduation, we were walking toward Gloria's home at 711 Claiborne Street, that famous address. Many days I crossed the tracks; many days we rode the big red bus to go out. My Mother-in-Law didn't think too much of me back then, and it was many years after we were married that she still didn't think too much of me either. The audience was is stitches laughing aloud. "Well back then I was "zero" on a scale of one to ten."

Well, when we were coming out of the graduation, all of a sudden, Mrs. Guichard was walking toward me then she said, "Darling, baby, Oh! It's so good to see you!" I had never in my life heard those words. The audience once again broke out with a boisterous laughter. So I'm confused because I got my diploma, and I've got my cap and gown, and the closer she got I'm trying to get ready for the embrace. Then she said, "Darling, the closer she got; her voice accelerated the decibels going up."

Baby, and just as I was about to embrace her, she walked right past me to embrace this six-foot-three handsome guy. Our quests could not contain their emotions any longer; the laughter and applause seemed to go on for minutes.

"They called him, Choo." Elvira, our high school classmate and bridesmaid in our wedding who was sitting in the front row, stood up saying, "He was good looking." I acknowledged he was good looking, and he was obviously Gloria's Mother's choice for the graduation date, not me. When we got to Gloria's house, no one was talking to me. I wasn't going to let all of those years that I had my radar on this girl prevent me from taking her out tonight. Mrs. Guichard was a tough person to deal with. If you thought Cinderella's Aunts were something, they were wimps compared to her. Everybody loved Choo; nobody had anything to do with me. Gloria, while walked toward me said, "Mother we are going out!" Mrs. Guichard said very abruptly, "You're going out with whom?" Gloria said courageously," Edgar and I are going out." Her Mother said unequivocally and quite forcefully, "If you ain't going out with Choo, you ain't going out at all!" At that point, I had to make a fundamental decision because her Mother was emphatic about Gloria, my Dream Girl not being able to go out, unless she went out with Choo, so I had to sharpen my negotiation skills. I wasn't going to let anybody rain on my big day after waiting nine years since the third grade and mess with my graduation night. So I stood up, stood up like a man, and didn't say a damn word! Our guests burst out in laughter. The audience went crazy with their boisterous yelling and applause. Even Gloria at that point was quite amused.

I knew that Gloria couldn't go out unless she went out with Choo, so guess who you went out that graduation night? I paused then said, "Gloria, Choo, and Edgar!" Our guests erupted into frenzy, and the laughter was deafening. I then walked over toward, Elvira, got her to stand up, then I said, "Elvira can testify!" Elvira raised her left hand and said "Yes, it was true." "I know it's a bit cumbersome and inconvenient, but I'm going to ask you to assist us in converting the seating arrangement into a dining one. We have some great food for you, and we are going to get you fed.

At this time, "I'm going to shut up and allow my Dream Girl, my sweetheart, my love share her thoughts of this incredible occasion. Gloria got up, saying, "You know he's in trouble, big trouble!" Gloria then said, "First I want to give all the glory and praise to the Lord, who's the head of our household." I want to thank everybody for coming, and I want to say something about my husband. "He's the most wonderful man that I know." She looked at me than said, "He's my best friend, my confident, my hero, my love, and most of all he's my Mister Everything. He's always there for you; he's the kindest person that you like to know. He seldom gets angry, and if he does, you have really done him something really bad. Gloria, on the other hand, might jump off the bandwagon because I'm not going to take too much."

Gloria then began telling our guests of an incident that she and Inez Boyd, one of our dearest friends and neighbors, which occurred at a snowball stand. Gloria told our guests the lady in line before them got two snowballs exactly like the ones we were planning to get. Gloria said, "The lady paid $3 for the two snowballs." Gloria continued, "When we got our two snowballs, exactly the same size and same flavors as the previous customer, the attendant charged me $3.02." Gloria said that she asked the snowball attendant, "Why was her bill two cents higher?" The attendant told her "Well, that's what she was charging me." Gloria responded, "Well that doesn't go like that," and she stated very emphatically, "I want my two cents!" The attendant returned the two cents to Gloria.

When Gloria and Inez were walking back toward her car, Inez said, "Glo, come on let's go," and Gloria said, "Nez, it not the two cents, it's the principal. While getting into the car, Gloria overheard the snowball attendant saying, "What's she's worrying about two cents for when she's getting into a Lexus?" Gloria told the attendant, "That's my damn Lexus and two cents!" The audience went ballistic with laughter. Gloria told the audience that Inez told her, "Let's go before we go to jail for two cents."

Finally, Gloria said, "I want to thank my children and my beautiful grandchildren. Oh; they just love their Meme and Poppee." "It's been a wonderful fifty years with Edgar. The only thing that we can't get along about is that TV remote control." She then gave our guests a demonstration of how I used the remote while describing a typical evening when we were watching TV together. Gloria said, "We'd be watching a movie, and all of a sudden the channels began going up and down, up and down. That's why he sits in the theater watching his programs, while I stay in the great room enjoying my selections without interruptions. Sometimes we looked at a football game together; however, during time outs or when there's another game on another station, he starts working that TV remote, switching back and forth like he's the network's chief operator." Finally, Gloria said with a great sense of adulation, "Edgar is wonderful; if I had to do it all over again, Edgar would be my choice all over again." Then Gloria turned and looked at me while walking over to me for a big kiss. "Fifty years, it has been a beautiful journey. You know, he's my best friend. We love and we have the same interest."

She than shook her head saying, "Not the garden, too much dirt for me, but I feed him when he's in the garden."

All of sudden as Gloria and I stood before our guests, our son, Edgar III, obviously full of emotions walked up to us, and Gloria said, "What you want to say crybaby?" Attempting to compose himself, Edgar III said, "It was really a blessing to be born with two wonderful and outstanding parents. The path was so easy for me and my sister to be successful because we had the best teachers in the world. It's a blessing to have my parents at the age that I am, and I hope that they can live to see many more." The three of us began embracing each other, and as usual I began wiping my tearful joyous eyes. Gloria's exclaimed, "Two crybabies, my two crybabies."

At that point of the celebration, I asked the guests to be patient for about ten minutes while we set up for dining. Then I acknowledged two of my former bosses, Fred Nodier, and his wife traveled from Lake Charles to be with us and Hershel Abbott. Hershel was our President and Fred was my General Manager, and I've got to say something about these two men. "Corporate America is some kind of place to work in. "Gentlemen at the top is a rare commodity, and the two men that are seated here today were corporate giants, but they were gentlemen. That is a rare commodity; thank you Hershel and thank you Fred. I then recognized in the audience the former medical consulting doctor for our Company, Dr. Ted Borghman, who was my primary physician and my very good friend.

After acknowledging and greeting our many guests, it was time to enjoy the delicious cuisine that Leah Chase prepared before leaving. As our guests began their departure, our family and my extended family began enjoying the celebration, dancing. When the cleaning up began in earnest, and we began to wind down and prepare for some well-deserved rest. The next day, Gloria and I, our children and grandchildren began opening the incredible gifts given to us by our many friends and associates.

Well, you've had a lot to read about this dreamer. I hope you will leave with the feeling that my experiences, situations, confrontations, grief, happiness, failures, and successes were many of the same that may have occurred in your life. Hopefully, you may conclude what you read about this dreamer reflects similar experiences in your life. I hope and trust that you will feel that your time was worthwhile in investing in my journey. Finally, most of all I trust your dreams and aspirations will be such that you too will be extremely blessed.

Sincerely,
Edgar Francis Poree, Jr.
The Dreamer

APPENDIX A

LETTER TO SISTER'S HUSBAND

Edgar F. and Gloria G. Poree, Jr.
6219 Providence Place
New Orleans, Louisiana 70126

Area Code (504) 283-3287   Cell (504) 451-0219

November 15, 1995

Dr. Robert Harrington
4600 Prentiss Avenue
New Orleans, Louisiana 70126

Dear Dr. Harrington:

November 15th is a very special day in the lives of the Poree-Harrington family. It was on this day some seventy years ago that Edgar Francis and Gertrude Boyd Poree were blessed with the birth of their first born, Edna Floe. There are not enough superlatives in all of the dictionaries that could adequately and appropriately describe and reflect the beauty, the spirituality and the worthiness of this modern day "Saint."

Edna was the "consummate" model of decency, of integrity, of character, of ethical behavior, unwavering faith and belief in Christ and an exceptional capacity to forgive. I know that this particular day weighs heavy on your heart, therefore we are all praying for you to endure through this moment of great loss. Although it is a time of reflection and from a humanistic point-of-view, a moment of great sadness; I encourage you to think about the great times, the exciting times that you and Edna Floe shared together. The many trips you took together, the cross country tour that you made, the numerous church conferences and the visits to your home country and the sharing of pleasantries among family members. Edna always looked forward to those trips with you.

I know for a fact, that the years that you and Edna were married, were the happiest and most fulfilling times of her life. There is no doubt in my mind that period of time Edna spent with you were her "Glory" days and that's a tribute to both of you. As the rebel of the family, I know that Edna was my "savior" in so many instances that I could not keep a count of. In every instance, Edna Floe would always find an explanation for my behavior even when it was obvious that I should have been scolded for misbehaving. There were times when I wanted to confront those that spoke unkindly about my family, she would intercede and always found some kind words for the enemy. Edna had an enormous capacity for "forgiveness" in her heart. There has never been anyone during my lifetime that exemplified such exemplary humility and capacity to forgive, like Edna Floe. Edna treated all, including those that I considered demons of deceit, with compassion and love.

As I reflect on the life of Edna Floe Poree Harrington, I smile, I give thanks to God for allowing me an opportunity to experience, to witness and to know that we were all made better and we were all truly blessed by having Edna Floe walk among us, counsel us, lead by example for us and finally loved us unconditionally. Edna Floe Poree-Harrington was and will always be in our hearts and soul our family's "Patron Saint."

Respectfully,
Edgar

APPENDIX B

TRIBUTE TO MY BELOVED WIFE

To My Beloved Wife
On this date over a half century ago,
The Creator in his infinite wisdom, his incredible vision and
His compassionate propensity;
Created the most incredible blessing and gift ever bestowed, to me.
That incredible blessing, that tremendous gift was
Gloria Mildred Theresa Guichard
It was a few years shortly thereafter when I first set eyes on this my
Greatest blessing and gift. It was at Joseph A. Craig
Elementary School
When I spotted her in Third Grade Lunch Line.
Bingo! That's it, she's the One!
I knew it then, in Third Grade and more importantly
I know it now, more than a half-century later I have experienced
The ultimate gratification and appreciation and adulation
Of the most incredible blessing and tremendous gift
That the Creator bestowed on the Twenty-fourth of
October in the year
Of our Lord in 1936.

How Do I Describe Gloria Mildred Theresa Guichard
It's as easy as saying your ABC's

G	Gorgeous	Physically and internally
L	Loving	Uncompromising
O	Outspoken	Candid-She's honest, frank to the point
R	Resolve	Never worried about what others had
I	Incredibly Independent	Needs no explanation
A	Absolute	If she says it-believe it
M	Mother (Meme)	Loving, firm, focus, compassionate
I	Intuitiveness	She has incredible instincts
L	Loyalty	Uncompromising
D	Devoted	To live with me for 40 +years incredible
R	Responsible	Maintaining Proper Perspective all times
E	Endurance	Coping with Edgar, Edgar, III and Troy
D	Dependable	She's always there to be counted upon
T	Toughness	She's not afraid to tell it like it is
H	Heartthrob	My Sweetheart
E	Elegance	Needs no explanation
R	Resourceful	She makes whatever the situation, better
E	Educator	Master Teacher Role Model
S	Spirituality	Unwavering Faith in God
G	Genuine	She's the real thing
U	Unsurpassable	She's the Ultimate Lady/Woman
I	Integrity	Uncompromising
C	Character	Impeccable
H	Honesty	What you see is what you get
A	Alluring	Seductive
R	Radiant	All of the Time
D	Delightful	Charming and Witty

Today, Tuesday, October 24, 2000 is

Gloria Mildred Theresa Guichard Poree's Day

From the Boy who chased you since Third Grade to the Man who has Lived his "Dream" with you for over Forty Years, Still Aspiring Still Loving You and Being with You,
I wish You

Happy Birthday My Beloved Sweetheart-My Wife

With Al My Love Forever

Edgar

APPENDIX C

Phil Johnson's Special Tribute

The Saga of Edgar Poree

It began on a bright and dry summer's day;
he fell in love with Southern Bell.
The year was 1971; he pledged his heart and soul
To Murray Fincher, the vows were done, and he was part of the payroll.
From then till now he's never looked back,
although he was allowed a few yells
When his old Southern charmer gave birth to a pack,
of delightful Baby Bell.
The birth changed the way phone business was done
First South Central, then BellSouth, kind of snazzy.
But for Edgar the phone biz was always such fun
Besides, his taste always leaned to the jazzy.

His very first job was a landmark decision:
Traffic manager of South Central Bell.
It involved hard work and much supervision.
And gave him a chance to excel.
He oversaw a management team of 30 members or more
Not to mention an employee work force that numbered 18 score.
His job on the personnel assessment team always brought him thanks.
He recommended candidates for promotion into management ranks
He managed the company's public and governmental affairs.
In fact, he was chief spokesman for BellSouth.

Dreamer Who's Been Extremely Blessed

He stroked the media, was never caught unawares
Small wonder they called him, "The Man with the Golden Mouth"

All in all he was well respected, even by the Bros in the Hood.
With that professional take-charge air he projected.
They just knew he had to be good.
But one day their belief was shaken,
as the company parking lot they passed.
A lot of doubts were awakened, did they see through his act, at last?
What they saw was Edgar helping a lady park,
while in coat and tie resplendent.
"Traffic manager my foot," they began to bark.
"He ain't nothing but a parking lot attendant."
That really happened!

Edgar believes in education and pursues it with a passion.
To him, it's the story of civilization and never out of fashion.
It all came together at Xavier U, with math and music and speech.
An intellectual trip on full scholarship,
where nothing exceeded his reach.
Then came payback time, with diploma in his pocket.
He filled a breach and left to teach for eight years at Johnson C. Lockett.

That brings us up to his Southern Bell, where he began to flower
Truth to tell, in his zeal to excel, whole assignments he'd quickly devour.
He's on more boards then Weyerhaeuser sells.
Symphony, Arts Council, Board of Trade.
He gets things done, to him, it's fun, he never fails to persuade
He collects boards like kids collect stamps.
In sheer volume alone, he's one of the champs:
He's got the DDD, the C of C, TCA and SUNO,
And the BBB, the PPC, the WTC and UNO.
Another he's got, I kid you not, is known by its letters-BS
But you stay cool, I'm no fool, The BS stands for Business School.
"Shame on you"

Edgar's also a motivational speaker, given 1600 talks o'er the years.
Now please, let's be fair, that's a lot of hot air.

Edgar Francis Poree Jr.

From 1600 talks o'er the years.
He won the Weiss Award, a most sincere and prestigious prize.
And the Leadership Council called him "Role Model of the Year,"
A decision impeccably wise.

Total Community Action and Goals To Grow-
he had a learning role in each.
The Neighborhood Corps he shaped to show,
a form of municipal outreach
He had help in all this from the real Southern Belle
Lovely Gloria, His bride from above
He saw her quite unremittingly fell, so hopelessly was he in love.

They, too, were blessed with baby bells,
Sweet Deidra and Edgar III
Troy and Alexis, grand-baby Bells,
Make up the rest of this great family.

In closing, I give my friend Edgar Poree
My dearest, sincerest good wishes this day.
I must end this celebration on over achieving,
So I bid him a loving and heartfelt Good Evening.

APPENDIX D

50TH ENGAGEMENT ANNIVERSARY POEM

It Seem As If It Was Only A Moment Ago

That I waited patiently, in a long line,
To use the <u>telephone.</u>
Anxious, nervous, yet determine to call,
That very special phone number back <u>home</u>

My anticipation, exceed my <u>reservation</u>
The closer I got to the phone
My emotions felt an incredible <u>sensation.</u>
I was about to pop the most ambitious question in my life,
To the young lady that I yearned and dreamed of being my wife

Only three more soldiers waiting in front of me,
I looked at my watch it was quarter after three.
At last it was my turn to use the phone,
Nervously, I dialed the number at her home

When Guich said "Hello," I could hardly wait to know,
Would this be my moment
To ask, "Would you marry me?"
I looked at my watch it was twenty-nine after three.
I asked, "Gloria Guichard would you marry me?

Edgar Francis Poree Jr.

There was a moment of silence,
Then she said, "Yes" at thirty after three!

Man, I was so excited, emotional as can be,
Cause the girl of my dreams would forever be with me!
So on Valentine Day, in the year of 1959,
I was rewarded the most beautiful lady that anyone could find.
Fifty years later, I still feel the same,
This lady of mine's is at the top of her game.

Pittsburg Steelers won the NFL Super Bowl,
For fifty years, Guich has given me love and treasures, untold!
So on this Valentine Day
For fifty years I can truly say,
My love, respect and admiration for you,
my darling continues to grow,
It Seems As If It Was Only A Moment Ago,
Not fifty years, since you said Hello!

So on this day I just want to say
HAPPY 50TH ENGAGEMENT ANNIVERSARY
HAPPY VALENTINE DAY
Love Always and Forever,
Edgar

APPENDIX E

50TH WEDDING ANNIVERSARY CELEBRATION PROGRAM

A Musical Interlude
Presiding   *Pastor Hadley Edwards*
                                   Bethany United Methodist Church
Prayer   *Pastor Edwards*
Welcome   *Mrs. Tyra Mitchell Poree*
Musical Selection   *Mrs. Minnie Raby*

Entrance of Edgar Francis Poree, Jr.

Entrance of Mrs. Gloria Poree
Escorted by Edgar Francis Poree, III

Musical Selection   *Mr. Vernon Ward*
Reading   *Troy Dion Pierre, II*
Musical Selection   *Alexis Kirsten Pierre*
"Did You Know?"   *Edgar Francis Poree, III*
Tribute to Parents   *Ms. Deidra Poree Pierre*
Musical Selection   *Mrs. Minnie Raby*

Presentation of Couple
Thanks from Celebrants
Congratulatory Wishes from Guests
Reception Immediately Following

APPENDIX F

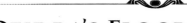

Deidra's Floor Chart of Daddy and Mother

EDGAR'S—FATHER GLORIA'S—MOTHER

Daddy	Executive	Mother	Executive tress
Daddy	Educator	Mother	Educator
Daddy	#1Cheerleader	Mother	Cheering from sideline
Daddy	Artist	Mother	Critic
Daddy	Actor	Mother	First Row
Daddy	Decorator	Mother	Support
Daddy	Landscape	Mother	Support
Daddy	Best Dressed	Mother	Best Dressed
Daddy	Chef	Mother	Chef
Daddy	Story Teller	Mother	Woman of few words
Daddy	Furniture Builder	Mother	We, can afford furniture man, now!
Daddy	Speaker-Orator	Mother	Reviewer
Daddy	Dancer	Mother	Watching from sideline, while hand Aunt Elvira shaking to the floor, sweating with Sticking clothes
Daddy	Interior Decorator	Mother	Property Manager
Daddy	Libra	Mother	Scorpio
Daddy	Salt	Mother	Cayenne Pepper
Daddy	Disciplinarian	Mother	Tyson
Daddy	Entrepreneur	Mother	CEO
Daddy	Author	Mother	Investor

Dreamer Who's Been Extremely Blessed

Daddy	Reviewer	Mother	Support
Daddy	Peace Maker	Mother	Negotiator
Daddy	Martin	Mother	Malcolm X
Daddy	Loves large crowds	Mother	Small crowds
Daddy	With the Jobs	Mother	Are you getting paid, man taking on all kind of jobs
Daddy	Leader	Mother	Leader
Daddy	Shopper-TV's, Electronics You name it	Mother	Shopper

Both Loving Parents

T-H-A-N-K   Y-O-U   P-A-R-E-N-T-S

T	Thanks, Truth, Trusting, Thinking
H	Humble Helping
A	Ambition, Abundant, Able
N	Noble, Never Neglected
K	Knowledge, Kind

Y	Yet, Youthful
O	Obedient, Opportunity, Overflow
U	Unfailing, Understanding, Useful, Uncut

P	Package, Persevere, Patient, Power, Priceless
A	Achieve All
R	Radiant, Real, Royal, Raw, Reasonable, Rare
E	Entertaining, Eager, Excellent, Exceptional
N	Nurturing, Noble, Neighborly
T	Taught, Trained (Highly) Total Package, Treasure
S	Successful, Saved, Selective, Sorrell

APPENDIX G

A SPECIAL MOTHER'S DAY MESSAGE

On this day we acknowledge, those who labored so hard,
For nine long months, for that girl or boy.
For Father to brag about what they had done,
While, Mother's daily chores wasn't much fun.
Carrying bundles of joy for such a long time,
Is enough to blow any normal person's mind.
Not Mothers. They continue to function as usual, everyday,
While Fathers' daily routine, complaining in every way.
I've been blessed with a sweetheart, a friend,
an incredible beautiful wife,
Who was willing to take a chance, making a real sacrifice.
Selecting me as her mate, for the rest of her life.
Oh! How fortunate I am to have, like no other,
A beautiful, caring love one, a very special Mother.
I thank God for all the many years, he's blessed me with you.
The Mother of our children, the beacon light of our lives,
Your Motherly attributes encourages and inspires.
So on this special day, I just want to say,
Your support, your love and strength, unlike no other,
Thank you my love, our children's most incredible Mother!
Thank you Meme, our grandchildren's super Grandmother.
Gloria Mildred Theresa Poree, you're the greatest, of all Mothers.

So on this very special occasion, I just want to say,
I love you and adore you in a very special way.
From Deidra, Edgar, III, Troy and Alexis to,
may God continue to bless you,
HAPPY MOTHER DAY
My Sweetheart, God knows I love You.
Love always and forever,
Edgar

APPENDIX H

A Message of Thanks

Touching Shoulders with Leah Chase

There's a comforting thought at the close of the day,
Of our 50th Wedding Anniversary, at Gertrude's Place,
Originally scheduled in Gloria's Courtyard
The rains came, making it impossible to be in the cards.

Rain didn't dampen the thrills and excitement in our hearts and soul,
November 21, 2009, festivity was worth millions untold.
What a thrilling, memorable occasion, for Gloria and I,
Tears of joy and adulation trickled down our cheeks, from our eyes.

Flashes of jubilation rang throughout our bones,
From the pastor's opening prayer, till the last melodic song.
Leah Chase, I came to you, for help in a really big way,
After Gloria discovered by plans of cooking for our
50th anniversary day.

I was in deep deep trouble, didn't know which course or route,
Although you had a party scheduled, you agreed to help me out.
Your willingness to help me, brought thrills through and through,
Leah Chase, I'm so grateful and blessed,
for touching shoulders with you.

Dreamer Who's Been Extremely Blessed

Leah, did you know you were great, did you know you were strong?
Did you know there were those leaning hard?
Did you know they waited, listened and prayed,
and were thrilled by your simplest word.
Leah, did you know that they longed, for the smile on your face,
For the sound of your voice ringing true,
Did you know they grew stronger and better because,
they touched shoulders with you?

Gloria and I were fortunate to live, during a time that we did,
To know such a beautiful, caring person as you,
Like our marriage, our friendship grew more endearing over 50 years,
Sharing good times, laughter, misfortunes, grief and even tears.

Since those $1.39 half-chicken dinners with two plates
and two 15 cents bottles of Barq's,
Your generosity made our 50th Anniversary such a great success.
As usual your culinary dishes were "Five Stars," the very best.
We thank you from the debts of our hearts, and we will always be true,
Cause, we were certainly blessed,
Lear Chase
Once we touched shoulders with you.
Sincerely,
Edgar and Gloria Poree

APPENDIX I

A Few Featured Speaking Engagements

American Business Women's Association Banquet
Anna B. Casey's Seminar
Sidney N. Collins Vocational Technical Institute Commencement
Cooperative Office Education Seminar
Dillard University Convocation
Delgado Community College Development Conference
Grambling State University Convocation
International Association of Business Communicators
International Facility Management Association
Jefferson County Administrative Conference
Lilly Endowment Educational Development Seminar
Links' Expanding the Vision of Student Development Conference
Louisiana State University Urban Studies Conference
Loyola University Institute of Human Relations Symposium
Tulane University Kappa Delta Pi Honor Society
Southern University at New Orleans Class Night Celebration
Southern University/Shreveport Commencement
Talladega College Convocation
Teacher of the Year Awards
Tennessee State University Motivational Conference
Beauregard Jr. High's Honors Program
Beecher Memorial Methodist Church's Men's Day
Bell Jr. High Honors Exercise
Judah P. Benjamin Promotional Exercise

Dreamer Who's Been Extremely Blessed

Bethany United Methodist Church Black History Celebration
Bethel A.M.E. Church Boyinton United Methodist Church
Camphor United Methodist Church
Carver Community School Honors Awards
Carver Middle School Achievement Day
G. W. Carver Sr. High Commencements *3
Christian Faith Ministries Conference
Joseph S. Clark Hi School Commencements *2
Mary D. Coghill Promotional Exercise
Cohen Sr. High Honors Exercise
Counseling and Placement Center Workshop
Destrehan High School Commencement
Frederick Douglas Black Cultural Testimonial Awards
Dunn School Promotional Exercise
Warren Easton High School Commencements *2
Helen Edwards School Awards
Greater New Orleans Federation of Churches Prayer Breakfast
First Street United Methodist Church Men's Day
Alcee' Fortier Sr. High School Commencement
Rivers Frederick Jr. High Awards Day
Future Business Leaders of America Conference
Grace United Methodist Church Black History Service
Guste School Promotional Exercise
Haven United Methodist Church Men & Women's Day
Murray Henderson Promotional Exercise
Velena C. Jones School Promotional Exercise
John F. Kennedy Sr. High School Commencement
Dr. Martin Luther King's Celebration
Kohn Jr. High School Achievement Day
L.B. Landry Sr. High Black History Tribute
Lawless Sr. High School Honors Awards
Living Witness Church of God in Christ
Livingston Jr. High School Honors Awards
Johnson C. Lockett Promotional Exercise
John McDonogh Sr. High School Commencements * 3
McDonogh #35 Sr. High School All Sports Banquet
Eleanor McMain Jr. High School Awards Ceremony
Greater New Orleans National Council of Jewish Women
Mt. Zion United Methodist Church Ecumenical Conference

National Conference of American Association of Blacks in Energy
New Hope Baptist Church Men's Day
New Zion Baptist Church Laymen's Day
New Orleans Public Kaleidoscope Black History Series
New Orleans Public School Counselor's Workshop
Francis T. Nicholls Sr. High School Commencement
Nievah Baptist Church Anniversary
Notre Dame Seminary Symposium
Palmer School Promotional Exercise
Peck Memorial Methodist Church Laymen's Day
Phillips Jr. High Honors Exercise
Public Policy Forum
Presbyterian Institute of Industrial Relations Conference
Sarah T. Reed Sr. High School Commencement
Rutledge College Commencement
St. Charles Parish School Conference
St. James A, M. E. Church Men's Day
St. John Institutional Baptist Church Men's Day
St. Joseph the Worker Catholic Church
St. Landry United Methodist Church Men's Day
St. Mary's Academy Sr. High School Commencement
St. Paul A.M.E. Church Anniversary
St. Paul Lutheran Church Black History Service
School Business Partnership Awards Banquet
Total Community Action Head Start Annual Workshop
Trinity Methodist Church Student Recognition Service
Unite Negro College Fund Southern Regional Conference
United Negro College Fund Lou Rawls Parade of Stars Awards
United Teacher of New Orleans Annual Awards Luncheon
United Way Federal Combined Kickoff Rally
University of New Orleans Symposium
Urban League Equal Opportunity Day
Booker T. Washington Sr. High School Honors Awards
Carter G. Woodson Jr. High School Awards
World of Work Youth International Exposition Conference
Xavier University Student Motivational Conference
YMCA Annual Black Achievers Awards Ceremony

Multiple Commencements

APPENDIX J

Awards, Boards, and Committees

"Award of Excellence for Outstanding Service"—National Black Child Foundation
"Citizen of the Year Award"-Spectator News Journal
"Distinguish Citizen Award"—Kappa Alpha Psi Fraternity Inc'
"Hall of Fame Honoree"—Palmer School
"Weiss Award"—National Conference for Community and Justice
"Note of Distinction Award"—Lafon Home's Jazzy Night
"Outstanding Distinguish Award"—Downtown Development District
"President Leadership Circle Award"—Telecommunication Company's President
"Spirit of Greatness Award"—Christian Faith Ministries
"International Leadership Award"—Toastmaster International
"Head Start Appreciation Award"—Total Community Action
"Parade of Stars Award of Excellence"—UNCF Lou Rawls
"Friend of Education Award"—United Teachers of New Orleans
Southern Baptist Hospital Foundation
Tulane University's A.B. Freeman Business School Council
Southern University at New Orleans Foundation
Park and Parkway Commission of New Orleans
University of New Orleans Higher Education Council
Better Business Bureau
New Orleans Council on Aging
State of Louisiana Humanities
Salvation Army

Downtown Rotary
The Board of Trade
Christian Ministries Foundation
Louisiana Colleges
Louisiana Science Center
Dryades Street YMCA
The World Trade Center
Metro YMCA
New Orleans Symphony Orchestra
The Arts Council of New Orleans
The World Trade Center
Bethany United Methodist Church Administrative
BellSouth Telecommunication Federal Political Action Committee
Southern University at New Orleans Neighborhood Coordinating Committee
Phillip Randolph Institute Planning Committee
United Teacher of New Orleans Scholarship Committee
National Alliance of Business College Student Development Committee
United Negro College Fund Community Development Committee

Appendix K

Family Photos

Mother: Gertrude Poree
1924

Father Edgar f. Poree
1951

Mother Gertrude B. Poree
1967

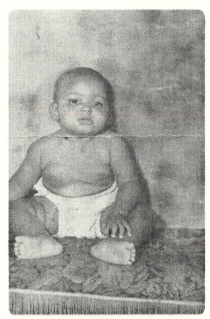

Baby Edgar Jr.
1937

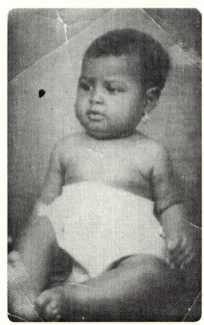

Baby Gloria Guichard
1937

Poree Siblings
1937

Edgar, Jr. 6 yrs. old
1942

Poree Family
1950

Fiancee Gloria
1959

Our Wedding
1959

Wedding Party
1959

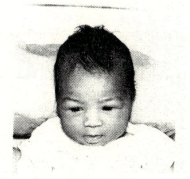
Daughter Dana Ann
1967

Xavier U's Opera Carmen
1968

Edgar, Jr.
1972

Kim Fields & Edgar, Jr.
1984

Family Portrait
1994

50th Anniversary
Edgar, III & Mother
Nov. 2009

50th Anniversary Troy Dion, II
Nov. 2009

50th Anniversary Alexis Kirsten
Nov. 2009

50th Anniversary Edgar, III
Nov. 2009

50th Anniversary Deidra
Nov. 2009

50th Anniversary
Nov. 2009

50th Anniversary
Nov. 2009

50th Anniversary
Nov. 2009

Gloria & Edgar at Patron Party
2010